Official

The THREE STOOGES™ ENCYCLOPEDIA

Official
The THREE STOOGES™
ENCYCLOPEDIA

The Ultimate Knucklehead's™ Guide to Stoogedom—from Amalgamated Association of Morons to Ziller, Zeller, and Zoller

Robert Kurson

CB
CONTEMPORARY BOOKS

Library of Congress Cataloging-in-Publication Data

Kurson, Robert.
  The official Three Stooges encyclopedia / Robert Kurson.
      p.   cm.
    ISBN 0-8092-2930-7
    1. Three Stooges (Comedy team)—Miscellanea.   2. Three
Stooges films—Miscellanea.   I. Title.
  PN1995.9.T5K87   1998
  791.43'028'092273—dc21   97-46511
                                                          CIP

Cover design by Todd Petersen
Interior photographs courtesy Comedy III Productions, Inc.
Interior design by Hespenheide Design

Published by Contemporary Books
A division of NTC/Contemporary Publishing Group, Inc.
4255 West Touhy Avenue, Lincolnwood (Chicago), Illinois 60646-1975 U.S.A.
Copyright © 1998 by Comedy III Productions, Inc.
Printed in the United States of America
International Standard Book Number: 0-8092-2930-7
  18   17   16   15   14   13   12   11   10   9   8   7   6   5   4   3   2   1

This book is dedicated to the memory of my dad,

Jack D. Kurson,

who woke me up in plenty of time on Saturday mornings

to eat a good oatmeal breakfast, watch the Stooges,

and ask whether I happened to notice that

"even though the Stooges find themselves in every possible

situation in every possible location, they never seem to think

there's anything unusual about that?"

Contents

Acknowledgments

The author would like to thank the following people for their kind and generous contributions to this book:

Amy Kurson, for her undying patience, warm support, and keen editorial judgment during many months of a nothing-but-Stooges lifestyle. It is the rare man, indeed, who is married to a brilliant and beautiful woman who can also recite the Stooges' "Maha" routine by heart.

Annette Kurson, the finest writer I know, who taught me the importance of words and who never wavered in her support for this project or her willingness to devote endless hours to its success.

Ken and Becky Kurson, two terrific writers whose laughter while reading along gave me confidence I wouldn't have found elsewhere.

Jane, Larry, Mike, and Sam Glover, who believed before anyone else that there was a Stooges book inside me.

Rob Feder, Elliott Harris, and Bob Mazzoni, my colleagues at the *Chicago Sun-Times*, from whom I have learned much about good writing, professionalism, and friendship. No one has a better eye for Stooge photos—or for poking— than Elliott does.

Ken Williams of Irmo, South Carolina, without whose die-hard research and gentlemanliness this project would not have been possible.

Bela G. Lugosi, Kathy, Arlene, and the folks at Comedy III Productions for their constant cooperation, assistance, and good cheer.

Matthew Carnicelli and Craig Bolt, my editors at Contemporary, who somehow fused the slapstick to the proper to turn out a beautiful book.

Harry Ross, one of the great Stooge minds of all time, who was a wealth of knowledge and a true pal in helping the book come to fruition.

Andrew Beresin, my law school roommate, attorney, and dear pal whose tireless tenacity breathed life into this project.

Pals Jason Steigman, Mitch Cassman, Rich Hanus, Ken Goldin, Jeff Lescher, Ken Andre, Jordan Heller, and Brad Ginsberg for years of good humor and good times.

Randi Valerious and Celestine Jeffreys, for their help and friendship, and to cousins Sam, Jeff, and Allen for stoking the Stooge flame in me when I was a kid.

My brother Eric Davis, who never needed more than a word or two to prompt him to recite Stooge plotline and dialogue as if he wrote the shorts himself.

Bill Gilger, an all-around mensch, Stooge fan, and heck of a nice guy.

Finally, my agent, Shari Lesser Wenk, for believing in me and this project, and always coming out swinging on my behalf. Every author should be so lucky.

It is an indictment every Stooge fan bravely endures: "All those men do is hit each other!"

To critics, the Stooges represent nothing more than flying pies and pokes to the eyes. They see no utility in a monkey wrench to the head, nothing constructive in using an oversized pair of scissors to pull a fellow man along by his nose.

Critics will always warn that there are better ways to get a friend's attention

Moe demonstrates a basic Stooge survival skill (*Pop Goes the Easel*, 1935).

than by jabbing him in the backside with a knitting needle.

They're missing the best part of the Three Stooges: the language.

The meat and potatoes of the Three Stooges is in their fists, but the flavor is in the language. After the last pie has flown, after the last eye has been poked, the words of the Stooges remain.

Moe, Larry, and Curly could stay at the Biltmore Hotel, but they invariably check in to the "Hotel Costa Plente" or the "Motel Snazzy Plaza." They could, one would suppose, drink Dewers or Gold Label but for some reason opt for "Old Homicide" instead. The Stooges never marry Susan, Katherine, and Betty; their true loves are "Aggie, Maggie, and Baggie."

Stooge films are rich in funny words, slogans, signs, songs, and people. Many of the terms have their origins in the slapstick style of vaudevillian comedy ("She was bred in Old Kentucky," Curly sings, "but she's just a crumb up here!"), but they are as fresh today as they were fifty years ago. Stooges fans are a passionate lot who

Is there really any comparison? The Stooges battle for the affections of three bathing beauties in a candid shot taken during the 1930s.

love language and care about details. They appreciate a murder suspect named Antonio Zucchini Salami Gorgonzola de Pizza.

The entries in Part II of *The Official Three Stooges Encyclopedia* are arranged alphabetically. Under "A," for example, one finds the entry **Aggie, Maggie, and Baggie** and the following definition: "Was it worth battling three brutish cavemen in *I'm a Monkey's Uncle* and *Stone Age Romeos* for the fair hands of Aggie, Maggie, and Baggie? Moe and Larry think so. Shemp gets Baggie."

Part III categorizes the entries in Part II. Love that episode when the

Stooges swing a presidential election but can't remember the names of the candidates? Just check "Politicians" to find "Hammond Egger" and "Abel Lamb Stewer." Want all the words to the song the Stooges use to teach the alphabet to a college classroom? Simply check the "Songs" category to discover "Swinging the Alphabet."

Part IV groups the book's entries by film. Say that you're paging through the *Encyclopedia* and come across the name of legendary wrestler "Ivan Bustoff" from the film *Grips, Grunts and Groans*. You remember him and want to know more about the film. Just flip to Part IV and check out the listings under *Grips, Grunts and Groans* to find other entries like "Hangover Athletic Club," "Kid Pinky," and "Wild Hyacinth Perfume."

Part V is a minireference library that provides a synopsis and key gag for every film the Stooges ever made. From Curly leading a procession of ducks in *A Ducking They Did Go* to Moe defrosting a frozen Curly over an open fire in *Violent is the Word for Curly* to the live and ornery clam chowder that won't allow the Stooges to eat in peace in *Dutiful but Dumb*, the immortal plots and gags are in the bag.

A few notes on what you *won't* find in *The Official Three Stooges Encyclopedia*: Peripheral people, places, or things that add nothing to plot or humor have been omitted. For example, if Moe reminds Larry that they must be in New York by noon, "New York" will not appear in the book. If, however, Moe reminds Larry that they must be in Moronica by noon,

Would you stop for these three professors (*Violent is the Word for Curly*, 1938)?

rest assured that "Moronica" will be included.

A few Stooges films, especially those done later in their careers, were remakes of earlier films and often used stock footage from the previous film. Therefore, some entries and key gags will pertain to more than one film.

Classic Stooge one-liners appear throughout the book. Though most of these jokes are used in dozens of films, the book will attribute them to only one film for the sake of brevity. In these cases, it's the humor of the joke that is important, not the exhaustive cataloging. Some photographs in the book were snapped between takes on the set

Clearly a bargain!

of classic Stooge shorts. The poses in these pictures, therefore, don't always match identically what appears in the films—but they sure are funny, anyway.

Finally, it is possible that I missed an important entry or two along the way. If you believe you've discovered a missing gem, send it to me in care of Contemporary Books, 4255 West Touhy Avenue, Lincolnwood, IL 60646-1975, or E-mail me at RK41144@aol.com. Don't remember what 41144 stands for? You're holding *The Official Three Stooges Encyclopedia*—look it up!

Official The THREE STOOGES™ ENCYCLOPEDIA

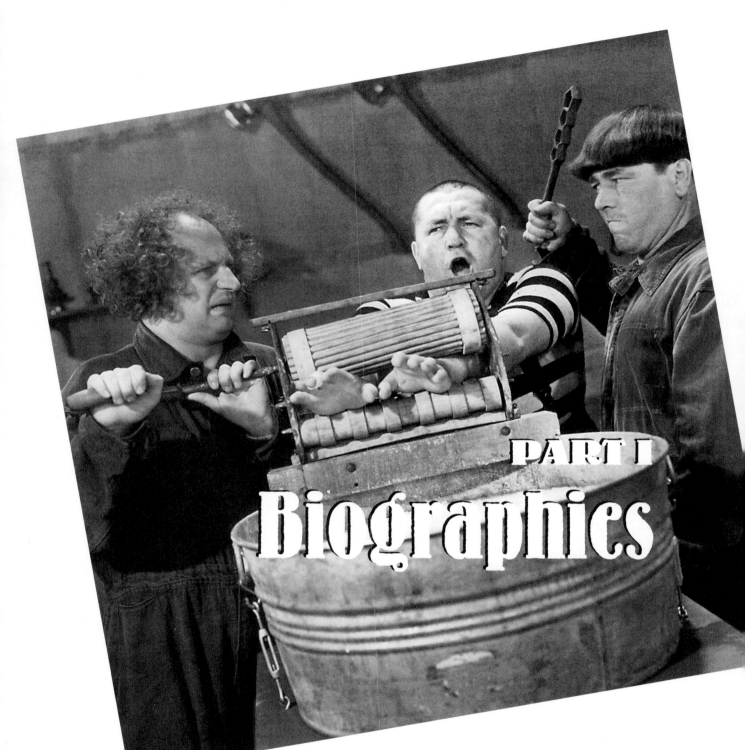

PART I
Biographies

A Brief Career Overview

It might be ages before scientists trace the slapstick gene. But something spicy was stirring in the bloodstream of the Horwitz family of Brooklyn near the turn of the century.

Photographs of Jennie and Solomon Horwitz provide no hints. The handsome-looking couple— he of barrel chest and raging mustache, she of wire-rimmed spectacles and pursed smile—look like any number of young couples of the day: optimistic and ready to make an imprint on the world. Soon they would have children who, God willing, would earn a nice living as skilled laborers or even professionals.

Jennie and Solomon didn't have a hint.

The couple produced five children, all boys. The first two, Irving and Jack, grew up to assume respectable careers. The other three—Samuel, Moses, and baby Jerome—turned out a bit different. They grew up to become Stooges.

By 1909, at age twelve, long-haired and elfin Moses (Moe) was earning bit parts in various films at Brooklyn's Vitagraph Studio, honing the role for which he was destined: the bully, the tough guy, the kid who let his fists do the talking. By 1916, he and older brother Samuel (Shemp) had scratched out a twelve-minute blackface routine and were playing vaudeville under their new, Americanized stage name "Howard and Howard." The pay was lousy and the conditions worse, but Moe, nineteen, and Shemp, twenty-one, had finally realized their dream: a career in showbiz.

Back home, fortunes were smiling on the Horwitz family. Jennie had become successful in real estate, and her youngest son, Jerome (Curly), had emerged as the apple of her eye. Quiet and unassuming, Jerome (or "Babe," as brother Moe called him) had dreamy waves of chestnut hair, an angel's grace on the ballroom dance floor, and a gorgeous tenor worthy of the finest vaudeville halls. But that summer was also to be painful for the thirteen-year-old Curly.

After borrowing Moe's rifle to go hunting one day, Curly accidentally fired a shell into his ankle. The injury caused the boy to limp for the rest of his life—a handicap Moe believed led to bigger problems later in his young brother's life.

Not every puppet grows up to be Howdy Doody.

The injury, however, did nothing to diminish Curly's fascination with show business. During his teenage years, he took great delight in watching Moe and Shemp fine-tune a vaudeville act that was becoming stunningly sharp in its timing and execution. With a break here or there, it looked certain to Curly that his brothers would go on to vaudevillian stardom.

That break came in 1922, when Moe ran into Charles Ernest Lee Nash, a long-lost boyhood pal. Nash had not fared well in business but seemed to be doing brilliantly in vaudeville under the name Ted Healy. As serendipity would have it, Healy was looking for a hot, young talent and immediately recruited Moe. The two created an instant sensation, and in no time Healy was earning $3,500 a week. In the first of many miserly mistakes, Healy paid Moe a weekly salary of only $100.

Despite the inequitable pay, Moe teamed with Healy until 1925, when a mystery guest in the audience at the

Orpheum Theatre in Brooklyn dazzled Healy with an uncanny instinct for improvisation and a singular ability to bounce himself off the theater's vaunted, slapstick-stained walls. Healy had no choice but to hire Shemp and reunite the Howard brothers.

But providence had even bigger plans for these emerging stars. While killing time in 1925 before a performance in Chicago, Healy, Moe, and Shemp drifted to a nearby theater where they caught sight of a daffy-looking character whose frazzled hair, herky-jerky violin gesticulations, and mad Russian dance moves caused the New Yorkers' jaws to drop. Without so much as a try-out, Healy offered the man $90 a week (plus an additional $10 to lose the violin) to join the act. Larry Fine accepted and became the original third Stooge.

Born Louis Feinberg on Philadelphia's south side in 1902, Larry was barely out of diapers when he began singing, dancing, and otherwise schmaltzing it up for adoring parents and friends. As a child, Larry had burned his arm with acid, an injury that required an unfortunate skin graft—and a very fortunate approach to therapy. In order to repair damaged nerves, Larry was given a violin and told to practice, practice, practice.

Before long, Larry had turned virtuoso, developing an instinct for music and a facility with instruments that seemed to assure his future as a professional musician. But there was another side to Larry.

Larry loved to box, and he was good at it. Moe later speculated that it was this training as a lightweight pugilist that conditioned Larry to absorb a lifetime worth of punishment as a Stooge. It undoubtedly also developed the footwork, speed, timing, and agility that Stoogedom so rigorously demanded. Every punch Larry took in the ring prepared him for a far more rewarding thump as a Stooge.

With Larry on board, the act became "Ted Healy and His Three Southern Gentlemen" and then "Ted Healy and His Stooges." With each new name, the team tore it up on the vaudeville circuit, garnering glowing press reviews as they toured the country. Though Moe, Larry, and Shemp were gradually becoming the focal point of the act, Healy continued to pay them the standard $100 rate while he took in thousands for a single performance. The Stooges' resentment continued to build.

By 1930, the film world was ready for the team now called "Ted Healy and His Racketeers." Fox Studios put up the money for the Rube Goldberg–penned movie *Soup to Nuts*, after which the studio offered Moe, Larry, and Shemp a seven-year contract. But according to Moe, Healy sabotaged the deal, and the trio—enraged and determined to make it on their own—broke from the wildly popular Healy.

The break did not last long. Though Healy had begun drinking heavily and was floundering with replacement stooges, Moe and Larry agreed to rejoin forces so long as their pal agreed to stop boozing. Shemp, however, wasn't so optimistic. Believing Healy to be a lost cause, and with a standing offer to play the character of Knobby Walsh in a Joe Palooka film for Vitaphone, Shemp bade farewell to the Stooges and made his way to a film career in California.

Things looked grim for the act, which depended on the interplay between Healy and three stooges, not two. Healy, Moe, and Larry needed to replace Shemp, not an easy task under the best of circumstances. In the first of a lifetime of savvy personnel decisions, Moe called on a name that would change the face of comedy forever: Curly.

Now twenty-nine, Curly had developed into a limber, graceful, whirlwind of potential but had virtually no show-business experience. Except for a stint as a comic musical conductor for the Orville Knapp Band, his exposure to the stage had consisted of studying the precision timing of brothers Moe and Shemp. He knew their routines and, boy, could he sing. Beyond that, he'd have to wing it—and cut his wavy hair.

Curly developed at the speed of light. By 1934, after only two years with the group, Healy and his Stooges had made five short comedies and five features for MGM. More than ever, things looked sweet for the trio and their leader. But Moe began to sense what Shemp had felt earlier. Frustrated with the $100 a week salaries and feeling more confident than ever that they would do better alone, Moe convinced his partners to walk. It was a risky move that might easily have backfired; Healy was still the big star, not the Stooges. But Larry and Curly stuck by Moe and stepped into the overwhelming wonderland of Hollywood filmdom. They were now, simply, the Three Stooges.

The Stooges signed a deal with Columbia to appear in a single two-reeler, or "short" as the 16-to-18-minute films were known. Shorts were added attractions offered by movie theaters and shown before the main feature. (Columbia's short-film department was to become a mighty powerhouse of the genre and produced some of the finest two-reelers in the business before shutting its doors in 1958.)

The first Three Stooges short, *Woman Haters*, didn't even star the Three Stooges. Marjorie White, a dollish blonde, was billed above Moe, Larry, and Curly in a musical version of the battle of the sexes. Even more unusual, the film was done entirely in rhyme and featured Larry as the prominent Stooge. Many Stooge fans dislike *Woman Haters*, as Moe, Larry, and Curly flash little of the manic charisma and distinct personas that would soon make them stars. (White died tragically in a car crash shortly after filming *Woman Haters*.)

It didn't take long for the Stooges to find their groove. Their next short, *Punch Drunks*, was frenetic and furious, a hilarious story of a struggling boxing manager (Moe) who discovers that whenever a certain fuzzy-haired fiddler (Larry) plays "Pop Goes the Weasel," the waiter in a local diner (Curly) goes berserk. Behind the power of Larry's violin and Moe's training regimen, Curly (as K. O. Stradivarius) goes on to become the heavyweight champion of the world.

Here, finally, was a chance for the Stooges to settle into the prototype roles that would forever define the group: Moe would be boss, the brains of the outfit with the muscle to back it up. Larry would be the middleman, the guy with just enough smarts to understand Moe's orders but not quite enough to get them right. Curly would be, well, Curly, a roly-poly bundle of whirling, swirling, graceful energy capable of delivering a smorgasbord of fantastical grunts, squeals, and double-talk. It was a formula that took the world of two-reel comedies by storm.

The Stooges' next short, *Men in Black*, guaranteed the team's success at Columbia and was even nominated for an Academy Award. The film's classic line, "Dr. Howard, Dr. Fine, Dr. Howard!" still holds a place in the repertoire of nearly every kid who has ever attempted a Three Stooges impression.

By the late 1930s, it was clear to Columbia that the Stooges were a sensation. Fan mail poured in from all over the world, and theater owners began to insist that they receive Three Stooges shorts before agreeing to screen some of Columbia's feature-length films. Personal appearances by the Stooges—at home and abroad—were packed to the rafters.

But that didn't guarantee that studio bosses treated the team fairly. The Stooges were required to make eight shorts a year at a salary of about $8,000 per picture, a figure that never increased *in twenty-four years*, despite the fact that the Stooges were earning millions for Columbia. By claiming—near contract renewal time—that the short-subjects unit was not earning its keep, Columbia caused the Stooges untold anxiety about their futures. When the inevitable eleventh-hour offer came through, Moe was too drained emotionally to ask for a raise.

Ballet is graceful, but less so if the ballerinas don't get along (Rhythm and Weep, 1946).

The Stooges, fortunately, did not allow the strain of Columbia's financial double-dealings to bleed the energy and humor from the films. In fact, the shorts got funnier. Beginning around 1938, Stooges scripts began to make increasingly brilliant usage of sight gags, sound effects, and verbal humor. To the delight of fans everywhere, Moe was now coming up with a fistful of mattress stuffing after pulling Larry's hair, eye-pokes were being accompanied by the wince-inducing strains of two plucked ukulele strings, and the Stooges—especially Curly—were now getting as many laughs for the crazy things they said as the crazy things they did.

Not everyone was thrilled with the Stooges. Some viewers objected that the trio was too violent and demanded to know where—if not from Moe—adorable little junior had learned the two-fingered eye-poke. Others argued that cream pies were never intended to fly and that hammers were meant to be used on nails, not skulls. Most reasonable people of the day, however, were happy to take the Stooges at face value—especially if that face was as silly as Curly's.

Even those for whom slapstick was too manic found much to love in the Stooges. Despite the trio's penchant for annihilating each other, they were always kind to children, pets, and down-and-outs; if a character took abuse from the Stooges, odds were that he or she was wealthy, powerful, or bossy—and had it coming.

And they tried hard. Whether called to guard a haunted house or ordered to confront an ornery crew of Wild West gunslingers, the Stooges stuck around to get the job done. While it is true that they ran away from dozens of monsters, gorillas, and henchmen during their career in film, it was always in an effort to avoid being murdered, not for lack of desire to complete the mission.

Through the years, the Stooges worked an increasing amount of their Jewish heritage into their films. Many was the time that a Yiddish phrase or expression found its way into a toast such as "Ver G'harget" ("Drop Dead"), an address like 123 Meshugana (Crazy) Avenue, or an insult such as "Huck mir nisht a chynick, and I don't mean efsher!" ("Don't bother me, get off my back and I don't mean maybe!").

The Stooges' golden age lasted from about 1938 to 1945, when nearly every film they made seemed to be flawlessly written, paced, performed, and directed. Moe, Larry, and Curly were equally hilarious as western gunslingers, opera stars, even vicious dictators. No one in Hollywood—or anywhere else—skewered Hitler as mercilessly and smartly as did Moe in *You Nazty Spy* (1940) and *I'll Never Heil Again* (1941). Into the mid-1940s, it appeared that nothing could derail such a finely honed team functioning at the very top of its powers.

But watch Curly in *If a Body Meets a Body* (1945). His timing is a hairbreadth off-kilter, there are ribbons of deliberation in his usually instinctive and graceful movements, and his high-pitched voice warbles instead of rings. He returned to his masterful self in his next film, *Micro-Phonies* (1945), a true Stooge classic and as brilliant a job as Curly ever pulled off. But as 1945 turned into 1946, Curly was never to be the same.

He struggled through the next ten films but seemed unable to make his body do what had come so naturally before. On the final day of filming *Half-Wits Holiday* in 1946, Curly suffered a stroke that put an end to one of the great comedic film careers of all time. At forty-three, Curly was finished as a Stooge.

Moe's initial reaction to Curly's retirement was to retire the Stooges. How, he reasoned, could anyone hope to replace such a vastly talented, multidimensional innovator? Hollywood agents pitched various substitute stooges but Moe didn't blink. There was only one man who knew the routines, whose comedic clock ticked lockstep with that of Moe and Larry, who had Stooge in his bloodstream and slapstick in his genes. If the Stooges were to continue, it would be with Shemp and no one else.

By this time, Shemp had established himself as a first-rate comedic film actor, starring in countless shorts, series, and feature-length films alongside such notables as W. C. Fields, John Wayne, and Abbott and Costello. But when Moe called, Shemp answered. After fifteen years, the original Three Stooges were reunited.

Maybe Moe, Larry, and Curly look skeptical because they've seen this show before.

Shemp had awesome shoes to fill; to his credit, he never tried to imitate or replace Curly. Instead, Shemp allowed his own savvy, streetwise persona to emerge, and the results were brilliant. It is easy to see why young Stooge fans take immediately to the childlike wonder projected by Curly. But one of the thrills of developing a mature love for the Stooges is in coming to appreciate the herky-jerky mannerisms, natural sound effects, and overall skittish disposition that Shemp brought to every role.

From 1947 to 1955, Shemp made numerous classic two-reelers with the Stooges, but not quite as many as might first appear. Budget cutbacks at Columbia forced longtime director Jules

White to recycle some shorts after 1952 by splicing a few new scenes into a heavy volume of stock footage from older shorts. The results were films like *Scotched in Scotland* (1954) and *Bedlam in Paradise* (1955), which were near clones of earlier films. With Shemp working at the top of his game, these retreads were too often a waste of a great comic's potential.

After a long bout with illness brought on by his stroke, Curly died in 1952 at the age of forty-eight. During the eight-film shooting schedule in 1955, tragedy again struck the Stooges. Shemp, who had attended the prizefights one evening with a troop of buddies, got into a friend's car and began telling jokes. Suddenly, his head slumped forward and, with a smile on his face, Shemp died of a heart attack. Once again, the fate of the Stooges hung precariously in Moe's saddened heart.

Moe's first choice to replace Shemp was Joe DeRita, a bowling ball–shaped burlesque veteran whom Moe and Larry knew from Harold Minsky's stable. But Minsky wouldn't turn DeRita loose, so Moe was forced to look elsewhere.

His next choice was Joe Besser, another chubby vaudevillian who had starred in his own series of Columbia two-reelers. Besser was everything his predecessors were not: whiny, trembling, and allergic to violence. His trademark whimpers, "Not so *hard!*" and "Oooh, you crazy!" never seemed to gel with the legacies left by Curly and Shemp. In 1958 Columbia closed its short-subjects unit; after twenty-four years and 190 shorts, the Three Stooges were finished making two-reelers for good.

But a funny thing happened on the way out of Columbia. Television had come to the forefront of American culture, and new generations of kids were falling in love with the Stooges in an entirely new way. Without having to venture to a theater to see a short and then waiting months before a new episode arrived, Stooge fans could watch their heroes on a daily basis for free. Thanks to television, the Stooges were becoming more popular than ever.

This time, Joe DeRita was available, and the Stooges were cooking yet again. Round and crew-cutted, "Curly Joe" bore a remarkable likeness to Curly, and with him the Stooges revived their career. They played to packed houses—even stadiums—across the country, made countless TV appearances, and starred in six feature-length motion pictures, always in the role of good guys.

During production of the made-for-TV *Kook's Tour* in 1970, Larry suffered a stroke that put him out of Stooge commission. Though Moe considered longtime Stooge role player Emil Sitka to replace Larry, he thought better of the idea and decided to retire the Stooges permanently. Larry died in January of 1975, and Moe died shortly thereafter, while working on his autobiography.

Today, more people in the United States can name all three Stooges (57 percent) than can name a single member of the U.S. Supreme Court (52 percent). Comic Jay Leno insists that if you ask a man to list the three men he most admires in history, he will invariably reply, "Abraham Lincoln, Albert Einstein . . . and Moe." There are few kids today who can't produce—on demand—a brilliant impression of Curly's trademark "Woo-woo-woo" or Shemp's immortal "Heep-eep-eep-eep."

Despite the rantings of a few crusty moralizers, the Three Stooges have become a vital thread in the American tapestry. The Stooges bridge generations; there is not a program around in which you'll catch more grandparents and grandkids mesmerized together in front of the television set. They bridge the sexes; contrary to popular belief, women love the Stooges, too, but are simply a bit more reluctant than men to poke a co-worker's eye in the workplace. And they bridge race, class, and culture; if you can snore like Shemp or drop to the ground and spin like Curly, exotic people from strange lands will welcome you as one of their own.

In fact, if you look hard enough, you'll realize that just about all the world's a Stooge.

Who's Who

··

THE BIG GUYS

Moe Howard

(June 19, 1897–May 4, 1975)

Moe was bossy.

But to know Moe simply for the punishment he inflicted is to know only a fraction of the Stooge.

Yes, Moe administered his share of eye-pokes and double face-slaps. And it is true that Moe emphasized his opinions by using sharp and jagged garage tools in ways not recommended by the manufacturer. But can any fair-minded person argue that the other Stooges didn't have it coming? Whether a man works in a downtown office or as a laborer in the field, there are only so many mistakes he can tolerate from inept partners before using an ax to express his displeasure. Moe, it turns out, was only human.

Interestingly, Moe often absorbed more abuse than he dished out. Take *Corny Casanovas*, in which Moe is knocked off a ladder, shoved underwater in a bucket, poked by the handle of a mop, shot in the scalp, smashed into a wall after laying down on a fold-out bed, nailed by a tack, shot in the rear end with dozens of carpenter's tacks by Larry's machine gun, forced to swallow a

pile of tacks, and given shoe polish instead of shaving cream with which to shave. You've had days like that, too; did you not become as grumpy as Moe?

Pacifist critics will be interested to learn that Moe had a tender side, too. He rarely hesitated, for example, to offer compliments, as when acknowledging Larry's good ideas by remarking, "You're a very intelligent imbecile." And no Stooge was more romantic. It was love that caused Moe to fire his pistol up the chimney at a philandering Shemp, and it was Moe who arranged dates for Larry and Shemp with his girlfriend Aggie's two sisters, Maggie and Baggie. (In fairness to Moe, he hadn't yet seen Baggie.)

Educators argue that there is no redeeming value in the Three Stooges, but they have missed Moe's talents as a linguist. His facility with the insult, while not the optimal way to impress academics, must nonetheless be recognized as a remarkable intellectual achievement. Moe reeled off more than 100 different invectives (see pages 56 and 57), but it was his uncanny ability to dismantle and reconfigure words into stinging insults that made his legend as a linguist. Before Moe, there was no such thing as a "hardboiled egghead," a "hot Airedale,"

(Shemp) and Jerome (Curly) went on to join him in making the Three Stooges the immortal comedy team they remain today. He married Helen Schonberger in 1925, and they produced two children, Joan and Paul. Moe's favorite Three Stooges film was the 1940 short *You Nazty Spy*, in which he bitingly spoofed Hitler. Moe died of lung cancer at age seventy-seven in 1975 while finishing work on his memoirs.

Larry Fine

(October 5, 1902–
January 24, 1975)

Like his bald and bushy head, Larry was a study in contrasts. Just when you thought you knew him, Larry would surprise you. His ethics, for example, zig-zagged across vast universes of morality. Unable to resist stuffing silverware into his tuxedo while a guest at swank parties, Larry might be deemed a common crook by law-enforcement types. Theologians, however, would argue that he lived a clean life, as when he took a disciplined stand after Moe offered him some "C-A-N-D-Y." "Nah," Larry replied firmly, "you know I don't smoke."

Larry's self-esteem could oscillate wildly. Often, he was self-effacing, as

or a "half-brother to a weasel." The English language misses Moe.

Moe was born Moses Horwitz in Bensonhurst, New York, and was one of five children. Two of his brothers, Samuel

Larry, with wife, Mabel, and daughter, Phyllis

when the Stooges were addressed as "gentlemen" by strangers. Larry's typically modest reply: "Who came in?" But equally often he was boastful, as when he bragged to a professor that there hadn't been a gentleman in the Stooges' family in fifty generations. He even had the gall to boast to a potential employer that the Stooges had graduated from detective school with the lowest temperatures in their class.

Larry is well remembered for his ability to follow orders. But parents who wish to raise obedient children might think twice about using him as a role model. Even Moe, who gave most of the orders, found painful Larry's attention to detail, as when Larry dropped a pile of metal pipes on his toes. Larry's rationale: "You told me to drop what I was doing. So I did."

Critics should go easy on Larry. Many was the time that he ventured into a stately mansion, only to proclaim that the joint reminded him of the reform school, evidence that his youth was at least partially misspent.

A rough childhood often produces reflective children; among the Stooges, Larry was the most philosophical. Faced in one film with execution at sunrise, Larry reasoned that he couldn't die since he had yet to see *The Jolson Story*. He displayed deep existential insight by telling a homicidal gangster not to kill him because death was too permanent.

Almost unknown as a conservationist (Larry refused to take baths because "it ain't spring yet"), he is also underappreciated as the Stooges' best idea man. When situations looked grim, it most often was Larry who suggested a way out. Had the Stooges made more films, some of his ideas might even have succeeded.

Larry was born Louis Feinberg in Philadelphia, and became an accomplished violinist and musician early in life. He married Mabel Haney and fathered two children, Phyllis and Johnny. Larry's favorite Three Stooges film was *Scrambled Brains* (1951). He died at age seventy-two in 1975.

Curly Howard
(October 22, 1903–January 18, 1952)

Deep down, don't we all wish we were Curly?

Curly never allowed the weight of the world (or the weight of his belly) to interfere with fun. He was immediate and of the moment, poised to pursue whatever new pleasure might present itself. Curly's joy resonated in the kitchen while stuffing turkeys, while using a straightedge razor and a hot towel to "shave" a block of ice, even on the gallows—cheering for himself—moments before being hanged.

Curly had fun.

That does not imply, however, that Curly was irresponsible. When asked to remind Moe to kill him later, Curly was always prompt to pull out a pencil and promise to make a note of it. When sent by Moe to bring back a flock of ducks, Curly assured everyone that "I'll be back in a quack with a quack . . . and I do mean quack!" He didn't perform all his duties flawlessly, but he always showed up to try.

Though Moe is the Stooge most noted for his temper, Curly could display a bit of the bile, too. Ordinary chefs, for instance, do not snap at critics by asking, "Are you casting asparagus on my cooking?" And few grown men express intellectual frustration by squealing, "I'm trying to think but nothing happens!" Occasionally, Curly would respond to criticism the way we all have: by declaring himself to be a victim of circumstance.

Curly was wonderful with animals and could certainly have made a name for himself in the veterinary sciences. Nowhere is this better illustrated than in *Rockin' Thru the Rockies*, in which Larry clobbers an unusual-looking fish with a metal pipe, only to be reminded by an eagle-eyed Curly that "that fish looks like Moe!" Few geese flew overhead without Curly imploring everyone to "look at the grouse!" Even during a reading lesson, after Moe recites the line "See the deer. Has the deer a little doe?" Curly is quick to interject as any animal lover would, "Yeah, two bucks." More than one homicidal gorilla took a fancy to Curly.

In the end, his real love was food. There is proof enough of this in *Three Little Pirates*, when the condemned Curly's thoughts turn hungry even as he is sentenced to death. Given the choice whether to die by burning or by being beheaded, Curly naturally selects the former, reasoning that "a hot stake is better than a cold chop." In court, after an angry judge cries "Order!" Curly replies that he'll take a ham sandwich. When the judge responds angrily, "Hold thy tongue," Curly answers as only a connoisseur could: "Not tongue—ham!" His joy at shooting a turkey from the sky is expressed simply in his declaration, "How I shall gobble this gobbler!" Like most food lovers, his sense of smell became highly developed; without realizing that he had sat upon a smoldering cigar, he remarked to a lovely woman that it "smells like somebody's frying onions." Curly lived for food.

Curly was born Jerome Lester Horwitz in Brooklyn, the fifth of five boys and younger brother to Samuel (Shemp) and Moses (Moe). Away from the camera, Curly possessed a delightful tenor and was an accomplished ballroom dancer. (Was there ever a more graceful comedian than Curly?)

As a boy, he accidentally shot himself in the foot while cleaning a rifle, causing agonizing pain that persisted into adulthood. Moe speculated that it was this pain—along with a fear that his short haircut made him less desirable to women—that caused his brother in later years to drink heavily. This drinking may have contributed to the stroke he suffered at age forty-two on the set of *Half-Wits Holiday* (1946), an illness that forced his retirement from the Stooges. Curly married four times and fathered two children, Marilyn and Janie (from different women) before dying at age forty-eight in 1952 of complications from further strokes.

Shemp Howard

(March 17, 1895–November 23, 1955)

In Jewish culture, a boy becomes a man when he turns thirteen. In Stooge culture, it happens when he learns to love Shemp.

A Stooge fan's first instinct is to compare Shemp with Curly. It was, after all, Shemp who replaced his younger brother after Curly fell ill and retired from the group in 1947. To some Curly lovers, this already made Shemp a bit of a badguy; no one, they claimed, could replace their hero.

They were right. It would have been impossible for anyone—even a comic actor as immensely talented as Shemp—to mimic the mesmerizing movements and irresistibly childlike persona that made Curly legend.

To his credit, Shemp never tried. Instead, he relied on skills

Shemp Howard

Shemp, with wife Gertrude (date unknown)

that already had established him as a great slapstick actor: an uncanny sense of timing, a savvy demeanor, and the apparent ability to move in 100 different directions at once. To watch Shemp shadow-box is to witness a mini-ballet in which an unfathomable whirlwind of bobs and weaves and double-slaps culminates, inevitably, in Shemp's own demise. Think that fancy footwork went unnoticed? Just tune in the popular television program *Seinfeld*, where Michael Richards's Kramer character pays homage every episode to all that Shemp did first.

Columbia was reluctant to hire Shemp as Curly's replacement, fearing he looked too much like his brother Moe (and perhaps not enough like brother Curly). But their minds soon changed as movie theater owners continued to demand Stooge shorts to attract customers.

Shemp, in the meantime, was bringing a newfound worldliness to the Stooges. He carried the air of a man who'd been around, a fellow who could toast gorgeous dames with gilded pickup lines such as "A couple of pip-pips, a little barbecue, and what have you!" When Moe warned him to stop making goo-goo eyes at a knockout blonde because the Stooges were in her home on business, Shemp informed him coolly, "I *mean* business!"

He was as cunning with men as he was charming with women. A master at controlling the crooked card tables of the Old West, he would rake in whopping poker jackpots with trademark poise and a casual "Come to Papa!" To colleagues who toasted him with a cheerful "Here's how," Shemp always declared suavely, "I know how!" Toughguys who insulted him were often told, "Them is fightin' words in my country!" When the brutes agreed to fight, however, Shemp used his wits instead of his fists, reminding them, "Well, we're not in my country."

As a top-flight physical comedian, Shemp was naturally concerned about his body. Nursing a bum leg, he told a physician not to amputate because "I've had it ever since I was a little kid." This concern for his own well-being often manifested itself in exaggerated symptoms, as when Shemp reported that "six

Is it real or isn't it? Only Shemp knows for sure (*Sing a Song of Six Pants*, 1947).

lions were tearing me apart bit-by-bit" after a frog had slipped down his shirt. Despite the Stooges' limited income, he tried to dress well, even asking Moe if his slip was showing when they wore kilts as Scottish detectives in *Hot Scots*.

Shemp was born Samuel Horwitz in Brooklyn. He was the third of five boys, two years older than brother Moe and eight years brother Curly's senior. His favorite Stooge film was his first, *Fright Night* (1947). He married Gertrude Frank in 1925 and had one son, Mort, before his death from a sudden heart attack in 1955 at age sixty.

Joe Besser
(August 12, 1907–March 1, 1988)

After Shemp died of a sudden heart attack in 1955, Moe and Larry were again forced to choose between hiring another Stooge or folding the tent. This time they selected Joe Besser, a roly-poly, chrome-domed vaudeville veteran who had enjoyed success on the Broadway stage in the 1930s and in his own series of Columbia short films from 1949 to 1956.

Joe made sixteen films with the Stooges, until Columbia closed the book on its short subjects department in 1958. Though Joe was quite earthly in appearance and mannerism, three of his sixteen Stooge films involved outer space. He remains best known for his plaintive whimpers, "Not so *hard!*" and "Oooh, you crazy!" Bravery was never Joe's forte, but he was always man enough to admit it. When asked by Moe in *Sappy Bullfighters* whether he was a man or a

mouse, Joe didn't hesitate to reply, "Squeak, squeak."

Unlike the other Stooges, Joe was not adept with his fists. He did, however, possess a cunning that served him well during sticky situations, as when jealous Latin lover José demanded to know how Joe dared to kiss his wife in front of him. "Turn around," Joe replied, "and I'll kiss her behind your back."

Joe was born in St. Louis and married Erna "Ernie" Kretschmer in 1932. He made his start in vaudeville as a teenager and soon found his way to Broadway, where he was discovered by executives at Columbia and signed to do his own series of two-reelers for the studio. During the 1940s, Joe appeared regularly on the legendary radio programs of Jack Benny, Eddie Cantor, and Fred Allen, and moved easily into regular television stints in the 1950s and 1960s on *The Ken Murray Show*, *The Joey Bishop Show*, and as the exasperated brat, Stinky, on *The Abbott and Costello Show*. He joined the Stooges in 1956 after Shemp—his close friend—died suddenly of a heart attack.

Joe's favorite Three Stooges film was *Flying Saucer Daffy* (1958). He called his association with the Stooges "the happiest years of my life in show business" and was front and center in 1983 when the Stooges were awarded a star on the Hollywood Walk of Fame. Joe died in 1988 at age eighty of heart failure.

"I go back fifty years with Joe Besser, when I played vaudeville with him," comic Milton Berle said after Joe's death. "He was one of a kind. He was very innovative, very creative. He was a darling of a man, very congenial."

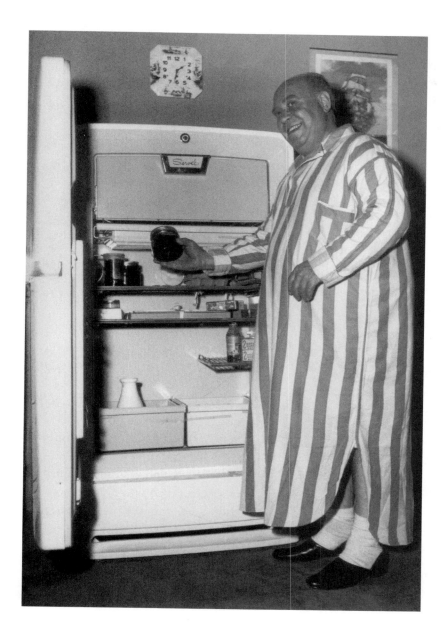

Joe appears to have had his share of experience with nighttime snacks.

Joe DeRita

(July 12, 1909–July 3, 1993)

Columbia closed its short features department in 1958, grounding all flying pies and forcing the Three Stooges to find another medium for their mayhem. But that wasn't the Stooges' only problem.

Joe Besser, who had joined the team for sixteen shorts, was forced to resign in order to tend to his ailing wife. For the third time since Curly fell ill in 1947, Moe and Larry faced the possibility that they had delivered their final slap.

Instead, they recruited a kindly faced, overgrown doughnut of a man,

That last case was a bit too much for Curly Joe to carry alone (*The Three Stooges Go Around the World in a Daze,* 1963).

Three of the roughest hombres ever to roam the Old West (*The Outlaws Is Coming,* 1965)

always a golden attribute when among Stooges. To Moe and Larry, he was just what the doctor ordered.

With crew cut in place and barrel belly front and center, DeRita looked enough like Curly to draw double takes even from seasoned Stooge fans. But Curly Joe, as he was called, proved to be very much his own Stooge.

Over the course of six years and six successful feature films, Curly Joe projected a warmth and, yes, intelligence that helped cast the Stooges in a new role: that of goodguys. Young children, especially, warmed to Curly Joe as they might to a doting grandfather; his relaxed delivery and soothing voice seemed perfectly suited to the ninety-minute feature-film format into which the Stooges were now venturing.

Curly Joe was born Joseph Wardell in Philadelphia to show business parents. Of the six men who filled the fabled shoes of Stooges, only Curly Joe was not Jewish (he came from French-Canadian and English stock).

Joe began his show business career as a dancer and quickly made his way to

Joe DeRita, to step into the most vaunted shoes in team comedy. DeRita was a veteran of burlesque and vaudeville, so he came steeped in the Stooges' rich tradition of precision timing and physical consequence. Despite his considerable girth, DeRita moved like a ballet dancer, the burlesque circuit, where he remained a mainstay for twenty-one years. His transition to film was a natural one. He was soon signed to a contract by MGM and also starred in a brief series of two-reelers for Columbia.

Curly Joe joined the Three Stooges in 1958 and made six feature films and countless, wildly popular public appearances with the team. His favorite Stooge film was *The Three Stooges Go Around the World in a Daze* (1963). He married Jean Sullivan in 1966 and died in 1993 at age eighty-three of pneumonia after a series of strokes.

"He used his stage experience," said Mr. DeRita's stepson, Robert Benjamin. "He made a lot of people happy in his life. He loved working with the Stooges."

Hercules has the strength of three men (*The Three Stooges Meet Hercules*, 1962).

OTHER NOTABLES

The great Stooge character actors were more than foils for flying fists; they were slapstick archetypes. Able to change identities faster than a superhero, these wonders of versatility perfected the cornerstone roles vital to classic slapstick and set the standard for generations to come.

Prince Shaam (Dick Curtis) and Mrs. van Bustle (Symona Boniface) discover how refreshing an ice-cold lemonade can be when prepared by a first-class waiter, butler, and chef (*Crash Goes the Hash*, 1944).

The Main Character Actors

Symona Boniface (1894–1950)

Stooge Films: 14 (1935–49) plus several remakes

Specialty: Refined society matron, quintessential party guest

Immortal Stooge Role(s): Vulnerable dowager Mrs. van Bustle (*Crash Goes the Hash*, 1944); opera-loving patron of the arts Mrs. Bixby (*Micro-Phonies*, 1945); blue-blooded partygoer Mrs. Smythe Smythe (*Half-Wits Holiday*, 1947)

Symona Boniface's characters epitomized upper-crust dignity, ladies who expected to live free from the hazard of flying cream pies.

They projected an air of pleasant refinement, delighted in attending the fanciest balls, were ready to presume that fellow party guests possessed pedigrees equal to their own . . . despite whatever strange behavior those guests might otherwise display.

Yet there was Boniface's Mrs. Smythe Smythe in *Half-Wits Holiday*, on the receiving end of desserts never intended for an aristocrat's face.

Stooge fans remember Boniface for one scene above all others. In *Half-Wits Holiday*, as she attempts to calm a jittery Moe (who knows that a dangling pie is about to fall from the ceiling), a concerned Boniface tells Moe, "Young man, you act as if the Sword of Damocles were hanging over your head!"

"Lady," Moe replies, "you must be psychic . . ."

Even after the pie hits Boniface square in the kisser, we realize Moe was right. She was a lady.

Boniface died in California in 1950.

Vernon Dent (1895–1963)

Stooge Films: 56 (1936–54) plus several remakes

Specialty: Unlimited

Immortal Stooge Role(s): Decapitation specialist Dr. D. Lerious (*From Nurse to Worse*, 1940); hardboiled police captain Mullins (*Shivering Sherlocks*, 1948); shifty attorney I. Fleecem (*Heavenly Daze*, 1948); diabolical jewel thief/doorman Hassan Ben Sober (*Malice in the Palace*, 1949)

At some point during each of their films, the Stooges collide with an obstacle that threatens their very existence. More often than not, that obstacle is Vernon Dent.

Straight man extraordinaire, Dent had don't-mess-with-me eyes and a regal air that cloaked a quick-fuse temper. Whether he portrayed a medieval king or a gritty detective, Dent projected the demeanor of a man who desired nothing more than to be left alone.

Dent's genius lay in his ability to plummet from grace at the slightest provocation. His characters did not suffer fools kindly, but his attempts to deal with the Stooges were often more injurious to himself than to them. A master of restraint, Dent always allowed the audience to realize that he was doomed without ever appearing to know it himself. That is the mark of the consummate straight man.

There was no character Dent couldn't play. He could be silly, gruff, boastful, or bashful. Even more impressive was his ability to transition seamlessly between personalities; his kings were as believable

Vernon Dent proves that not all military officers enforce discipline according to the government's strict codes of conduct (*Booby Dupes*, 1945).

This splendid chicken, ripe for stealing from Vernon Dent, would have fed four if the dog had considered sharing (*Half Shot Shooters*, 1936).

rewarding the Stooges as they were ordering their executions moments later. Watch Dent shift gears in *Shivering Sherlocks* when his line of merciless interrogation is flipped by Shemp, or study his facial expressions in *Squareheads of the Round Table* as Shemp unknowingly insults him. The Stooges were lucky to work so closely with so gifted a talent.

Dent died suddenly from a heart attack in 1963 at age sixty-eight.

Bud Jamison (1894–1944)

Stooge Films: 50 (1934–44)
Specialty: Policemen and butlers
Immortal Stooge Role(s): Jovial Confederate Colonel Buttz (*Uncivil Warriors*, 1935); furious French trapper Pierre (*Whoops, I'm an Indian!*, 1936); backslapping, heavy-brogued beat cop Officer O'Halloran (*Mutts to You*, 1938)

Jamison was the first great Stooge character actor and a master of foreign accents. The jumbo-sized Jamison was deadliest when playing authority figures who were just a smidgen too trusting. His hearty belly laugh and thick Southern drawl as Colonel Buttz made it seem only natural that he would reveal Confederate military secrets to the crafty Major Hyde (Curly) in *Uncivil Warriors*. His ruddy disposition as Irish beat cop Officer O'Halloran in *Mutts to You* explains why he became so smitten with fetching neighborhood lass Mrs. O'Toole (Curly, disguised and wanted for kidnapping).

Jamison was a Christian Scientist who reportedly refused medication upon falling ill at age fifty. He died in 1944 in Hollywood.

Christine McIntyre (1911–1984)

Stooge Films: 22 (1944–50) plus several remakes
Specialty: Unlimited
Immortal Stooge Role(s): Reluctant opera star Alice Bixby (*Micro-Phonies*, 1945); gorgeous speakeasy dame Nell (three films); thunder-fisted Miss Hopkins (*Brideless Groom*, 1947); biddy-to-beauty fountain of youth beneficiary Serena Flint (*All Gummed Up*, 1947); crooning, lovesick Princess Elaine (*Squareheads of the Round Table*, 1948)

When Columbia producers hired Christine McIntyre, no one expected anything more than another sweet-faced, curvy blonde as background ornamentation.

She made them think otherwise in a hurry. Even in brief early roles, it was clear that behind the angelic cheekbones lay a woman with a flawless sense of timing and an uncanny instinct for comic counterpoint. In the course of a few years, McIntyre became a fan favorite and developed into one of the great comedic actresses of all time.

McIntyre had no weaknesses. She was as capable playing the damsel in distress as she was playing the homicidal foreign spy, as comfortable batting an eyelash as throwing a roundhouse punch. Her allure was neither innocent nor vampy; there is not a single McIntyre character who gets by solely on looks or without a potent dose of wit and opinion. McIntyre was a modern woman long before it was fashionable.

McIntyre graduated from Chicago Musical College and used her lovely soprano in films like *Micro-Phonies* (to

Christine McIntyre as the enchanting Mrs. Leander (*Idle Roomers*, 1944)

sing "Voices of Spring") and *Squareheads of the Round Table* (in an aching duet with Cedric the Blacksmith). But, more important, the training seemed to have stamped her with an impeccable sense of rhythm and timing. McIntyre's interplay

with detective Shemp in *Who Done It?*—while each tries to poison the other's drink—is a masterpiece of finesse and nuance between two comic actors at the top of their games.

McIntyre made films with the Stooges and other Columbia short-feature artists until 1954, when she married radio pioneer J. Donald Wilson. She died of cancer in California in 1984.

Emil Sitka (1915–1998)

Stooge Films: 32 (1947–65) including feature films

Specialty: Unlimited

Immortal Stooge Role(s):

Curmudgeonly landlord Amos Flint (*All Gummed Up*, 1947); embattled justice of the peace J. M. Benton (*Brideless Groom*, 1947); jittery murder target Old Man Goodrich (*Who Done It?*, 1949); Shemp's wealthy uncle Phineas Bowman (*Gents in a Jam*, 1952)

Christine McIntyre stains Moe's reputation (*Three Pests in a Mess*, 1945).

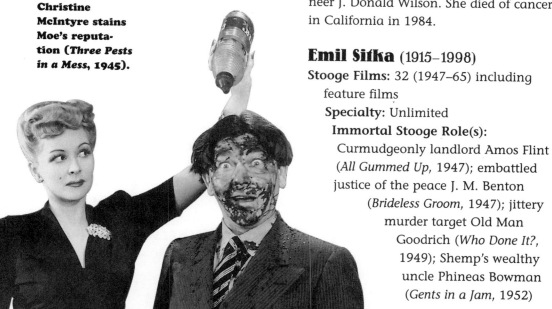

Emil Sitka

Emil Sitka seemed always to wobble and warble. Whether playing a savvy lawyer, a grumpy landlord, or a jittery inventor, Sitka infused his characters' psyches with disorienting ribbons of doubt and a perpetual shadow of suspicion.

Sitka had the funniest eyes in Stoogedom. Even when he didn't speak, his darting pupils seemed to foretell the chaos that would inevitably unfold before him. His ability to remain stoic and stately while playing butlers caught in pie fight crossfires is legendary.

Sitka is the only character actor to appear with all four incarnations of the Stooges (Moe and Larry plus Curly, Shemp, Joe, and Curly Joe). His first film—and Curly's last—was *Half-Wits Holiday*

(1947), and his career continued until *The Outlaws Is Coming* (1965), after which the Stooges finally hung it up for good.

Sitka is undoubtedly best known for his role as dumbstruck justice of the peace J. M. Benton in *Brideless Groom*. Struggling to overcome violent objections by a horde of women who demand to marry Shemp, Benton's warbling nuptials can still be heard above the din of slaps and punches:

"Hold hands, you lovebirds!"

Emil Sitka died in 1998.

Other Significant Players

Stanley Blystone (1895–1956)
Stooge Films: 14 (1935–52)
Specialty: The gruff boss
Immortal Stooge Role(s): Dirty-dealing card shark and homing pigeon owner Longhorn Pete (*Goofs and Saddles*, 1937); unforgiving Sergeant MacGillicuddy (*Half Shot Shooters*, 1936)

Dick Curtis (1902–1952)
Stooge Films: 12 (1938–51)
Specialty: Badguys
Immortal Stooge Role(s): Prince Shaam (*Crash Goes the Hash*, 1944); Badlands Blackie (*Three Troubledoers*, 1946)

Dudley Dickerson (1906–1968)
Stooge Films: 7 (1940–49) plus 1 remake
Specialty: Cook

Badlands Blackie (Dick Curtis) makes the lovely Nell (Christine McIntyre) an offer she cannot refuse (*Three Troubledoers*, 1946).

Dudley Dickerson looks ready for his own stretcher after uncovering the Stooges' ingenious hiding place (*From Nurse to Worse*, 1940).

Immortal Stooge Role(s): Stunned (and wet) cook (*A Plumbing We Will Go*, 1940)

Dudley Dickerson was the most frequently seen black actor in Stooge films. Though constantly cast as a skittish, bulging-eyed cook, porter, or janitor, Dickerson transcended the racial stereotyping common to the day by demonstrating a sense of comic timing equal to that of the Stooges. His instinct for allowing tension to hang just so long before relieving it with a trademark double take stamps him as an immortal in the slapstick genre.

Bess Flowers (1900–1984)

Stooge Films: 6 (1938–45)
Specialty: Fancy ladies
Immortal Stooge Role(s): Revenge-hungry society matron Muriel van Twitchett (*Termites*, 1938); nouveau riche art snob Maggie Smirch (*Tassels in the Air*, 1938); careless mother Mrs. Manning (*Mutts to You*, 1938)

Eddie Laughton (1903–1952)

Stooge Films: 15 (1935–45)
Specialty: Clerks, hangers-on
Immortal Stooge Role(s): Percy Pomeroy, prisoner #41144 (*So Long Mr. Chumps*, 1941)

Kenneth MacDonald (1901–1972)

Stooge Films: 12 (1946–55) plus several remakes

Specialty: Brainy badguys
Immortal Stooge Role(s): "Honest" Icabod Slipp (*Hold That Lion!*, 1947); cutthroat armored car bandit Lefty Loomis (*Shivering Sherlocks*, 1948); tribal chief and shrunken-head aficionado Varunu (*Hula-La-La*, 1951); corrupt campaign chief Wm. "Bill" Wick (*Three Dark Horses*, 1952)

It was serious trouble for the Stooges whenever they met up with a character played by Kenneth MacDonald. His crooks, always suave and debonair, could call upon both brain and brawn to dispatch meddlesome enemies like Moe, Larry, and Shemp.

MacDonald administered perhaps the soundest thrashing the Stooges ever took when, as shady estate executor Icabod Slipp in *Hold That Lion!*, he accused each of the Stooges of being the villainous Slipp, then battered them unconscious for the offense. Even out of suit and tie, MacDonald wreaked havoc. As single-minded witch doctor Varunu in *Hula-La-La*, he needed only a loincloth and a scowl to convince the Stooges he was dead serious about shrinking their heads.

Jacques ("Jock") O'Mahoney (1919–1989)

Stooge Films: 3 (1947–49)
Specialty: Bumbling and stumbling Romeos
Immortal Stooge Role(s): Uncoordinated gunslinger The Arizona Kid (*Out West*, 1947); lovesick Cedric the Blacksmith (*Squareheads of the Round Table*, 1948)

This procedure certainly could not have been part of Cedric the Blacksmith's (Jacques O'Mahoney) blacksmith training (*Knutzy Knights*, 1954).

Even wicked magician Mergatroyd (Phil Van Zandt) is enchanted by the Stooges' gallant treatment of this Coleslawvanian damsel (*Fiddlers Three*, 1948).

Phil Van Zandt (1904–1958)

Stooge Films: 13 (1940–58) plus several
  remakes
Specialty: Scheming royalty

Immortal Stooge Role(s): The Black
  Prince (*Squareheads of the Round Table*,
  1948); megalomaniac magician
  Mergatroyd (*Fiddlers Three*, 1948)

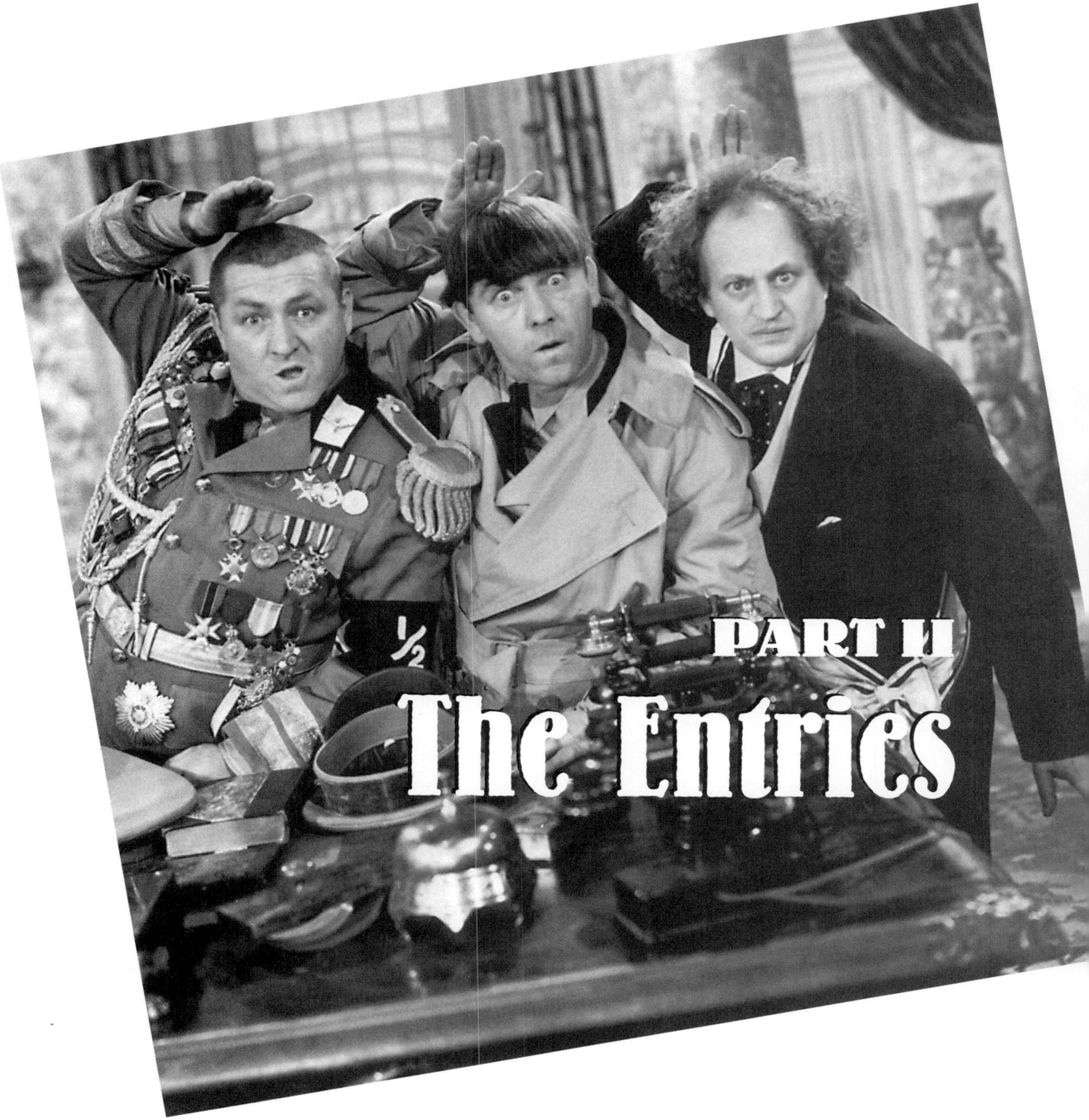

½

PART II
The Entries

How to Use Part II

Here's what you'll find in the typical entry in Part II:

1. The term itself, listed alphabetically and in **bold** type.
2. The movie in which the term appears, written in *italics*. Often, two movies are listed because some of the later Three Stooges films were remakes of earlier films and used many of the same terms.
3. Other relevant terms that appear elsewhere in the book, ***bold and italicized*** for easy reference.
4. Entries are alphabetized as they sound. Greedy landlord Amos Flint, for example, is listed in the "A" section, humorless physician Dr. D. Lerious in the "D" section, opera diva Señorita Cucaracha in the "S" section, etc.

5. Keep a sharp lookout for Immutable Stooges Laws, the ironclad rules that govern all Stooge films. They pop up in this section faster than Moe can execute a double slap, so keep your eyes peeled, puddin' head.

Example:

The Amateur Carpenter—
Though Shemp proved in film after film that his reading skills needed work, he is entrusted in *The Tooth Will Out* to extract the aching molar of a ferocious and desperate Western bandit. When Shemp consults the book ***The Amateur Carpenter*** instead of ***Practical Dentistry***, the odds are not with the bandit.

A

A.A.M. (Amalgamated Association of Morons) Local 6⅞—The Stooges couldn't be expected to throw pies under just any conditions; they needed protection. Thus their labor union, the Amalgamated Association of Morons, Local 6⅞. When a stuffy butler questions their integrity in *Half-Wits Holiday*, the boys flash their A.A.M. buttons and chant together: "We are morons, tried and true, let us do our call for you!" followed by assorted grunting, groaning, and impossible facial contortions.

A-1 Correspondence School of Detecting—As a grizzled veteran gumshoe, *Inspector McCormick* senses that the bumbling Stooges aren't ready for detective work in *Hot Scots* and *Hot Ice*. His worries are put to rest, however, when the boys remind him where they earned their stripes: the A-1 Correspondence School of Detecting.

A.B. Cloud & Co.—Spaceship sales firm that uses beautiful aliens *Tyra and Elektra* to distribute its business cards in *Flying Saucer Daffy*. Their simple but enticing pitch: "A.B. Cloud & Co.— Distributors Sputnik G.I.-8—New and Used Space Ships—*200 Vapor Blvd., Zircon*—Phone: *Bleep Bluep Blop*."

A-K-70—Curly's prison number in *Beer Barrel Polecats* and *In the Sweet Pie and Pie*. Though not in jail for a vehicular offense, the Stooges wear the identification numbers on license plates affixed to their chests. See also *B-K-68* and *O-K-67*.

A. Mouser—Manager of the *Lightning Pest Control Co.* in *Ants in the Pantry*. Mouser has the mind of a dirty rat and little command of the exterminator's code of ethics, ordering his three employees to drum up business by planting mice, ants, moths, and other pests in the homes of prospective clients.

A.P. Willis Company—The book Curly mistakenly uses to perform a marriage ceremony between the ill-tempered *Badlands Blackie* and his reluctant but beautiful bride *Nell* in *The Three Troubledoers*. Curly begins by reading an unconventional vow, "Do you take this horse collar for your lawfully wedded harness?"

A. Panther—Stingy owner of *Panther Brewing Company* in *Three Little Beers* who would have had far less trouble had he seen fit to invite *all* employees to his company's golf outing.

A to Z Express Company—Name of the Stooges' moving company in *The Ghost Talks* and *Creeps*. The Stooges try hard, but clients of this business might quibble with the term *Express*.

Abdul's Cactus Remedy—Get-rich-quick elixir originally concocted by Dr. Abdul (see also **Dr. Abdul's Medicine Show**) in *Phony Express*. The Stooges become sole distributors of the potion, trusting Abdul's claim that the potion "cures every ailment known to man or beast."

Moe's mystical turban and flowing robes only hint at the power contained in a bottle of Abdul's Cactus Remedy (*Phony Express*, 1943).

Abel Lamb Stewer—Not known for their political activism, the Stooges nonetheless get involved in the presidential campaign of shady Abel Lamb Stewer in *Three Dark Horses*. An exact count was never given, but Moe probably delivered some votes with his sign that read, *"Don't Be a Muttonhead— Vote for Abel Lamb Stewer for President."* See also *Hammond Egger*.

"A-Calling We Do Come"—A song of love and courtship sung by the Stooges

in *Musty Musketeers* (sung to the tune of "Farmer in the Dell"):

> *A-calling we do come*
> *To woo our maidens fair*
> *We bring them flowers and wile-away hours*
> *But get ye not in their hair!*

"About five-foot-five by five-foot-five"—Police departments around the world wish for more witnesses like Moe, who in *Quiz Whizz* provides this astonishingly precise physical description of the missing Joe. See also *Skin*.

"According to Darwin . . ."—The introductory title in *I'm a Monkey's Uncle*. It reads, "According to Darwin, our Ancestors Hung From Trees By Their Tails—And Thereby Hangs Our Tale." See also *"Any Similarity . . ."*

Achilles, the Heel—Shifty shakedown artist in *The Three Stooges Meet Hercules*.

Acme Escort Bureau—Upper-crust escort firm recommended to society matron *Muriel van Twitchett* in *Termites of 1938*. It is to Mrs. van Twitchett's disadvantage that Acme Escort's listing in the telephone directory is located so close to the Stooge-owned *Acme Exterminating Company*.

Acme Exterminating Company— IMMUTABLE STOOGES LAW #1: If fancy rich people have a problem that needs fixing fast, the Stooges will own a nearby business that will claim to solve the problem. In *Termites of 1938*, the Stooge-owned Acme Exterminating Company sounds like just the cure for a bug-infested family planning a ritzy party. The company's slogans, *"If You Got 'Em, We'll Get 'Em"* and "They Never Get Away From Us!" however, are optimistic at best. See also *"At Your Service . . ."*

Acme Service Station—Gasoline station where the Stooges provide enthusiastic but calamitous Super Service in *Violent is the Word for Curly.*

"Actual Photo of Flying Saucer Sets Country Ablaze"—Screaming headline in the **New York Gazette** announcing photographic evidence of alien life in *Flying Saucer Daffy.*

"Adam and Eve on a raft"—Moe's kitchen slang for two eggs on toast in *Playing the Ponies.* When the customer requests that the eggs be scrambled, Moe shouts to the kitchen, "Wreck 'em!"

"Adirondack . . ."—All three Stooges volunteer to become a jilted woman's lover in *Boobs in Arms*, but she will have only one. Moe solves the problem by pointing to each Stooge in rapid succession while chanting this catchy rhythmic rhyme:

> *Adirondack one zell, two zell, three zell, zam!*
> *The bucktail thenaget tickle and tam*
> *Eh, scram, the butcher man*
> *See, saw, buck, out!"*

Were it not for the hasty arrival of the woman's jealous husband, Curly would have celebrated his victory.

Admiral Hawkins's Flagship—Though unable to aim or even load a cannon, privates Moe, Larry, and Curly push, pull, and tweak the weapon until they man-age to sink Admiral Hawkins's flagship with a single blast in *Half Shot Shooters.*

Admiral H. S. Taylor—Officer in command at the *Republic of Televania Naval Base* in *Three Little Sew and Sews.*

Aggie, Maggie, and Baggie—Was it worth battling three brutish cavemen in *I'm a Monkey's Uncle* and *Stone Age Romeos* for the fair hands of Aggie, Maggie, and Baggie? Moe and Larry think so. Shemp gets Baggie.

Ajax—Impatient millionaire in *All the World's a Stooge* who indulges his trendy wife's wish to adopt a refugee child by providing her with three knicker-clad imps: Moe, Larry, and Curly.

Ajax Sportswear—On the run from the cutthroat principles of the **Cheatham Investment Company**, the Stooges take refuge in the Ajax Sportswear store, where Curly accidentally murders a mannequin in *Three Pests in a Mess.*

Alert Detective Agency—When the life of *Old Man Goodrich* is threatened in *Who Done It?*, detectives Moe, Larry, and Shemp from the Alert Detective Agency are hired to protect him. Goodrich lives, anyway.

Ali Ben Woodman and His Swinging Bedouins—Jazz combo featured on the radio during the Stooges' taxicab ride to Egypt in *We Want Our Mummy.* After the group's song, the radio announcer asks, "Do you need money? Borrow on your camel or elephant! No red tape, no cosigners."

Alice Bixby—Wonderful soprano in *Micro-Phonies* whose mother, opera patron **Mrs. Bixby**, refuses to allow her to perform. Under the alias **Miss Andrews**, Alice records a magnificent version of *"Voices of Spring,"* a song that launches her career as a singer and ends the short but glorious career of her lip-synching accomplice **Señorita Cucaracha** (Curly).

"All Parts in This Picture Are Played By the Three Stooges"—Opening title for *Self Made Maids*. See also **Moella, Larraine,** and **Shempetta.**

"All Unmarried Redheaded Maidens . . ."—See *"Proclamation . . ."*

Alma Matter—Beautiful registrar and instructor at the local school of criminology in *Blunder Boys*. She is also the daughter of **Watts D. Matter**, dean of the school.

Amarillo Beer—Made "For Thirsty Throats," Amarillo Beer is the sponsor of the sexy calendar the Stooges mistake for a map of **President Ward Robey**'s palace in *Saved by the Belle*.

The Amateur Carpenter—Though Shemp proved in film after film that his reading skills needed work, he is entrusted in *The Tooth Will Out* to extract the aching molar of a ferocious and desperate Western bandit. When Shemp consults the book *The Amateur Carpenter* instead of *Practical Dentistry*, the odds are not with the bandit.

"Amazing! Incredible! Horrific! . . ."—Tell-it-like-it-is carnival poster alerting citizens to the appearance of a colossal show in *Idle Roomers*. The entire poster reads, "Amazing! Incredible! Horrific! The Greatest Attraction of the Age—Lupe The Wolf Man—Alive-In Person."

Ambrose Rose Estate—A death in the Stooges' family can only mean one thing: a big inheritance that won't come easy. In *Hold That Lion!* and *Loose Loot*, a newspaper delivers the news: "Ambrose Rose Estate Released From Probate/Three Nephews Sole Heirs/Huge Estate Turned Over To Executor."

Amelia Carter—World-traveling lovely swooped up by the Stooges and **Phileas Fogg III** in *The Three Stooges Go Around the World in a Daze*.

"America's Gift to Indigestion"—See *Ye Colonial Inn*.

Amos Flint—Greedy landlord who is delighted at the prospect of evicting the Stooges from the **Cut Throat Drug Store** in *All Gummed Up* and *Bubble Trouble*. Only when the Stooges offer Flint a dose of their miraculous **Fountain of Youth** does the old geezer allow them to stay. And that is only before the potent potion turns him into a crying infant.

Amscray, Ixnay, and Onay—Scheming cabinet members who oust **King Herman 6⅞** of **Moronica** and bring **Moe Hailstone** to power in *You Nazty Spy*.

Amscray, Ixnay, and Umpchay—Devious cabinet members who attempt to return the throne of **Moronica** to **King Herman 6⅞** by eliminating dictator **Moe Hailstone** in *I'll Never Heil Again*.

Anacanapanasan, eenar, anasana-pacarscram—Seldom-used ingredients—at least in the art world—splashed by the Stooges on another painter's masterpiece in *Pop Goes the Easel*.

Anacanapon and piddledictatar—Specialty surgical tools requested by veterinarian Moe while preparing for canine surgery in *Calling All Curs*.

Anapanacag, cedascram falsyeth, anacanapon, and eenots—Ingredients expertly mixed by *Drs. Howard, Fine, and Howard* in an effort to cure the eccentric behavior of the patient in Room 81 in *Men in Black*. The Stooges' curiosity deprives the patient of a cure, since the doctors drink the medicine themselves.

Anesthesia—See *Kingdom of Anesthesia*.

"Ancient Egypt—In the Reign of the Great King Rootentooten"—Site of *Mummy's Dummies*. Opening title reads, "Ancient Egypt—In the Reign of the Great King Rootentooten." See also **King Rootentooten**.

Ancient Erysipelas—Site of *Matri-Phony*. *Matri-Phony* provides an insightful glimpse into why historians remain torn on the accuracy of ancient names used by the Stooges in their films. Here, "Mohicus" and "Larrycus" seem authentic, but scholars still can't pinpoint "Curleycue" to any known ancient time period. See also *Octopus Grabus*, *Mohicus*, *Larrycus*, and *Curleycue*.

"And lay you right down, too!"—Curly's reassuring afterthought in *Phony Express* after Moe promises an angry

sheriff that a bottle of miracle medicine will "pick you right up."

"And the rest of the day for myself!"—After Moe offers a charming toast in *Fuelin' Around* and *Hot Stuff* by exclaiming, "Top o' the morning to you," gentleman Shemp suavely adds, "And the rest of the day for myself!"

Anemia—See *State of Anemia*.

Angel—Ghastly hatchet man who works for crook *Lefty Loomis* in *Shivering Sherlocks* and *Of Cash and Hash*. Angel is, by even the most compassionate of standards, IQ-challenged, but seems content to bide his time sharpening his hatchet and mumbling to himself. One gets the feeling that nothing short of, say, three bumbling detectives could pry the troubled creature from his chair.

Angus and McPherson—Diabolical crooks who mastermind a plot to rob *The Earl of Glenheather* in *Hot Scots* and *Scotched in Scotland*.

Anna Conda—Wheelchair-bound hospital patient in *Men in Black* who is stopped by the Stooges in the hospital hallway and asked for her driver's license.

Annie and Fannie—As associates of the Three Stooges go, it was probably safer to be a pet than a friend. Annie and Fannie are the faithful fire department horses the Stooges take for a washing to a Turkish bath in *Flat Foot Stooges*.

Annie Oakley—Blond gunslinger with a marksman's eye, an angel's face, and an inexplicable desire to bail out yellow-bellied sheriff **Kenneth Cabot** and his three deputies in *The Outlaws Is Coming*.

"Another Broadway Turkey . . ."— See *"Theatre Chit Chat."*

Another turkey—Delectable dessert ordered by the Stooges after dining on turkey with champion wrestler **Ivan Bustoff** in *Grips, Grunts and Groans*.

"Antiques Made While-U-Waite . . ."—See *Ye Old Furniture Shoppe*.

Antonio Zucchini Salami Gorgonzola de Pizza—Sure the Stooges were wrong about him, but if you stumbled across an Italian organ grinder with a British accent named Antonio Zucchini Salami Gorgonzola de Pizza, wouldn't you be suspicious? Against the manifest weight of evidence, detectives Moe, Larry, and Shemp grill de Pizza on his role in the murder of **Slug McGurk** in *Tricky Dicks*.

"Any Resemblance . . ."—Mozart was not the only man to utilize variations on a theme. The opening disclaimers "Any Resemblance . . ." were used in several films. *You Nazty Spy* warns, "Any Resemblance Between the Characters in This Picture and Any Persons, Living or Dead, is a Miracle." *Back from the Front* cautions, "Any Resemblance Between the Characters in this Picture and Other Human Beings is a Dirty Shame." And *Don't Throw That Knife* warns, "Any Resemblance Between The Three Stooges and Regular Human Beings, Whether Living or Dead, is a Dirty Shame."

"Any Similarity . . ."—The opening disclaimer in *I'm a Monkey's Uncle* warns, "Any Similarity Between the Characters in this Picture and Real Monkeys is Definitely Unfair to the Monkeys."

Apex Construction Company—IMMUTABLE STOOGES LAW #2: If the Stooges breathe a sigh of relief after making an escape, the real fix is just ahead. In *How High Is Up?*, Moe, Larry, and Curly manage to flee from angry workmen, only to find themselves in line for a job with the Apex Construction Company on the unsteady girders of a 97-story skyscraper.

April, May, and June—When the Stooges foil swindlers from stealing the oil-rich land of **Widow Jenkins**, the portly woman awards them what no amount of oil can buy: her beautiful daughters April, May, and June. Curly, always a connoisseur of the fair sex, judges them to be "three of the prettiest months of the year!"

"Are you casting asparagus on my cooking?"—Great chefs consider themselves to be artists, and are naturally quite sensitive to criticism of their creations. Curly is no exception in *Busy Buddies*, in which he challenges a customer scornful of his pancakes by asking, "Are you casting asparagus on my cooking?"

"Are you married or happy?"—Enigmatic question asked by Curly as he "shaves" a block of ice in *An Ache in Every Stake*.

"Are you short of money? . . ."—
Punchy commercial playing on medieval
radio in *Squareheads of the Round Table*.
Because they are busy trying to save the
heads of the king and a noble blacksmith, the Stooges listen to only the first
part of the captivating ad:

> Are you short of money?
> Are you still wearing last year's rusty
>   old armor?
> Then see the Scowling Scotsman today!

Arizona Kid—Gallant but clumsy cowboy held captive by *Doc Barker*'s gang
in *Out West*. The Arizona Kid is justifi-
ably proud of his wavy blond locks, but
probably won't mention in his resumé
that he needed the Stooges to bust him
out of jail.

**"Armored Car Robbers Identified—
Café Workers Name Loomis
Gang"**—Shocking headline that appears
on the front page of *The Daily Record
Post* in *Shivering Sherlocks* and *Of Cash
and Hash*. The revelation is bad news for
the Loomis gang, but even worse news
for stoolpigeon café workers Moe, Larry,
and Shemp.

Arthur van Twitchett—Wealthy
sportsman whose hedonistic fishing trip
prompts his wife Muriel to call upon
three unorthodox escorts in *Termites
of 1938*.

Asbestos suit—Outfit that *Uncle
Mortimer* advises the recently deceased
Shemp to wear to prepare for the after-
life in *Heavenly Daze* and *Bedlam in
Paradise*.

"At a loss for adjectives"—
Restaurateur Moe's self-described reaction when he realizes partners Curly and
Larry have stolen hot dogs and silverware from the incoming owners of the
Flounder Inn restaurant in *Playing
the Ponies*.

"At the Front"—Title of the sketch performed by the Stooges in *Gents Without
Cents*, in which Curly is "volunteered"
by Moe and Larry to die for his country
in the line of military duty. See also
Hill 303.

"At Your Service . . ."—The Stooges
were expert at attracting business by
using snappy slogans and catch phrases.
As *Acme Exterminating Company*
employees in *Termites of 1938*, they
chant, "At your service day and night,
we do the job and do it right . . . Acme!"
In *We Want Our Mummy*, the Stooges promote their detective agency by chanting,
"At your service night and day, if we
don't get 'em you don't pay . . .
Excelsior!"

"Atomic Documents Missing . . ."—
See *Daily Gazette*.

Axis Partners—The scheming foreign
ministers who conspire with *Moe
Hailstone* to plan his conquest of the
world in *I'll Never Heil Again*. The
Partners include *Chizzilini*, the *Minister
of Rum* (or *Bay of Rum* as he is introduced), and *Napoleon*.

B

B. A. Copper—Unrealistic chief of detectives in *Tricky Dicks*, he gives the Stooges only twenty-four hours to capture the killer of **Slug McGurk**. He is probably unfamiliar with the methods of the Stooges, as their best work usually does not come when they are rushed.

B. Bopper—Brilliant but gullible curator of the **Museum of Natural History** in *Stone Age Romeos*. Bopper is prepared to pay the Stooges $25,000 for their film of modern-day cavemen until he overhears Moe bragging about pulling a fast one on the museum. It is at that point that Bopper loses his academic refinement, pulls violently on the Stooges' fake beards, and saves the museum's funds for more noble research projects.

B. K. Doaks—Theater producer of ten flop shows who instructs the Stooges to forcibly remove critic **Nick Barker** from the premier of his eleventh in *Three Hams on Rye*.

B-K-68—Moe's prison number in *Beer Barrel Polecats* and *In the Sweet Pie and Pie*, it is affixed to a license plate he wears. See also *A-K-70* and *O-K-67*.

Museum curator B. Bopper (Emil Sitka) is certain that cavemen still exist but doesn't realize how close to home they are (*Stone Age Romeos*, 1955).

B. O. Botswaddle—President of *Super Terrific Productions* film studio in *Three Missing Links*. Botswaddle is remarkably adroit in his choice of actors, casting Curly as a gorilla and Moe and Larry as Neanderthals in his upcoming blockbuster production, *Jilted in the Jungle*.

B.O. Pictures Corporation—Not the luckiest of movie studios, struggling B.O. Pictures calls upon the help of the Stooges in *Hula-La-La* and *Studio Stoops*. They are not currently in business.

B. O. Davis—Though *So Long Mr. Chumps* was made more than fifty years ago, students of crime still puzzle over the perplexing motives of B. O. Davis. Perhaps the most enigmatic character ever to cross the Stooges' paths, Davis rewards Moe, Larry, and Curly bountifully for the return of his lost oil bonds, then generously commissions them to bring him an honest man. Only when the Stooges are inside prison walls trying to bust free that innocent man do they learn that B. O. Davis is really *Lone Wolf Louie*, a notorious criminal with a truly odd modus operandi.

B-U-R-P—Distinctive call letters of the radio station that sponsors the *Mystery Motor Jackpot Show* in *A Missed Fortune*.

"The back of the drapes"—What an ornery Curly tells an interrogator is behind the drapes in *Matri-Phony*.

"Bad Lands"—Ominous sign nailed to a tree in *Goofs and Saddles*.

Badlands Blackie—Among the most sinister of badguys in Stooges films, Badlands Blackie has killed the last six sheriffs of *Dead Man's Gulch* and is anxious to kill the seventh, Curly, in *The Three Troubledoers*.

"The bag left me holding the babe!"—After *Molly the Glamour Girl* abandons a baby in the Stooges' pawnshop in *Three Loan Wolves*, Larry explains the sudden turn of events to partners Moe and Curly by declaring, "The bag left me holding the babe!"

Balbo the Magician—House magician at the swank *Kokonuts Grove* nightclub in *Loco Boy Makes Good*, and owner of a dazzling jacket Curly simply must try on.

Lucille Ball—Lucy was a young unknown when she played the sassy *Daisy Simms* in *Three Little Pigskins* (1934). But the experience, apparently, left a lasting impression. In Okuda and Watz's *The Columbia Comedy Shorts: Two-Reel Hollywood Film Comedies, 1933–1958*, Lucy remarks that "Working with . . . the Three Stooges was my first training in slapstick and real physical comedy. And I very much appreciated training with some real greats."

"A barking dog never bites . . ."—Shemp's defiant last words before a tough-talking Moe takes an angry bite out of his nose in *Pest Man Wins*.

Baron of Brains—See *Baron of Gray Matter*.

Baron of Gray Matter—Curly's title as bodyguard to *Queen Anne of Anesthesia* in *Restless Knights*; he is also referred to as *Baron of Brains*.

Barters—Stiff-as-a-board butler in *All the World's a Stooge*. Barters becomes even less enthralled with his employer's decision to adopt refugee children when those children turn out to be the Stooges.

Bay of Rum—One of the most versatile names in Stooges films. It was the nickname of the *Minister of Rum*, one of the *Axis Partners* in *I'll Never Heil Again*. It was also a treacherous body of water on the map of *South Starv-Vania* in *You Nazty Spy*. And in *Gents Without Cents*, the Stooges refer to the Bay of Rum in performing their song and dance routine for *Manny Weeks Theatrical Enterprises*.

Bear traps—IMMUTABLE STOOGES LAW #3: Bear traps in Stooge films will always find the rear end of Moe (various films).

Bearded Lady—The Stooges rarely look a gift horse in the mouth, especially when it talks. In *Even as I.O.U.*, crooked racetrack ventriloquists make longshot horse Bearded Lady "talk," and the Stooges, who have the rare ability to accept unusual natural phenomena, bet the ranch. Bearded Lady comes in, and the Stooges parlay their winnings into ownership of their own racehorse, the lethargic but mischievous *Seabasket*.

Becky—See *Onion Oil Company*.

Belief—IMMUTABLE STOOGES LAW #4: No Stooge will believe the first report that the other has seen a hideous, horrible monster (various films).

Bell—Reluctant wife of Moe who is being courted by irresistible pet shop owner Larry in *He Cooked His Goose* and *Triple Crossed*.

Belle and Zell—Kidnapped sisters of the beautiful *Nell* in *Pals and Gals*.

Bellevue Hospital—Where Curly nearly undergoes a "cerebrum decapitation" at the hands of *Dr. D. Lerious* in *From Nurse to Worse*. The hospital seems to have been state of the art; unlike other hospitals the Stooges visit, Bellevue's anesthetic of choice is ether, not a large wooden mallet to the head.

"Below the McMason McDixon line"—*The Earl of Glenheather* is not convinced that detective Shemp is truly a Scotsman in *Hot Scots* and *Scotched in Scotland*. Moe, however, allays his doubts by assuring him that Shemp hails from "below the McMason McDixon line."

"Beneath This . . ."—Epitaph on the gravestone in front of *Diggs, Graves, and Berry Undertakers* that Shemp uses for cover in *Shot in the Frontier*. It reads, "Beneath This Monumental Stone Lies 80 Lbs. of Skin and Bone." See also *"Here Lies . . ."* and *"Mama Loved Papa . . ."*

Betty, Hettie, and Nettie—Fair-minded Stooge-watchers know that Moe,

Betty, Hettie, and Nettie will need to get used to minor disagreements among their fiancés if they are to adjust smoothly to marriage (*Pardon My Backfire*, 1953).

Larry, and Shemp are not perfect and continue to wonder why they should have to capture three violent criminals in *Pardon My Backfire* to secure the love of Betty, Hettie, and Nettie?

Big Mike—IMMUTABLE STOOGES LAW #5: The thing that stands between every gangster and his loot is the Stooges. In *Fright Night* and *Fling in the Ring*, Big Mike puts in the fix on the big *Chopper Kane–Gorilla Watson* fight. But when the Stooges cross-up the crooked mobster, Big Mike pronounces a punishment that makes even the most macho viewer shudder: the Stooges will be going for a ride, "a *one-way* ride."

"The Biggest Chiselers in Town"— Sign on the Stooges' pottery business in *Matri-Phony*.

"The Biggest Grafters in Town"— Sign on the Stooges' tree surgery business in *Some More of Samoa*.

Bill—Until the film *Goofs and Saddles*, few people recognized the remarkable loyalty of the homing pigeon. When Curly attempts to send an incriminating note with a pigeon named Bill, the bird faithfully turns the note over to the Stooges' enemy *Longhorn Pete*, who doesn't take kindly to spies trying to expose his crooked cattle rustling operation.

Bill and Rosebud—Newlyweds in *Goof on the Roof* who abandon the spirit of young love after they return home to inspect the Stooges' redecoration of their apartment.

Bill Stein—Colorful prison radio announcer who promises to bring gallows spectators a "jerk-by-jerk" description of the Stooges' hanging in *In the Sweet Pie and Pie*. A true adherent to the "make the best of it" outlook on life, Stein tells listeners, "It's a beautiful day for a hanging!"

Biltless Hotel—Hotel where the Stooges track down the elusive *Eel* in *Blunder Boys*.

Birdie—Not the first talking horse in the Stooges' experience, but certainly the most pleasant. Birdie was the Stooges' reincarnated sister in *Hoofs and Goofs* and the sequel *Horsing Around*.

Black Bottom Café—Where testimony indicates the unfortunate *Kirk Robbin* was found dead in *Disorder in the Court*. The Stooges were never so smug as to ignore talking animals, and in this case it paid off. The three key witnesses for defendant *Gail Tempest* heed a parrot's advice, check the bird's foot for a letter, and discover a confession by the real culprit, *Buck Wing*.

Black Louie—Knife-throwing pirate in *Three Little Pirates*. Though the Stooges encountered more knife throwers than the average person, they never seemed to meet a master; knives thrown at them usually grazed just the tops of their heads.

Black Louie's Pirate Den—Temporary safe haven for the Stooges from the death sentence imposed by the *Governor of Dead Man's Island* in *Three Little Pirates*.

Black Prince—Master magician who has an obvious gift for conjuring but uses his talent for no good in *Squareheads of the Round Table* and *Knutzy Knights*. Fans of modern-day magic can see the influence of the Black Prince in the popular sabre-through-the-box routine, though today's magicians put a beautiful woman inside the box instead of three meddling court jesters.

Blackie—See *Badlands Blackie*.

Blackie's Place—*Badlands Blackie's* hideout in *The Three Troubledoers*.

Blackie and Doyle—Confidence men who dreamed up the phony *Canvas Back Duck Club* in *A Ducking They Did Go*. Though Blackie and Doyle would have hired any Joe off the street to sell its bogus duck-hunting memberships, they must have admired Larry's claim that the Stooges were "three of the best salesmen who ever sailed."

Blackjack and Lefty—Coldhearted members of the deadly *Killer Dillons* gang who resent the recent arrival of three mysterious desperadoes in *Punchy Cowpunchers*.

"Blacksmith Shop"—Sign on the barn where Sheriff Curly holds off gunslinger *Badlands Blackie* in *The Three Troubledoers*.

Bleep Bluep Blop—Easy-to-remember telephone number of spaceship sellers *A.B. Cloud & Company* in *Flying Saucer Daffy*.

Blue Point University—Football rival to *Boulder Dam University* in *Three Little Pigskins*.

Bologna and whipped cream—Scrumptious-sounding meal ordered by famished fireman Shemp in *Soup to Nuts*.

Bonny Banks—See *Glenheather Castle*.

Bonzo—Man's natural affection for gorillas is not buoyed by watching an ape-man commit a heinous robbery in *Dizzy Detectives*. But once it is disclosed that the no-good **Mr. Dill** has forced the animal into a life of crime—and that the poor gorilla goes by the name Bonzo—all is immediately forgiven on Bonzo's behalf.

"Boo-hoo"—Melancholy phrase sung in three-part harmony by the weeping Stooges after they lose their jobs in *Sappy Bullfighters*.

Bortch—Immutable Stooges Law #6: If a fight is going poorly, the Stooges will pleasantly pretend there is a phone call for the enemy, causing that enemy to graciously stop fighting to take the call. Nowhere is this better illustrated than in *Dunked in the Deep* and *Commotion on the Ocean*, when the Stooges distract foreign spy Bortch long enough to knock him out and tie him up.

"Botanical offshoot"—Never was Moe's aptitude for medicine more evident than in his diagnosis of injured dog *Garçon* in *Calling All Curs*. He says, "The preambulation of the pedal extremity is impeded by the insertion of a foreign botanical offshoot." Moe removes the splinter, which Curly promptly sits on. Moe's revised diagnosis: "Looks like botanical offshoot in the upholstery."

Boulder Dam University—Home to football legends *The Three Horsemen*, for whom the Stooges are mistaken in *Three Little Pigskins*.

Box 41144—Address to which Larry replies after reading an irresistible per-

sonal ad in *Gypped in the Penthouse*. See also *"Tired of being beautiful and alone . . ."*

"Boxcars"—Math was never Curly's strongest subject, but he makes a wonderful effort when asked by **Little Jimmy** in *Cash and Carry* how much six and six is. Curly's reply: "Boxcars!"

Bravuria—Noble land that is home to the Stooges and **Prince Charming** in *Snow White and the Three Stooges*.

"Breaker-uppers of the peanut brittle foundry"—Occasionally one of the Stooges will make vague reference to a fascinating event, leaving the viewer aching to know more. In *Monkey Businessmen*, for example, electrician Moe warns partners Larry and Curly to behave properly so that their employer, **Smiling Sam McGann**, does not catch on that they were the "breaker-uppers of the peanut brittle foundry." No further reference is made to such a mysterious occurrence in this film or any other, forcing the imagination to fill in details Moe regretfully never supplies.

Breath O' Heather Vat 106 Plus—Surprisingly strong scotch brewed from pharmaceuticals and mixed in an old boot in *Pardon My Scotch*. Not all tasters agree on its quality, but the potency of Breath O' Heather is questioned by none.

Bretta, croomithistle, papeeptoomin, and pickle juice—Ingredients used by Moe to mix the nerve-calming cocktail **eenar fraapini** in *Up in Daisy's Penthouse*.

"The Bride Wore Spurs"—The somewhat improvisational play performed in *Three Hams on Rye* for which the Stooges receive rave reviews.

"Brightens Old Bodies"—See *Brighto*.

Brighto—Medicine manufactured by the *Brighto Medical Company* and sold by the Stooges in *Dizzy Doctors*. The company claims that Brighto "Brightens Old Bodies," a slogan whose vagueness leads to decreased sales by the Stooges. There is nothing lacking in the Stooges' resolve to sell Brighto, however, as their motivational chant reveals:

> Brighto, Brighto
> Makes old bodies new
> We'll sell a million bottles
> (Curly) Woo woo woo woo woo woo woo!

Brighto Medical Company— Manufacturers of cure-all medicine

Brighto in *Dizzy Doctors*. The company made a nice product, but the labels should have been more explicit in warning that the medicine wasn't intended to be wiped on the uniforms of policemen.

Bronx Taxi Cab—Even in the Stooges' day, taking a taxi to Egypt was not the most cost-effective means of travel. But the Stooges are in a pinch in *We Want Our Mummy*, and are willing to pay Bronx Taxi Cab's *$2,198.55* fare.

The Bronx Taxi Cab Company should hire drivers who don't look so inconvenienced by a simple fare to Egypt (*We Want Our Mummy*, 1939).

Even Moe is astonished at the miraculous healing powers of Brighto (*Dizzy Doctors*, 1937).

The Brooklyn Building—Laxly guarded high-rise building where detectives Moe, Larry, and Curly track a larcenous ape in *Dizzy Detectives*.

Brooks Circus—Where *Schnapps* the horse nearly loses his life before being rescued by the Stooges in *Horsing Around*.

Brown—See *Captain Casey and Brown*.

Buck Wing—Sinister murderer of Kirk Robbin in *Disorder in the Court*. Although it might be unseemly to talk about the redeeming qualities of a fleeing murderer, Wing must be given credit for tying a written confession to *Polly* the parrot's foot.

Buffalow Billious—Curly in *Goofs and Saddles*. See also *"Wild Bill Hicup Due In"* and *Just Plain Bill*.

The Stooges are not the first businessmen surprised to find out what happens when you say no to gangsters like Butch McGee and his henchmen (*Three Loan Wolves*, 1946).

Bunion Eight—The car Shemp successfully identifies on the *Mystery Motor Jackpot Show* in *A Missed Fortune*. Plagued by a bum foot, Shemp declares, "My bunion aches!" and the $50,000 prize is his.

Burned toast and a rotten egg—Curly's lunch order in *Three Sappy People* and Larry's lunch order in *Beer Barrel Polecats*. When questioned about the unusual choice, Larry and Curly explain, "I got a tapeworm and it's good enough for him."

"The Busiest Place on the Map"—See *Cucaracha*.

Butch—The mouse-chasing bulldog in *Flat Foot Stooges*. Butch engages in a gruesome-sounding pursuit of a firehouse mouse, but lives, anyway. Butch is also the nickname for the baby the Stooges discover on a porch and care for in *Mutts to You*.

Butch McGee—President of the extortionist *Gashouse Protective Association* in *Three Loan Wolves*. He orders the shakedown of the Stooges' pawnshop, but the beating McGee receives at the hands of the Stooges cannot bode well for any reelection campaign he might be planning.

The *Buzzard*—As aviation engineers the *Wrong Brothers*, the Stooges build the *Buzzard*, an airplane with which they revolutionize flying by proving that three pilots is too many for any cockpit.

C

C-A-N-D-Y—What Moe promises Larry if he keeps up his excellent repair work in *Listen, Judge*. Moe has spelled the word so that Shemp doesn't catch on, but Larry is phonetically challenged. His response: "You know I don't smoke!"

C.M. & St. P. R.R.—In *Movie Maniacs*, the name of the railroad the Stooges board to reach Hollywood, where they hope to hit it big. The railcar reads, "C.M. & St. P. R.R./Consigned to Hollywood Storage Co./Hollywood, California."

Cackle fruit—Moe's appetizing term for eggs in *All Gummed Up*.

Cackle soup—Chef Curly's mouth-watering term for chicken soup in *Busy Buddies*.

Café Casbahbah—Ancient Egyptian restaurant run by the Stooges in *Malice in the Palace* and *Rumpus in the Harem*. Moe and Shemp's service is not first-rate, but Larry's cooking—especially his hot dogs—are surprisingly good, hinting at talents Larry himself might never have fully explored.

Café La-Mer-Essen—Countless romances have been born in charming cafés. In *Love at First Bite* and *Fifi Blows

Her Top, Shemp and Joe find true love at the Parisian Café La-Mer-Essen. (In Yiddish, "Lemiressen" means "Let's eat!")

"Cairo City Limits—Tunis 1500 mi."—Encouraging sign encountered by the Stooges in their hunt for the Egyptian mummy of **King Rootentooten** in *We Want Our Mummy*.

Calamity Insurance Company—Tight-fisted insurance agency whose unfair policies toward the handicapped force the Stooges to take action in *Hokus Pokus* and *Flagpole Jitters*. That the Stooges end up terrified and teetering on a skyscraper's flagpole should not lessen the value of their altruistic motives.

"CA MERAS PROH IBITED O NPENAL TYOF DEATH"—Menacing sign posted at the outskirts of **Vulgaria** in *Dutiful but Dumb*. Translated, it reads, "Cameras prohibited on penalty of death"—bad news for three eager photographers named **Click, Clack, and Cluck**.

"Can U Take It? Try Our Mush"—Tempting sign in the Stooge-owned Jive Café in *Busy Buddies*.

"Candid Cameraman . . ."—Anyone doubting the Stooges' value to society need only read the newspaper account of their photographic undercover mission in *Three Smart Saps*: "Candid Cameraman Exposes Corruption in County Jail/ Stevens Again Warden As Walker is Parked Behind Prison Bars."

Canned Corn—*Little Jimmy* needs an operation and only Curly's Brooklyn accent can save him in *Cash and Carry*. When Curly finds an empty "Canned Corn" in a junkyard, he thinks it to be "Canned Coin" and dutifully checks inside. His payoff: seed money for the operation.

Cannonball Express—Locomotive that the crooked *Icabod Slipp* hops in *Hold That Lion!*

Cantina de Rosa—In *Cookoo Cavaliers*, the Stooges intend to buy a saloon but mistakenly purchase the Cantina de Rosa, a beauty salon that caters only to women who cannot afford to lose all their hair.

Canvas Back Duck Club—Phantom duck hunting club concocted by con men *Blackie and Doyle* in *A Ducking They Did Go*. Although the club is a sham, the Stooges are remarkably successful in selling memberships to the mayor, police chief, and governor.

*Those priceless moments before the big duck hunt (**A Ducking They Did Go**, 1939)*

Captain Andrews—Air Force officer whose appetite for pretty women obscures his ability to judge the battle-worthiness of *Professor Danforth*'s combination helicopter-tank-submarine in *The Three Stooges in Orbit*.

Captain Burke—Enlisting officer who is unsympathetic when he discovers that the Stooges have signed up for the army by mistake in *Half Shot Shooters*.

Captain Casey and Brown—Gruff policeman and crack newspaper reporter who investigate the Stooge-concocted kidnapping of Hollywood starlet *Dolly Devore* in *Studio Stoops*. When Brown introduces himself to the Stooges by saying, "I'm Brown from the *Sun*," Shemp replies, "Oh, that's too bad. Are you peeling?"

Captain Daley—Humorless superior who is slugged by Sergeant Mullins in *Punchy Cowpuncher*. Mullins also was aiming for the Stooges.

Captain Dodge—Moe in *Uncivil Warriors*. See also *Lieutenant Duck* and *Major Hyde*.

Captain Gorgonzola—Captured commanding officer in *Wee Wee Monsieur*. Though the Stooges never meant to enlist in the French Foreign Legion, they rescue the Captain using nonmilitary-issue Santa Claus suits as disguises.

Captain Kidd's Kid's Treasure—The loot the Stooges hope to discover in *Cash and Carry*. The Stooges never had much luck buying treasure maps from shady-looking individuals, but this time things look different. After using unsafe blasting techniques to knock down a wall, Moe, Larry, and Curly uncover mountains of gold bars and cash, every inch of which the U.S. Treasury will want returned.

Captain Mullins—No-nonsense cop who makes liberal use of a lie detector while questioning the Stooges about an unsolved robbery in *Shivering Sherlocks* and *Of Cash and Hash*. Though he catches the Stooges in some untruths (Shemp did, in fact, steal a quarter from Moe's shoe) Mullins carelessly grabs the lie detector himself, and is unable to truthfully account for his own whereabouts when asked by Shemp where he was at 11 P.M. the evening before.

Captain Roarke—Driven by a fierce loyalty to his homeland *Anemia* in *Fuelin' Around* and *Hot Stuff*, Captain Roarke is assigned to kidnap brilliant, wild-haired *Professor Snead*. In his excitement, however, Roarke plucks the wild-haired Larry and his two assistants, Moe and Shemp. Though Roarke means well, the Anemian military brass is not amused, and reclassifies the loyal captain to the lowly rank of private.

Car 314—See *Cannonball Express*.

"Cards for All Occasions"—Description on the box of greeting cards the Stooges sell in *Boobs in Arms*.

Carey—Giant canary who romances Shemp in *Cuckoo on the Choo Choo*. Beauty was often sufficient to seduce the Stooges, but Carey the canary is neither pretty nor shapely. Only the lovesick Shemp knows for sure what was so alluring about the six-foot bird.

Carnation Pictures—Movie studio commandeered by the Stooges in *Movie Maniacs*. The studio's motto: "Carnation Pictures from Contented Actors."

Carol Danforth—Breathtaking daughter of *Professor Danforth* whose face is responsible for launching her father's combination helicopter-tank-submarine in *The Three Stooges in Orbit*.

Carrot County Fair Champion Milking Contest—Local cow-milking contest offering a $100 prize in *Busy Buddies*. Most Three Stooges films do not raise immense ethical questions, but it's inescapable here: Is it acceptable for Curly to win the Carrot County Fair Champion Milking Contest by milking a "cow" that is really Moe and Larry hiding inside a costume and pouring out a gallon of milk?

"Casey the Plumber"—Sign on the truck the Stooges hijack in *A Plumbing We Will Go*.

Castor and Earle Revue—When the Castor and Earle Revue fails to perform in *Gents Without Cents*, it opens the way for the Stooges and their famed *"Niagara Falls"* routine.

Cedric the Blacksmith—Every woman dreams of a romance like the one enjoyed by *Princess Elaine* in *Squareheads of the Round Table* and *Knutzy*

MOE'S INSULTS

Self-esteem is not a character trait normally associated with the Three Stooges. Yet, who had more self-esteem than Larry, Curly, Shemp, Joe, and Curly Joe, the five men on the receiving end of an endless barrage of insults by Moe?

From "Airedale" to "Worm," the razor-tongued Moe fired more than 100 of his verbal poison arrows directly into the hearts of his partners. Did any partners quit the Stooges? Did any of them break down and cry (besides Joe Besser)? If the ability to withstand Moe's charge that one has "mashed potato muscles" or is "half-brother to a weasel" isn't self-esteem, then there exists no self-esteem at all.

Listed below are the various affronts, barbs, disdains, indignities, invectives, stingers, and zingers hurled by Moe throughout his career with the Three Stooges.

Airedale	Applebrain	Applehead	Baboon
Baby hippopotamus	Beanbrain	Beetlebrain	Birdbrain
Birdbrained idiot	Blubberhead	Bonehead	Bubblebrain
Bunionhead	Buttonhead	Caterpillar	Cementhead
Chipmunk	Chiseler	Chowderhead	Chucklehead
Clumsy idiot	Clumsy ox	Dewhead	Dimwit
Dope	Dumb cluck	Dumb ox	Dumbbell
Dummy	Earthworm	Egghead	Empty skull
Featherbrain	Featherbrain imbecile	Flatbush flathead	Frozen dainty

● ● ●

Knights. Her suitor, Cedric the Blacksmith, risks execution for courting a lady so far above his station. Yet Cedric will not be silenced, nor will the three troubadours he recruits to serenade the princess with the now classic *"Oh, Elaine."* Even Elaine's crusty father cannot help but agree when Shemp reminds him that "millions of women marry Smiths every year."

Cedric the Clam—Rare crustacean owned by pet shop proprietor Larry in *He Cooked His Goose*. Larry claims that Cedric is the only trained clam in the world and proves it by having Cedric snap seven times when asked the number of days in the week. Cedric's next trick is less friendly: when Larry asks the clam to demonstrate how he treats those he dislikes, Cedric sprays Shemp

General nuisance	Goosebrain	Grapehead	Half-brother to a weasel
Half-wit	Halibut	Head-clunker	Hot Airedale
Idiot	Ignoramus	Imbecile	Ironhead
Jughead	Knothead	Knucklehead	Lamebrain
Latherhead	Laughing hyena	Little Man	Lug
Lunkhead	Man O' war	Mangy floormop	Mashed potato muscles
Matzohead	McNothing	Mental midget	Mongoose
Mophead	Moron	Musclebound	Musclebrain
Nesthead	Nitwit	Numbskull	Onionhead
Overstuffed bologna	Oysterbrain	Pebblebrain	Petty larceny Stooge
Picklebrain	Picklepuss	Porcupine	Porpoise
Puddin' head	Pussywillowbrain	Rain-in-the-face	Rat
Rummy	Sap	Sawdusthead	Scissorbill
Scrabblehead	Skillethead	Skunk	Sleepyhead
Slug	Snoring hyena	Softboiled egghead	Spongehead
Spotted raccoon	Squashbrain	Squirrelbait	Stoop
Stupid	Stupid idiot	Stupid Stooge	Tadpole
Termite	Titmouse	Tub O' lard	Turniphead
Two-ounce brain	Useless	Weaselbrain	Wiseguy
Worm			

● ● ●

in the face with a stream of seawater. When a frustrated Shemp asks Cedric to do the trick again, the clam shows true loyalty to Larry and sprays Shemp again.

"Census Takers Report Here"—Sign hanging outside City Hall in *No Census, No Feeling*. The sign is clearly written, but probably too small to read for those who might be running from the police and a homicidal angry shopkeeper.

Cerebrum Decapitation—Nonroutine procedure ordered by medical examiner *Dr. D. Lerious* to treat Curly's conviction that he is a dog in *From Nurse to Worse*.

"Certainly; we're all incompetent!"—Curly's confident interjection after a woodshop customer asks if his priceless Chinese cabinet will be in competent hands with the Stooges.

Cess, Poole, and Drayne—Not very elite law firm handling the estate of the Stooges' uncle **Ambrose Rose** in *Hold That Lion!* and *Loose Loot.*

"The Characters in this Picture . . ."—Opening title in *I'll Never Heil Again.* It reads, "The Characters in this Picture are All Fictitious. Anyone Resembling Them is Better Off Dead."

Charger—Majestic horse used by *Lady Godiva* to swoop up her love, the *spirit of Sir Tom*, in *The Ghost Talks.*

Cheatham Investment Company—Shortsighted entrepreneurial firm in *Three Pests in a Mess.* Though the Stooges show great potential as inventors, the Cheatham Investment Company loses interest in them immediately after discovering they are not, in fact, in line for a $100,000 sweepstakes prize. See also *I. Cheatham.*

"A Chicken in Every Pot with Egger"—Campaign slogan of presidential candidate Hammond Egger in *Three Dark Horses.* See also *"Cuddle Up a Little Closer with Hammond Egger."*

Chief Growling Bear—Short-fused Indian chief in *Rockin' Thru the Rockies* who leaves this ominous ransom note: "Dear Hatchet Face: We takem paleface squaws. You get new face, maybe next time we takem you. Chief Growling Bear. P.S. Tell three coyotes with you if no gone by sunset we scalp em . . . close to the shoulder!"

Chief Kelly—Feisty fire department chief in *Flat Foot Stooges* who is plenty satisfied that his men can continue to fight fires with horse-drawn fire trucks.

Chief Leaping Lizard—See *"Darling Husband . . ."*

Chief Rain in the Puss—No-fun Indian chief with scalp-'em instincts in *Back to the Woods.*

Chili pepperinos—Blazing-hot snack fed to lethargic racehorse *Thunderbolt* in *Playing the Ponies.* Though not a long-term substitute for proper workouts and training, the chili pepperinos make even Thunderbolt look like Secretariat for a day.

Chisel Inn Hotel—Sparkling new inn remodeled by the Stooges with paint, nails, and sheer determination in *Loco Boy Makes Good.*

Chizzilini—One of the devious Axis Partners plotting the overthrow of ruthless dictator *Moe Hailstone* in *I'll Never Heil Again.*

Chopper—Snappy nickname of murder suspect *Gilbraith Q. Tiddledewadder* in *Tricky Dicks.*

Chopper Kane—Ferocious boxer trained by the Stooges in *Fright Night* and *Fling in the Ring.* Chopper's a cinch to win his upcoming bout with *Gorilla Watson*, but gambling gangster *Big Mike* has "advised" against that. The Stooges' solution: plenty of creampuffs and a beautiful woman to soften up the Chopper.

Christmas Day—One of Shemp's cunning aliases in *Blunder Boys*. See also *Groundhog Day*, *Independence Day*, *Labor Day*, *New Year's Day*, and *St. Patrick's Day*.

Circle Follies Theatre—Where the Stooges corner the crooked *Icabod Slipp* in *Loose Loot*.

City Assessor—Office that gives the Stooges their start as census takers in *No Census, No Feeling*.

City Dump—It might not be much, but it's home to the Stooges in *Cash and Carry*.

City Pound—Location to which the Stooges and other stray dogs are taken for fumigation in *From Nurse to Worse*.

Clarence Cassidy—Good-guy gunslinger whose stumblebum heroics only make it tougher for the Stooges to capture bank bandit *Red Morgan* and his cutthroat gang in *Merry Mavericks*.

Claude A. Quacker—Friend of the Stooges in *Pardon My Clutch* and *Wham-Bam-Slam!* Claude might have been considered a pioneer in holistic medicine for recommending that Shemp treat his frazzled nerves with rest and relaxation. But when he also sells his mechanically unsound car to his friends, Quacker's real motives are immediately evident.

Clayhammer—Stodgy butler who disdainfully greets the arrival of three unlikely escorts to his employer's home in *Termites of 1938*. Curly is unshaken by Clayhammer's shabby treatment, calling him "Sledgehammer" before joining his fellow escorts.

Click, Clack, and Cluck—As eager photographers Click, Clack, and Cluck in *Dutiful but Dumb*, the Stooges accept all assignments, including photographing an invisible-ray machine located in *Vulgaria*.

Cliff—Flimflam man who, along with bogus invalid *Mary*, plans to cheat an insurance company out of $25,000 in *Hokus Pokus*.

Clinton Arms Hotel—Secret location where kidnappers have stashed lovely starlet *Dolly Devore* in *Studio Stoops*.

Clipper—No-good swindler who convinces the vulnerable *Widow Jenkins* to part with her oil-rich property in *Oily to Bed, Oily to Rise*.

Clogging—IMMUTABLE STOOGES LAW #7: Clogged fountain pens, bags of birthday cake icing, and other items easily stuck in their containers will only discharge after a Stooge looks directly into the container (various films).

Cloud 49—Departure point for the heavenly train used by Shemp to return to Earth in *Heavenly Daze* and *Bedlam in Paradise*. Its destinations: the Big Dipper, Mars, Venus, Earth, and Kukamonga.

Clux Dog Soap—Soap of choice for the Stooge-operated *K-9 Dog Laundry* in *Mutts to You*.

Cocktails—IMMUTABLE STOOGES LAW #8: Cocktails mixed by the Stooges will smoke, flame, and burn holes in wooden tables, but will still be enjoyed by those who drink them (various films).

Coffin Nail Cigarette Contest—Curly's commitment to entering contests pays off when he wins $50,000 in the Coffin Nail Cigarette Contest in *Healthy, Wealthy and Dumb*. The contest is sponsored by the Coffin Nail Cigarette Company, located at *1010 Tobacco Road*, Virginia, Texas.

Coleslawvania—Kingdom in which the Stooges serve as royal fiddlers in *Fiddlers Three* and *Musty Musketeers*. See also *"A small kingdom . . ."*

Collision mats—Chef Curly's scrumptious term for pancakes in *Busy Buddies*.

Colonel Buttz—Renowned officer of the Confederate army in *Uncivil Warriors* who appreciates Curly's recipe for a cocktail called *nip and tuck*: One nip, Curly explains to the Colonel, and they tuck you away for the night.

Colonel Henderson—Owner of a problematic car that only gets more problematic when the Stooges work on it in *Higher than a Kite*.

Colossal Insurance Company—See *Dr. D. Lerious*.

Columbia Uniform Supply Company—Business located next to *The Doggy Pet Shop* in *A Plumbing We Will Go*.

Columbus—Mechanically unsound car sold to the Stooges by *Claude A. Quacker* in *Pardon My Clutch* and *Wham-Bam-Slam!* When Quacker tells the Stooges the car is a Columbus, Shemp replies, "Never mind who you bought it from, what make is that?"

"Come to Papa!"—Shemp's victory cry as he uses both arms to rake in a colossal poker pot in *Out West* and *Pals and Gals*.

Complete Outfitters—Haberdasher where the Stooges purchase Curly's hat in *3 Dumb Clucks*.

"Completely illogical, preponderantly impracticable, and moreover, it stinks"—*Professor Quackenbush*'s opinion of a colleague's theory in *Half-Wits Holiday* and *Pies and Guys* that heredity determines social distinction.

Coney Island Curly—Anyone questioning the Stooges' bravery hasn't seen *The Three Troubledoers*. When the lovely *Nell* warns Curly about murderous *Badlands Blackie*, he doesn't run or whimper, but boldly states that there's nothing to fear with "Coney Island Curly" in town.

Congo—Innocent gorilla in *Spooks* who cannot be blamed for his violent reaction to a mad professor's plan to transfer his brain into that of a human.

Consolidated Fujiyama California Smog Bags—Dubious product in which Joe invests his jackpot winnings in *Quiz Whizz*. In fairness to Joe, the film was made in 1958, when far less was known about the ill effects of smog.

Corabell, Dorabell, and Florabell—The Stooges' fiancées who stage a sit-down strike in *The Sitter Downers*. Though

The lucky Florabell, Corabell, and Dorabell in the days when chivalry reigned (*The Sitter Downers*, 1937)

never acknowledged by modern feminists, the spirit of Corabell, Dorabell, and Florabell can still be seen in strong-willed women everywhere.

"Councilman Goodrich Threatened With Death—Promise to Clean Up Vice and Corruption Brings Threat From Racketeers"—Startling newspaper headline that kick-starts detectives Moe, Larry, and Shemp into action in *For Crimin' Out Loud*.

Count Alfred Gehrol—Fiendish spy who invites *Admiral H. S. Taylor* to lunch at his home in *Three Little Sew and Sews*. Gehrol gets more than he bargained for when a different navy "tailor"—Curly—shows up in the Admiral's place.

Count of Five—Moe in *Restless Knights*.

Countess Schpritzwasser—Regal guest at a party marking the Stooges' entrée into society as gentlemen in *Half-Wits Holiday* and *Pies and Guys*.

"A couple o' pip pips, a little barbecue, and what have you!"—Detective Shemp shows off his regal manner and seductive charms by offering this toast to a devious knockout blonde in *Who Done It?* and *For Crimin' Out Loud*. She tries to murder him, anyway.

Cousin Basil—Immutable Stooges Law #9: If a beautiful woman is in love with a Stooge, she either is convinced that he has money or believes him to be someone else. Immutable Stooges Law #10: When a beautiful woman is in love with a Stooge, he will believe her affections to be only natural. In *Brideless Groom* and *Husbands Beware*, a lovely woman thinks the man in her apartment to be her beloved cousin Basil. The graciousness of her welcome changes when she learns that the man is Shemp.

Cow—In order to teach Curly to milk a cow in *Busy Buddies*, Moe relies on a simple diagram that illustrates these basic parts of the animal: spare ribs, chopped liver, filet of sole and heel, hash, meat loaf, franks, wieners, hot dogs, sukiyaki, hamburger, meatballs, "weiner schnitzell," corn beef, auto club steaks—meats every Thursday—salami.

Coyote Creek—Where the action unfolds in *Punchy Cowpunchers*.

Coyote Pass—Sleepy Western town where the Stooges set up a dental practice in *The Tooth Will Out*. Little is known about Coyote Pass other than that it had flexible dental licensing guidelines.

Creampuffs—What *Chopper Kane* claims is his favorite fruit in *Fright Night* and *Fling in the Ring*.

Croakers Sanitarium—Institution that attempts to treat Shemp's hallucinations in *Scrambled Brains*. It fails.

Crosby Building—Very temporary quarters for the fraudulent *Canvas Back Duck Club* in *A Ducking They Did Go*.

Crumb's Pies—Decoy product carried by the Stooges while working undercover as detectives for the *Super Slueth Detective Agency* in *Spooks*.

Crushed eyebrows—The injury Shemp declares he is suffering while being used as a headfirst battering ram in *Fright Night* and *Fling in the Ring*.

"Cry in This"—Inscription embroidered on the handkerchief Shemp gallantly hands to a weeping woman in *Don't Throw That Knife*.

Cucaracha—Home to the Stooges' beauty parlor in *Cookoo Cavaliers*.

Cucaracha is, the welcome sign says, "the busiest place on the map."

"Cuddle Up a Little Closer with Hammond Egger"—Campaign slogan of presidential candidate *Hammond Egger* in *Three Dark Horses*. See also *"A Chicken in Every Pot with Egger."*

"Cures Every Ailment Known to Man"—See *Abdul's Cactus Remedy*.

Curleycue—Immutable Stooges Law #11: If a Stooge poses as a woman, he is certain to attract a suitor. In *Matri-Phony*, Curly (as Curleycue) shows sufficient skill with makeup and red wig to distract the redhead-loving ruler of *Erysipelas*, *Octopus Grabus*.

Curly Q. Link—Curly as nephew and heir of deceased millionaire *Professor Bob O. Link* in *If a Body Meets a Body*.

"Curly Q. Link Sought . . ."—Newspaper headline announcing the search for the heir of deceased *Professor Bob O. Link* in *If a Body Meets a Body*. It reads, "Curly Q. Link Sought/Heir to Three Million."

Curlylocks—Curly as a Confederate soldier in *Uncivil War Birds*.

Cut Throat Drug Store—Stooge-run pharmacy in *All Gummed Up* and *Bubble Trouble*. It is here that the Stooges create perhaps their greatest invention, a **fountain of youth** potion that transforms the old into young, with only occasional side effects.

D

Daily Chronicle—Newspaper in *Dizzy Detectives*. Headline reads, "Mysterious Burglaries Panic City/Police Shakeup as Ape Man Strikes Again."

Daily Gazette—Newspaper in *Crime on Their Hands*. Headline reads, "Punjab Diamond Stolen/Daring Bandits Raid Museum In Daylight." Also, newspaper in *Commotion on the Ocean*. Headline reads, "Atomic Documents Missing/Suspects Being Screened/Top Drawer Secret Data Stolen." Finally, the tabloid in *Quiz Whizz* that announces Joe as the winner of a $15,000 TV jackpot.

Daily News—Newspaper that hires the Stooges as reporters in *Crash Goes the Hash*. Managing Editor **Fuller Bull** deserves credit for his bold hiring of the Stooges, none of whom has a journalism degree.

The Daily Press Post—See *"Manning Baby Disappears!"*

The Daily Record Post—See *"Armored Car Robbers Identified—Café Workers Name Loomis Gang."*

Daily Star-News—See *"Flying Saucer Photographer Awarded City's Highest Honor."*

Daily Star Press—Rival newspaper to the *Daily News* in *Crash Goes the Hash*.

Dainty Dolly Dish Company—Fragile business that rejects the Stooges in *The Tooth Will Out*, thereby inspring three of the most curious dental careers in the history of dentistry.

Daisy—Shapely blonde known affectionately as "Daisy-Waisy" by the Stooges' amorous father in *3 Dumb Clucks* and *Up in Daisy's Penthouse*. The seductive but gold digging Daisy might have succeeded in bumping off "Popsie-Wopsie" but for the dedication of his three sons, whom the still-vital octogenarian probably still has not forgiven.

Popsie-Wopsie cannot resist the charms of the conniving Daisy-Waisy (Lucille Lund) (3 Dumb Clucks, 1937).

Daisy Simms—Sassy-tongued dame—played by Lucille Ball—who thinks three college phenoms would be just what the doctor ordered for boyfriend *Joe Stack*'s football team in *Three Little Pigskins*. See also *Lucille Ball*.

Dandy Dawson—Dastardly mastermind of the plot to kidnap glamorous Hollywood starlet *Dolly Devore* in *Studio Stoops*.

"Danger Dynamite Caps . . ."—IMMUTABLE STOOGES LAW #12: When an ominous warning is posted, the Stooges will either misread or miss the warning entirely and then enact the precise behavior warned against. In *Dunked in the Deep*, the Stooges use liberal force in cracking walnuts on a wooden crate that reads, "Danger/Dynamite Caps/Do Not Jar, Strike, Shake, Or Drop/Highly Explosive."

"Dangerous—Keep Away . . ."—Warning on a door in *Three Hams on Rye*. Shemp is on the right track by trying to sound the letters out, but misreads the warning as, "Dang-a-roos—Kip Awah." A case study in IMMUTABLE STOOGES LAW #12 (see *"Danger Dynamite Caps . . ."* above).

Dapper Dan—As leader of a gang of burglars in *Crime on Their Hands* and *Hot Ice*, Dapper Dan is accustomed to crossing society's boundaries. But that does not make him qualified to perform life-threatening stomach surgery simply because Shemp has swallowed the priceless *Punjab Diamond*.

"Darling Husband . . ."—It's not *Pierre*'s day in *Whoops, I'm an Indian!* First he is outsmarted during a gambling game

with the Stooges, then he returns home to find a note that reads, "Darling Husband, I am running away with my true love, Chief Leaping Lizard. Love and kisses, you rat. Your loving wife, Fifi. P.S. You will find the can opener in the tool chest."

Darwin—Light-fingered monkey who is trained to steal by three beautiful gold diggers in *Healthy, Wealthy and Dumb* and *A Missed Fortune*. The Stooges could have been spared the heartache of dealing with the robbery-minded Darwin had the manager of the *Hotel Costa Plente* seen fit to prohibit primates as guests.

Davenport Seats—Author of the book "How to Become a Babysitter," which is relied upon by the Stooges in *Baby Sitters Jitters*. Seats is not a well-known authority, but it is still hard to imagine him recommending that grown men sleep in a baby's crib.

Day and Nite Plumbers—Stooges' business in *Vagabond Loafers* and *Scheming Schemers*. Their admirable work ethic is reflected in the name of their business, but it's likely the Stooges' plumbing work would have been better had they concentrated on either day plumbing or night plumbing.

Dead Man's Gulch—Site of *The Three Troubledoers*. The lawless Western town has a population of 202, but when the Stooges mosey in and hear three gunshots, the population sign is immediately changed to read 199.

Dead Man's Island—Landing spot for the Stooges' shipwrecked craft, *Garbage Scow #188 N.Y.C.* in *Three Little Pirates*.

Though most men shipwrecked on Dead Man's Island might have panicked, Moe proves himself a master psychologist by uncovering the **Governor of Dead Man's Island**'s weakness for "gifts from strange lands."

"Dead Man's Island 1672"—Opening title in *Three Little Pirates*.

"Dead or in Bad Shape"—According to the wanted poster, any hombre tough enough to bring in the Stooges "Dead or in Bad Shape" was entitled to a bountiful reward in *Whoops, I'm an Indian!*

"Dear General Muster . . ."—Letter of distress attached by the Stooges to **Bill**, a double-crossing homing pigeon in *Goofs and Saddles*. The urgent message reads as follows:

> *Dear General Muster,*
> *Have located rustlers. Send 1000 troops immediately if not sooner.*
> > *Love and Kisses,*
> > *Buffalow Billious, Wild Bill Hicup,*
> > *Just Plain Bill*
> *P.S. Send a change of underwear.*

"Dear Hatchet Face"—See *Chief Growling Bear*.

"Dear Old Mexico"—Curly's poetic tribute to the country in which the Stooges perform their comedy bullfighting act in *What's the Matador?*:

> *Dear Old Mexico!*
> *The warmth of your chili will bring new zest*
> > *to my breast*
> *And vice-a-versa!*

"Decker 117, Opponents 0"—The saloon's chalkboard tells a violent tale in *Horses' Collars*, where outlaw **Double Deal Decker** has just tangled with two rough gunfighters. (Moments before, the sign read, "Decker 115, Opponents 0.") Next up for Decker: three tough hombres from parts unknown.

"Delegates Welcome to Convention City"—Banner announcing the upcoming political convention in *Three Dark Horses*.

The DePeysters—The real damage done by con men is on the psyches of their prey. In *Bedlam in Paradise*, the DePeysters are ready to pay $50,000 to Moe and Larry for a worthless **fountain pen that writes under whipped cream**. Although the recently deceased and heaven-sent Shemp saves the day, it is unlikely that the DePeysters' entrepreneurial spirit will rise so majestically again.

Mr. DePeyster (Vic Travers), butler Spiffingham (Sam McDaniel), and Mrs. DePeyster (Symona Boniface) enjoy a song with the Stooges between takes on the set of *Heavenly Daze* (1948).

"Deposit Dogs Here"—Sign on the Stooges' dog-washing business in *Mutts to You*. See also *K-9 Dog Laundry*.

Derstick, anacanapooner—Great sculptors are nothing without their tools, a fact avant-garde artist Moe knows well in *Self Made Maids*. Though he seems gruff while ordering fellow artists Larry and Shemp to retrieve his tools, it is clear that he cannot continue work on a marvelous statue without a derstick and anacanapooner.

Desmond of the Outer Sanctorum—The bone-chilling character Shemp creates in order to frighten Moe and Larry while inside the haunted *Smorgasbord Castle* in *The Ghost Talks* and *Creeps*. Shemp's Method acting is a bit too convincing even for him; when he spots his reflection in the mirror, the sight nearly frightens him to death.

Diana—Lovely redhead whom emperor *Octopus Grabus* determines to marry in *Matri-Phony*. Diana is saved that terrible fate when Curly uses an ingenious redhead disguise to distract the emperor, a nearsighted cad who falls head over heels in love with Curly.

Diane—Gorgeous, shapely, and a little bit sassy, kings desire her in *The Three Stooges Meet Hercules* but she wants only *Schuyler Davis* . . . if he'll stop acting like such a milquetoast.

"Dice, Dancing, Dames, Drinking, and Dunking"—The various attractions advertised at villain *Double Deal Decker*'s saloon in *Horses' Collars*. See also *Double Deal's Five "D" Delight*.

Diggins—Shady lawyer who recommends to clients *Tiska, Taska, and Baska* that they marry the soon-to-be-executed Stooges in order to receive a $10 million legacy in *In the Sweet Pie and Pie*. Though the setting of the film is never disclosed, Diggins's advice surely would warrant disbarment in any state.

Diggs, Graves, and Berry Undertakers—In an ironic turn, the Stooges survive deadly bullets by ducking behind gravestones at Diggs, Graves, and Berry Undertakers in *Shot in the Frontier*.

Dillon Gang—Menacing hombres in *Punchy Cowpunchers*. The capture of the *"Killer Dillons"* requires the combined firepower of the Stooges, a blond cowboy named *Elmer*, the *U.S. Cavalry*, and especially the lovely *Nell*.

"Direct From Three Hot Weeks in Kansas"—Sign advertising the traveling road show *Nell's Belles* in *Rockin' Thru the Rockies*.

"Distilled Monday"—Boastful advertising claim printed on bottles of *Old Homicide* liquor in *Out West*.

"Distilled Yesterday"—Marketing slogan inscribed on bottles of *Old Panther* liquor in *Love at First Bite*, *Shot in the Frontier*, *Gypped in the Penthouse*, and *Tricky Dicks*. Although not as well aged as *Old Homicide* (*"Distilled Monday"*), Old Panther is the most popular liquor among the Stooges and their thirsty acquaintances.

"Divorce Evidence Manufactured . . ."—Motto that appears on the office door of the Stooges-owned **Super Slueth Detective Agency** in *Spooks*: "Divorce Evidence Manufactured to Your Order. Don't Knock, Walk In."

"Do Not Disturb"—Sign hanging from a drunken Shemp's neck in *Cuckoo on the Choo Choo*. The way Shemp snores, it's best to heed the advice.

Doc Barker—Hard-hearted villain with a soft spot for innocent **Nell** in *Out West* and *Pals and Gals*.

Dr. A. Yank—Few American health professionals are as well-trained as Dr. A. Yank, the dentist visited by the Stooges in *I Can Hardly Wait*. Yank's degrees: D.D.S., Ph.D., C.O.D., F.O.B., and P.D.Q.

Dr. Abdul's Medicine Show—Marketing vehicle for Dr. Abdul's all-purpose elixir in *Phony Express*. It's improper to cast aspersions on Abdul's credentials, but had his potion worked as advertised ("cures every ailment known to man and beast") the Stooges might have avoided subsequent violence at *Peaceful Gulch*.

Dr. Ba Loni Sulami—Witch doctor and inventor in *Three Missing Links*. Sulami concocts a powerful love potion that, unfortunately for Curly, doesn't distinguish between men and gorillas.

Dr. Belcher—See *"Try Dr. Belcher's . . ."*

Dr. Bright—Inventor of **Brighto** in *Dizzy Doctors* who is not so bright at hiring capable salesmen.

Dr. D. Lerious—Investigating physician for the **Colossal Insurance Company** in *From Nurse to Worse*. Lerious holds several degrees: M.D., C.C.C., F.H.A., W.P.A., and A.W.O.L., but has inadequate training in veterinary science. When Curly acts like a dog to establish his insanity and collect insurance, the doctor is too easily convinced and orders a brain transplant.

"Doctor Dippy's Retreat"—Logo on the ambulance driven by the men in white who retrieve escaped eccentric millionaire **Mr. Boyce** in *Rhythm and Weep*.

Dr. Gezundheidt—Physician who, despite his experienced demeanor, looks truly shocked to hear cuckoo birds singing when he examines Shemp's head in *Scrambled Brains*.

Dr. Graves—Idealistic hospital superintendent in *Men in Black*. He takes a chance on three eager interns when they promise to devote their careers *"For duty and humanity."*

Dr. Howard, Dr. Fine, Dr. Howard—If there is one thing that proves the Stooges do, in fact, contribute to the social good, it is their consistent instinct to heal. As Dr. Howard, Dr. Fine, and Dr. Howard, the Stooges work toward wellness in *Men in Black* (as physicians), in

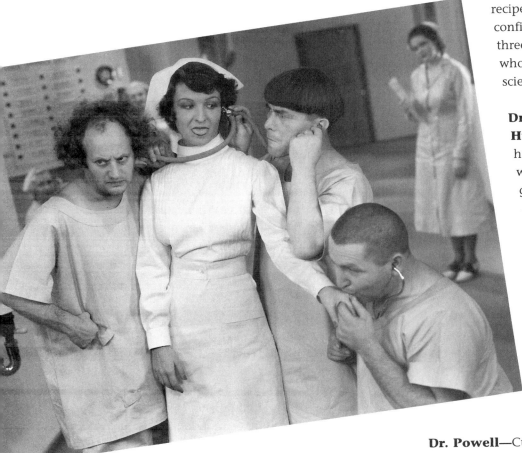

recipe for rocket fuel, but the confidence she inspires in three maintenance workers who like to dabble a bit in science, too.

Dr. Jekyll and Mr. Hyde—Mad scientist and his bloodthirsty assistant who attempt to perform a gorilla-to-human brain swap in *Spooks*.

Dr. Mallard—Swindler who operates *Mallard's Rest Home and Clinic* in *Monkey Businessmen*. Mallard promises to treat the Stooges' frazzled nerves, never realizing that their malady might be contagious.

Dr. Powell—Curator of the Egyptian Room at the *Museum of Ancient History* in *We Want Our Mummy*. Powell dedicates himself to the return of the priceless mummy of *King Rootentooten*, even if it kills three detectives who know even less about the mummy's deadly curse than does Powell.

Dr. Y. Tug—Multidegreed dentist in *I Can Hardly Wait*. Like partner **Dr. A. Yank**, Tug has earned a D.D.S., Ph.D., C.O.D., F.O.B., and P.D.Q.

Dr. York—Quick-thinking physician who recommends three unorthodox psychiatrists to treat the eccentric behavior of his friend's wife in *Three Sappy People*.

Dr. Howard, Dr. Fine, and Dr. Howard draw upon the latest medical techniques to treat a stricken nurse (*Men in Black*, 1934).

Calling All Curs (as veterinarians), and in *Some More of Samoa* (as tree surgeons).

Dr. I. Yankum—IMMUTABLE STOOGES LAW #13: Whenever someone searches desperately for a professional, he will mistake a Stooge for that professional. In *All the World's a Stooge*, window washer Moe is mistaken for esteemed dentist Dr. I. Yankum, a result that still makes dental professionals wince.

Dr. Ingrid—Stunning blond scientist whose greatest achievement at the **National Space Foundation** is not her

Drs. Hart, Burns, and Belcher—On the run with an injured accomplice in *A Gem of a Jam*, three desperate bank robbers are in no mood to hear the Stooges explain that they are janitors, not Drs. Hart, Burns, and Belcher. A textbook example of IMMUTABLE STOOGES LAW #13: Whenever someone searches desperately for a professional, he will mistake a Stooge for that professional. (Drs. Hart, Burns, and Belcher also run the *Croakers Sanitarium* in *Scrambled Brains*.)

Drs. Lyman and Walters—Creative physicians not strictly tied to the Western approach to medicine. They are treating *Little Betty Williams*, a girl suffering deep depression after the kidnapping of her father in *Nutty but Nice*. Their proposed cure: a cheer-up visit by three singing waiters whose jokes are livelier than their harmonies.

Dogfish—Remarkable fish that barks lustily when Moe pulls it from his line in *I'm a Monkey's Uncle* and *Stone Age Romeos*. Though the fish looks delicious, Larry wisely warns of potential health consequences by declaring, "I hope it ain't got fleas!"

"Dogs Washed While U Wate . . ."—Sign advertising the Stooges' dog washing business in *Mutts to You*. It reads, "Dogs Washed While U Wate 50 cents—Clipping Curling Simonizing $1.00—Moe-Curly-Larry Props." See also *"Deposit Dogs Here."*

The Doggy Pet Shop—Store adjacent to the *Columbia Uniform Supply Company* where the Stooges are discovered fishing from a fish tank in *A Plumbing We Will Go*.

Dollar Day—Promotion conceived by Curly to promote the Stooge-owned Ye Olde Pottery and Stoneworks in *Matri-Phony*. The idea, Curly says, will "put a pot in every palace."

Doctors Walters (John Tyrell) and Lyman (Vernon Dent) call in three unorthodox specialists to help lift the forlorn spirits of an ailing little girl (Nutty but Nice, 1940).

Dolly Devore—Glamorous blond starlet rescued by the Stooges in *Studio Stoops*.

Dolores—Mexican beauty who mistakenly carries off the Stooges' suitcase in *What's the Matador?* Traveling to Dolores's home to retrieve the case is a small problem for the Stooges. Explaining their presence in her bedroom to insanely jealous husband *José* is a much larger problem.

"Don't Be a Muttonhead—Vote For Abel Lamb Stewer for President"—Name-calling in politics is not a new phenomenon, as is proved in this campaign slogan from *Three Dark Horses*.

"Don't Chop the Wood . . ."—Like the best ice cream trucks of today, the Stooges' fish truck in *Booby Dupes* played a charming tune, which Curly identifies as "Don't Chop the Wood, Mother; Father's Coming Home with a Load."

"Don't let 'em kill you till we get there!"—The best detectives don't simply solve crimes; they also inspire confidence in their clients. When terrified *Old Man Goodrich* phones the Stooges and begs them to prevent his murder in *For Crimin' Out Loud*, Moe inspires hope in the trembling senior citizen by declaring, "Don't let 'em kill you till we get there!"

"Don't look at me!"—Shemp's wary reply in *Three Dark Horses* after Moe declares that he is hungry enough to eat a horse.

"Don't worry; you smell . . . good!"—A triple date with three lovely cavewomen awaits the Stooges in *I'm a Monkey's Uncle*, and naturally Shemp wants to smell good. Moe does his part to reassure his nervous pal, telling him, "Don't worry; you smell . . . good!"

Dopey Dan's Daily Double—Horseracing tout sheet peddled by Curly in *Even as I.O.U.*

Dora and Flora—Shemp's aesthetically challenged sisters who marry Moe and Larry in *Husbands Beware*.

Double Deal Decker—Villainous ranch rustler and owner of *Double Deal's Five "D" Delight* in *Horses' Collars*. Decker's defeated many a meddler in his day, but none who, like Curly, goes crazy at the sight of a mouse.

Double Deal's Five "D" Delight—One-stop establishment offering *"Dice, Dancing, Dames, Drinking, and Dunking"* in *Horses' Collars*.

"Double Featur"—It's tough to start a business, but the Stooges seem to have a good thing going with their new Mexican beauty salon in *Cookoo Cavaliers*. Just after opening, four lovely showgirls arrive for a makeover and dye job—the result, no doubt, of the enticing hand-painted sign on the salon window: "Double Featur—Bleeching and Manakures—Hair Washed or Dry Cleened and Press."

"Dububb, zedubb, wubbub, dewubb dee-dub-wub"—Larry's astute translation in *Hold That Lion!* and *Loose Loot* when asked what Shemp—trapped inside a goldfish bowl—is mumbling.

Duke of Durham—Larry in *Restless Knights*. He is also referred to as the Duke of Mixture when brought before her royal highness, **Queen Anne of Anesthesia**. See also **Baron of Gray Matter** and **Count of Five**.

Duke of Mixture—See *Duke of Durham*.

"Dump No Rubbish Here"— IMMUTABLE STOOGES LAW #14: A mannequin will always be mistaken by the Stooges for a human being and will then be beheaded, dismembered, or otherwise killed. In *Three Pests in a Mess*, the Stooges try to dispose of a "murdered" mannequin in dumpsters marked "Dump No Rubbish Here."

Dungen—Sourpuss sailor whose crotchety attitude toward the Stooges in *Back from the Front* might be forgivable if he weren't really a high-ranking German spy with a particular appetite for the Stooges' execution.

Curly provides a sobering reminder that it's always unsafe to step between two men engaged in a swordfight (*Back from the Front*, 1943).

E

Eagon's Rehearsal Hall Theatre—
Where the Stooges and newfound girl-friends *Hilda, Wilda, and Tilda* rehearse their variety act in *Rhythm and Weep*.

The Earl of Glenheather—Ruddy-cheeked Scottish nobleman who hires the Stooges to guard his cobwebbed castle in *Hot Scots* and *Scotched in Scotland*.

"Earthmen Return Home From Venus! World Honors First Travelers in Space"—See *New York Globe*.

Edam Neckties—Proud sponsor of the radio broadcast of the Stooges' hanging from *Hangemall Prison* in *In the Sweet Pie and Pie*. *Bill Stein*, the radio voice of the hangings, reminds listeners that Edam Neckties has three convenient locations: *Skagway, Alaska*; *Little America*; and *Pago Pago*.

Earysyphillus—The disease Shemp claims is being transmitted as Moe bites his ear in *Don't Throw That Knife*.

The Eel—Evasive thief the Stooges track to the *Biltless Hotel* in *Blunder Boys*. Little is known about the Eel, who is among the few criminals ever to escape the wily Stooges.

Eenar fraapini—Exotic cocktail mixed by Moe to calm groom-to-be Shemp's nerves in *Up in Daisy's Penthouse*. Though many ingredients used to make an eenar fraapini are not readily available, the recipe is presented here for posterity: Mix liberal amounts of **bretta, croomithistle, papeeptoomin, and pickle juice.** Shake well.

Eenginzoemen, anacanapanasan—Key missing ingredients that the Stooges finally add to their miraculous *Fountain of Youth* in *All Gummed Up* and *Bubble Trouble*. The result: youth everywhere!

Effie—Amorous bearded lady who finds the circus's freak show to be just the right place for romance with Curly in *Three Little Twirps*.

Egbert—Stooges' adopted son in *Three Loan Wolves*. Yes, Egbert speaks to his pawnbroker fathers with a bit of sass in his voice, but if that is the only problem with a child who was pawned by a woman named *Molly the Glamour Girl*, the Stooges should count their blessings.

18—Curly's football uniform number in *No Census, No Feeling*.

Eighteen blondes and twelve redheads—The company a hopeful Larry says he intends to attract during his lunchbreak in *Three Little Sew and Sews*.

81C—When budding detectives Shemp and Larry rough up the wrong man in

Blunder Boys, Moe orders them to prepare for the dreaded "81C," a punishment whereby Moe extends two fingers on each hand while Shemp and Larry reluctantly run forward and poke their own eyes into the menacing digits.

Electricity—IMMUTABLE STOOGES LAW #15: Power outages are most likely to occur during the critical moments of Stooge fights in haunted houses (various films).

Elementary Chemistry—Title of book Moe is reading in the laboratory in *Fuelin' Around* and *Hot Stuff*. While it is true that the Stooges were forced at gunpoint to create a super rocket fuel, the results prove that some skills cannot be learned from a book.

"The Elevator Dance"—Fancy dance Larry promises he will demonstrate to Ted Healy and a rapt audience in *Soup to Nuts*. After Larry stays motionless for what seems like an eternity, Healy demands an explanation for this strange "Elevator Dance." Larry's reply: "There's no steps to it!"

1122 Lillyflower Terrace—Curly's tranquil-sounding address in *Healthy, Wealthy and Dumb*.

Elite Café—Employer of the Stooges in *Shivering Sherlocks* and *Of Cash and Hash*.

Ella, Bella, and Stella—You can't marry women as desirable as Ella, Bella, and Stella without some jealous thugs wanting to kill you in a high-noon shootout. The ***Noonan Brothers*** are

quick draws in *Shot in the Frontier*, but the Stooges wear their holsters proudly and win the dames in the end.

Elmer—Dashing cowboy in the tradition of the great Gary Cooper in *Punchy Cowpunchers*. Elmer is nuts about the cowboy's solitary life, his guitar, and the lovely ***Nell***—in that order. Nell, however, isn't nuts about Elmer's priorities, and rearranges them by hurling a vase directly at the cowboy's trademark golden locks.

Elmo Drake—Musclebound trucking foreman who works alongside the Stooges at the ***Seabiscuit Food Corporation*** in *Muscle Up a Little Closer*. When Joe's fiancée ***Tiny*** finds her engagement ring to be missing, all suspicions turn toward Drake, a roughneck who manhandles the Stooges before finally succumbing to the awesome strength and wrestling technique of Tiny herself.

Elvis—The Stooges' semicooperative pet skunk in *The Outlaws Is Coming*.

Emir of Shmow—Wrongful owner of the ***King Rootin' Tootin' Diamond*** in *Malice in the Palace* and *Rumpus in the Harem*. The Emir of Shmow is a case study in the role of the subconcious in guilt. Although able to read the funny pages while wearing the stolen Rootin' Tootin' Diamond on his turban, the Emir is immediately terrified at the sight of an otherwise silly looking twelve-foot-tall, six-armed Santa Claus (the Stooges) who demands the return of the gem.

Enchiladas, spaghetti, artichokes, onions, celery, olives, radishes, pigs feet, and herring—Banquet prepared by the Stooges for their new baby in *Sock-A-Bye Baby*.

"Engine 1 M.F.D."—Wording on the Midland Fire House in *Flat Foot Stooges*.

Erysipelas—See *Ancient Erysipelas*.

Escape routes—IMMUTABLE STOOGES LAW #16: While fleeing for their lives from bandits, ghouls, or angry bosses, the Stooges will select the escape route least likely to provide the desired relief (various films).

Eureka!—Shemp's declaration after solving a difficult problem in *Baby Sitters Jitters*. Moe's reply: "You don't smell so good, either."

Ever Rest Pet Cemetery—Macabre grounds where the Stooges try to dispose of a mannequin they think they murdered in *Three Pests in a Mess*.

"Every man for himself!"—Curly's noble declaration after brave noblemen Moe and Larry proclaim, "One for all and all for one" in *Restless Knights*.

"Everything From a Needle to a Battleship . . ."—Sign in the Stooges-owned *Cut Throat Drug Store* in *All Gummed Up* and *Bubble Trouble*. It reads, "Everything From a Needle to a Battleship—We Also Sell Drugs—Soda Fountain."

"Examination Room"—Ambiguous sign on the door to the army's enlistment headquarters.

Executive clemency—See *President of the United States*.

The Emir of Shmow (Frank Lackteen) learns a painful lesson about messing with men in Santa Claus suits (*Malice in the Palace*, 1949).

Exhaust valves—IMMUTABLE STOOGES LAW #17: When consuming too much liquid too quickly, the body of a Stooge will discharge that liquid through the ears (various films).

"Exit Tunnel 12"—Gate through which the Stooges pass in *No Census, No Feeling*. The passage, according to a sign on the gate, is for *"Players Only,"* forcing the Stooges to disguise themselves as "Halfback," "Quarterback," and "Hunchback."

F. B. Eye—With a cunning criminal like *The Eel* on the loose in *Blunder Boys*, veteran police captain F. B. Eye knows he can't afford to save his three promising new detectives for a tidier case. Although the Stooges lose their jobs for allowing The Eel to slip through their hands at the *Biltless Hotel*, it must be remembered that The Eel was dramatically ahead of his time by using women's clothing as a disguise.

F.B.I.—When his lovely daughter *Princess Alicia* is kidnapped in *Fiddlers Three* and *Musty Musketeers*, an outraged *King Cole* orders his guard to call the F.B.I.—detectives Flannigan, Brannigan, and Iscovitch.

Facts and Figures Magazine—Brazenly named publication that pays Moe and Larry $10,000 for a phony photograph of a spaceship in *Flying Saucer Daffy*.

Fairport Theatre—See *"Free Auto."*

Faith, Hope, and Charity—Protecting colonists from Indians is a job for an entire army, not three lone soldiers. This is understood instinctively by Faith, Hope, and Charity, three beautiful pilgrims who give inspiration to the Stooges in *Back to the Woods*.

The Farmer in the Dell—Jubilant song sung by the Stooges to celebrate their decision to become farmers in *The Yoke's On Me* (sung to the tune of "The Farmer in the Dell," with Curly's joyous interjections in parentheses):

> *The farmer in the dell (onions!)*
> *The farmer in the dell (potatoes!)*
> *We'll make nice vegetables*
> *Like farmers in the dell (tomatoes!)*

(It is best left for an expert to comment on the effects of the Stooges' father's decision to smash tomatoes in their faces after the song's last verse, but even the casual observer can see it didn't help the Stooges' business.)

"Feel Tired? . . ."—Advertisement on the back of Larry's **Onion Oil Company** uniform in *Slaphappy Sleuths* that reads, "Feel Tired? Take Stun. Stun is Nuts Spelled Backward."

Feet—Immutable Stooges Law #18: After a Stooge's foot is continuously twisted by Moe, that foot will unwind at dizzying speeds like an airplane propeller (various films).

Felix Famous Concentrated Soap—It is not the good fortune of those who eat Shemp's cooking in *Baby Sitters Jitters* that the words "soup" and "soap" look so much alike.

Felix Stout's Bar—Schoolteachers might argue that the Stooges should have been walking, not running, past Felix Stout's Bar while searching for a sick girl's missing father in *Nutty but Nice*. But to feel sorry for the man out front who is repeatedly run over while carrying buckets of beer is to forget the Stooges' noble purpose.

Fido—If the military awarded the Purple Heart to dogs, Fido would be a worthy recipient. Trusted navy pal and bunkmate to the Stooges in *Back from the Front*, Fido shows rare courage after the Stooges sink their own ship, paddling courageously to tow his masters' lifeboat while they recover from the blast.

Field Marshal Herring—Curly's role as right-hand henchman to ruthless dictator *Moe Hailstone* in *I'll Never Heil Again*.

Fife of Drum—See *Count of Five*.

Fifi—Demure French maid whom Curly woos while taking the census inside a fancy house in *No Census, No Feeling*. Though not as prolific as the great French poets, Curly offers Fifi a glass of punch and this heartfelt sonnet:

> *Roses are red*
> *And how do you do?*
> *Drink four of these*
> *And woo woo woo woo!*

(Fifi is also the Parisian lovely Shemp and Joe fall for at the *Rue de Schlemiel* and *Rue de le Pew* in *Love at First Bite* and *Fifi Blows Her Top*, respectively, and is the French maid in *Pest Man Wins* who alerts *Mrs. Castor* to the presence of pests in the home by delicately informing her, "Madam, there is mouses in the houses!")

50 cents or 3 for $1—Reward money offered by authorities for the Stooges'

capture in *Phony Express*. See also *"Wanted for Vagrancy."*

Fifty generations—The amount of time in *Half-Wits Holiday* Larry claims has passed since there has been a gentleman in the Stooges' families. Moe's reply: "Quit bragging."

"5736" and "Mr. No One"—Super-secret code names for the crooks who take over a prison in *Three Smart Saps*. Under normal circumstances, ingenious crooks like "5736" and "Mr. No One" would triumph over authorities with little more than a thought. But when their sinister plan includes kidnapping the father of the Stooges' fiancées, it is simply a matter of moments before justice—and romance—will prevail.

Filch—Weasely right-hand man to devious con artist *Vickers Cavendish* in *The Three Stooges Go Around the World in a Daze*.

Filet of sole and heel—Delicious-sounding seafood dinner prepared by Moe in *Space Ship Sappy*. The dish—a black work boot cooked over an open fire—is probably best enjoyed without contemplating its ingredients.

"Filmed in Glorious Black and White"—Dramatic opening title in *The Three Stooges Meet Hercules*.

Final blow—IMMUTABLE STOOGES LAW #19: The Stooges will apply the final knockout blow to a dazed enemy by blowing heartily on that enemy's chest (various films).

Filet of sole and heel (*Space Ship Sappy*, 1957)

"Finders Keepers"—Policy clearly posted inside ***The Lost Mine*** in *Cactus Makes Perfect*. Two violent bandits who watch the Stooges discover the mine, however, aren't persuaded by signs.

Fine powdered alum—It would be easy to assign sole blame to Curly for preparing fruit punch with fine powdered alum instead of powdered sugar at a society party in *No Census, No Feeling*; after all, a group of ladies made unable to speak by severe puckering of the lips is a serious situation. But one must always remember to ask what fine powdered alum was doing near the powdered sugar in the first place.

First National Bank—Inevitable holdup target of **Red Morgan**'s bandits, which the newly deputized Stooges are assigned to guard in *Phony Express*.

The Fishmarket Duet—Song-and-dance troupe revived in *Dunked in the Deep* by its founding members, Shemp and Larry. Trapped aboard an ocean freighter, the duet make the best of things by launching into "***Number Four***

in the Blue Book," a catchy little tune that Shemp says he and Larry sing "for the halibut." Unfortunately, only the first stanza survives, as Moe interrupts the performance with a violent crescendo:

> *We're off to see the sea*
> *To see what we can see!*

$5,000 Benson County Sweepstakes—Feature race won miraculously by the Stooge-owned horse *Thunderbolt*—despite running for a time in the wrong direction—in *Playing the Ponies.*

Fix-All Fixers, Ink.—Stooges' handyman business in *They Stooge to Conga.* Larry's sign reads, "Fix-All Fixers, Ink. General Handiwork Our Speshalty."

Fleur de Polecat—Trapped in an operating room and posing as surgeons, Moe and Larry decide to knock out a violent thug with a heavy dose of ether. The thug, however, enjoys and recognizes the smell, recalling it as his favorite scent, Fleur de Polecat.

Fleur de Skunk—*Moe Hailstone*'s cologne of choice in *You Nazty Spy,* and Moe's favorite powdered fragrance in *Cookoo Cavaliers.*

Fleur de Stinkun—Powerful aftershave used liberally by Curly as he prepares for his introduction into high society in *In the Sweet Pie and Pie.*

Flint—Well-bred butler at the **Mrs. van Bustle** residence who confers the ulti-

mate insult upon meeting Moe, Larry, and Curly in *Crash Goes the Hash.* Says Flint indignantly, "Such levity; you remind me of the Three Stooges!"

Flipper's Fluffy Fablongent Flapjacks—Every Stooge could cook, but none was more flamboyant than Larry. In *Rusty Romeos,* Larry takes a drab-looking box of Mrs. Flipper's Fluffy Pancake Mix and whips them into the tempting Flipper's Fluffy Fablongent Flapjacks. (In Yiddish, *fablongent* means "all mixed up" or "totally confused.")

Flo, Mary, and Shirley—Show business is rich with stories of chance meetings and fateful partnerships. One of the most successful occurred in *Gents Without Cents,* in which the Stooges' upstairs neighbors are three beautiful dancing girls who make the perfect complement to their promising *"Niagara Falls"* stage routine.

Flounder Inn—Stooge-owned restaurant in *Playing the Ponies.* In a society that rewards risk-taking and ambition, it is hard to criticize the Stooges for boldly trading the Flounder Inn to con men for a broken-down horse. But with delicious specials like **Lobster with Frog Legs**, one can only speculate as to the real potential of this interesting eatery.

"A Flying Field Somewhere in Somewhere"—The film *Higher Than a Kite* opens with the sign, "A Flying Field Somewhere in Somewhere," which is appropriate, since the Stooges soon find themselves straddling a missile headed for Germany.

"Flying Saucer Photo Alerts Capitol"—Premature headline in the *Washington Chronicle* alerting citizens to Joe's photograph of a flying saucer—really a dirty paper plate—in *Flying Saucer Daffy*. Though not as serious in consequence as "Dewey Defeats Truman," the *Chronicle's* rush to headline is an early example of the embarrassment sure to occur when a newspaper jumps the gun.

"Flying Saucer Photographer Awarded City's Highest Honor"—Headline in the *Daily Star-News* announcing Joe's second, and this time authentic, photograph of a flying saucer in *Space Ship Sappy*.

Folger Apartments—Where the Stooges track **Junior**'s father in *Baby Sitters Jitters*.

"Football To-day. Tigers Vs. Cubs. Positively No Admittance"—Sign in *Three Little Pigskins* announcing the big football game between **Boulder Dam University** and **Blue Point University**.

It's curious that NFL teams still have not adopted the Stooges' revolutionary kicking formation (*Three Little Pigskins*, 1934).

"For Duty and Humanity!"—High-minded principle to which new physicians *Dr. Howard, Dr. Fine, and Dr. Howard* pledge themselves in *Men in Black.* "For Duty and Humanity" does not predate the more traditional Hippocratic oath, but medical schools report its increased popularity among students born after the Stooges made *Men in Black.*

Foreign Legion Headquarters—Paris-based recruiting station that enrolls the Stooges in *Wee Wee Monsieur.*

Forgiveness—IMMUTABLE STOOGES LAW #20: If Moe says he forgives you, the worst is yet to come (various films).

"Fort Scott, Kansas, 1868—The Heroic Men of the U.S. Cavalry"—Successive scene titles in *Punchy Cowpunchers.* It is to Fort Scott that the dashing **Elmer** travels to summon three of the U.S. Cavalry's best to foil *"The Killer Dillons."*

Fountain of Youth—Unorthodox methods—like mixing potions in a boot—have prevented the Stooges from being recognized as inventors of historical significance. But no one can dispute that they were visionaries. The Fountain of Youth, a serum designed to transform the elderly into the young in *All Gummed Up* and *Bubble Trouble,* would surely be on store

The tentative, critical moments just before the Stooges succeed in inventing the Fountain of Youth (*Bubble Trouble,* 1953)

shelves today but for the greedy **Amos Flint**, who, in an early experiment, drank too much and turned into an infant.

Fountain pen that writes under whipped cream—Worthless gadget that con men Moe and Larry nearly sell for $50,000 to **The DePeysters** in *Heavenly Daze* and *Bedlam in Paradise*. The Stooges' effect on generations of investors must be traced to this film, since no other attempts to market a fountain pen that writes under whipped cream have surfaced since.

$4.85—No U.S. president will ever mention it, but Curly and Shemp's experience with the tax system brought many of this country's inequitable tax laws to light. In *Healthy, Wealthy and Dumb* and *A Missed Fortune*, Curly and Shemp's $50,000 prize money is reduced to $4.95 after taxes ($4.85 for Shemp), a result regretted as much by the owner of a fancy hotel where the Stooges celebrated as by the Stooges themselves.

$4.95—See *$4.85*.

400 Shekels—Price **Radames** pays the Stooges for a used chariot in *Mummy's Dummies*. This would have been a reasonable deal for Radames had even one item on the chariot worked as advertised.

418 Meshugena Avenue—Posh address of the Stooges' fiancées in *G.I. Wanna Go Home*. ("Meshugena" is Yiddish for "crazy.")

489 Shekels—Fair-sounding price for one of the Stooges' factory-rebuilt chariots in *Mummy's Dummies*.

41144—See *Percy Pomeroy* and *Box 41144*.

1410 South America Way—Site of the Stooges' nouveau hair salon, the **Cantina de Rosa**, in *Cookoo Cavaliers*.

1414 Bleecker Street—Address of the plumbing-troubled **Norfleet Mansion** in *Scheming Schemers*.

"Four slices of burned toast and a rotten egg"—Low calorie dessert ordered by Moe in *Punch Drunks*. When waiter Curly questions his choice, Moe explains that he has a tapeworm and it's "good enough for him."

"Free Auto"—Visible language on a poster used by a crook to wipe his shoe in *Oily to Bed, Oily to Rise*. When the crook tosses the sticky poster onto a nearby car, the Stooges think the car to be free and drive off. The entire poster reads, "Free Auto Given Away Every Saturday—Fairport Theatre."

"Friday the 13th"—Most gunfighters would cancel a high noon shootout if the ticking clock read "Friday the 13th." Even more would cancel if they tried to turn back the clock and it read, *"No Use—You're Doomed."* These things happened to Larry in *Shot in the Frontier*. He and the Stooges still fought. That should settle any questions about the Stooges' bravery.

Frontier Inn—Hotel where a New York–based talent scout stays in *Rockin' Thru the Rockies.*

"A frozen dainty"—Moe's analysis of Curly's condition after pulling him out of a truck full of ice in *An Ache in Every Stake* and *Violent is the Word for Curly.*

Fuller Bull—Managing Editor at the *Daily News* who hires the Stooges in *Crash Goes the Hash* to get the scoop on the society wedding of **Mrs. van Bustle** to **Prince Shaam**.

Fuller Grime—General manager of **Onion Oil Company** who enlists private detectives Moe, Larry, and Shemp to solve a series of robberies at his service stations in *Slaphappy Sleuths.*

Fuller Rath—General Manager of **Carnation Pictures** Studio in *Movie Maniacs.* Although Fuller was obviously a name associated with power in the 1940s and 1950s (see **Fuller Bull** and **Fuller Grime** above), the name seems inexplicably to have lost favor in the present day.

G.C.M.—Unfortunate diagnosis given to a canine patient at the Stooge-run dog hospital in *Calling All Curs*. Although Larry describes it in layman's terms as a "bad case of Scavengeritis," it turns out that G.C.M. is a common affliction at the hospital more formally known as "Garbage Can Moocher."

G. Y. Prince—It's tempting while watching *Quiz Whizz* to criticize Joe for investing his jackpot prize money in *Consolidated Fujiyama California Smog Bags*. But can any of us say that amid the excitement of making a big investment we would have noticed the suspicious initials of the product's eager pitchmen, G. Y. Prince and *R. O. Broad*?

Gail Tempest—Shapely nightclub dancer wrongfully charged with the murder of *Kirk Robbin* in *Disorder in the Court*. Tempest's courtroom strategy is unorthodox, but the verdict proves that her decision to dance in a sexy outfit to the music of three dubious key witnesses was brilliantly conceived.

A gallon of gasoline, two tumblers of bicarbonate of soda, an ounce of iodine, and a pinch of mustard—Curly's ready-made recipe for bleaching hair in *Cookoo Cavaliers*.

Gallstone—Curly's role as field marshal in *You Nazty Spy*.

Garbage Scow #188 N.Y.C.—Stooge-manned craft of dubious seaworthiness that shipwrecks on *Dead Man's Island* in *Three Little Pirates*. Although the boat lands the Stooges on hostile ground, its one-of-a-kind construction lends credence to Moe's life-saving yarn that Curly is the *Maharajah of Canazzi*, a mystic who brings strange gifts from strange lands.

Garçon—Prized canine patient kidnapped from the Stooges' dog hospital in *Calling All Curs*. Most veterinarians would not have chosen to replace the fluffy Garçon by gluing mattress stuffing to an ordinary mutt, but true pet lovers cannot help but appreciate the Stooges' sense of duty in such a case.

Garden Theatre—Venue that inexplicably rejects the Stooges' song and joke act in *Rhythm and Weep*. Larry is painfully aware that the Garden is the twenty-sixth theater the Stooges have been thrown out of this month, prompting Moe to lament, "What is there left for us?" Larry's realistic response: "Four more theaters." Also, the place where the Stooges are hired to hang posters for *The Great Svengarlic*'s hypnotist show in *Flagpole Jitters*.

Gashouse Protective Association—Roughneck gang that puts the payola arm on the Stooges' pawnshop in *Three Loan Wolves*. The gang's resulting black eyes and bruised egos show what happens to extortionists who mess with pawnbrokers who know a thing or two themselves about dishing out physical punishment.

Gawkins—Butler in *Ants in the Pantry* who demonstrates an active faith in God. After his master's home becomes overrun by mice, ants, moths, and other pests, Gawkins can hardly believe his luck when three traveling exterminators present themselves for hire, telling the Stooges, "Heaven must have sent you!"

Gazette Journal—Newspaper in *The Sitter Downers* that announces the Stooges' protest against the nonconsenting father of their fiancées. It reads, "Suitors in Third Week of Sit Down Strike/Persistent Lovers Win Nation's Sympathy as Gifts Pour In."

"Gee, Moe, I'm sorry, Moe, what Moe can a fella say? That's all there is, there ain't no Moe!"— Rhythmic apology sung in scat by Shemp after he pries a bucket from Moe's head in *Corny Casanovas*.

"General Handiwork Our Speshalty"—See *Fix-All Fixers, Ink.*

"General Motorcycle: 17½, Anacanapana Steel: 25¼, Tsimmis Incorporated: 17"—Stock prices read by Larry as Moe unravels the tape used to bind *Professor Jones* in *Outer Space Jitters*.

General Muster—Commanding officer who sends *Wild Bill Hicup* (Moe), *Buffalow Billious* (Curly), and *Just Plain Bill* (Larry) to thwart cattle rustler *Longhorn Pete* in *Goofs and Saddles*.

"The genius!"—Shemp's awestruck declaration upon seeing a genie burst forth from a magic lamp he has rubbed in *Three Arabian Nuts*.

George B. Bopper—Distressed father in *Spooks* who hires three crack detectives to locate his missing daughter. Although Bopper erred in neglecting to inquire as to the Stooges' comfort around haunted mansions, he must be given a concerned parent's pardon.

George Lloyd—Jealous husband who seeks revenge on his wife by kidnapping adorable baby *Junior* in *Baby Sitters Jitters*. The willingness to kidnap is not a desirable trait in a father, but Lloyd shows admirable parental potential when he forgives Junior for clubbing his toes with an oversize hammer.

George Morton—President of the Voters League who intends to endorse his friend *Judge Henderson* in *Listen, Judge*— until the Stooges serve an explosively delicious birthday cake at Henderson's party.

"Gevalt!"—Moe's impassioned cry for help as his spaceship goes out of control in *Space Ship Sappy*. ("Gevalt!" is a Yiddish declaration meaning "Oh, my God!" or "What in the world!")

"Gezundheidt!"—Larry's polite reply to the baby he has burped in *Baby Sitters Jitters*.

Ghinna Rumma—Skittish thief in *Malice in the Palace* and *Rumpus in the Harem* who, along with cohort *Hassan Ben Sober*, plots to steal the glorious

King Rootin' Tootin' Diamond from the *Emir of Shmow*.

Ghost Town Hotel—Temporary safe haven for the Stooges while being chased by claim jumpers in *Cactus Makes Perfect*.

Giggle water—Moe's affectionate term for the champagne he sips in *Flying Saucer Daffy*.

Gilbraith Q. Tiddledewadder—Attention-hungry actor who falsely confesses to **Slug McGurk**'s murder in *Tricky Dicks*. Tiddledewadder goes by the dashing nickname "Chopper," a sad example of the damage well-meaning parents can do when they foist unusual names like Gilbraith on their children.

Gilda—Loyal daughter of **King Herman 6⅞** who risks her life by planting an exploding billiard ball on the pool table of ruthless dictator **Moe Hailstone** in *I'll Never Heil Again*.

Gilmore Stadium—Action-packed site of the big football game in *Three Little Pigskins*.

The Gin of Rummy—Moe's secret identity in *Three Little Pirates*, he is the interpreter for the **Maharajah of Canazzi**, and the only person standing between the lives of the Stooges and a horrible death at the hands of the execution-happy **Governor of Dead Man's Island**.

Gin smothered in bourbon—Curly's cocktail of choice in *Three Sappy People*.

Ginsberg, Rosenburg, Goldstein, and O'Brien—Real estate brokers in *G.I.*

Wanna Go Home. With four partners, this business is obviously successful, although the sign in front doesn't immediately suggest it: "Nothing to Buy, Nothing to Sell, We've Gone Fishing, You Can Go . . . Fishing Too."

"Give me that fillum!"—Heartsick wail that erupts repeatedly from the soul of **Bortch** in *Dunked in the Deep* and *Commotion on the Ocean*.

"Giveth them the works"—Military instructions carried by the Stooges to the colonies in *Back to the Woods*.

Gladys—The Stooges' faithful mule in *The Three Troubledoers*. Gladys carries the gear of three men without complaint, prompting Moe to stop in a sleepy town to buy her some shoes. Curly is even more grateful, suggesting that Moe throw in a pair of bedroom slippers, too.

Gladys Harmon—Golden-hearted owner of the struggling **Elite Café** in *Shivering Sherlocks* and *Of Cash and Hash*. In *Shivering Sherlocks*, the Stooges are enraged that customers continue to take advantage of Gladys by running up colossal tabs at her café, and demand to see who the culprits are. An inspection of the checks, however, reveals three names that appear with alarming regularity: Moe Howard, Larry Fine, and Shemp Howard.

Glenheather Castle—Spooky palace guarded by the Stooges in *Hot Scots* and *Scotched in Scotland*. The opening title reads, "Glenheather Castle—On the Bonny Banks of Scotland—But 'Tis Late and the Bonny Banks are Closed."

"Go two miles north and make a left-hand turn at the pool room"—Precise set of directions Curly gives to a homing pigeon in *Goofs and Saddles*.

Goiter—Curly has a wonderful idea in *Beer Barrel Polecats*. He will smuggle a keg of beer into prison to quench the Stooges' thirst. His plan looks to be in danger, however, when a suspicious guard asks about the gigantic lump under his coat. Curly, always a quick thinker, provides a ready reply that puts the man at ease: "Goiter."

Gold Collar Button Retriever—Brilliant gold-finding contraption invented by Curly in *Cactus Makes Perfect*. The retriever relied on an intricate interplay between bow-and-arrow and alarm clock, and would have changed the nature of the great western gold rush had it been invented a few decades earlier.

"Gold, gold, we want gold . . . zoot!"—Inspiring chant recited by the Stooges during their hunt for gold in *Cactus Makes Perfect*.

Goldberg, Ginsberg, Rosenberg, and O'Brien—Latin American booking agents for the Stooges' comedy bullfighting act in *What's the Matador?*

Goldstein, Goldberg, Goldblatt, and O'Brien—Booking agents for the Stooges' smash vaudeville act in *A Pain in the Pullman*.

"Gone to Lunch—Moe, Larry, Curly"—Many critics of the Three Stooges are quick to label face-slapping and eye-gouging as bad manners, but they rarely mention the many instances in which the Stooges demonstrate textbook etiquette. One such occasion occurs in *Disorder in the Court*, when the Stooges leave this polite note during the climax of the country's most sensational murder trial.

"Gone to Rest Under the Spreading Chestnut Tree"—Message left by blacksmith **Will Idge** in *Fiddlers Three* and *Musty Musketeers*.

The Good Ship Pfifernill—Although not nearly as well known as the *Nina*, *Pinta*, and *Santa Maria*, *The Good Ship Pfifernill* found America, too, and delivered to it three common criminals deported from England in *Back to the Woods*.

The Goon—Immutable Stooges Law #21: If there is an important science experiment in the works, the scientist will consider the Stooges to be perfect subjects for the experiment. In *Outer Space Jitters*, the **Grand Zilch of Sunev** already controls one zombie, The Goon, but wants to create three more for his collection.

"A gorg goggle yata benefucci timini garanga para dickman hee ha June 22nd"—Shemp is not a natural-born secretary, as proven by this baffling sentence he reads back after taking dictation from Moe in *Studio Stoops*.

Gorilla Watson—*Chopper Kane*'s would-be boxing opponent in *Fright Night* and *Fling in the Ring*. Stooge films leave few questions unanswered, but *Fright Night* and *Fling in the Ring* are notable exceptions. The Gorilla Watson–Chopper Kane fight had the makings of a classic until greedy gangster **Big Mike** caused the cancelation of the fight, leaving viewers wondering to this day just how good Watson could have been.

"Got Ants in Your Plants? We'll Kill 'Em!"—Take-no-prisoners motto of the **Lightning Pest Control Company** in *Ants in the Pantry* and *Pest Man Wins*.

Gottrox Jewelry Company—Robbery target of felonious hypnotist **The Great Svengarlic** in *Flagpole Jitters*.

Government of Urania—Department of Inferior—Military arm of the Uranian government, which assigns duties to undercover spies Moe, Larry, and Shemp in *Hot Stuff*.

Governor of Dead Man's Island— IMMUTABLE STOOGES LAW **#22:** If the Stooges come into contact with the ruler of a land, that ruler will eventually order their executions. The Governor of Dead Man's Island in *Three Little Pirates* has a weakness for trinkets and treasures, which Moe and Curly (as the **Maharajah of Canazzi**) masterfully seize upon to escape certain execution.

Grand Zilch of Sunev—Charming but murderous ruler of the planet *Sunev* in *Outer Space Jitters*. Along with right-hand man **The High Mucky Muck**, the Grand Zilch plans to turn the Stooges into zombies.

The Great Svengarlic—Crooked hypnotist in *Flagpole Jitters*. As evidenced by his motto ("He'll Steal Your Breath Away!"), Svengarlic could have made a beautiful living through stage hypnosis alone; indeed, there might be only a handful of hypnotists in the world who can make three men crawl out on a skyscraper's flagpole. His decision to use his gift for criminal purposes, however, is a sorry end to a promising career and a bane to the reputation of honest hypnotists everywhere. (An honest Svengarlic appears in a similar role in *Hokus Pokus*, proof that on-the-level hypnosis will be more rewarding in the long run.)

Even on the planet Sunev, the Stooges know how to subdue a crook like the Grand Zilch of Sunev (Gene Roth) (*Outer Space Jitters*, 1957).

Even busy bullfighters cannot help but take time to admire Greta (Greta Thyssen) (*Sappy Bullfighters*, 1959).

Greta—Shapely blonde who lands the Stooges a comedy bullfighting job in *Sappy Bullfighters*. Her jealous husband José, however, is not so magnanimous.

"Gritto spelled sideways is Ottri-guh-guh"—Though nosy maintenance man Moe should have kept his hands off expensive studio equipment in *Micro-Phonies*, he demonstrates an uncanny affinity for the microphone during a commercial he "broadcasts" for Gritto soap:

> *Use Gritto, radio friends, the soap that gives your hands that dishpan look! How will the old man know you've been working if your hands don't have that dishpan look, hmm? Put a box of Gritto in a glass of water and listen to it fizz! Remember, Gritto spelled sideways is Ottri-guh-guh."*

*See also **Sandra Sandpile**.*

Groundhog Day—One of Shemp's cunning aliases in *Blunder Boys*. See also *Christmas Day*, *Independence Day*, *Labor Day*, *New Year's Day*, and *St. Patrick's Day*.

Gyp the People—It isn't easy to feel sorry for a crook, but even those toughest on crime have to sympathize with the plight of Gyp the People in *So Long Mr. Chumps*. Strictly minding his own business, People is held at gunpoint by Curly as part of the Stooges' plan to get themselves thrown in jail. In self-defense, Gyp takes the gun and turns it on Curly, but that's not how it looks to the local beat cop who hauls the hard luck crook—and not the Stooges—to jail.

Gypsom Good Inc., Antiques—One look inside the Gypsom Good antique store and it's easy to see why the felony-minded *Ape Man* chose to rob it in *Dizzy Detectives*. But the Stooges know fine quality, too, and pose ingeniously as watchmen inside the store to trap the crooked simian.

H

H₂O—Curly's prison uniform number in *Beer Barrel Polecats* and *So Long Mr. Chumps*. Also, jockey Larry's number while riding racehorse **Thunderbolt** in *Playing the Ponies*. As men who excelled in neither math nor science, it was the Stooges' misfortune to continually receive fractions and chemical equations as uniform numbers. Even their labor union, the *Amalgamated Association of Morons*, was affiliated with local 6⅞. (Also, Curly's affiliation number with the *Needlock Appliance Corporation* in *I Can Hardly Wait*.)

H²O²—Moe's gritty football uniform number in *Three Little Pigskins*.

Haffa Dalla—Arab in *Malice in the Palace* and *Rumpus in the Harem* who, along with accomplices *Hassan Ben Sober* and *Ghinna Rumma*, recruits the Stooges to recover the *King Rootin' Tootin' Diamond* from the light-fingered *Emir of Shmow*.

Half a pint of ectowhozis (may substitute with ectowhatsis), 4 grams of alkabob, shishkabob, jigger of sastrophonia, carbolic acid, squirt of haratang—In one of the great moments in the history of chemistry—really in the history of science—the Stooges concoct a super rocket fuel with these ingredients in *Fuelin' Around* and *Hot Stuff*.

Halliday—Moe's role as a cunning detective in *Blunder Boys*. See also *Tarraday* and *St. Patrick's Day*.

Hammond Egger—Rarely can a politician point to a single cause to explain defeat in an election. Crooked presidential candidate Hammond Egger, who trusted three strange delegates to cast the deciding votes in *Three Dark Horses*, is the exception.

"Hammond Egger Wants Your Vote"—Stooge-written theme song for the crooked presidential campaign of candidate *Hammond Egger* in *Three Dark Horses* (chanted with fervent enthusiasm):

> Hammond Egger wants your vote
> Shout his praises from your throat
> You'll eat steak instead of stew
> Five, four, three, two!

"Hang Hitler!"—Stooges' defiant salute to German naval officers aboard the **S.S. Shickelgruber** in *Back from the Front*.

Hangemall Prison—Site where the Stooges are to be hanged for committing the Mushroom Murders in *In the Sweet Pie and Pie*. Prisons since Hangemall have become less liberal; nowadays, cheering by other inmates during hangings is strictly forbidden.

Hangover Athletic Club—Rough-and-tumble gym where the Stooges train fearsome wrestling champion *Ivan Bustoff* in *Grips, Grunts and Groans*. The training regimen does not contribute to Bustoff's success in the ring, but Curly's phony beard and a certain perfume save the day.

"Happy 10th Anniversary"—Succinct but heartfelt inscription on the cake in *Pardon My Backfire*.

Happy Haven Hotel—It is true that the proprietor of the Happy Haven abruptly ejected the Stooges from his hotel in *Loco Boy Makes Good*. But the hotel also should be remembered for offering the kinds of lodging available only in a bygone era. Its motto: "Rooms $1 A Month—Free Showers When It Rains."

Harold the Ape—Acts of compassion by gorillas toward men don't occur only on public television specials. In *Crime on Their Hands* and *Hot Ice*, Harold the Ape—a gorilla untrained in medicine and surgery—relies on simple affection to diagnose Shemp's need to be rescued from the angry scalpel of crook *Dapper Dan*.

Hassan Ben Sober—Deflated recipient of a prophetic note in *Malice in the Palace* and *Rumpus in the Harem*. It reads, "Hassan Ben Sober—You Are Late—I Got the Diamond—You Got the Gate—(signed) Omagosh, Emir of Shmow."

"Have You Sore Feet? Try Tic-Tac. Good for the Toe"—Snappy advertising slogan on the back of Shemp's *Onion Oil Company* uniform in *Slaphappy Sleuths*.

Hayfever, spotted fever, buck fever, colic, rickets, graying teeth, musty silverwear, dandruff, and lumbago—According to Moe in *Phony Express*, *Doctor Abdul's Cactus Remedy* will cure these ails. And, he promises, it will also shine old silverware.

Hazel—See *Onion Oil Company*.

"He don't smoke, drink, nor chew!"—Curly's indignant response in *Mutts to You* after *Officer O'Halloran* asks if Curly's baby is still on the bottle.

"He drew twenty years with one stroke of the pen"—Finding themselves unexpectedly in art school in *Pop Goes the Easel*, Moe brags that his own father used to draw, a report Curly clarifies by remarking, "Sure, he drew twenty years with one stroke of the pen."

"The Heat Is On"—Sultry number sung by *Tiny Landers* in her triumphant nightclub debut in *Sweet and Hot*.

Heavenly Express—Train that departs from *Cloud 49* in *Heavenly Daze* and *Bedlam in Paradise*. Its destinations: the Big Dipper, the Middle Dipper, Earth, Mars, Venus, Kukamonga, and all points south.

Heebah, Reebah, and Sheebah—Anyone convinced that chivalry is dead hasn't seen *Rumpus in the Harem*. When three men dress as a gigantic Santa Claus to attempt a death-defying recovery of a stolen diamond, that is not for money and that is not for glory. That can only be to prevent the ransoming of their sweethearts Heebah, Reebah, and Sheebah to the wicked *Sultan of Pish Posh.*

Helen Blazes—Sultry seductress sent by the devil to entice Shemp in *Bedlam in Paradise.* With ethical dramas as powerful as that featuring Helen Blazes, it is shocking that the American clergy continues to refrain from invoking Stooges films in its sermons.

"He'll feblonger him"—Larry's bold prediction on behalf of boxer *Chopper Kane* in *Fling in the Ring.* (In Yiddish, "He'll make him punch drunk.")

"He'll Steal Your Breath Away!"—Sensational claim made by optimistic but misguided hypnotist *The Great Svengarlic* in *Hokus Pokus* and *Flagpole Jitters.*

"Hello ma, hello pa. It wasn't much of a fight. I stood like that . . . but not for long"—Curly's dramatic broadcast over a hospital's intercom system in *Dizzy Doctors.*

Hemoglober, sulfademus—Specialty surgical tools Moe calls for while performing an impromptu operation—at gunpoint—on the bullet wound of a gangster in *A Gem of a Jam.*

Hendrix Jewelry Store—Pricey boutique robbed by murderous crooks *Mr. Jerry Pip and Steve* in *A Snitch in Time.*

"Henna color at all!"—Comforting reassurance provided by hair stylist Larry in *Cookoo Cavaliers* after a showgirl asks if he can make her hair "henna" color.

"Here Lies A Father of 28; He Might Have Had More But Now It's Too Late"—Mournful epitaph on the gravestone Larry hides behind in *Shot in the Frontier.* The stone is located in front of *Diggs, Graves, and Berry Undertakers.* See also *"Beneath This . . ."* and *"Mama Loved Papa . . ."*

"Here This Week—The Great Hypnotist Svengarlic—He'll Steal Your Breath Away—A Stellar Attraction—Scientific—Educational—2 Performances Daily"—Awe-inspiring poster hung by the Stooges in *Hokus Pokus* and *Flagpole Jitters.* Although the Stooges were more intuitive than average poster hangers, even they could not have anticipated Svengarlic's newest trick: hypnotizing and then convincing them to risk life and limb by climbing the unsturdy flagpole of a nearby skyscraper.

"Here Today, Pawn Tomorrow"—No-nonsense motto of the Stooges' pawnshop in *Three Loan Wolves.*

Herman's Great Combined Shows—Immutable Stooges Law #23: If there is a knife or spear thrower practicing in the vicinity, the Stooges will find and anger him. In *Three Little Twirps*, the Stooges join Herman's Great Combined Shows, a circus that features the *Sultan of Abadaba,* a spear thrower who stretches basic carnival ethics by using three human targets without a moment's rehearsal.

"Hey You No Smoking"—Warning sign hanging on the wall in *No Dough Boys.* When Moe scolds Curly for

THEMES

Like great classical music, Three Stooges films are filled with recurring themes. Listed below are some of the most common Stooge occupations, nemeses, and settings; try mixing and matching one listing from each category and see if you don't remember a Stooge film along just those lines.

STOOGE OCCUPATION	NEMESIS	SETTING
Spies	Enemy spies	Haunted house
Detectives	Crooks	Jail
Vagrants/bums	A misunderstood gorilla	Train/boat
Janitors/handymen	Ghosts/spooks	Jail
Cooks/butlers/waiters	High society	Palace
Doctors/dentists	Police	Mansion
Husbands/boyfriends	Wives	Jail
Royal subjects	Boss	Hospital

brazenly ignoring the sign, Curly replies, "It says *you*, not me!"

"Hi, Lorna; how ya doone?"—Perhaps more than any other Stooge, Shemp was a master in the ways and means of a gentleman. In *Hot Scots* and *Scotched in Scotland*, for example, Shemp is introduced to lovely Scottish lass **Lorna Doone**, to whom he extends the noble greeting, "Hi, Lorna; how ya doone?"

"High altitude, low prices. No matter what you got you'll lose it at Mallard's."—Slick ad campaign conducted by the crookedly run *Mallard's Rest Home and Clinic* in *Monkey Businessmen.*

The High Mucky Muck—Polite but bloodthirsty right-hand man to the **Grand Zilch of Sunev** in *Outer Space Jitters.*

"Highly polished mahogany and termites with big blue eyes"—Detective Moe uses a high-powered magnifying glass to gather evidence but doesn't realize that he is inspecting detective Larry's head in *Who Done It?* and *For Crimin' Out Loud.* His analysis: "Highly polished mahogany and termites with big blue eyes."

Hilarious Hash Slingers—Showbiz moniker used by the Stooges while working as singing waiters in *Nutty but Nice.*

Their motto: "America's Gift to Indigestion."

Hilda, Wilda, and Tilda—On the brink of suicide in *Rhythm and Weep*, the Stooges find these beautiful girls atop a skyscraper about to commit their own triple suicide. Since the girls are dancers and the Stooges musicians, the suicide is off and romance is on.

Hill 303—Deadly setting for the play the Stooges perform in *Gents Without Cents*. Curly's character is no coward, yet even he blanches when given these directions to Hill 303: Go through Skeleton Pass, over Murder Meadow to Massacre Junction; then follow the trail to Poison Creek, around Funeral Mountain, and head directly for *Dead Man's Gulch*.

Hollywood Storage Company—IMMUTABLE STOOGES LAW #24: When traveling, the Stooges will select the train, bus, plane, or ship least likely to reach their intended destination. In *Movie Maniacs*, the Stooges are aspiring actors who set out by train to conquer Hollywood. The railcar they board, however, is destined for the Hollywood Storage Company.

"Home on the Farm"—Anyone who doubts that song can comfort the heartbroken soul hasn't heard Shemp's reflective rendition of "Home on the Farm" in *Gypped in the Penthouse* (sung to the tune of "Home on the Range"):

> Home, home on the farm
> In Georgia our farm had such charm
> And mama's so sweet

> Cooks good things to eat
> In Georgia down on the farm.

"Home on the Range"—Although the Stooges have just used their yodeling talents to rescue a kidnapped girl in *Nutty but Nice*, they don't forget their beginnings as singing waiters, belting out this version of an American classic:

> Home, home on the range
> Where the roasts and the pies we do bake
> Our apple pie's fine
> I'll take custard for mine
> And now everything is okay.

"Home Sweet Home"—In today's era of jailhouse riots and prisoner revolts, it is refreshing to see this sign hung on the Stooges' jail cell in *3 Dumb Clucks*.

Honest Moe, Honest Shemp, and Larry—Sales force for *The Smiling Egyptians*, the Stooges' used chariot dealership in *Mummy's Dummies*. While it

Honest Moe, Honest Shemp, and . . . Larry on the prowl for crooked palace guards (Mummy's Dummies, 1948)

appears from Moe's introduction of his salesmen that Larry might have sold some unsteady chariots during his career, it is astonishing to see how forthright used vehicle salesmen were about their reputations in ancient times.

Hook, Line, and Sinker—Ingenious name for the Stooges' fish vending business in *Cookoo Cavaliers*. Entrepreneurs pay advertising agencies big dollars to create catchy and provocative corporate signatures like this, but the Stooges were savvy enough to realize the marketing potential in their own names: Larry Hook, Moe Line, and Curly Sinker.

Hopping—IMMUTABLE STOOGES LAW #25: When one Stooge has injured his foot and is hopping about in pain, the other Stooges will clap, stomp, and otherwise create an on-the-spot klezmer dance (various films).

Hordred the Huntsman—Bumbling but tenderhearted assassin in *Snow White and the Three Stooges*.

Horses—IMMUTABLE STOOGES LAW #26: Stooge-owned horses possess an unusual recessive gene that causes their middles to sag dangerously close to the ground (various films).

"Horseradish"—IMMUTABLE STOOGES LAW #27: If there are chemicals anywhere in the vicinity, the Stooges will discover and immediately mix them in an unconventional container such as a boot. IMMUTABLE STOOGES LAW #28: All chemicals mixed by the Stooges will have the effect of burning through whatever they touch, including floor boards, steel prison bars, and the human body. In *All Gummed Up* and *Bubble Trouble*, the impatient **Amos Flint** is scalded by a Stooge-brewed concoc-

With a surefire name like Hook, Line, and Sinker, it's difficult to imagine how the Stooges failed in the fish business (*Cookoo Cavaliers*, 1940).

tion that leaves the blistering imprint "Horseradish" on his back.

"Horsethieves!"—Inflammatory charge made by three angry cavemen after the Stooges steal their girls in *I'm a Monkey's Uncle* and *Stone Age Romeos*.

Hospital—Place where Shemp tells census-taker Moe he was born in *Don't Throw That Knife*. His explanation: "I wanted to be near my mother."

"A hot stake is better than a cold chop"—The *Governor of Dead Man's Island* has sentenced the Stooges to die but generously allows them to select the method of execution: beheading or burning at the stake. Curly immediately chooses burning. His explanation: "A hot stake is better than a cold chop."

Hotel Costa Plente—When you win $50,000 in the *Coffin Nail Cigarette Contest*, you don't celebrate at Motel 6. The Stooges check into the Hotel Costa Plente in *Healthy, Wealthy and Dumb* and *A Missed Fortune* with dreams of high living and regal treatment, but check out to the realities of gold-digging dames and taxes that leave them only **$4.95**.

Hotel Snazzy Plaza—Most reasonable people can empathize with the mortified management of the posh Snazzy Plaza, who probably overreact a bit to news of a wolfman running loose around their hotel. But the wolfman's capture in *Idle Roomers* is clearly a police matter, not a job for three bellboys who are still mastering the basics of moving suitcases and garment bags.

Maintenance man Larry moistens his mop (*Three Missing Links*, 1938).

"Hours 2 to 5 or by Appointment"—Sign on the office of *Doctor Ba Loni Sulami*, a witch doctor in *Three Missing Links*. Doctors like Sulami graduate from medical school and immediately think they can keep bankers hours. Perhaps had he invested more time, Sulami's love potion might have worked only on humans like Curly, not on untamed gorillas attracted to Curly.

"How I shall gobble this gobbler!"—IMMUTABLE STOOGES LAW #29: Bullets fired carelessly into the sky will always hit and drop a succulent turkey, duck, or other ready-to-eat delicacy at the Stooges' feet. In *Back to the Woods*, Curly's old English muzzleloader discharges and delivers a wonderful turkey, which prompts Curly to exclaim, "How I shall gobble this gobbler!"

If only Shemp had placed that pipe on the left . . . (*Vagabond Loafers*, 1949)

An advancement in filtration systems made brewing beer easy in the Stooges' day (*Beer Barrel Polecats*, 1946).

How to Be a Plumber—Even those schoolteachers who recoil from the methods of the Stooges must admire Moe for reading books to hone his craft. Still, the owner of the **Norfleet Mansion** has a right to wonder why Moe hasn't read *How to Be a Plumber before* accepting a complicated plumbing job in *Vagabond Loafers* and *Scheming Schemers*.

How to Become a Babysitter—IMMUTABLE STOOGES LAW #30: The instructional lessons in how-to books will not translate well when read by the Stooges. Although the Stooges read *How to Become a Babysitter* in *Baby Sitters Jitters* with the best intentions, author **Davenport Seats** could not have recommended that three grown baby-sitters take a nap in their charge's own crib.

How to Make Panther Pilsner Beer—Mouthwatering instruction manual penned by J. Panther Pilsner in *Beer Barrel Polecats*. See IMMUTABLE STOOGES LAW #30.

"Howard, Fine and Besser—Stage Screen and Radar"—Inscription on the Stooges' traveling case in *Fifi Blows Her Top*. Although the film is rich in detail about the Stooges' triple whirlwind romances with three beauties, fans have long lamented that the Stage, Screen, and Radar show advertised on their case was never actually performed in the film.

"Huck mir nisht a chynick, and I don't mean efsher"—Emerging from a Chinese laundry in *Mutts to You*, fugitive Larry must convince an angry police-man that he really is Chinese. Larry nearly pulls it off, telling the cop, "Huck mir nisht a chynick, and I don't mean efsher." Had the cop spoken Yiddish he might have known that Larry had told him, "Don't bother me, get off my back, and I don't mean maybe!"

Hugo—Nazi henchman who mistakes the Stooges—temporarily— for three Japanese sabo-teurs in *No Dough Boys*.

Hugo Gansamacher—Brilliant but eccentric psychiatrist played by Moe in *Sweet and Hot*. It is not clear whether Gansamacher owed his loyalties to the Freudian or Jungian school, but his cure for stage fright was positively revolutionary.

Hyden Zeke Detective Agency—Detective agency that pits the Stooges against the hard-hearted *Double Deal Decker* in *Horses' Collars*.

No clue is too small for three new sleuths from the Hyden Zeke Detective Agency (*Horses' Collars*, 1935).

I

"I Am Starving . . ."—There is often no greater motivator than hunger, as evidenced by the sign Curly carries in *Pop Goes the Easel*. It reads, "I Am Starving—Must Have Work—If I Can't Get Anything Else." See also *"Must Have a Job . . ."* and *"Stop Look and Listen. . . ."*

"I can do very nicely with a highball!"—Although Curly does not seem to be a sports fan in *Violent is the Word for Curly*, he doesn't hesitate to weigh in this way after Moe and Larry declare that *Mildew College* could do well with football and basketball.

"I can't die; I haven't seen *The Jolson Story*!"—Men cling to life for a myriad of reasons, but none seems more rational than Larry's in *Squareheads of the Round Table*, in which he laments, "I can't die; I haven't seen *The Jolson Story*!"

I. Cheatham—Underhanded president of the *Cheatham Investment Company* in *Three Pests in a Mess*.

"I didn't know it was Monday!"—Curly's delighted reaction in *Three Little Beers* when he spots two beauties on the golf course washing their golf balls.

I. Doolittle—Police inspector in *Dizzy Detectives* who is under great public pressure to capture an ape man committing a string of baffling burglaries.

I. Fleecem—Attorneys rarely criticize each other in public. Privately, however, they'll tell you that lawyers like I. Fleecem do irreparable damage to the reputation of the bar. Fleecem's handling of Shemp's estate in *Heavenly Daze* and *Bedlam in Paradise* is a case study in legal malpractice. And as president of *Skin and Flint Finance Corporation* in *Sing a*

Attorney I. Fleecem (Vernon Dent) negotiates a fee with his clients (*Heavenly Daze*, 1948).

Song of Six Pants and *Rip, Sew and Stitch*, Fleecem's fervor to foreclose on the Stooges' struggling tailor business conjures images of the unreformed Ebenezer Scrooge in *A Christmas Carol*.

"I got it for my bar mitzvah!"— Moe's expression of gratitude after bandit **Mad Bill Hookup** compliments his rifle in *Guns A Poppin*.

"I got my eyes closed"—Although Curly might have been fitter had he dropped a few pounds, he was a man keenly in touch with his body. In *Calling All Curs*, for example, it takes Curly only a moment to deduce why he cannot see after Moe has poked him in the eyes. His explanation: "I got my eyes closed."

"I got sick of the dough and thought I'd go on the loaf"—Curly's explanation in *Uncivil Warriors* for why he quit his job at the bakery.

"I got Stetson; which one is she?"— After asking **Corabell, Dorabell, and Florabell** to marry them in *The Sitter Downers*, the Stooges realize they haven't chosen a particular bride among the three. The solution: have the girls toss their names into a hat and allow the Stooges to pick. Curly, however, is faced with a dilemma when he digs deep, pulls out his choice, and declares, "I got Stetson; which one is she?"

"I hope it didn't hit the pool room"—Always a conscientious soldier, this is Moe's remark after the Stooges fire a missile without aiming precisely in *Half Shot Shooters*.

"I know how!"—Shemp's triumphant retort in *Gypped in the Penthouse* after Larry proposes the toast, "Here's how."

I. M. Greecy—President of the **Onion Oil Company** in *Slaphappy Sleuths*. Although Greecy is never seen on-screen, it is reasonable to give him credit for coining the company's unforgettable trademark motto, **"In Onion There is Strength."**

"I mean business!"—Detective Shemp is positively smitten with his client's niece in *Who Done It?* and *For Crimin' Out Loud*, but detective Moe isn't charmed by his flirtation and gruffly reminds him that the Stooges are conducting business. Shemp's hasty reply: "I mean business!"

"I Must Not Eat Out of Garbage Cans"—Sign beside a dog hospital's garbage can in *Calling All Curs*. It is intended as a gentle reminder for a canine who suffers from **G.C.M.**, a disease more commonly known as Garbage Can Moocher.

"I shoot an arrow into the air, where it lands I do not care; I get my arrows wholesale!"—Inspired chant recited by Curly before he fires his bow-and-arrow-based **Gold Collar Button Retriever** in *Cactus Makes Perfect*.

"I shot a seven, but they wouldn't give me the money!"—Curly's frank reply in *Three Little Beers* when asked on the golf course what he had shot recently.

"I want a good dirty fight; now shake hands and come out gouging"—Referee's instructions to an

Have you seen their ball? (*Three Little Beers*, 1935)

already nervous Curly Joe in his world championship wrestling match with the **Mighty Itchy-Kitchy** in *The Three Stooges Go Around the World in a Daze.*

"I Was Born in Brazil"—Many of the world's great chefs sing while preparing meals, and Curly is no exception. While whipping up celery for a newfound baby in *Sock-A-Bye Baby*, Curly sings this song:

> *I was born in Brazil and I grew on a tree*
> *When they shook the tree then I fell down*
> *Then they put me in a bag*
> *And they fastened on a tag*
> *And they shipped me off to New York town.*

"I used to play in five flats but I got kicked out of the last one"—Gifted musicians often boast of their accomplishments—especially around attractive women—and pianist Shemp is no exception in *Gypped in the Penthouse* when he remarks "I used to play in five flats but I got kicked out of the last one."

Icabod Slipp—While it is disrespectful to criticize the dead, it must be acknowledged that Shemp's uncle *Ambrose Rose* showed poor judgment in naming Icabod Slipp—or anyone from the firm of *Slipp, Tripp, and Skipp* Investment Brokers—as executor of his estate in *Hold That Lion!* and *Loose Loot.*

"Ice with Personality—Coal with Oomph"—Dynamic slogan of the

Honest Icabod Slipp (Kenneth McDonald, right) has big plans for the Stooges' moolah—and for their health (*Loose Loot*, 1953).

Stooge-owned *Zero Ice & Coal Co.* in *An Ache in Every Stake*.

"If It's a Good Picture, It's Out of Whack!"—Signature motto of *Whack Magazine*, employers of photographers *Click, Clack, and Cluck* in *Dutiful but Dumb*.

"If We Solve Your Crime It's a Miracle"—Boastful catchphrase of the *Miracle Detective Agency*, for whom the Stooges tackle cases in *For Crimin' Out Loud*.

"If You Buy a Home Like This it's a Miracle"—Compelling billboard advertising *Miracle Homebuilders, Inc.* in *Even as I.O.U.*

"If You Got 'Em—We'll Get 'Em!"— One of two powerhouse slogans of the Stooge-owned *Acme Exterminating Company* in *Termites of 1938*.

"If you have a knick knack with a nick in it, we'll knock the nick out of the knick knack with Brighto"— Only a man who truly believed in his product—or who desperately needed the money—could have made this heartfelt sales pitch, as Larry did while selling *Brighto* in *Dizzy Doctors*.

"If you were over here I'd give you this!"— Moe's ominous warning to Curly as he slaps a befuddled Larry in *Mutts to You*.

Igor the Ape—IMMUTABLE STOOGES LAW #31: All gorillas, orangutans, and other apes will fall in love with Curly and Shemp, but will not develop the same affection for Larry and Moe. In *A Bird in the Head*, Igor's crush on Curly is bittersweet, as both are the intended victims of *Professor Panzer's* plan to transfer Curly's brain into Igor's head.

"I'll be back in a quack with a quack . . . and I do mean quack!"—It is a rare man who can inspire confidence in strangers, but that is precisely what Curly does for a short-tempered police chief in *A Ducking They Did Go*. The chief has bought a membership in the *Canvas Back Duck Club* from the Stooges, but has good reason to believe there are no ducks anywhere nearby. Curly has reason to believe the same, but relies on sheer optimism to allay the chief's fear by announcing, "I'll be back in a quack with a quack . . . and I do mean quack!"

"I'll make a note of it!"—Curly might have approached his work in an unorthodox manner, but he was always conscientious. When Moe orders Curly to "Remind me to kill you later" in *Cash and Carry*, Curly enthusiastically looks for a pencil and replies, "I'll make a note of it!"

"I'll take a ham sandwich"—Curly's reply in *Back to the Woods* to an angry English judge who demands "order" in the courtroom. When the judge responds angrily, "Hold thy tongue," Curly replies, "Not tongue; ham!"

"I'll take a milkshake . . . with sour milk!"—Shemp may be a teetotaler in *Punchy Cowpunchers*, but he's a desperado, too. Standing at the bar with *"The Killer Dillons"* looking on, Shemp retains his toughguy image by ordering one of the Wild West's most notorious drinks: the milkshake with sour milk.

"I'm a pedestrian!"—After Moe declares himself to be a Democrat in *Half Shot Shooters*, Curly acknowledges his own party affiliation by declaring, "I'm a pedestrian!"

"I'm a victim of circumstance!"—Curly's no-frills explanation for the courtroom disturbance he is accused of creating in *Disorder in the Court*.

"I'm Brown from the *Sun*"—See *Captain Casey and Brown*.

"I'm glad he can't smell them any closer!"—No Stooge understood military tactics like Curly. In *Uncivil Warriors*, the Stooges are introduced to an officer who, they are told, can smell spies a mile away. Although the Stooges are spies, Curly doesn't worry for a moment, declaring, "I'm glad he can't smell them any closer!"

"I'm going to get myself a cheap lawyer!"—Larry's menacing promise to *Doc Barker*'s gang after he is abruptly apprehended in *Out West* and *Pals and Gals*.

"I'm losing my mind!"—Painful declaration by Moe after being shot in the behind with dozens of carpenter's tacks in *Corny Casanovas*. See also *"You're tearing my heart out!"*

"I'm poisoned!"—Moe's self-diagnosis after being kissed by Curly in *Dizzy Detectives*.

"I'm too pleasingly plump as it is"—Curly's candid explanation for needing to lose a few pounds in *Flat Foot Stooges*.

"I'm trying to think, but nothing happens!"—Curly's discouraging report after Moe has ordered the Stooges to think of a way to recover a kidnapped dog in *Calling All Curs*.

"Impossible"—Moe's quick reply in *Brideless Groom* when a roughed-up Shemp asks, "You wanna spoil my looks?"

"In Days of Old . . ."—Not enough credit is given to the role of opening titles in Stooge films, which often create the delicate ambience necessary to set a historic scene. Nowhere is this more evident than in the two medieval period pieces, *Squareheads of the Round Table* and *Knutzy Knights*. In *Squareheads*, the opening title reads, "In Days of Old When Knights Were Bold and Suits Were Made of Iron"; in *Knutzy Knights*, it reads, "In Days of Old When Knights Were Bold—The Guys Were Hot But the Gals Were Cold."

"In Onion There is Strength"—Bold advertising slogan of the **Onion Oil Company** in *Slaphappy Sleuths*. Probably coined by company president **I. M. Greecy**, although this is only speculation.

"In the Spring . . ."—Romantic opening title in *The Sitter Downers*. It reads, "In the Spring Three Young Men's Fancies Lightly Turn to Thoughts of— You Know."

"Incomprehensible and utterly impractical"—See *The Inventors Association*.

Independence Day—One of Shemp's cunning aliases in *Blunder Boys*. See also *Christmas Day*, *Groundhog Day*, *Labor Day*, *New Year's Day*, and *St. Patrick's Day*.

Inky, Blinky, and Dinky—Moe (Inky), Larry (Blinky), and Curly (Dinky) as merchant mariners in *Back from the Front*.

"Inspector"—Although Stooge-owned businesses did not return profits in every quarter, they were often textbook examples of the kind of teamwork taught in today's prestigious business schools. In *Mutts to You*, for example, Larry never insists on actually washing dogs at the Stooges' **K-9 Dog Laundry** (although this obviously would be the most fulfilling duty for anyone associated with such an establishment). Instead, he wears a hat that reads "Inspector," a testament to putting profits above personal pride.

Inspector McCormick—Scotland Yard bigwig who is unmoved by the Stooges' burning desire to become detectives in *Hot Scots* and *Hot Ice*.

Instant Glue—Precursor to the super sticky, Crazy Glue–type products of today, Instant Glue "sticks anything"—especially Moe—in *Income Tax Sappy*.

Intent to Commit Mayhem—Heinous crime for which Moe stands trial in *Idiots Deluxe*. Exhibit A, a well-worn axe, seems to incriminate Moe, but his testimony about being driven nuts by Larry and Curly impresses the judge, who renders a verdict of not guilty and, to the chagrin of Larry and Curly, a return to Moe of Exhibit A. (Moe is also charged with Intent to Commit Mayhem in *Guns A Poppin*.)

The Inventors Association—Shortsighted outfit in *Cactus Makes Perfect* that informs Curly that his **Gold Collar Button Retriever** is "incomprehensible and utterly impractical." Once the Stooges use the odd-looking contraption to discover a lost gold mine, however, the practical aspect of the invention is immediately apparent.

Investors Inc.—Managed by president **G. Y. Prince** and treasurer **R. O. Broad**, this fly-by-night investment firm peddles tempting but worthless **Consolidated Fujiyama California Smog Bags** to an unsuspecting Joe in *Quiz Whizz*.

Ironhead—*Ivan Bustoff*'s scheduled wrestling opponent in *Grips, Grunts and Groans*. It is unknown whether the vicious Ironhead realizes that Curly has disguised himself and replaced the drunken Bustoff, but one thing is certain: Ironhead inflicts the maximum amount of punishment on opponents regardless of name or possible disguise.

"Is it true that the time and space are calculated by the interplanetary magnetism to solar radiation?"—The first—and last—question Professor Feinstein (Larry) accepts from the student body at **Mildew College** in *Violent is the Word for Curly*.

"Is my slip showing?"—The Stooges traveled to many parts of the world and encountered many foreign customs, some of which took a bit of getting used to. In *Hot Scots* and *Scotched in Scotland*, for instance, Shemp betrays some discomfort with the kilt he is wearing by asking Moe, "Is my slip showing?"

Isle of Stromboli—Fantastical vacation paradise where an amorous Shemp promises to honeymoon with ugly nurse *Nora* in *Scrambled Brains*.

"Isn't he quisn't!"—Larry is thrilled to meet a talking unicorn in *Have Rocket, Will Travel*, and promptly proclaims, "Ain't he quaint!" Moe, wanting to make a positive impression with the wondrous animal, reminds Larry that he should use the word "isn't" instead of "ain't." Larry's revised opinion of the unicorn: "Isn't he quisn't!"

"It ain't spring yet!"—Larry's forceful objection in *Healthy, Wealthy and Dumb* and *A Missed Fortune* after being ordered by Moe to take a bath.

"It don't say anything, you gotta look at it"—Although this was not the reply Moe was seeking, Shemp can only answer one way when asked what his watch says in *For Crimin' Out Loud*: "It don't say anything, you gotta look at it."

"It must be something else"—Moe's unshakable opinion in *Pardon My Clutch* and *Wham-Bam-Slam!* after the Stooges' friend *Claude A. Quacker* suggests that an ailing Shemp might be suffering from "excessive use of the gray matter of the brain."

"It was nothing, Mademoiselle. All it took was genius, determination, and raw courage."—Most men fresh from a trip to Venus would boast outrageously, but Larry plays it debonairly when describing his journey to a stunning French blonde in *Have Rocket, Will Travel*.

"It's in His Left Pocket"—If Curly seems occasionally to lack trust in others, perhaps it is due to an experience like that in *Cactus Makes Perfect*, where his own undershirt betrays him with its imprinted clue as to where he is hiding fifty dollars.

"It's our duty to posterior"—Larry's solemn confirmation after Moe declares that the Stooges must never reveal a secret rocket fuel formula in *Fuelin' Around* and *Hot Stuff*.

"It's putrid!"—After Moe and Larry celebrate a brilliant idea in *All Gummed Up* and *Bubble Trouble* by exclaiming, "It's tremendous!" and "It's colossal!," Shemp makes it unanimous by adding, "It's putrid!"

"It's sharp medicine, but it's a sure cure for all diseases"—While most men on death row tremble and sob, Shemp bravely watches his executioner sharpen an axe in *Squareheads of the Round Table* commenting reflectively, "It's sharp medicine, but it's a sure cure for all diseases."

Ithaca—Dual locations where the action unfolds in *The Three Stooges Meet Hercules*. The Stooges, it turns out, are safer in New York than in ancient Greece.

Ithaca Pharmacy—The Stooges' place of employment—and where a mischievous time machine is born—in *The Three Stooges Meet Hercules.*

Ivan Bustoff—Legendary wrestler trained by the Stooges in *Grips, Grunts and Groans.* Although Bustoff is not known to be an inspiration to athletes of today, much could be learned from him about toughness and guts. While today's sports stars miss a game for a hangnail or stubbed toe, Bustoff cancels his championship bout only after his trainers dropped several iron dumbbells onto his head.

"I've had it ever since I was a little kid"—Compelling reason Shemp gives for wanting to avoid a leg amputation in *Out West* and *Pals and Gals.*

Ixnay—See *Amscray, Ixnay, and Onay* and *Amscray, Ixnay, and Umpchay.*

....

J. B. Fletcher—Bigwig chief of Hollywood's **B.O. Pictures Corporation** in *Studio Stoops*.

J. J. Figbee—No-nonsense IRS man who comes looking for his share of Joe's $15,000 TV jackpot money in *Quiz Whizz*.

J. M. Benton—Justice of the peace in *Brideless Groom* and *Husbands Beware*. The romantic effect of his lyrical refrain, "Hold hands, you lovebirds!" is somewhat diminished when one of Shemp's prospective brides crashes a birdcage onto Benton's head.

J. P. Morse—Crotchety head of the **National Space Foundation** in *Have Rocket, Will Travel* who remains stuck in his old-fashioned belief that maintenance men like the Stooges shouldn't dabble in creating rocket fuels.

J. O. Dunkfeather—Students of American drama rightfully point to Thornton Wilder's *Our Town* as the paradigmatic use of a narrator to tell a dramatic story. As a narrator, J. O. Dunkfeather is less well known, but described for his audience an equally moving story about mysterious flying pies in *Spook Louder*.

J. Panther Pilsner—Author of the invaluable pamphlet *How to Make Panther Pilsner Beer* in *Beer Barrel Polecats*. Pilsner cannot be blamed for the calamity that resulted from the Stooges' use of his book, as neither Larry, Moe, nor Curly appeared to follow its directions carefully.

J. L. Cameron—Managing editor of the *Daily Gazette* in *Commotion on the Ocean*. Cameron might have been the fiercest news hawk of his day, but he should have been more diligent in discouraging the reporter-at-large fantasies of the three janitors who struggled just to clean his office. Cameron is also managing editor of the *Daily Gazette* in *Crime on Their Hands*.

J.T.—IMMUTABLE STOOGES LAW #32: Those who sample Stooge-brewed liquors will be immediately astonished—and injured—by the drink's potency. In *Pardon My Scotch*, J.T. is a bootlegger who is ready to pay nearly any price after tasting the Stooges' special homemade scotch, a recipe made from drugstore supplies and mixed for flavor in an old boot.

"Jack and Jill"—Improvisation is a cornerstone of American artistic creativity, but it is not solely the domain of jazz musicians and workshop actors. As fiddlers in *Fiddlers Three*, the Stooges proved they can weave new magic out of old standards, as with this interpretation of the classic children's rhymes, "Jack and Jill" and "Jack Spratt":

Jack and Jill went up a hill
Jack Spratt could eat no fat
Jack, Jack, Jack, Jack
Jack be nimble, Jack be quick
Jack jump over the candlestick
Jack jump over the candlestick
Jump!

Their working of *"Simple Simon,"* also in *Fiddlers Three*, is even more avant-garde but every bit the interpretive classic as "Jack and Jill."

Jackie—Curly's character in *Woman Haters*.

From that distance, the turkey is a sitting duck (G.I. Wanna Go Home, 1946).

Jake—Immutable Stooges Law #33: If the Stooges are about to dine on turkey, a parrot will crawl into that turkey and make it "walk" away. Nowhere is this more classi-

cally illustrated than in *G.I. Wanna Go Home*, where Jake, the Stooges' pet parrot, fulfills his natural role perfectly.

Jane—Immutable Stooges Law #34: An indelible set of lip prints will be left by all women who plant kisses on the face of a Stooge. In *Gypped in the Penthouse*, Jane is dating Moe, Larry, and Shemp simultaneously, a job she could have made easier on everyone had she left less obvious evidence of her lips on the face of Larry.

"Jap Sub Blown Up . . ."—Shocking newspaper headline from *The Times Press* in *No Dough Boys*. The full headline reads, "Jap Sub Blown Up Offshore—U.S. Coast Guard Deals Death Blow—3 Japanese Soldiers Escape—Citizens Warned to Keep a Sharp Lookout."

Jerkington—Pewter-faced, humorless butler who waits upon the haunted mansion in *If a Body Meets a Body*. Not nearly the bon vivant that butler **Sappington** was in *Half-Wits Holiday*, it is hard to imagine a man less suited to attend to the needs of guests—even in a haunted mansion—than the moribund Jerkington.

Jerry—Some of life's most bittersweet moments are the result of a friendship gone sour. Such was the case in *From Nurse to Worse* with Jerry, a man who advised the Stooges to act crazy in order to defraud an insurance company—but never warned them about doctors who order lobotomies for patients who act *too* crazy.

Jessie, Bessie, and Tessie—IMMUTABLE STOOGES LAW #35: Triple-decker bunk beds used by the Stooges will be assembled with low-grade materials and dubious craftsmanship. In *G.I. Wanna Go Home*, the Stooges gallantly choose the weaker-looking triple bunk for themselves, leaving new wives Jessie, Bessie, and Tessie to hope for a better fate on their sturdier triple bunk.

Jiffy Fixers—IMMUTABLE STOOGES LAW #36: The last time an item will function properly is the moment before the Stooges decide to repair it. As Jiffy Fixers in *Listen, Judge*, the Stooges don't balk at repairing a doorbell simply because they are not doorbell specialists; as their sign clearly indicates, they are generalists, and a bargain at that: "Jiffy Fixers—We Repair Everything—It's Done in a Flash for Very Small Cash."

Larry proves that men with curls get the girls (Marjorie White) (*Woman Haters*, 1934).

Jilted in the Jungle—Title of the film in which Curly co-stars (as a gorilla) in *Three Missing Links*. The making of *Jilted in the Jungle* illustrates clearly IMMUTABLE STOOGES LAW #31: All gorillas, orangutans, and other apes will fall in love with Curly and Shemp, but will not develop the same affection for Larry and Moe.

Jim—Larry's character in *Woman Haters*.

Jimmy Collins—Cuddly baby left on the Stooges' porch in *Sock-A-Bye Baby*.

Jive Café—Critics of the Stooges' style of business management delight in explaining why Stooge-owned businesses don't turn a profit. But sometimes success in business is just a matter of timing, nothing more. Had the Stooges, for example, opened their swinging Jive Café from *Busy Buddies* today, when trendy coffeehouses catering to well-heeled bohemian types thrive, perhaps customers would better have appreciated the café's theme, "A Speed Feed, A Short Snort."

"Jive Dinners, 4 Bits—Bloop Soup, Reat Meat, Jake Cake, Hava Java"—Dinner specials written on a chalkboard menu in the Stooges' sensibly priced *Jive Café* in *Busy Buddies*.

Joe—Troublemaking but talented monkey who is a valued member of the Stooges' stage act in *A Pain in the Pullman*. Had Joe learned to keep his hands off the toupées of others, there's

no telling how far the Stooges could have gone in show business.

Joe Stack—Roughneck gambler in *Three Little Pigskins* who recruits the Stooges to play football, but whose astronomical wager on the upcoming game causes him to overlook obvious clues that football is not the Stooges' best sport.

"Joe Stack's Tigers to Meet Cubs in Professional Football Classic"—IMMUTABLE STOOGES LAW #37: Whenever a championship sporting event is being played, the Stooges will figure decisively in its outcome. In *Three Little Pigskins*, this newspaper headline announces the season's biggest football game without ever mentioning that big-time thug *Joe Stack* stands to lose $50,000 if his three newfound, unorthodox players fail to come through.

Joe Strubachincoscow—Impatient draft board officer in *Dizzy Pilots* who writes to tell the Stooges that the army awaits if they do not complete construction on their revolutionary new airplane, *The Buzzard*.

Joe's Beanery—Lunch joint the Stooges frequent in *No Dough Boys*. Had the waiter minded his own business or simply asked them, he would have determined that the Stooges were not Japanese soldiers, just models posing for a photographer.

Joe the Monkey has the Stooges well trained in matters of morality (*A Pain in the Pullman*, 1936).

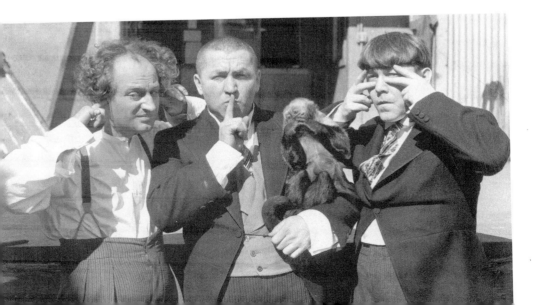

Joe's Minstrels Songs and Dances— IMMUTABLE STOOGES LAW #38: The plausibility of a disguise will not figure into the Stooges' decision to use that disguise. Trying to evade *Doc Barker*'s gang in *Pals and Gals*, the Stooges think fast—but not realistically—after they tumble into a box of costumes from Joe's Minstrels Songs and Dances. The short-tempered gang, it appears, have seen a minstrel show or two in their time.

"Joe's Traveling Store General Merchandise"—Inscription on the covered wagon in *Goofs and Saddles* and *Pals and Gals*. Until the Stooges made necessity the mother of invention in their films set in the Old West, little was known about the high-speed escape potential of the covered wagon.

John Bradley—Viewers of *Three Arabian Nuts* often feel heartsick for John Bradley, the antique collector who gave Shemp a magic genie lamp simply because the thing looked like a hunk of junk. But few ever credit Shemp for rubbing the lamp in the first place, an act that would not have occurred to a blue blood like Bradley.

Johnny, Frankie, and Mabel—Names used by Moe (Johnny), Curly (Frankie), and Larry (Mabel) while posing as adorable imps in *All the World's a Stooge*.

Johnson—Perpetually frustrated stage manager in *A Pain in the Pullman* who apparently was never schooled in handling the eccentric behavior of three aspiring actors . . . or their mischievous monkey.

"Join the Army and See the World— or What's Left of It"—Advertising pitch displayed outside army recruiting headquarters in *Boobs in Arms*.

Jones' Drugstore—Birthplace of the highly potent, Stooge-concocted **Breath O' Heather Vat 106 Plus** scotch in *Pardon My Scotch*.

José—Mexican strongman and jealous husband who misinterprets the presence of the Stooges in his bedroom in *What's the Matador?* and *Sappy Bullfighters*.

Juanita, Conchita, Pepita, and Rosita—Four splendid showgirls who perform at the **Cantina de Rosa** across

With body-guards like Moe and Larry, Curly can afford to delight in the wonders of another man's wife (*What's the Matador?*, 1942).

the Mexican border in *Cookoo Cavaliers.* Curly is smitten upon meeting the foursome, but retains enough composure to observe that "They must be hungry; they all end in ita!"

Judge Henderson—Fair-minded magistrate who acquits the Stooges of chicken-stealing in *Listen, Judge.* Henderson is less benevolent, however, after the Stooges devastate his home with sloppy repair work and the hazardous baking of an exploding birthday cake.

Judge Woodcock R. Strinker—The judge who, according to newspapers of the day, will preside over the **Ambrose Rose** estate in *Hold That Lion!* and *Loose Loot.*

Judith—Enchanting daughter of **Colonel Buttz** in *Uncivil Warriors.*

Jumbo Mexican Jumping Beans—Immutable Stooges Law #39: All ingredients necessary for Stooge-prepared recipes will be shelved dangerously close to ingredients that produce disastrous results if consumed. In *All Gummed Up,* Shemp mistakenly spills Jumbo Mexican

Jumping Beans into his precisely mixed Fountain of Youth formula, causing him not to grow younger but to jump wildly about the room.

June East—See *Little Red Book.*

Junior—Immutable Stooges Law #40: The Stooges will attempt to confirm that unloaded guns are indeed unloaded by pointing the barrel at lethal parts of each other's anatomy and pulling the trigger. Immutable Stooges Law #41: All guns believed by the Stooges to be unloaded will be loaded. In *Baby Sitters Jitters,* Shemp relies too heavily on a woman's assurance that a pistol is empty and confidently pulls the trigger, leaving an unbecoming bullet trace along the sensitive scalp of a suddenly furious Moe.

Just Plain Bill—Larry in *Goofs and Saddles.* See also **Buffalow Billious** and **Wild Bill Hicup.**

"Just straight salary"—What Moe tells an inquisitive boss in *Slaphappy Sleuths* when asked if he ever got a commission in the army.

K-9 Dog Laundry—Technologically ambitious dog-washing business owned by the Stooges in *Mutts to You*. While high-reaching in its aim to automate the process, the K-9 Dog Laundry proves that Henry Ford's assembly line concept does not translate smoothly to every type of business.

K. O. Bossy—Menacing alias taken by Curly upon entering the **Carrot County Fair Champion Milking Contest**. Moe and Larry intend to help K. O. Bossy when they climb into a cow costume armed with gallons of ready-to-pour milk, but cheat themselves—and everybody watching—of a chance to see how K. O. Bossy would have milked under honest conditions.

K. O. Stradivarius—There are only a handful of names in the history of sport that still strike fear into the hearts of men. K. O. Stradivarius—Curly's ring persona in *Punch Drunks*—is one of those names. No boxer stood a chance against Stradivarius . . . so long as trainer Larry played *"Pop Goes the Weasel"* on the violin.

Katrina—Scandinavian beauty whose heart Moe captures in *Love at First Bite* and *Fifi Blows Her Top*.

"Keep Our City Clean"—Sign to which the Stooges pay limited attention while working as a cleanup crew in *So Long Mr. Chumps*.

Kelly—Strong-armed assistant to **Colonel Henderson** in *Higher Than a Kite*. The dour-faced Kelly is in no mood to hear the Stooges' aviator fantasies; he

Fight manager Moe has prodigy K. O. Stradivarius (Curly) primed and ready to fight . . . so long as Larry shows up with violin to play "Pop Goes the Weasel" (*Punch Drunks*, 1934).

SOUND EFFECTS

Imagine how much fun it would be if the real world sounded like a Three Stooges film. A horn would honk if you bumped your nose. A cloth would tear when someone pulled your hair. And when you drank a particularly potent beverage, auto horns, whistles, bells, cuckoo clocks, and skidding tires would announce your discomfort to everyone within earshot.

Here are some of the most common—and funniest—sounds heard in Stooge films along with their real-life origins.

EVENT	CREATED BY
Hair pulled from the scalp	Ripping a cloth
Gulping/drinking	Emptying water from a gallon glass jug
Eye poke	Plucking ukelele strings
Bird chirping after victim is knocked out	The whistling of director Jules White
Face slap	Cracking a whip
Punch to the stomach	Banging a kettledrum
Punch to the nose	Squeezing a rubber bulb bicycle horn
Twisting ears, limbs, neck	Toolbox ratchets
Knock to the head	A wooden tempo block
Sitting on an open flame or hot iron	Butter frying in a pan
Slipping or tripping	Slide whistle
Swallowing a potent drink	Auto horns, whistles, bells, cuckoo clocks, and skidding tires

● ● ●

wants the squeak in the Colonel's car fixed fast. Moe, always confident in the Stooges' craftsmanship, assures him that "We'll squelch that squeak in nothing flat."

Kenneth Cabot—Earnest and honest magazine editor who wears his heart on his sleeve . . . even if it serves as a target for the Wild West's nastiest bandits in *The Outlaws Is Coming*.

Ketchup—Larry's "favorite fruit," as he attests in *Wham-Bam-Slam!*

Kid Pinky—Up-and-coming boxer with whom Curly spars in *Grips, Grunts and Groans*. When Curly first lays eyes on the slender Pinky, he decides the catcher's mask and chest protector he is wearing won't be necessary. He is wrong.

"The Killer Dillons"—Dramatic subtitle in *Punchy Cowpunchers* that introduces some of the meanest hombres the Stooges will ever tangle with, the **Dillon Gang**.

Killer Kilduff—Boxing champion dispatched by **K. O. Stradivarius** in *Punch Drunks*.

King Cole—One must empathize with King Cole in *Fiddlers Three* and *Musty Musketeers*. When your own magician **Mergatroyd** kidnaps your lovely daughter, the **Princess Alicia**, any king would be grateful for three brave fiddlers who aren't intimidated by a little black magic from a bullying court sorcerer.

King Herman 6⁷/₈—Figurehead ruler of the nation of **Moronica** in *You Nazty Spy* and *I'll Never Heil Again*. Herman is overthrown by **Moe Hailstone** in *You Nazty Spy*, only to be returned to power in *I'll Never Heil Again*.

King Putentakeit—Egyptian king whose coffin Shemp uses to hide himself in *Mummy's Dummies*. Mummies in general are not particularly handsome, but Shemp still cannot feel proud when one of the crooks opens the coffin door and declares, "Good old Putentakeit, he sure was an ugly old cuss!"

King Rootentooten—Among the most fair-minded kings in Stooge films, Rootentooten understands both the value of human life and a healthy smile. When the Stooges cure his toothache in *Mummy's Dummies*, Rootentooten promptly forgives them for selling defective used chariots and cancels their impending executions for the crime.

King Rootin' Tootin' Diamond—First-time viewers of *Malice in the Palace* and *Rumpus in the Harem* inevitably wonder about all the commotion surrounding the King Rootin' Tootin' Diamond: Why did the **Emir of Shmow** steal it? Why are so many, like **Hassan Ben Sober** and **Ghinna Rumma**, so desperate to get it back? And why do three brave souls disguised as a gigantic, six-armed Santa Claus make a perilous journey to secure its return? Then they see it glimmering atop the turban of the Emir of Shmow in its 100-carat glory and they know. From that point forever, they know.

King Rutentuten—Mummified king the Stooges search for in *We Want Our Mummy*.

King Winter Outfitting Co.—IMMUTABLE STOOGES LAW #42: As salesmen, the Stooges will carry whatever line of goods ensures the fewest sales. In *Saved by the Belle*, the Stooges represent a line of snazzy winter clothing made by the King

Winter Outfitting Co. of Ticonderoga, New York. Sales would surely have been brisker, however, had they chosen a territory other than **Valeska**, a "thriving kingdom in the tropics."

Kingdom of Anesthesia—Domain of the kidnapped **Queen Anne of Anesthesia** in *Restless Knights*, where the penalty for allowing a queen to be kidnapped is execution by firing squad.

Kingdom of Moronica—See *Moronica*.

Kirk Robbin—Murder victim in *Disorder in the Court*. If Robbin could have spoken, he would have implicated **Buck Wing** in the murder, not lovely nightclub dancer **Gail Tempest**, who nearly takes the fall for the crime.

Kiss the Moonbeams Off My Elbow—Publicity ace Shemp has big plans for lovely Hollywood starlet **Dolly Devore** in *Studio Stoops*, especially a starring role in the upcoming blockbuster *Kiss the Moonbeams Off My Elbow*.

Kitty—Giggling and gorgeous blonde the Stooges use to fatten up their fighter in *Fright Night* and *Fling in the Ring*. Kitty doesn't know much about boxing, but even she's concerned with the staggering number of creampuffs the Stooges feed **Chopper Kane**.

Knights of Columbus—What woodsman Curly pledges to hunt after Moe commits to hunting elk in *Whoops, I'm an Indian!*

Knives—IMMUTABLE STOOGES LAW #43: Knife throwers will narrowly miss the

Stooges' heads, but will always ruin their hats (various films).

Knucklehead—Perhaps Moe's grandest insult, and one he was able to apply masterfully no matter how delicate the situation. Though he had plenty of practice using the term in short films, Moe's most humanitarian use of "knuckle-head" occurred aboard a spaceship in the feature *Have Rocket, Will Travel*, where the barb helped inspire Larry and Curly Joe to keep looking for an abandoned monkey left for dead.

Kokonuts Grove—Fabled nightclub at the newly remodeled *Chisel Inn Hotel* (formerly *Ye Olde Pilgrim Hotel*) in *Loco Boy Makes Good*. Kokonuts Grove will always be remembered for the Stooges' nightclub act, *"Nill, Null, and Void,"* and their signature line, *"Three Hams Who Lay Their Own Eggs."*

Kraft's College of Arts—Temporary place of respite for the police-fleeing Stooges in *Pop Goes the Easel*.

Krispy Krunchies—Sponsor of the popular radio program on whose airwaves opera sensation *Señorita Cucaracha* (Curly) and her two accompanists, *Señors Mucho and Gusto* (Larry and Moe), are scheduled to appear in *Micro-Phonies*.

That was close! (*An Ache in Every Stake*, 1941)

L

L.B.S., F.O.B., N.U.T.Z.—Fancy medical credentials don't guarantee a doctor's competence, but when you're suffering you'll take a man with every degree there is. With Shemp agonizing from a serious case of frazzled nerves in *Wham-Bam-Slam!*, the Stooges are grateful—at first—for the arrival of self-educated friend *Claude A. Quacker*, a man who didn't attend medical school but whose business card alone inspires confidence. It reads, "Claude A. Quacker, L.B.S., F.O.B., N.U.T.Z.—Health Restorer and Advisor—214 E. 5th St.—Phone P.U. 3411."

L-R-L-R-L-R-L 1-1-2-3-2-2-1—Combination scrawled on a scrap of paper and discovered by the Stooges in bank robber *Terry Hargen*'s pocket in *Sing a Song of Six Pants* and *Rip, Sew and Stitch*. For all his notoriety, Hargen is undone by basic laziness; had he memorized this simple combination, the incriminating scrap of paper would never have been uncovered by three tailors more interested in alterations than crime.

La Stinkadora—The slippery *Eel* was not the first burglar to successfully disguise himself as a woman. But he is likely the first to jeopardize the deceptive effect of the disguise by smoking an ultramacho brand of cigar, the odious La Stinkadora, in *Blunder Boys*.

Labor Day—One of Shemp's cunning aliases in *Blunder Boys*. See also *Christmas Day*, *Groundhog Day*, *Independence Day*, *New Year's Day*, and *St. Patrick's Day*.

Lady Godiva—Blond beauty whose noble purpose—and hourglass figure—inspired the *Spirit of Sir Tom* to wait 1,000 years for her return in *The Ghost Talks*.

Lake Winapasakee—Hometown listed by both Larry and Curly when interviewed by census-taker Moe in *No Census, No Feeling*. Although Curly seems to have fond memories of the place, he has a tough time spelling it, saying, "W . . . O . . . Woof! Make it Lake Erie; I've got an uncle there!"

Larraine—Stooge fans tend to be a rough-and-tumble crowd, which makes it embarrassing for them to admit that the Stooges often look fetching when dressed in drag. Still, there is no denying the womanly appeal of Larry—as the lovely Larraine—in *Self Made Maids*. See also *Moella* and *Shempetta*.

Larrycus—Larry's ancient Erysipelean moniker in *Matri-Phony*.

Larry's Pet Shop—None of us would be immune to feelings of power and splendor if we owned our own pet store. But Larry, owner of Larry's Pet Shop in *He Cooked His Goose* and *Triple Crossed*, went too far by messing with the wives and fiancées of dear friends. No matter how many goldfish a man sells, no matter how much profit a man makes on a bag of dog food, no man should ever send his best friend's wife a card that reads, ***"Merry X-Mas, Your Pet Man Larry."***

Last in Kadora—Reading skills don't count only in the classroom; they are vitally important in the real world, too. Had Shemp read the **La Stinkadora** cigar label correctly in *Blunder Boys*— rather than as Last in Kadora—perhaps the felonious **Eel** would have been captured and his reign of robbery halted forever.

"Last Year"—In *Three Little Twirps,* the date Moe estimates Curly last attended the fourth grade.

Latherneck Shaving Cream—Product that the Stooges are paid to advertise—in ridiculous costume—in *No Dough Boys.*

"Laughing Gas"—Inscription on experimental bombshell fired by the Stooges in *Boobs in Arms*. The experiment works, though not on the enemy.

"Law Officers on the Way . . ."— Newspaper headline in *Merry Mavericks* announcing the arrival in town of three legendary marshals. Although the Stooges don't know yet that they, themselves, are those marshals, the headline predicts big things from them nonetheless: "Law Officers on the Way—Famous Marshal and Deputies Expected Soon to Clean Up the Town."

Leander's Carnival—Traveling sideshow in *Idle Roomers* that features insane **Lupe the Wolf Man**. Because of unfortunate incidents in old time carnivals like Leander's, the first thing carnival managers learn today is that insane wolfmen need special care; you don't check them into posh hotels, you don't use flimsy cages to hold them, and you certainly don't put them anywhere near three bellhops who will inevitably play the music that drives most wolfmen crazy.

Lefty Loomis—It is truly a shame that armored car robber Lefty Loomis chose a crooked path in life. His ability to control hair-triggered, ghastly hatchet murderer **Angel** in *Shivering Sherlocks* and *Of Cash and Hash* hints at a sensitivity and compassion that might truly have been used toward the benefit of society.

Leiloni Baggiagaloupe—Spicy waitress at the Italian restaurant where love blooms for Larry in *Fifi Blows Her Top*. He also knows her simply as **Maria**.

"Let's Fall in Love"—Lilting ditty sung by **Tiny Landers** in her barn in *Sweet and Hot.*

Liar's Club 27th Annual Convention—Gala event honoring Moe, Larry, and Joe for their story about a trip to the planet **Sunev** in *Space Ship Sappy.*

Lieutenant Duck—Larry in *Uncivil Warriors*. See also **Captain Dodge** and **Major Hyde**.

Lightning Pest Control Company— Exterminating business that employs the Stooges in *Ants in the Pantry* and *Pest Man Wins.*

Lily of the Alley—If your cavewoman was coming to visit, you wouldn't slap on any old cologne, and neither does Moe in *I'm a Monkey's Uncle*. For this special occasion, caveman Moe uses only the finest fragrance, Lily of the Alley.

Limburger cheese—Lesser men would recoil upon being served a Limburger cheese sandwich, but Moe is delighted to receive one in *Cuckoo on the Choo Choo*, declaring Limburger to be his "favorite fruit."

Limburger cheese spread—IMMUTABLE STOOGES LAW #44: Guests at Stooge-attended society balls will not appreciate the playful spirit of the less genteel in attendance. In *All the World's a Stooge*, Curly makes a forgivable mistake when he applies Limburger cheese to his chest instead of medicinal *Salve*, but the blue bloods in the crowd don't see it that way.

Link, Mink, and Pink—Sausage firm cooked up by the lightning-quick imagination of Moe in *If a Body Meets a Body*. Although the Stooges own no such firm, Moe understands the impression such a grand fib makes on a rough, gruff detective asking some very grueling questions.

"Listen to that exhaust!"—Larry's expression of concern for the performance of the Stooges' car in *Mutts to You*. Although the vehicle doesn't have an engine, the huffing-and-puffing Curly is doing his best to push the car from behind.

Little America—See *Edam Neckties*.

Little Betty Williams—Daughter of *Mr. Williams* who goes into a deep depression when her father is kidnapped by crooks in *Nutty but Nice*. **Drs. Lyman and Walters** say that Betty will die if she doesn't cheer up, leaving the Stooges no choice but to find the girl's missing daddy through the lost art of yodeling.

"Little Fly upon the Wall"—Poets will tell you that writing and reading a poem require different skills, that it is the rare poet who does both effectively. Curly is one of those poets in *All the World's a Stooge*, in which he stirringly recites this poem:

> *Little fly upon the wall*
> *Ain't ya got no clothes at all?*
> *Ain't ya got no shimmy shirt?*
> *Ain't ya got no petti-skirt?*
> *Boo, fly, ain't ya cold?*

Little Jimmy—Handicapped boy in *Cash and Carry* who entrusts his entire $62 savings to the Stooges to invest so that he can have a leg operation.

"Little Miss Muffet"—Traditional nursery rhyme performed by the Stooges in *Fiddlers Three*. See also *"Jack and Jill"* and *"Simple Simon."*

Little Red Book—A man might own no more intimate a personal possession than his little black book. In *You Nazty Spy*, the viewer is treated to that most rare opportunity, a glimpse into Curly's little red book, where the following entries conjure images of storybook romances from times past:

> *June East, 110 Goodnecking Place,*
> *Whoopee 4430*
> *Ruby Clutch, Oh Ooog, has car—often runs*
> *out of gas! Woo Woo Woo!*
> *Tessie, Oomph 269*

"Liver and milk . . . and a banana split"—Nutritious lunch ordered by a ravenous Moe in *Soup to Nuts*. Shemp, however, doesn't think much of Moe's choice; besides, he tells his pal, "There's only one banana left, and it's too old to do the splits."

Lobo City—Lawless setting for *Whoops, I'm an Indian!*

Lobo Jail—Safe haven taken by the Stooges from the enraged *Pierre* in *Whoops, I'm an Indian!*

Lobster with Frog Legs—Succulent delicacy offered as "Today's Special" at the Stooges' *Flounder Inn* restaurant in *Playing the Ponies*.

Lone Wolf Louie—Revealing real name of confidence man *B. O. Davis* in *So Long Mr. Chumps*.

Long hallways—IMMUTABLE STOOGES LAW #45: Where there exists a long hallway with many opposing doorways, there will be a daring chase involving the Stooges (various films).

Longhorn Pete—IMMUTABLE STOOGES LAW #46: Only after a crook, thief, or bandit has foiled all other branches of the military will the Stooges be called in to defeat that crook. In *Goofs and Saddles*, Longhorn Pete's cattle-rustling operation has mushroomed sufficiently to warrant the arrival of lawmen *Wild Bill Hicup*, *Buffalow Billious*, and *Just Plain Bill*.

Longhorn Saloon—IMMUTABLE STOOGES LAW #47: The Stooges will stumble upon a dishonest card game in every saloon they enter. IMMUTABLE STOOGES LAW #48: No one beats the Stooges at a crooked card game. In *Goofs and Saddles*, the Longhorn Saloon serves as the hangout for notorious cattle rustler *Longhorn Pete*, a man who plays a game of poker nearly as corrupt as that of the Stooges.

"Look at the grouse!"—Master painter Moe poses his lovely model for a painting in *Pop Goes the Easel* by telling her to glance skyward and look at the grouse. Curly, however, comments that his gaze toward the heavens reveals nothing. Moe tries to provide a measure of inspiration by kicking Curly from behind a couple of times, but Curly still sees only air. Finally, Moe resorts to hitting Curly squarely on the head, causing a sudden bout of clarity and Curly's revised report, "Look at the grouse!"

"Look in these shoes for some toes!"—Moe is understandably distressed when a car falls on his foot in *Pardon My Clutch* and *Wham-Bam-Slam!* But he remains lucid enough to alert Shemp and Larry to "Look in these shoes for some toes!"

Lord Larryington and Sir Moeington—Regal identities assumed by tuxedo-wearing con men Moe and Larry in order to impress an easy mark in *Heavenly Daze*.

Lorna Doone—Fetching blond secretary to *The Earl of Glenheather* in *Hot Scots* and *Scotched in Scotland*. Moe is immediately impressed with Doone, calling her "a charming bit of thistledown."

Los Arms Hospital—Institution with a liberal intern program in *Men in Black*. Los Arms takes a chance on three green physicians who pledge their lives "For Duty and Humanity!" Also the hospital in *Dizzy Doctors* where the Stooges peddle the cure-all **Brighto**.

The Lost Mine—Warehouse containing tons of gold, which, until Curly invented the **Gold Collar Button Retriever** in *Cactus Makes Perfect*, was unseen by human eyes.

Louie, Max, and Jack—Second set of triplets to Moe, Larry, and Joe in *A Merry Mix-Up*.

Love Tales—Syrupy romance magazine that vicious boxer **Chopper Kane** reads while being deconditioned by his trainers, the Stooges, in *Fright Night*.

Luana—*Raribongan* princess engaged to shrunken-head afficionado **Varunu** in *Hula-La-La*. Luana is as much opposed to her upcoming marriage as the captured Stooges are to the upcoming shrinking of their heads, so a partnership is struck: Luana avoids her wedding and the Stooges' craniums live to see another day.

Lubazac, whozica, pashcunyakas, cotton—Finely honed surgical tools used by Moe to repair an ailing tree in *Some More of Samoa*.

Too little credit has been given to the Stooges for their bravery at the dinner table (*Income Tax Sappy*, 1954).

Luke, Morris, and Jeff—Third set of triplets to Moe, Larry, and Joe in *A Merry Mix-Up*.

Lulu—Breathtaking daughter of Professor Quackenbush (see **Professors Rich and Nichols, Quackenbush and Sedletz**) in *Half-Wits Holiday* and secretary to Quackenbush in *Pies and Guys*. Lulu cheerfully agrees to assist the professor in teaching the Stooges to become gentlemen, but does not choose her words carefully enough when instructing them to "do *exactly* as I do."

Lulu Belle, Mary Belle, and Ringa Belle—The history of warfare overflows with tales of interrupted romance and battlefield longings for one's sweetheart. The Stooges were not immune to this timeless tale of woe, suffering separation anxiety from fiancées Lulu Belle, Mary Belle, and Ringa Belle as the Civil War breaks out in *Uncivil War Birds*.

Lupe the Wolf Man—Hideous monster in *Idle Roomers* who goes berserk when exposed to music. In today's age, a troubled wolfman like Lupe is cared for in a convalescent facility, not booked to appear in a traveling sideshow like *Leander's Carnival*.

No bellhop should have to handle live cargo, especially if that live cargo happens to be homicidal Lupe the Wolf Man (*Idle Roomers*, 1944).

 **M**

M. Balmer—Though never seen on-screen, M. Balmer's presence in *Shot in the Frontier* is as constant as the stoic sign that hangs outside his business: "*Diggs, Graves, and Berry Undertakers*—M. Balmer, Mgr."

Mabel—Gold-digging blonde who is simultaneously engaged to Moe, Larry, and Joe in *Rusty Romeos*.

McPherson—See *Angus and McPherson*.

McSniff—Larry's alias while posing as a Scottish distiller in *Pardon My Scotch*.

McSnort—Curly's alias while posing as a Scottish distiller in *Pardon My Scotch*.

McSnuff—Moe's alias while posing as a Scottish distiller in *Pardon My Scotch*.

"A Maid on a Night Out Winding a Grandfather Clock with Her Left Hand"—A dab of red here and a splash of blue there and Curly, posing as a painter in *Wee Wee Monsieur*, has created his masterpiece, a curious painting entitled, "A Maid on a Night Out Winding a Grandfather Clock with Her Left Hand."

Maisy, Mimi, and Minnie—The Stooges' girlfriends in *False Alarms*. Maisy is friendly, Mimi seems nice, but Minnie is not mini.

Mad Bill Hookup—Impolite bandit on the run from authorities in *Guns A Poppin*. Not only does Hookup dare to fire his six-shooter at the local sheriff, he has the gall to do it in the Stooges' log cabin, where Moe is vacationing to calm his frazzled nerves.

John Lester Johnson does not appear intimidated despite the mighty poses struck by the Stooges (*Wee Wee Monsieur*, 1938).

Madame de France—Immutable Stooges Law #49: An inheritance from a well-to-do relative will never have the soothing effect upon the Stooges the dearly departed intended. In *Slippery Silks*, the Stooges inherit the swank fashion boutique "Madame de France" from **Uncle Pete**, a well-intentioned man who should have realized that high style and international flair cannot be left in a will.

"Madcap Wins Ten Thousand Dollar Sweepstakes"—Irresistible newspaper headline that inspires the Stooges to trade their struggling restaurant, the *Flounder Inn,* for the glamorous business of horse racing in *Playing the Ponies*.

Mademoiselle—Moe's not-entirely-complimentary name for finicky French designer **Omay** in *Tassels in the Air*.

Maha—Life-saving routine performed by Moe and Curly to distract an execution-minded governor in *Three Little Pirates*. A lesson to all kids in the value of learning a foreign language, the exchange went like this:

Moe: *Maha?*

Curly: *A-ha?*

Moe: *You like to speak that?*

Curly: *I like to talk that!*

Moe: *Ras Bañas ya-tee benafucci a timi nicaronja. That, how you say, that Pickle Puss, he askee taskee what dee chit vat syke you gottik?*

Curly: *Naathing!*

Moe: *Naathing?*

Curly: *Yooks!*

Moe's translation: The Maharajah says he is the bearer of a rare jewel.

(The Maha routine was reprised by Moe and Curly Joe in *The Three Stooges Go Around the World in a Daze*.)

Maharajah of Canazzi—Curly's secret identity in *Three Little Pirates*. Called **Maha** for short, Curly's brilliant interplay with **The Gin of Rummy** (Moe) saves the day for three castaways whose facility with language spares them a grisly fate.

Main 2468—Simple-to-remember telephone number that Shemp must dial in order to reach the local authorities in *Dopey Dicks*. Like many of us, Shemp chooses to commit the number to memory but soon forgets it. Unlike many of us, Shemp was being stalked by a head-hungry, murder-minded mad scientist when he chose to foresake pencil and paper.

Maintenance Men's Quarters—Where the Stooges call home—before calling Venus home—in *Have Rocket, Will Travel*.

Majestic Fight Arena—Historic boxing venue scheduled to host the championship match between **Gorilla Watson** and Stooge-managed **Chopper Kane** in *Fright Night* and *Fling in the Ring*.

Major Filbert—Humorless Confederate officer sent to sniff out Union spies in *Uncivil Warriors*. The Stooges' attempts to distract Filbert with jokes and mirth go unappreciated, testament to the major's legendary nickname, "Bloodhound Filbert."

Major Hyde—Curly in *Uncivil Warriors*. See also **Captain Dodge** and **Lieutenant Duck**.

Mallard's Rest Home and Clinic—Convalescent retreat run by crooks in *Monkey Businessmen*.

"Mama Loved Papa . . ."—Most tombstones just give the basics: name, dates, and relatives. There are a few, however, that impart the wisdom of the ages, such as the one Moe hides behind in *Shot in the Frontier*. It reads, "Mama Loved Papa, Papa Loved Women, Mama Caught Papa with Two Girls In Swimmin'."

Mame—When a millionaire introduces preciously dressed refugee children Moe, Larry, and Curly to their new "mammy" in *All the World's a Stooge*, the Stooges eagerly recite their own rendition of "Mame":

Larry (Mabel):	*Who darned our socks and washed our shirts When we were helpless little squirts?*
Curly (Frankie):	*Mame!*
Moe (Johnnie):	*Who kept the buttons on our clothes Who scrubbed our ears and blew our nose?*
Curly (Frankie):	*Mame!*
Curly (Frankie):	*Oh, Mame It's your little boy, Sammy Comin' home from Alabamy Put on those eggs and hammy Don't flim-flammy, Mame Mame!*

"The Management Reserves the Right to Refuse $1,000 Bills"—Optimistic sign posted inside the Stooge-

owned *Shangri-La Upholstering Company* in *Hugs and Mugs*.

Mandy—Careless maid employed by society matron *Muriel van Twitchett* in *Termites of 1938*. It was Mandy who phoned the *Acme Exterminating Company* instead of *Acme Escort Bureau*.

"Manning Baby Disappears!"—Staggering headline in *The Daily Press-Post* that poises a nation to turn on whichever three men happen to be blamed for the crime in *Mutts to You*.

Manny Weeks Theatrical Enterprises—Behind every star is a promoter who believed in that star when no one else did. In *Gents Without Cents*, Manny Weeks had the foresight to cast the Stooges in a star-studded stage pro-

Before the Maharajah, most people believed it was impossible to engage in a swordfight while wearing bifocals and a turban (**Three Little Pirates**, 1946).

duction. His reward: the immortal *"Niagara Falls"* routine.

Manuel—Mexican gentleman, showgirl manager, and proprietor of the *Cantina de Rosa* in *Cookoo Cavaliers*. Manuel is very much the likable sort . . . until the Stooges finish bleaching the hair of his top three attractions.

Map of Unknown Lands Where Cavemen Are Still Supposed to Exist—In *Stone Age Romeos*, museum curator B. Bopper entrusts the Stooges with a priceless map showing the suspected location of modern-day cavemen. In the interest of science, the names of those lands and waterways are listed here: Schnozzle Mountain, Wing Ding, Kegoboozia, Ferblongent, Rigor Mortis, Hang Gover, Schnozzle Mts., Bourbon River, Giva-Dam, Straights of Rye, Isle-Liquor, *Bay of Rum*, Skull Islands, Drop Dead Sea, Mish Mosh, Pish Posh, Hot Sea, Tot Sea, Canabeer, Gunga Din, Drinka Gin, Eye Land, Coney Island, Tail Land, Shmow Lake, Yule Liquor, Udopia, He Land, She Land, We Land.

Maria—Spicy waitress Larry seduces over a bowl of spaghetti and meatballs in *Love at First Bite* and *Fifi Blows Her Top*.

Marigold, Narcissus, and Petunia—Wives of the Stooges in *Pardon My Clutch* and *Wham-Bam-Slam!* who understand—temporarily—Shemp's need to take a relaxing vacation.

Marshal Bommell—Nazi henchman in *Higher Than a Kite*. Bommell is prepared to execute spy Curly but must continu-

ally stop to salute the picture of the Führer that is stuck to Curly's posterior.

Marshal Boring—Nazi commander who takes a fanciful shine to Larry—who is dressed in drag—in *Higher Than a Kite*. Although Boring is tough on the outside, he draws upon a soft place somewhere inside, calling Larry his "little begonia."

Mary—Among the most sinister dames ever to cross the Stooges' paths. Mary not only cheats an insurance company by feigning disability, but manipulates the Stooges' big hearts (and affection for blondes) so that they vouch for her condition in *Hokus Pokus* and *Flagpole Jitters*. Also, the newlywed wife of Larry and pioneering feminist in *Woman Haters*. The feisty and physically capable Mary does not sit idly by when she discovers the pledge Larry made as part of his induction into the Woman Haters Club.

Mary Bopper—Slick blonde whose brain is nearly transferred into a gorilla's skull by *Dr. Jekyll and Mr. Hyde* in *Spooks*. Only the heroics of the Stooges stop the hideous experiment by the mad doctor and his cutthroat assistant.

"Mary, Mary, Quite Contrary"—Beat version of the children's classic as recited by Curly in *Nutty but Nice*:

> *Mary, Mary, quite contrary*
> *How does your garden grow?*
> *With silver bells and cockle shells*
> *And one measly petunia!*

Maskazino cherry—Sweet-tasting treat Curly is delighted to find in the punch bowl in *Hoi Polloi*.

Mattie Herring—History is crowded with rulers tempted by the charms of seductive women. *Moe Hailstone* is no exception in *You Nazty Spy*, in which secretary Mattie Herring has more than typing on her treasonous mind.

Matzohs—Although Larry is not the shipping foreman in *Muscle Up a Little Closer*, he knows precisely what is in the newly arrived shipment from Japan: matzohs. And Moe seems happy to hear it, remarking, "Oh, just in time for Thanksgiving!"

Maxey—Bile-bloated proprietor of Maxey's Place in *Yes, We Have No Bonanza*.

Maxey's Place—Western musical saloon where the Stooges work as singing waiters in *Yes, We Have No Bonanza*.

"Mazel Tov!" and "L'Chaim!"— Declarations of joy from reluctant soldiers, the Stooges, upon discovering that World War I has ended in *Half Shot Shooters*. Curly also wishes Moe "Mazel Tov!" in *Calling All Curs* after the Stooges discover that prized pooch *Garçon* has given birth. (In Hebrew, *mazel tov* means "congratulations" and *l'chaim* means "to life.")

"Me, three!"—Shemp is not the type to be left behind when there is courting to be done, especially in *I'm a Monkey's Uncle* and *Stone Age Romeos*. After Moe declares that he will be searching for love, and Larry says, "Me, too!" Shemp makes it unanimous by exclaiming, "Me, three!"

Meadows—Well-bred butler who waits upon the pest-infested home of *Mrs. Castor* in *Pest Man Wins*.

"Meet my bare hand"—Moe's response—accompanied by a startling slap—after Larry remarks that the Stooges might encounter a bear in *Ants in the Pantry*.

"Men at Work"—No one has done more for the reputation of the classic "Men at Work" sign than the Stooges, who showcased it gloriously in five films. In *3 Dumb Clucks*, Curly politely hangs the sign in his prison cell before drilling an escape hole; in *Violent is the Word for Curly*, Larry places the sign in front of a car primed to receive the Stooges' patented *"Super Service"* treatment; in *Tassels in the Air*, the Stooges place the sign near an antique table they are preparing to paint; in *Listen, Judge*, the sign keeps a nosy homeowner at bay; and in *How High Is Up?*, the Stooges use the sign to inform passersby not to awaken the three men under the *Minute Menders, Inc.* truck.

Mergatroyd—Viewers of *Self Made Maids* seem shocked that Mergatroyd, the Stooges' cutely named triplets, resemble Moe, Larry, and Shemp so closely. But a closer look at the babies' mothers, *Moella*, *Larraine*, and *Shempetta*, explains everything.

Mergatroyd the Magician—You can warn amateur magicians endlessly about abusing magic for evil purposes, but nothing humbles them like watching the downfall of the evil Mergatroyd in

One benefit of sneaking into a magician's box (*Fiddlers Three*, 1948)

Fiddlers Three and *Musty Musketeers*. Although a brilliant illusionist, Mergatroyd's plot to kidnap and marry *Princess Alicia* alters his legendary timing, causing three brave fiddlers to burst forth from his magic box to save the day.

"Merrie Olde England"—Quaint opening title that sets the scene in *Back to the Woods*.

"Merry X-Mas, Your Pet Man Larry"—Amorous Christmas greeting sent by playboy pet shop owner Larry to the sweethearts of his pals in *He Cooked His Goose* and *Triple Crossed*.

Metropole Flower Shop—With romantic visions of sweethearts *Corabell,*

Dorabell, and Florabell dancing in their eyes, the Stooges leave the Metropole Flower Shop with more optimism than is warranted in *The Sitter Downers*.

"Mexico—Where Men are Men and Women are Glad of It"—Zesty opening title in *Sappy Bullfighters*.

Mickey Finn Gang—Actual perpetrators of the brutal *Mushroom Murders* for which the Stooges were to be hanged in *In the Sweet Pie and Pie*. Only Mickey Finn's confession saved the Stooges from the gallows, a point that still troubles ardent supporters of the death penalty.

Mickey Moe the Murderin' Masseur—Formidable nickname

Moe confers upon himself in *Three Loan Wolves*.

Midland Fire Department—
Stooges' fire-fighting unit in *Flat Foot Stooges*. The department's entrance requirements are never explicitly listed, but the Stooges' unorthodox approach to battling blazes hints that firefighter exams in Midland were flexibly graded.

Mighty Itchy-Kitchy—Extra-beefy Sumo wrestler in *The Three Stooges Go Around the World in a Daze* who doesn't appreciate taking a beating from Curly Joe.

Mike Lipincranz—
Coveted dramatic role played brilliantly by Moe in the **Stooge Follies** stage show in *Rhythm and Weep*. It is not known whether Curly or Larry auditioned for the part, but since the Lipincranz character is required to dish out a variety of extreme physical punishments, Moe must have been the natural choice from the start.

Mildew College—Immutable Stooges Law #50: If the Stooges wander anywhere near a university, laboratory, or other place of higher learning, they will be mistaken for esteemed professors from that place of higher learning. In *Violent is the Word for Curly*, three visiting scholars to prestigious Mildew College don't have Ph.D.s, but teach the all-girl student body a musical

Curly Joe has the Mighty Itchy-Kitchy (Iau Kea) just where he wants him—about to break a hand (*The Three Stooges Go Around the World in a Daze*, 1963).

version of the alphabet they won't soon forget.

Millie—Lovely woman engaged to Shemp in *He Cooked His Goose* and to Joe in *Triple Crossed*. Larry tries to seduce Millie away, even calling her "Millie my little dilly," but she manages to stay true to her man, anyway.

"Mingle or I'll mangle!"—Moe knows that the Stooges' success as nightclub hosts in *Loco Boy Makes Good* will depend on good customer relations. He therefore asks Curly to mingle with the guests, but when Curly balks, Moe explains himself in no uncertain terms: "Mingle or I'll mangle!"

Minister of Propaganda—Like every ruthless dictator, *Moe Hailstone* understands the power of public opinion. That's why he doesn't hesitate to appoint the cunning Larry as Minister of Propaganda in *You Nazty Spy*. (Also, while posing as one of Hitler's henchmen in *Back from the Front*, Larry's briefcase reads, "Minister of Propaganda— Specialist in Lies and Bunk.")

Minister of Rum—Official title of the *Bay of Rum*, one of the *Axis Partners* in *I'll Never Heil Again*.

Mink, skunk, and porcupine— The array of elegant furs Moe promises to lavish upon the lovely *Lulu* as he woos her in *Half-Wits Holiday* and *Pies and Guys*.

Minute Menders, Inc.—Stooges' handyman business in *How High Is Up?*

Mirabel Mirabel—Glamorous actress who shows great range by starring opposite Curly—who plays the part of a wild gorilla—in the film *Jilted in the Jungle* in *Three Missing Links*.

Miracle Detective Agency— IMMUTABLE STOOGES LAW #51: Criminals being tracked by detectives Moe, Larry, Curly, and Shemp will inevitably hide out in a haunted mansion. In *For Crimin' Out Loud*, the Stooges trail some thugs to a spooky house, where Shemp's "trusty little shovel" ultimately works its magic on the craniums of the crooks.

Miracle Massage Reducing Machine—Fantastical thinning contraption sold door-to-door by the Stooges in *Spook Louder*.

Miracle Homebuilders, Inc.— Construction company advertised on a billboard made to look like a house in *Even as I.O.U.* Miracle's motto: *"If You Buy a Home Like This It's a Miracle."*

Miss Beebee—Mostly lovely dental school instructor in *The Tooth Will Out*, Miss Beebee's protruding front teeth compel the candid Shemp to refer to her as "Miss Buckshot."

Miss Dinkelmeyer—Voice student in *Brideless Groom* whose love for *Professor Shemp Howard—Teacher of Voice* is stronger than her pipes.

Miss Emma Blake—Unfortunate woman who happens to be enjoying a scrumptious fish dinner at precisely the moment the Stooges are starving for a bite to eat in *Commotion on the Ocean*.

Miss Hopkins—IMMUTABLE STOOGES LAW #52: The most devastating punch thrown in a Stooge film will be delivered by a delicate woman. In *Brideless Groom* and *Husbands Beware*, breathtaking blonde Miss Hopkins mistakes Shemp for her darling *Cousin Basil*, a mixup that, when realized, causes unfortunate consequences for Shemp's kisser.

Miss Janie Bell—IMMUTABLE STOOGES LAW #53: Cakes baked by the Stooges will explode. IMMUTABLE STOOGES LAW #54: Cakes eaten by the Stooges will contain feathers that must be coughed up. In *Three Hams on Rye*, the lovely Miss Janie Bell prepares a cake that Moe declares to be "light as a feather!" Only after the Stooges cough up bushels full of actual feathers does anyone look askance at Miss Janie Bell's talents as a baker.

Miss Jones—Heavenly shaped angel who works the pearly gates with **Uncle Mortimer** in *Heavenly Daze* and *Bedlam in Paradise*.

Miss Kelly—Spunky daughter of fire **Chief Kelly** in *Flat Foot Stooges*. When Miss Kelly discovers that diabolical fire engine salesman **Reardon** is sabotaging her father's firehouse, she lands one of history's great haymakers on the stunned crook's kisser.

Miss Lapdale—Larry's hourglass-shaped secretary in *He Cooked His Goose* and *Triple Crossed*. Feminists may object to Miss Lapdale's willingness to take dictation while seated in Larry's lap, but by film's end the surprising Lapdale is just about the only woman whom playboy Larry has not seduced.

Miss Scudder—Although he danced with princesses, rubbed elbows with starlets, and escorted debutantes, Moe was never more smitten with a woman than he was with Miss Scudder in *A Snitch in Time*. Although pretty and pleasant, Miss Scudder must have possessed deeper qualities that touched the usually grumpy Stooge. By film's end, Moe puts on an unforgettable exhibition of punching, slapping, and poking to insure that his two helpers fixed Miss Scudder's furniture to his high standards.

Miss Shapely—IMMUTABLE STOOGES LAW #55: No life-threatening predicament, illness, threat, or danger will derail the Stooges' flirtations with a beautiful woman. In *Monkey Businessmen*, the Stooges check into **Mallard's Rest Home and Clinic** to relax, a goal made more challenging by the pulse-raising form of curvaceous Miss Shapely.

Mlle. Zora—Eye-catching fortune teller with the seductive walk in *They Stooge to Conga*. Mlle. Zora apparently has true psychic powers, as she slaps Curly's face before he has a chance to ask her a question.

"Modes Modernistique"—Show-stopping line of high fashion wear designed by the Stooges in *Slippery Silks*. Every "Modes Modernistique" dress was made of finely crafted wood and was elegantly adorned with drawers, handles, and cabinets, a testament by the three former carpenters to sticking with what you do best.

Moe Hailstone—Moe in his role as ruthless dictator in *You Nazty Spy* and *I'll Never Heil Again*.

Moella—One of three fetching models painted and courted by the Stooges in *Self Made Maids*. Moella bore an eerie resemblance to Moe, proving the old wives' tale that romance runs deep between partners who look alike. See also **Larraine** and **Shempetta**.

Mohicus—IMMUTABLE STOOGES LAW #56: Whenever a life-threatening situation requires the services of one brave soul, Moe will step forward to volunteer Curly as that brave soul. In *Matri-Phony*, Mohicus forces **Curleycue** to pose as a redheaded beauty so that **Diana**, the real redheaded beauty, can escape the clutches of lustful governor **Octopus Grabus**.

Molasses, Tabasco, seltzer, eggs, paint, and paint remover—Power-packed ingredients Moe adds to **Old Homicide** to fashion a Mickey Finn in *Out West* and *Pals and Gals*.

Molly the Glamour Girl—Heartless hussy who hocks a baby at the Stooges' pawnshop in *Three Loan Wolves*.

Montgomery M. Montgomery—Alias used by a cutthroat crook as part of a plot to murder the Stooges and steal their TV jackpot winnings in *Quiz Whizz*. When the Stooges are told to arrive at Montgomery's home acting like children,

Joe joyously exclaims, "Oh boy, we'll be Montgomery's wards!"

Moose and Chuck—Gangster **Big Mike**'s heinous henchmen in *Fright Night* and *Fling in the Ring*.

"The morbid the merrier!"—After Moe refuses to apply for a gravedigger's job because it is too morbid, Curly presents this alternate viewpoint in *If a Body Meets a Body*.

Moronica—Every century or so a country influences world events far in excess of its size or population. Moronica, where the action unfolds in *You Nazty Spy* and *I'll Never Heil Again*, is one such country. As host to ruthless dictator **Moe Hailstone** and his two henchmen, Moronica (or Moronika, as it appears in a banner and on a map in *You Nazty Spy*) saw the uprising and downfall of a political regime that could have changed the course of history forever.

Moronica (Larry)—Larry's alias while dressed as a demure beauty in *Higher Than a Kite*. The Stooges escape execution when Nazi officer **Marshal Boring** becomes smitten with Moronica, a textbook example of IMMUTABLE STOOGES LAW #11: If a Stooge poses as a woman, he is certain to attract a suitor.

"Moronica for Morons" —See *"Moronika for Morons."*

Joey-Woey and knickered pals Moe and Larry charm millionaire Montgomery M. Montgomery (Gene Roth) (*Quiz Whizz*, 1958).

"Moronica Uber Alles"—See *"Moronika for Morons."*

"Moronika for Morons"—Behind every world power is a trademark patriotic slogan, a motto that inspires fervent loyalty among the masses, and Moronica is no exception. Its concise but potent slogan in *You Nazty Spy* is "Moronika for Morons." (It also appears in *I'll Never Heil Again*, with the spelling "Moronica." A hanging shield in *I'll Never Heil Again* reads "Moronica Uber Alles.")

"The mortar the merrier!"—Larry's happy declaration after an angry Moe warns that he could have used a mortar to hit Shemp in *All Gummed Up* and *Bubble Trouble.*

The most beautiful cave in Mesopotamia—Lavish gift a sleep-talking Moe promises to the cavewoman of his dreams in *I'm a Monkey's Uncle* and *Stone Age Romeos.*

Mother's Pies—Pastry business in *Dizzy Doctors* that happens to schedule a delivery during the Stooges' spirited escape from police.

"The mouth is in the front!"—Startlingly basic pointer given by dentist Moe to dentist Shemp in *The Tooth Will Out.*

Mr. and Mrs. Allen—Thieving couple who might have made off with the priceless *Van Brocklin Painting* had they been able to sidestep three crafty plumbers with a nose for crime in *Vagabond Loafers.*

Mr. and Mrs. Leander—Carnival promoters in *Idle Roomers.* The Leanders violate every law of veterinary ethics by keeping a wild wolfman inside a hotel despite the damage it is capable of inflicting on an innocent bellhop—or even three innocent bellhops.

Mr. and Mrs. Manning—Wealthy couple who communicate poorly in *Mutts to You.* Had Mrs. Manning simply told her husband that she was temporarily placing their baby on a porch, the Stooges could have stuck to their dog washing business and avoided the police manhunt that goes with scooping up an abandoned child.

Mr. Baines—Head honcho of movie studio *B.O. Pictures* in *Hula-La-La.*

Mr. Beedle—In *A Bird in the Head*, Moe senses boss Beedle's concern with the Stooges' paperhanging qualifications, and quiets him with the kind of reassurance that only an artisan can convey: "Don't worry," Moe tells Beedle, "you won't know the joint when you get back."

Mr. Bell—Overprotective father of *Corabell, Dorabell, and Florabell* in *The Sitter Downers.* You'd think that a father would be grateful to marry his daughters to the likes of Moe, Larry, and Curly, but Mr. Bell somehow seems bent on having his girls grow into spinsters.

Mr. Boyce—Eccentric millionaire who promises to finance the Stooges' song-and-joke act in *Rhythm and Weep.* The fact that Boyce turns out to be an escaped rest home patient should not diminish the public's opinion of him as an expert judge of showbiz talent.

Mr. Cash—Undercover tax collector and master of the phony beard who busts up the Stooges' crooked tax advisory business in *Income Tax Sappy*.

Mr. Dill—No-good crook who forces an innocent gorilla to do his dirty work in *Dizzy Detectives*.

Mr. Dinkelspiel—Immutable Stooges Law #57: Landlords who rent rooms to the Stooges will not take into account the Stooges' charming personalities when making eviction decisions. In *Hoofs and Goofs*, crusty landlord Mr. Dinkelspiel cannot allow himself to go with the flow when he suspects (correctly) that the Stooges are keeping a horse in their upstairs apartment. Fortunately for the Stooges, Dinkelspiel is also myopic; after he inspects a cabinet without finding a horse inside, he allows the Stooges to stay another day.

The wealthy Mr. Morgan (Vernon Dent) prepares to settle things with his fists, but will that really bring back his priceless Chinese cabinet (*Slippery Silks*, 1936)?

Mr. Gingy—Stooges' Parisian landlord in *Wee Wee Monsieur*. Gingy is owed many months back rent, but is not yet ready to accept Curly's painting—***A Maid on a Night Out Winding a Grandfather Clock with Her Left Hand***—in lieu of payment.

Mr. Graves—Inventor of the death ray machine in *Spook Louder* that he claims will destroy millions. With so many lives in the balance, it is flattering—but curious—that he chooses to hire the Stooges to guard his house.

Mr. Heller—Cunning alias used by the devil to convince Moe and Larry to market a worthless ***fountain pen that writes under whipped cream*** in *Bedlam in Paradise*.

Mr. Herbert—Finicky director of the blockbuster film ***Jilted in the Jungle*** in *Three Missing Links*. Herbert is against his boss's idea of casting Curly as a gorilla and Moe and Larry as Neanderthals—until he sees the three janitors clean the man's office.

Mr. Jerry Pip and Steve—Tough-sounding crooks who tangle with the Stooges in *A Snitch in Time*. Like most thugs who mix it up with the Stooges, Mr. Jerry Pip and Steve are probably still rotting behind bars somewhere.

Mr. Jones—Drugstore owner who dabbles in bootlegging in *Pardon My Scotch*.

Mr. Morgan—Unsportsmanlike owner of a Chinese cabinet

worth $50,000 that is broken by three apprentice woodworkers in *Slippery Silks*.

Mr. No One—See *5736 and Mr. No One*.

Mr. Norfleet—Jittery millionaire in *Scheming Schemers*.

Mr. Philander—Pianist in *Pest Man Wins* who plays bravely despite the cat that Larry and Shemp have slipped inside his piano.

Mr. Romani—Show me a man who was scolded as a child for breaking a toy, and I'll show you a man who gets angry at his three helpers for accidentally smashing a Chinese cabinet worth $50,000. Mr. Romani, owner of **Romani Artistic Woodwork**, demonstrates little appreciation for the concept of accident in *Slippery Silks*, and even less appreciation for the Stooges' noble attempt to glue the box back together.

Mr. Scroggins—Scroogian landlord who threatens foreclosure of **Ye Olde Pilgrim Hotel** in *Loco Boy Makes Good*.

Mr. Singapore—Impatient proprietor of **Singapore Joe's Palace Hotel** in *Saved by the Belle*.

Mr. Smellington—It's one thing for a theatre director to reject an artist. It is quite another to suggest that those artists jump off the city's tallest building. But that is precisely what **Garden Theatre** director Mr. Smellington suggests to the Stooges in *Rhythm and Weep*, never considering how badly it might hurt a song-and-joke troupe to tell them they are the worst act he's ever heard in his life.

Mr. Stevens—Father of Stooge fiancées **Stella, Nella, and Bella** in *Three Smart Saps* who is imprisoned by racketeers inside his own jail.

Mr. Wallace—Fresh-scrubbed reporter for **The Times** who is assigned to interview the enigmatic **J. O. Dunkfeather** about mysterious flying pies and the Master Spy Ring in *Spook Louder*.

Mr. Williams—Kidnapped father of **Little Betty Williams**. All those yodeling lessons from childhood pay off for Mr. Williams when fellow yodeler Curly zeroes in on the kidnappers' hideout in *Nutty but Nice*.

Mr. Wilson—Slave-driving editor of **Whack Magazine** in *Dutiful but Dumb*. In direct contravention of a boss's duty to look out for his employees, Wilson knowingly sends shutter-challenged photographers **Click, Clack, and Cluck** (Moe, Larry, and Curly) to **Vulgaria**, a country that uses firing squads to execute anyone caught taking pictures.

Mr. Winthrop—Oddball millionaire who cares more about his rare **Puckerless Persimmon Tree** than about his own failing health in *Some More of Samoa*.

Mr. Zero—Spirited member of the **Woman Haters Club 87** who delivers the club's first invocation in *Woman Haters*.

Mrs. Bedford—Livid dog owner in *Calling All Curs* who worries more about the disappearance of her prize-winning pooch **Garçon** than she does about the feelings of the three veterinarians who allowed the dog to be kidnapped from under their noses.

Mrs. Bixby—Wealthy society matron and generous sponsor of the *Krispy Krunchies* radio program in *Micro-Phonies*. Mrs. Bixby falls in love with the singing of soprano *Señorita Cucaracha* and simply must hire the opera star at any cost. Moe knows that the delicate señorita is really Curly dressed in a fetching outfit, but he accepts the proposition graciously, ignoring the baritone objections of the newly wealthy soprano.

Mrs. Burlap—Socialite whose refined demeanor is not enough to overcome the wiggling mouse dropped down her dress by the Stooges in *Ants in the Pantry*.

Mrs. Castor—Society matron whose plan to impress lunch guests is derailed by the simultaneous arrival of ants, mice, moths, and three exterminators in *Pest Man Wins*.

Mrs. Catsby—Blue-blooded patroness of academia who never intended her endowment at *Mildew College* to be used to support the unorthodox teaching methods of Professors Moe, Larry, and Curly in *Violent is the Word for Curly*.

Mrs. Crump—Battle-ax landlady in *Baby Sitters Jitters* who has little patience for tenants behind on their rent.

Mrs. Dennis O'Toole—A lovely dress, flattering pantyhose, and thick brogue transform fugitive Curly into Mrs. Dennis O'Toole, a robust new mother whose Irish charms and dainty ways bewitch *Officer O'Halloran* in *Mutts to You*.

Mrs. Flipper's Fluffy Pancake Mix—See *Flipper's Fluffy Fablongent Flapjacks*.

Mrs. Gottrocks—Distinguished guest at a party marking the Stooges' entrée into society as gentlemen in *Half-Wits Holiday* and *Pies and Guys*.

Mrs. Hammond Eggerley's Theatrical Apts.—Rickety thespian boardinghouse where the Stooges and their pet monkey *Joe* reside in *A Pain in the Pullman*. For actors out of work, the Eggerley place wasn't all bad, as the sign out front attests: "26 Rooms—2 Bath Tubs—Rates $4.00 Per Week Up—Mostly Up."

Mrs. Henderson—Society matron who hastily hires the Stooges as cook, butler, and waiter in *Listen, Judge*. A textbook example of IMMUTABLE STOOGES LAW #58: The Stooges will arrive at the homes of wealthy socialites just before a big party is to commence and just after the cook, butlers, and maids have quit.

Mrs. Magruder—Although Moe calls his landlord "Mrs. Battle-ax" in *Gents in a Jam*, the crusty Magruder does allow the Stooges to work off their overdue rent by painting their own apartment, a proposition far more risky than that offered by any other Stooge landlord.

Mrs. Morgan—IMMUTABLE STOOGES LAW #59: Pie will be served at all society parties, balls, and other quaint get-togethers attended by the Stooges. In *Slippery Silks*, an infuriated *Mr. Morgan* discovers that his enemies, the Stooges, are fitting Mrs. Morgan for a custom-designed dress.

With rage in the room and pie on the plates, Mrs. Morgan will soon see the dark side of her strong-armed husband.

Mrs. Pendall—Society matron who recommends snooty interior decorator *Omay* to *Thaddeus and Maggie Smirch* in *Tassels in the Air*.

Mrs. Smythe Smythe—Refined guest who attends a party marking the Stooges' entrée into society as gentlemen in *Half-Wits Holiday*.

Mrs. Throttlebottom's Chicken Coop—Lofty establishment allegedly robbed by the Stooges in *A Plumbing We Will Go*. The evidence doesn't stick, but even the biggest Curly fans will be suspicious at the mounds of chicken feathers that fly from his jacket after acquittal.

Mrs. van Bustle—It is a story as old as the ages: a wealthy millionairess is duped by the charms of a gold-digging schemer posing as the prince of a faraway land. This is the fate of Mrs. van Bustle in *Crash Goes the Hash*, but her story has an unusually happy ending. Able to cast off residual feelings of shame and embarrassment, Mrs. van Bustle develops a new, more powerful love for an undercover photographer with a bald head, round stomach, and no apparent mutual interests.

Mud—IMMUTABLE STOOGES LAW #60: Mud that is stuck in the ear of a Stooge can be dislodged only by blowing vigorously into that Stooge's other ear (various films).

Mugsy—Lead-fisted mobster who tracks a priceless string of pearls to the Stooge-owned *Shangri-La Upholstering Company* in *Hugs and Mugs*.

Muriel van Twitchett—Society matron who seeks revenge on her inattentive husband by hiring escorts to accompany her to a party in *Termites of 1938*. When the Stooges show up instead, the revenge is all her husband's.

Muscle Manor—Testosterone-laden gymnasium in *Fright Night* where the Stooges train boxer *Chopper Kane* for his championship bout with *Gorilla Watson*.

Muscles—IMMUTABLE STOOGES LAW #61: All henchmen, bodyguards, and sidekicks will have names even more intimidating than their looks. In *Crime on Their Hands* and *Hot Ice*, Muscles stands by *Dapper Dan* in his effort to surgically recover the swallowed *Punjab Diamond* from the stomach of detective Shemp.

Museum of Ancient History—Musty museum that employs Egyptologist Professor Wilson in *We Want Our Mummy*.

Museum of Natural History—Museum headed by ambitious curator *B. Bopper* in *Stone Age Romeos*. Most museums are content to let their curators dust displays and arrange school field trips. But the Museum of Natural History has a rare one in Bopper, who offers the Stooges $25,000 from the museum's coffers if they can prove that cavemen still exist.

Mushroom Murders—IMMUTABLE STOOGES LAW #62: Law enforcement officials struggling with unsolved crimes will

The three men falsely accused of the Mushroom Murders (*In the Sweet Pie and Pie, 1941*)

pin those crimes on the Stooges. Convicted for the grisly Mushroom Murders in *In the Sweet Pie and Pie*, the Stooges are ready to meet the hangman's noose, but are bailed out by the confession of guilt-ridden *Mickey Finn*, the true perpetrator of the crime.

"Must Have a Job . . ."—Larry's yeoman work ethic is never more proudly displayed than on the sign he carries in *Pop Goes the Easel*. It reads, "Must Have a Job—Will Do Anything—Position as Bridge Instructor Preferred."

"My Beautiful Jane"—Tenderhearted love sonnet sung by an adoring Moe in *Gypped in the Penthouse*:

> *Ah, my beautiful Jane*
> *While it's in my brain*
> *May I deign to gain*
> *To ask you not refrain*
> *The chance to make us twain!*

My ex-wife and ten bartenders—The eleven income tax deductions to which Shemp feels he is entitled in *Income Tax Sappy*.

"My, what a beautiful head of bone you have!"—Irresistible pickup line dished out by a bathing beauty to navy captain Curly in *Booby Dupes*.

"Mysterious Burglaries Panic City— Police Shakeup as Ape Man Strikes Again"—Startling headline in the *Daily Chronicle* that increases pressure on police inspector *I. Doolittle* to solve a baffling series of crimes in *Dizzy Detectives*.

Mystery Motor Jackpot Show— Shemp's $50,000 grand prize for winning the "Mystery Motor Jackpot" radio show in *A Missed Fortune* should be remembered for the intellectual achievement it represented, not for the brevity with which Shemp hung on to the money.

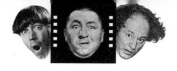

N

Naki, Saki, and Waki—Deceptive aliases adopted by the Stooges while posing as three Japanese soldiers in *No Dough Boys*.

National Express and Storage Company—Innocent-looking storage facility where three larcenous ladies go to pick up a string of stolen pearls in *Hugs and Mugs*.

National Space Foundation—American institution in *Have Rocket, Will Travel* that should have recognized that even janitors like the Stooges can concoct a top-secret rocket fuel if given a lab, volatile ingredients, and the affections of a beautiful blond scientist.

NBC—Immutable Stooges Law #63: The three-gong NBC theme will sound whenever a Stooge is hit in the head by three horseshoes, bowling balls, or other deadly objects (various films).

Needlock Appliance Corporation—Firm for which the Stooges work in *I Can Hardly Wait*. The Needlock Appliance Corporation is never seen on-screen, but the Stooges wear buttons that proudly proclaim their affiliation: Moe is member *13*, Curly is member H_2O, and Larry is member *6⅞*.

Nell—Every man dreams of having a dame like Nell in his life. Pretty, loyal, and able to throw a wicked punch at an ungentlemanly outlaw, Nell is the epitome of womanhood in no fewer than six Stooge films. In *Out West*, Nell refuses to sit by daintily while **Doc Barker**'s gang gets away with the murder of her pappy; instead, she recruits three tough-looking hombres to execute a plan of revenge that includes the rugged-but-imprisoned **Arizona Kid** and even the **U.S. Cavalry**. In *Pals and Gals*, Nell knows she could easily slip away from the villainous **Doc Barker** but won't desert her locked-up sisters **Belle and Zell**. In *The Three Troubledoers*, Nell resists marrying bandit **Badlands Blackie**, relying instead on courageous Sheriff Curly to free her captive father. In *Punchy Cowpunchers*, Nell calls upon the handsome golden locks and noble gallantry of cowboy **Elmer** to thwart the desperado **Dillon Gang**. In *Rockin' Thru the Rockies*, Nell shows her musical side as she leads her song-and-dance troupe **Nell's Belles** to the big-time stages of San Francisco. And in *Horses' Collars*, Nell places her trust in the quick-draw skills of three hombres sent from parts unknown to rescue an I.O.U. from dirty **Double Deal Decker**.

Nell's Belles—Most showbiz newcomers face obstacles on the road to stardom, but few battle wild bears and angry Indians to get there. In *Rockin' Thru the Rockies*, the all-woman song-and-dance troupe Nell's Belles has its hands full while traveling to San Francisco, despite the best intentions of their three brave escorts.

Nerve tonic—One of many medications Moe takes for a case of frazzled nerves in *Idiots Deluxe* and *Guns A Poppin*. See also *Vitamins A.P.U.*

"Never in the history of motion pictures has the U.S. Cavalry been too late"—Soothing reassurance provided by a cavalry man to a worried *Arizona Kid* in *Out West*.

New Year's Day—One of Shemp's cunning aliases in *Blunder Boys*. See also *Christmas Day*, *Groundhog Day*, *Independence Day*, *Labor Day*, and *St. Patrick's Day*.

New York Gazette—Newspaper in *Flying Saucer Daffy* that prints the screaming headline, *"Actual Photo of Flying Saucer Sets Country Ablaze."*

New York Globe—Newspaper that gives the Stooges' trip to Venus front page attention in *Have Rocket, Will Travel*. The headline reads, *"Earthmen Return Home from Venus! World Honors First Travelers in Space."*

"Niagara Falls"—Immortal dramatic vignette performed by the Stooges in *Gents Without Cents*. Scholars of drama, psychology, and geography have yet to determine why Moe and Larry go berserk upon hearing the name "Niagara Falls," but the routine is reproduced below nonetheless for fresh study and consideration:

> *Niagara Falls!*
> *Slowly I turned . . . step-by-step . . .*
> *   inch-by-inch . . .*
> *I walked up to him, I smashed him like this,*
> *   I hit him, I bopped him,*
> *I tore him to pieces, and I knocked him down!*

"Nice cold hotcakes smothered in vinegar"—Mouthwatering breakfast prepared lovingly by the Stooges for wheelchair-bound *Mary* in *Hokus Pokus* and *Flagpole Jitters*.

"A nice salami sandwich smothered in sour cream with cherry jelly, pickle in the middle, and some mustard on top"—As guests on *Sunev* in *Outer Space Jitters*, the Stooges do not do their best to conform to the planet's customs. When offered a regal meal of clam shells and battery acid, the impolite Stooges request instead "a nice salami sandwich smothered in sour cream with cherry jelly, pickle in the middle, and some mustard on top."

"Nice soup from a nice, juicy bone"—Curly's delectable description of the meal he prepares for his starving pals in *If a Body Meets a Body*.

Nick Barker—Drama critic in *Three Hams on Rye* who routinely pans shows produced by *B. K. Doaks*. After the Stooges consume and cough up a cake made of feathers during Doaks's new play, Barker proclaims the show to be an absolute "sensation."

Nikko—IMMUTABLE STOOGES LAW #64: All hideously deformed monsters employed by criminals will dislike the Stooges. In *Who Done It?* and *For Crimin' Out Loud*, the Stooges make a good-faith effort to avoid a confrontation with the bloodthirsty Nikko, but Nikko is lustily committed to their murders, anyway. In *A Bird in the Head*, Nikko is assistant to the mad *Professor Panzer*, and is only too happy to assist Panzer in transplanting the puny brain of an unfortunate paperhanger into the skull of a wild ape.

Nill, Null, and Void—Stooges' nightclub act in *Loco Boy Makes Good*. Their tag line, *"Three Hams Who Lay Their Own Eggs,"* only hints at the show-stopping entertainment ahead.

919 Circle Avenue—Posh address of the *Circle Follies Theatre* in *Loose Loot*.

90 Proof—Alarming reading taken from a thermometer in Curly's mouth while he awaits the arrival of beautiful nurses in *Monkey Businessmen*.

"95 percent temper; 5 percent mental"—Although he favored the eye-poke and double stomach punch, Moe was also capable of using simple math to deliver a crushing blow. When Curly declares himself to be temperamental in *Saved by the Belle*, Moe uses raw numbers to confirm it: "95 percent temper; 5 percent mental."

$97—Amount demanded by the pastry man before he'll deliver another pie on credit to the Stooge-owned *Jive Café* in *Busy Buddies*.

Nip and Tuck—See *Colonel Buttz*.

"No, but I know a big fence in Chicago"—Curly's worldly reply to a

Shemp prepares to teach Nikko (Duke York) that pulling hair is not an honorable way to go about being a goon (*For Crimin' Out Loud*, 1956).

woman in *In the Sweet Pie and Pie* who asks if he is familiar with the Great Wall of China.

"No Honeymoon No Work/Unfair to Union Husbands"—More in the mood for love than for the home construction work, newlywed Curly carries this two-sided picket sign reflecting the Stooges' unwavering—for the moment—policy in *The Sitter Downers*.

"No, I'll wait; maybe I'll get potatoes"—Larry's optimistic response after

Moe asks if he intends to eat an entire chicken alone.

"No Hunting, Fishing, or Swimming"—Spoilsport sign posted by Indian **Chief Rain in the Puss** in *Back to the Woods*. Other area signs include "No Camping," "No Shooting," "No Fires," "No Smoking," and "Scram."

"No, Milwaukee"—Larry's response in *Half Shot Shooters* when asked by a commanding officer if he was born in America.

"No Peddlers"—The mark of any great salesman is his ability to improvise. That rare skill is classically demonstrated in *Spook Louder*, in which the Stooges rebound from a ringing rejection to sell the same customer an item she truly needs, a "No Peddlers" sign for her front door.

"No qualms or trepidations . . ."—In an effort to calm the professor who has trained them to become gentlemen in *Half-Wits Holiday*, the Stooges offer these reassurances at a party that marks their debut into society:

> Curly: *Professor Quackenbush, have no qualms or trepidations.*
> Larry: *We will justify your faith in us indubitably, sir.*
> Moe: *Professor, the vicissitudes we have encountered have elevated us to a lofty position.*

(The pie fight that ensues, however, takes a bit of the luster off these remarkable statements.)

"No Smoking—No Hunting—No Fishing—No Nothing Go Home"—Restrictive sign on the grounds where the Stooges have gone to smoke, hunt, fish, and escape home in *Idiots Deluxe*.

"No Use—You're Doomed"—We all wish, at some critical moment in our lives, to turn back the hands of time. But few of us meet with the kind of unsympathetic clock that Larry encounters when he tries to reset the hands of time in *Shot in the Frontier*. Its grim message to a panicked Larry: "No Use—You're Doomed."

"No Burpoline"—Inventors take too little advantage of the great ideas available in Stooge films. One day, however, someone will market the revolutionary product advertised on the radio in *Sing a Song of Six Pants* and *Rip, Sew and Stitch*: "No Burpoline—the only gasoline containing bicarbonate of soda."

"No, but I get a little attack there every time I eat too much"—Fish salesman Curly's answer to a customer who asks if he has a haddock in *Cookoo Cavaliers*.

"No Dogs or Babies Allowed"—Prominently posted policy at the Stooges' apartment in *Mutts to You*, an unlucky film in which the Stooges work as dog washers and happen upon an abandoned baby.

"No Sale"—The cash register's sad reaction when Curly crashes into it headfirst in *Busy Buddies*.

Noazark Shipbuilding Company—
Even the greatest acts are born of humble beginnings, and so it was with the Stooges' stage act, "Two Souls and a Heel," which debuted at Noazark Shipbuilding Company in *Gents Without Cents*.

"Nobody lives here, either!"—Keen observation made by Joe in *Space Ship Sappy* after Moe and Larry observe that the planet **Sunev** is deserted and uninhabited.

Noonan Brothers—In *Shot in the Frontier*, the Noonan Brothers don't take kindly to strangers who mosey in and marry their dames, another western dispute to be settled by bullets and the quick-draw powers of the Stooges.

Nora—Homely sanitarium nurse with whom delirious patient Shemp falls madly in love in *Scrambled Brains*. Also, one of two pretty Stooge accomplices in *Cuckoo on the Choo Choo*.

Norfleet Mansion—Stately residence with imperfect plumbing in *Vagabond Loafers* and *Scheming Schemers*. The mansion's only problem is a missing diamond ring; the plumbing doesn't turn imperfect until after the Stooges arrive.

"Not Responsible for Hats and Coats"—Artistic inspiration cannot be planned; when the impulse flares, the artist must create. That should be kept in mind by all nonartists who sympathize with the butler in *Tassels in the Air*, upon whose back the Stooges paint the poignant message, "Not Responsible for Hats and Coats."

"Not since I was a baby"—Moe's forthright testimony in *Idiots Deluxe* and *Guns A Poppin* when asked by a judge if he had ever been indicted.

"Nothing to Buy, Nothing to Sell, We've Gone Fishing, You Can Go . . . Fishing Too"—Information-packed sign hung outside the real estate offices of **Ginsberg, Rosenburg, Goldstein, and O'Brien** in *G.I. Wanna Go Home*. A testament to the extra mile the firm is willing to go, since most businesses are content to hang a simple "Closed" sign during off-hours.

Number Four in the Blue Book—See *The Fishmarket Duet*.

Number 22—One of hundreds of greeting cards written and peddled by the Stooges in *Boobs in Arms*. After they hurl an angry potential customer down a sidewalk opening, the Stooges toast him with card number 22, which goes like this:

> *Greetings little shut-in*
> *Don't you weep or sigh*
> *If you're not out by Christmas*
> *You'll be out the Fourth of July!*

N'Yuk-N'Yuks—Sponsor of the Stooges' children's television program, *"The Three Stooges Scrapbook,"* in *The Three Stooges in Orbit*. The product's irresistible motto: "The Breakfast of Stooges."

O-K-67—Larry's prison number in *Beer Barrel Polecats* and *In the Sweet Pie and Pie*, it is affixed to a license plate he wears. See also *A-K-70* and *B-K-68*.

O. U. Gonga—Forward-thinking dean of the *Wide Awake Detective School* in *Scotched in Scotland*. Unlike many deans who are content to attend school banquets and act as passive figureheads, Gonga takes an active role in the success of his students. He won't hesitate, for example, to assign even his three worst students to monumental cases, such as guarding the precious relics in spooky *Glenheather Castle*.

O'Brien's Kosher Restaurant—Eclectic restaurant advertised on Curly's army uniform in *Boobs in Arms*. Their pitch: "When You Get Back Eat at O'Brien's Kosher Restaurant—Soup, Salad, Entrée, Coffee, Desert—All This and Herring Too—40 cents."

Octopus Grabus—Redhead-loving emperor of *Ancient Erysipelas* in *Matri-Phony*. History's great rulers are often undone not by enemy armies, but by their own personal shortcomings, and Grabus is no exception. His severe near-sightedness is disastrous for wooing redheads, one of whom, *Diana*, is savvy enough to substitute a brave Erysipelian potter named *Curleycue* to distract the amorous emperor.

Odius—Bossy king of ancient Ithaca in *The Three Stooges Meet Hercules*.

Officer O'Halloran—Stout cop whose taste for robust Irish women nearly allows Curly—disguised as the lovely *Mrs. Dennis O'Toole*—to escape with a kidnapped baby in *Mutts to You*.

Oga—Dastardly count who is faithful to the evil queen in *Snow White and the Three Stooges*.

The cunning Count Oga (Guy Rolfe) sniffs out three half-baked spies (*Snow White and the Three Stooges*, 1961).

Rock bands were not the first musical groups to clash over artistic differences (*Idiots Deluxe*, 1945).

Martians Ogg and Zogg seem to share at least one disciplinary approach with their earthly nemeses (*The Three Stooges in Orbit*, 1962).

Ogg and Zogg—Martians in *The Three Stooges in Orbit* who, unfortunately, fit all the worst Martian stereotypes: they're unreasonable, don't speak English, aren't very handsome, and are devoted to conquering Earth.

"Oh, Elaine"—Among the most impassioned songs of courtship ever sung, "Oh, Elaine" evokes truths about romance, danger, and friendship that touch a universal chord. Sung in stirring three-part harmony by the Stooges on behalf of their heartsick friend ***Cedric the Blacksmith***, the listener can only wish he or she were the intended recipient, rather than the lovely ***Princess Elaine*** in *Squareheads of the Round Table* and *Knutzy Knights*:

(Sung to the classical strains of ***Sextetrum Lucia***, with Elaine's part in parentheses.)

> *Oh, Elaine, Elaine, come out, babe*
> *Take a look who's standing here, right here*
> *The big boy is here, we see the coast is clear*
> *He wants to see you, so come out on your*
>   *front porch.*
>
> *Oh, Elaine, come out, oh, please come out*
> *Time is short, the guards are hanging about*
> *Your Cedric's here, no kiddin', Cedric's here.*
>
> *(I see, I see my darling Cedric standing there*
> *I know, I know that I will soon be in his arms*
>   *again.)*

*She knows, she knows that she will soon be
in his arms again!
(Nee, but flee, the Black Prince is lurking
near!
I will raise the shade, the lovely shade, when
the coast is clear.)*

"Oh, I don't know; I've been around!"—The brave **Señorita Rita** has gone out on a limb for the Stooges in *Saved by the Belle*. During an interrogation of the Stooges by an army general who might order their executions, Rita remarks that Curly certainly looks innocent to her. Curly's reply: "Oh, I don't know; I've been around!"

"Oh, thank you. I couldn't dance a step last year."—Larry's gracious reply after a society lady in *Hoi Polloi* tells him that his dancing is "atrocious."

"Oh, woe is Moe!"—Larry's lament in *Idiots Deluxe* after believing Moe to have been eaten by a grizzly bear.

"Old Holland Cheese . . ."—Tempting taste treat advertised on the Stooges' handbills in *Dunked in the Deep*. It's not clear who designed the handbills, but if the intent was to make the mouth water, the writer succeeded: "Old Holland Cheese in Five Delicious Flavors . . . Amsterdam, Rotterdam, Beaver Dam, Boulder Dam, and Giva Dam—Only on Sale at Open Air Markets."

Old Homicide—A drink is only as good as its weakest ingredient. Moe understands this bartending principle instinctively in *Out West* and *Pals and Gals*, when he expertly mixes the potent liquor Old Homicide with just the right complement of **molasses, Tabasco, seltzer, eggs, paint, and paint remover**.

Old King Cole—Delightful rhyme recited by royal fiddlers Moe, Larry, and Shemp in *Fiddlers Three*. It is reproduced here for the first time in its entirety:

*Old King Cole is a merry old soul
Yes he is, it's plain to see
He called for his pipe
He called for his bowl
And he always called for his fiddlers three.*

*Oh, Old King Cole, you're a merry old soul
Without a care and fancy free
Please call for your pipe
Please call for your bowl
And here are your fiddlers three, that's we!*

Old Man Goodrich—Terrified geezer who desperately dials detectives Moe, Larry, and Shemp to prevent his murder in *Who Done It?* and *For Crimin' Out Loud*. Goodrich should have learned to dial faster.

Old Panther—Not to be confused with **Panther Pilsner Beer**, Old Panther was serious stuff that packed a wallop in *Love at First Bite*, *Shot in the Frontier*, *Gypped in the Penthouse*, and *Tricky Dicks*. Although not as delicate as some finely aged liqueurs, Old Panther's recent vintage (**"Distilled Yesterday"**) allowed it to mix easily in rubber boots and metal pails.

Omagosh—Regal surname of the **Emir of Shmow** in *Malice in the Palace* and *Rumpus in the Harem*.

Omay—Haughty French interior decorator for whom Moe is naturally mistaken in *Tassels in the Air*.

"On the end of a rope"—During a dance with a charming lady in *An Ache in Every Stake* and *Three Smart Saps*, Curly brags that his own father died dancing—on the end of a rope.

Onay—See *Amscray, Ixnay, and Onay*.

½—Larry's football uniform number in *Three Little Pigskins*. Also, the number that appears on Curly's arm patch in *You Nazty Spy*.

$100—Stratospheric prize money offered to the first-place finisher in the **Carrot County Fair Champion Milking Contest** in *Busy Buddies*.

106⅞—A sick patient is often the best judge of his own condition, and this is certainly true of the ailing Moe in *Idiots Deluxe* and *Guns A Poppin*. His self-estimated temperature: 106⅞.

111 Riverside Drive—Deceptively serene-sounding address of the spooky mansion where murdered **Professor Bob O. Link**'s will is to be read in *If a Body Meets a Body*.

118 6th Street, San Francisco, California—If ever there opens an honesty hall of fame, this address will be among the first inductees. This is the office where the Stooges return lost oil bonds belonging to **B. O. Davis** in *So Long Mr. Chumps*. But the honesty doesn't end there. Davis then commissions the Stooges to bring him an honest man for employment, making 118 6th Street a timeless monument to telling the truth.

$140—Estate left behind by the recently deceased Shemp in *Heavenly Daze* and *Bedlam in Paradise*.

I thought *you* added the yeast (*Beer Barrel Polecats*, 1946).

185—Astonishing number of bottles of beer brewed by the bootlegging Stooges in *Beer Barrel Polecats* after each takes it upon himself to add yeast to the recipe.

1,000—The number of reasons that Shemp acknowledges exist for not drinking alcohol in *Baby Sitters Jitters*. However, Shemp says between swigs of champagne, "I can't think of one right now."

$1,000—Lofty sum wagered by Professor Quackenbush (See **Professors Rich and Nichols, Quackenbush and Sedletz**) in *Half-Wits Holiday* on the principle that any three nitwits can be taught to be gentlemen. Quackenbush loses.

1,000 Shilbleenas—Staggering reward offered to the Stooges by **Hassan Ben Sober** for the recovery of the **King Rootin' Tootin' Diamond** in *Malice in the Palace* and *Rumpus in the Harem*.

1,000 Shilbleenas Virgin Tax— Astronomical ransom demanded by the **Sultan of Pish Posh** in exchange for his promise not to add the Stooges' girls to his harem in *Rumpus in the Harem*.

Onion Oil Company—Gasoline conglomerate in *Slaphappy Sleuths* being brought to its knees by a string of robberies at its service stations. General manager **Fuller Grime** knows that without the help of three undercover detectives, it is certain Onion Oil will be forced to stop offering the kinds of prices that made it famous: "Ethel 30¢ Per Gal.—Becky 26¢ Per Gal.—Hazel 22¢ Per Gal."

"Only when I take bicarbonate"— Curly's polite reply in *Three Smart Saps* when asked by a pretty dance partner if he "rumbas."

"Open 10 to 3"—Business hours of the holdup-ready **First National Bank** in *Phony Express*.

Operator 12—Larry's code name as a deep undercover spy in *Uncivil Warriors*. See also **Lieutenant Duck**.

Operator 13—While thoroughly entertaining in *Uncivil Warriors*, Curly was also a master spy. His explanation for the whereabouts of the missing Operator 13—that the man swam across the river and died of Potomac Poisoning—must be taken with a grain of salt.

Operator 14—Moe's code name as a deep undercover spy in *Uncivil Warriors*. See also **Captain Dodge**.

Operator 15—Curly's code name as a *very* deep undercover spy in *Uncivil Warriors*. See also **Major Hyde**.

"Opportunities in Mexico . . ."— Enticing sign hanging in the window of **Pedro Ruiz Business Opportunities** in *Cookoo Cavaliers*. The sign reads, "Opportunities in Mexico—Business Always Good—Today's Special—Beauty Shop in Cucaracha—$300."

"The Orient . . ."—There is something romantic about the Far East that makes the land irresistible to any who venture there. Poets, writers, and photographers have long tried to capture the seduction of this wondrous place, but none has done it better than the writer of the opening title in *Rumpus in the Harem*, who wrote, "The Orient—Where Men are Men and Women are Glad of It."

Original Two-Man Quartet—
IMMUTABLE STOOGES LAW #65: Trombone players in Stooge films will not have full control of the instrument's slide. In *Idiots Deluxe* and *Guns A Poppin*, Larry and Curly's (Larry and Joe in *Guns A Poppin*) noisy two-man drum and trombone act is damaging enough to poor Moe's case of shattered nerves. But an airborne trombone slide that lodges around Moe's neck is more than any man on the verge of a nervous breakdown should be expected to endure.

Oscar the Dummy—Padded boxing dummy that manages to beat up Moe, Larry, and Shemp in *Fright Night* and *Fling in the Ring*. Had the Stooges worked together rather than shoving the wobbly Oscar at one another, they might have given the dummy a better fight.

"Our Leader—President Ward Robey—The People's Friend"—
Propagandist sign that hangs under the portrait of President Ward Robey in *Saved by the Belle*. The Stooges don't think Robey or his generals are very friendly as they await execution on trumped-up charges.

P

Painless Papyrus—There are times when Moe's quick wit and precision thinking astonish even the most ardent skeptics. There is no better example of such an occasion than in *Mummy's Dummies*, where the Stooges are moments from being thrown to the lions by *King Rootentooten* for selling a faulty used chariot. Noticing that the king has a terrible toothache, Moe's brain kicks into gear and spits out an ingenious plan: Shemp will pull the tooth. At first the king is wary but Moe is prepared, assuring him that dentist Shemp is known across Egypt as Painless Papyrus.

Paint—IMMUTABLE STOOGES LAW #66: No Stooge paint job is complete until Moe's face and rear end have been covered (various films).

Pago Pago—See *Edam Neckties.*

Pamo Hair Remover—Potion with unpleasant potential that is handled too liberally by hairdressers Moe, Larry, and Curly in *Cookoo Cavaliers*.

"The Panics of 1936"—Stage review that is desperate for a substitute act—even a substitute act featuring three amateurs and their far more talented monkey—in *A Pain in the Pullman*.

Panther Brewing Company—Brewery in *Three Little Beers* that sponsors a lovely annual golf tournament but neglects to offer lessons to employees—like the Stooges—who might still have an unpolished game.

Panther Pilsner Beer—Flagship product of the *Panther Brewing Company* delivered by the Stooges in *Three Little Beers*. Little indication is given as to Panther Pilsner's taste, body, or smoothness, but one thing appears certain: it was among the most problematic beers of its time to deliver.

Parasites—What Moe tells the queen the Stooges were looking over while in Paris in *Restless Knights*. Also, the scenery shown to Joe by his loving Parisian sweetheart Fifi in *Fifi Blows Her Top*.

"Paris—Somewhere in France"—Opening title in *Wee Wee Monsieur*. Although the film's setting is imprecisely communicated, one aspect of Parisian life clearly emerges: it was legal for landlords to maim deadbeat tenants like Moe, Larry, and Curly.

Paté D'Fagua—Savory delicacy ordered by a restaurant guest in *Loco Boy Makes Good*. Larry, as the man's waiter, has committed the cardinal sin of his trade by being unfamiliar with the menu, telling the hungry patron, "I'll see if the band can play it." Also, Curly's term for the fine turkey luncheon the Stooges are served in *All the World's a Stooge*.

"Patents Bought and Sold"—Sign on the door of the shady patent office in *Three Pests in a Mess*.

Paul Pain—Melodramatic actor and self-described "heartthrob of millions" in *A Pain in the Pullman*. Pain might have had full command of the stage, but he is a mere understudy when dealing with the toupée-stealing tendencies of the Stooges' monkey *Joe*.

Peaceful Gulch—Deceptively placid name for a town turned on its ear by the lawless antics of bandit *Red Morgan* and his thugs in *Phony Express* and *Merry Mavericks*.

Peaceful Gulch Saloon—Now-legendary site of the showdown between *Red Morgan*'s gang and three scrappy new deputies in *Phony Express* and *Merry Mavericks*.

Pebble—Yeoman's name Larry answers to before rising meteorically to the position of *Minister of Propaganda* in *You Nazty Spy*.

Pedro Alvarez—Mexican promoter who demands that talent agent *Shamus O'Brien* deliver him a top notch American act in *What's the Matador?* Instead, he gets the Stooges.

Pedro Ruiz Business Opportunities—Border town brokerage that sells the Stooges a Mexican beauty salon in *Cookoo Cavaliers*. Proprietor Pedro Ruiz is a nice enough fellow who speaks decent English, but he must learn the difference between a saloon and a salon.

Penciltucky Railroad Company—Where the action unfolds in *Cuckoo on the Choo Choo*.

Penciltucky Railroad Company No. 428—Railroad detective Moe's squad car unit in *Cuckoo on the Choo Choo*.

Pepe—Faithful canine owned by *Greta* and her jealous husband *José* in *Sappy Bullfighters*.

Percival DePuyster—Larger-than-life movie star who shuns paparazzi in *Dutiful but Dumb*. Photographers Moe and Larry fail in their assignment to snap a picture of DePuyster with his glamorous new fiancée, but Curly manages to work his head under a sterling silver platter on DePuyster's dinner table, shocking the appetite from the star and his sweetheart as they prepare to enjoy their meal.

Percy Pomeroy—Every prisoner dreams of having three strange men bust him out of jail, but only a very few—like Pomeroy—ever see that dream become glorious reality. In *So Long Mr. Chumps* and *Beer Barrel Polecats*, Pomeroy (a.k.a. Prisoner *#41144*) is astonished to hear from his prison cell what must sound like angels: the beckoning voices of Moe, Larry, and Curly, three men of principle who won't rest easy until the innocent Pomeroy is freed.

Perfect Underwear Company—Business where Larry arranges a job for Shemp as a traveling salesman in *He Cooked His Goose*. Although no salesman ever tried harder than Shemp, one gets the distinct impression his sales would have skyrocketed had he refrained from modeling the underwear himself.

Phantom Gang—Murderous band of thugs who attack the person and property of innocent *Professor Goodrich* in *Who Done It?* Whatever else you say about the Phantom Gang, one thing is certain: they were politically correct, employing both a woman and a hunchback when most gangs of the time were staffed only by males in tip-top shape.

Phileas Fogg III—Great grandson to Phileas Fogg and a regular English gentleman. Fogg follows in his ancestor's steps by traveling around the world in eighty days—this time without spending a farthing—in *The Three Stooges Go Around the World in a Daze.*

Philip Black—Owner of the *Ever Rest Pet Cemetery* in *Three Pests in a Mess.* Mr. Black should think twice about showing up at his cemetery dressed as an undertaker . . . just in case three jittery men happen to be there disposing of a body.

Phony beards—IMMUTABLE STOOGES LAW #67: Phony knee-length beards worn by the Stooges will fool homicidal crooks for a moment, but not much longer (various films).

Pianos—IMMUTABLE STOOGES LAW #68: No grand piano will remain open while a Stooge inspects the wires inside (various films).

Pier 7—Fateful meeting place in *Dunked in the Deep* and *Commotion on the Ocean* where roughneck foreign spy *Bortch* meets his Waterloo—the Stooges.

Pierre—Hulking trooper Pierre is having a bad day in *Whoops, I'm an Indian!* After being bilked by the Stooges in a crooked game of chance, Pierre discovers that wife **Fifi** has left him for Indian *Chief Leaping Lizard.* His vow to kill all Indians becomes an unlucky break for the Stooges, who have just constructed Indian disguises to avoid detection by a local sheriff.

Piggy—Never have the Stooges seemed so proud to be uncles as with Piggy, the adorable colt born to the Stooges' reincarnated sister, **Birdie**, in *Horsing Around.*

Pig's feet smothered in lubricating oil, raw potatoes boiled in pure varnish, and head cheese garnished with rusty nails—In the Stooges' day, condemned men were not allowed the luxury of selecting a last meal before execution, as proven by this final feast thrust upon prisoners Moe, Larry, and Shemp in *Hot Stuff.*

Pinch Penny Market—Grumpy landlord **Amos Flint** is faced with a dilemma in *All Gummed Up* and *Bubble Trouble*: Should he stay loyal to longtime tenants the Stooges, or rent the **Cut Throat Drug Store** to the Pinch Penny Market for three times the rent? The speed with which Flint opts against the Stooges makes it obvious that his choice was vengefully made.

Pip Boys Lary Moe & Shemp—IMMUTABLE STOOGES LAW #69: Blazing-hot appliances will not be used by the Stooges with the degree of caution recommended by the manufacturer. As tailors the Pip Boys in *Sing a Song of Six*

Pants and *Rip, Sew and Stitch*, the Stooges utilize blazing hot irons and steam presses to fix problems with each other rather than with the wrinkled slacks and ill-fitting shirts that are the real enemies of tailors everywhere.

Platt Field—Site of the big football showdown between *Boulder Dam University* and *Blue Point University*, as advertised on signs carried by the Stooges in *Three Little Pigskins*.

"Players Only"—See *"Exit Tunnel 12."*

Plaza D'Toros—IMMUTABLE STOOGES LAW **#70**: Curly's head will always be a notch harder than the next hardest object in the vicinity. In *What's the Matador?*, the Plaza D'Toros arena hosts one of history's most closely contested bullfights, a stand-off between Curly and an ornery bull that is decided by a violent collision of the heads. The bull, one hopes, was not permanently injured by its defeat.

+4—They say that prison depersonalizes the inmate, a truth to which Moe can attest in *So Long Mr. Chumps* and *Beer Barrel Polecats*. Although still a human being, inmate Moe is issued the sterile uniform number +4, an identifier that reflects none of the special leadership skills or rock-busting talents he utilizes so effectively from behind bars.

"Plymouth City Limits . . ."—Gracious sign of welcome that greets the Stooges' arrival in *Back to the Woods*. Typical of early Pilgrim hospitality, the sign reads, "Plymouth City Limits—Come Again—Plymouth Chamber of Commerce."

Poison gas—Moe's term for the skunk the Stooges are about to fire at a band of rival cavemen in *I'm a Monkey's Uncle* and *Stone Age Romeos*.

Police Station Section 13 Detective Bureau—Police branch manned by three unorthodox but gritty detectives in *Tricky Dicks*. Their assignment: crack the *Slug McGurk* murder case in twenty-four hours—or else.

Polly—Most parrots involved in murder trials don't make nearly the impact Polly does in *Disorder in the Court*. Unwilling to sit idly in her cage while *Gail Tempest* is wrongfully tried for the murder of *Kirk Robbin*, Polly implores the court to "Find the letter! Find the letter!" And indeed, there it is, tied to her foot and implicating the real perpetrator, *Buck Wing*.

"Pop Goes the Weasel"—Most great fighters hone their craft with years of hitting the heavy bag and countless rounds of sparring. For Curly, a.k.a. *K. O. Stradivarius* in *Punch Drunks*, just a few bars of "Pop Goes the Weasel" transform the former overweight into a champion heavyweight overnight.

Popping Corn—Additive Shemp mistakenly adds to a customer's radiator—with appetizing results—in *Slaphappy Sleuths*.

Popsie—Also known as Popsie-Wopsie, the Stooges' philandering father in *3 Dumb Clucks* and *Up in Daisy's Penthouse*.

"Post No Bills"—Those of us without wooden legs don't contemplate the pitfalls of our handicapped brethren until we see a sign like the "Post No Bills" sign nailed to the wooden leg of a party guest in *Three Sappy People*.

Potomac Poisoning—See *Operator 13*.

Practical Dentistry—It was obvious from the moment Shemp picked up the book *The Amateur Carpenter* that the molar of an angry and suffering bandit would not be extracted smoothly. The more interesting question raised in *The Tooth Will Out* is whether Shemp would have gotten the correct tooth had he read the book he intended, *Practical Dentistry*.

"Practically unoccupied"—*Professor Panzer*'s preliminary diagnosis upon inspecting Curly's skull in *A Bird in the Head*.

President of the United States—Compassionate chief executive officer in *Cash and Carry* who makes *Little Jimmy*'s leg operation a reality. The President—unlike the Stooges—does not tap into the vaults of the U.S. Treasury in order to finance the surgery, but does understand the mistake the Stooges made in thinking the vaults contained buried treasure. He offers the Stooges *"executive clemency,"* a generous offer to which Curly fearfully replies, "Oh no, not that!"

President Ward Robey—IMMUTABLE STOOGES LAW #71: Parrots will always work against the best interests of the Stooges. In *Saved by the Belle*, the Stooges are traveling salesmen about to be released after resolving a misunderstanding with a Valeskan general. As the Stooges prepare to depart, Curly's parrot

yelps, "Why don't you search them, General?" advice upon which the general acts swiftly. He finds a telegram that reads, "Get rid of present wardrobe," but his limited English produces a different translation: "Get rid of President Ward Robey," an offense punishable by death in *Valeska*.

Press-Press-Pull—Say what you will about the intelligence of the Stooges; no men ever made more brilliant use of bathroom knobs. Barred from entering the big event in *Three Little Beers* and *Even as I.O.U.*, the Stooges duck into a men's room and emerge at the event's press gate flashing impressive credentials. Moe's button says "press" and he is allowed to enter. Larry's button says "press" and he is allowed to enter. Curly's button says "pull," but he enters anyway.

Prince Boris—Scheming prime minister who plots the abduction and overthrow of *Queen Anne of Anesthesia* in *Restless Knights*.

Prince Charming—Gallant and daring, Prince Charming refuses to abandon stepfathers Moe, Larry, and Curly Joe even after he discovers that he has become king in *Snow White and the Three Stooges*.

Prince Gallant III of Rhododendron—Boys today who fantasize about becoming princes rarely consider the downside of royalty. They could learn a sobering lesson from the experience of Prince Gallant, a romantic soul whose plans to wed the fair *Princess Alicia* are derailed by jealous magician

Mergatroyd in *Fiddlers Three* and *Musty Musketeers*. Gallant has the heavens to thank for three brave fiddlers who save the day, but aspiring boys should realize that most kidnapped princes would not be so lucky.

Prince Shaam—In *Crash Goes the Hash*, Prince Shaam is able to convince wealthy *Mrs. van Bustle* that he cares only for her, but the Stooges aren't so easily duped, and catch the prince with his paws in van Bustle's safe. Curly's reward: the hand of the newly single millionairess.

"Prince Shaam of Ubeedarn Engaged to Widowed Socialite—Van Bustle Heiress to Wed Royal Blueblood"—Shocking headline in the *Daily Star Press* that scoops the competing *Daily News* and causes editor *Fuller Bull* to spare no expense in hiring three ace reporters, even if those reporters are three laundry men he thinks work for the competition.

Princess Alicia—*Coleslawvanian* princess in *Fiddlers Three* and *Musty Musketeers*.

Princess Elaine—Princess of unequaled beauty in *Squareheads of the Round Table* and *Knutzy Knights*. Elaine's grace and charm cause *Cedric the Blacksmith* to risk his life—and the lives of three brave minstrels—by serenading her. Incidentally, some have speculated that Elaine might have been adopted, as her stunning good looks do not appear to be shared by her father the king, a man who, Shemp says, "has the puss of a snapping turtle with a bellyache."

"Proclamation . . ."—Rulers generally know what they want, and Erysipelian emperor *Octopus Grabus* is no exception in *Matri-Phony*. His royal decree makes no apologies for its directness as it hangs outside the Stooge-owned Ye Olde Pottery and Stoneworks. It reads, "All Unmarried Redheaded Maidens Between the Ages of 18 and 22 Report at Once to the Emperor . . . Object Matrimony."

"Prof. A. K. Rimple No. 60"—In keeping with the traditions of modern flight, *Professor A. K. Rimple* identifies his spacecraft with this simple serial number in *Space Ship Sappy*.

Professor A. K. Rimple—Since the advent of NASA, access to outer space has been limited to astronauts. But in the Stooges' day, a chance meeting with a spaceship builder like Professor Rimple in *Space Ship Sappy* could mean a trip to the planet *Sunev*, even for three sailors who mistake the rocket for a newfangled-style house.

Professor Bilbo—Immutable Stooges Law #72: No magician, regardless of skill or reputation, can prevent the Stooges from bursting forth during the disappearing woman trick. In *A Plumbing We Will Go*, street illusionist Professor Bilbo has mesmerized a large crowd, but his payoff might have been bigger had the reappearing "woman" not been replaced by three ne'er-do-wells ducking from the law.

Professor Bob O. Link—Even stingy millionaire Bob O. Link would have bequeathed his nephew *Curly Q. Link* more than *67 Cents Net* had he anticipated the trauma Curly would endure prowling a haunted mansion in search of his killer in *If a Body Meets a Body*.

Professor Danforth—Eccentric old coot in *The Three Stooges in Orbit* whose top secret invention, a combination helicopter-tank-submarine, might have been more favorably received by the air force had he chosen someone other than the Stooges to fly it.

Professor Fuller—Enthusiastic art instructor at *Kraft's College of Arts* in *Pop Goes the Easel*. Moe proudly reports to Fuller that the Stooges have been using some of his brushes.

Professor Hicks—Eggheaded academic who insists in *Violent is the Word for Curly* that money designated for an athletic program at **Mildew College** would be better spent on the salaries of three esteemed European professors. Had the three *real* professors shown up, he might have been right.

Professor Jones—Like most professors, Jones has his mind on the theoretical, not the practical. While his scientific focus facilitates a trip with the Stooges to the planet *Sunev*, it doesn't help a whit when battling murderous planet rulers like the **Grand Zilch of Sunev** in *Outer Space Jitters*.

Professor Panzer—Another case of a brilliant mind wasted on the pursuit of evil. Panzer is committed to transplanting Curly's brain into the skull of *Igor the Ape* in *A Bird in the Head*. But in his mad quest for infamy he neglected to choose an ape who wouldn't fall in love with its benefactor.

Professor Repulso—IMMUTABLE STOOGES LAW #73: Professional musicians will give a substandard performance at recitals attended by the Stooges. In *Ants in the Pantry*, Professor Repulso, a guest at a

It was Professor Danforth's (Emil Sitka) idea to paint the Stooges, but he doesn't seem to think much of it (*The Three Stooges in Orbit*, 1962).

TOP TEN FILM TITLES

They range from silly (*Cuckoo on the Choo Choo*) to plain (*I Can Hardly Wait*) to strange (*Wham-Bam-Slam!*). Three Stooges film titles are a cornucopia of creativity that practically beg to be ranked, adjusted, and re-ranked.

Listed below are one man's opinion of the top ten Stooge film titles. The selection process, be assured, was not easy; the agony of choosing between *Oily to Bed, Oily to Rise* and *Loco Boy Makes Good* cannot—and should not—be described to innocent readers. Just sit back and enjoy.

(In alphabetical order)
Beer Barrel Polecats
Idle Roomers
Loco Boy Makes Good
Sing a Song of Six Pants
So Long Mr. Chumps
Squareheads of the Round Table
They Stooge to Conga
Three Hams on Rye
The Tooth Will Out
What's the Matador?

● ● ●

swank society party, plays a piano filled by Larry with cats. The result: his sharps screech and his flats meow.

"Professor Shemp Howard— Teacher of Voice"—Lyrical lettering on the door of Shemp's classroom in *Brideless Groom* and *Husbands Beware*.

Professor Snead—Brilliant and bushy-haired inventor of top secret rocket fuel for whom Larry is mistaken in *Fuelin' Around* and *Hot Stuff*. The real Snead never reveals his revolutionary formula, but given the potency of Larry's substitute concoction, Snead's formula was probably obsolete anyway.

Professor Tuttle—When you become the only professor to know the whereabouts of the priceless mummy of **King Rootentooten**, it should come as no surprise when you are kidnapped. In *We Want Our Mummy* this obvious lesson was lost on Professor Tuttle, who endangered not only himself but three brave detectives who took a taxicab all the way to Egypt to rescue him.

Professors Feinstein, Frankfurter, and Von Stueben—Erudite identities stolen by the Stooges in *Violent is the Word for Curly*. Although the Stooges have no formal degrees, their uncanny ability to teach the alphabet to appreciative students at **Mildew College** is a model for modern secondary education.

Professors Rich and Nichols, Quackenbush and Sedletz— Distinguished scholars who use the Stooges to study evolution in *Hoi Polloi* (Rich and Nichols) and in *Half-Wits Holiday* and *Pies and Guys* (Quackenbush and Sedletz). Each pair places a high-stakes wager on whether three bumbling laborers can be taught to be gentlemen. Those who wager "yes" learn an important lesson about environment and heredity. Those who wager "no" win the bet.

Professor Quackenbush (Milton Frome, left) probably wishes he hadn't wagered with Professor Sedletz (Gene Roth, right) that he could turn these plumbers into gentlemen (*Pies and Guys*, 1958).

Puckerless persimmon tree—Some humorless types think the Stooges to be an uneducated lot. But who else—including geography majors—would know that the only place to find the rare puckerless persimmon tree featured in *Some More of Samoa* is on the exotic island of **Rhum Boogie**?

"Pump in four more slices!"—Moe's directive in *An Ache in Every Stake* upon determining that Larry has not added enough gas to a recently deflated birthday cake.

"Pungfauthadrednock with the bicuspid canafran"—Painful-sounding diagnosis made by Shemp in his first case as a dentist in *The Tooth Will Out*.

Punjab Diamond—No one should forgive the crooked *Dapper Dan* for stealing the priceless Punjab Diamond in *Crime on Their Hands* and *Hot Ice*. But those critical of his decision to operate without anesthesia after Shemp swallows the rock should consider that as the fourth-largest diamond in the world, the Punjab was not likely to be passed in a more natural manner.

Professor Shemp Howard is a virtuoso voice instructor, but he's no better than average at tuning pianos (*Husbands Beware*, 1956).

"Punjab Diamond Stolen . . ."—
Newspaper headline in *Crime on Their
Hands* that reads, "Punjab Diamond
Stolen—Daring Bandits Raid Museum In
Daylight."

Puppo Dog Biscuits—The mark of a
great chef is his ability to improvise. As
undercover photographers in *Crash Goes
the Hash*, the Stooges can't balk when
ordered to prepare canapés for tony
guests at a society party, but prove themselves to have great culinary vision by
substituting Puppo Dog Biscuits when no
proper canapé base can be found.

Quatro the Magnificent—Although born into royalty, Prince Charming is raised a ventriloquist and magician by the Stooges, who have rescued him from the hands of an assassin in *Snow White and the Three Stooges*. His stage name: Quatro the Magnificent.

Queen Hotsytotsy—Not much is known about this ancient Egyptian queen from *We Want Our Mummy*, except that she was willing to look beyond the physical limitations of her husband, *King Rutentuten*. Rutentuten, the Stooges discover after an extensive search in a haunted tomb, was a midget.

Queen Anne of Anesthesia—IMMUTABLE STOOGES LAW #74: A person will be most at risk the moment after he or she commissions the Stooges as bodyguards. With the sinister *Prince Boris* plotting her overthrow, Queen Anne shows faulty instincts by commissioning the Stooges as royal bodyguards.

?—Curly's football uniform number in *Three Little Pigskins*. Although Curly's inventive footwork in the film obviously has influenced today's superstar running backs, modern football teams nonetheless require all uniform numbers to range from zero to 99.

"Quiet—Do Not Disturb"—Even with the mayhem they cause, the Stooges often show sensitivity toward those not inclined toward noise and commotion. These regal manners are demonstrated in *Dizzy Doctors*, when the Stooges place a "Quiet—Do Not Disturb" sign next to a hospital patient trying to break Rip Van Winkle's record.

Quinto—Ventriloquist's puppet who proclaims his master's love for **Snow White** in *Snow White and the Three Stooges*.

"Quit bragging"—See *Fifty generations*.

On the lookout for King Rutentuten (We Want Our Mummy, 1939)

R

R. O. Broad—Swindler of *Investors Inc.* who sells worthless *Consolidated Fujiyama California Smog Bags* to an unsuspecting *Joe* in *Quiz Whizz*.

Radames—Chief of the Palace Guard in *Mummy's Dummies* who, after swindling *King Rootentooten*, has the gall to complain about being swindled himself by three small-time used-chariot dealers.

Radio KGBY—Historic radio station where opera star *Señorita Cucaracha* (Curly) is discovered by wealthy and influential music lover *Mrs. Bixby* in *Micro-Phonies*.

Ralph—Immutable Stooges Law #75: A person who answers a door that is being knocked on by a Stooge will have his forehead knocked on by that Stooge after the door is opened. Although Ralph is assistant to an insane professor who experiments with beheadings in *Dopey Dicks*, his head is most at risk while answering a door being knocked on by Moe.

Ralph Dimsal—Grouchy boss of the Stooges in *The Three Stooges Meet Hercules*, he roughs up *Schuyler Davis* but loves *Diane*.

"Ramonones Sequidimes," by Fleeacrons—There is no record in the history of music to confirm the existence of the composition "Ramonones Sequidimes" or the composer "Fleeacrons," but that does not stop Moe from announcing that the Stooges will perform it in *Termites of 1938*.

Rance Roden—Underhanded land grabber in *The Outlaws Is Coming*. Roden is willing to slaughter millions of buffalo to own the Wild West, so it is his pleasure to add the hides of three pesty deputies to his endangered-species list.

Rancho Golf Club—Site of the *Panther Brewing Company*'s annual golf tournament in *Three Little Beers*. Until the Stooges' entry into the tournament, the Rancho was among the most beautifully manicured courses in the country.

Randolph Stuart III—Cunning alias of one *Vickers Cavendish*, con man extraordinaire in *The Three Stooges Go Around the World in a Daze*.

Raribonga—Anthropologists still don't know much about the island of Raribonga, from the film *Hula-La-La*. But it is safe to assume that when three dance instructors of dubious grace are sent to teach the natives to rumba, that island has not yet lifted itself from the ranks of the Third World.

Reardon—Diabolical fire engine salesman in *Flat Foot Stooges*.

On the lookout for head-shrinking Raribongan natives (*Hula-La-La*, 1951)

Recruiting Headquarters—IMMUTABLE STOOGES LAW #76: No Stooge escape is final. IMMUTABLE STOOGES LAW #77: No matter how clear the coast, the Stooges have not seen the last of their enemy. In *Boobs in Arms*, Moe, Larry, and Curly narrowly escape the clutches of a jealous husband by joining an anonymous-looking bread line. The line, however, leads into an army recruiting center, which happens to employ the very same jealous husband so eager for revenge on the Stooges.

Red Dog Canyon—Most adult children think that their filial duty ends when they write a check to the local nursing home. But they could learn a valuable lesson by watching *Oil's Well That Ends Well*, in which Moe, Larry, and Joe risk life and limb prospecting for uranium at the Red Dog Canyon. Their goal isn't riches or fame, just the money to pay for dear old dad's operation.

Red Dog Saloon—Western speakeasy where trouble brews alongside the beer in *Out West*, *Pals and Gals*, and *Punchy Cowpunchers*.

Red Morgan—Notorious bank bandit whose crooked capers are put on ice when the gunslinging Stooges mosey into town in *Phony Express* and *Merry Mavericks*.

Republic of Cannabeer, P.U.—Nation whose draft board is losing patience with the Stooges in *Dizzy Pilots*. Its representative, *Joe Strubachincoscow*, gives the Stooges only thirty days to complete work on their revolutionary aircraft, **The Buzzard**. This short deadline seems unfair until one sees The Buzzard and realizes how many years—even centuries—of work still remain.

Republic of Televania Naval Base— Top-secret military site where espionage and intrigue figure dramatically in the lives of three Navy dry cleaners in *Three Little Sew and Sews*.

Rhum Boogie—Exotic island in *Some More of Samoa*. Travel buffs are invariably seduced by the film's opening title, which paints an irresistible picture of a tropical paradise: "Rhum Boogie—Where the Natives Live in Bamboo Huts on Milk From Contented Coconuts."

"Rich Oil Man Gets Divorce Yesterday—Gets New Bride Today"— Racy headline announcing the wedding of Shemp Howard, Sr., to **Daisy Flowers** in *Up in Daisy's Penthouse*.

Rita—Reluctant fiancée of the *Governor of Dead Man's Island* in *Three Little Pirates*. Rita finds it necessary to bust the Stooges out of jail despite their state-of-the-art collection of jailbreak tools.

Rite Bar—The sixteenth establishment the Stooges have visited in a desperate

and unsuccessful search for a glass of beer in *Beer Barrel Polecats*.

Roast Stooge—Nonscrumptious-sounding item on the natives' menu in *Some More of Samoa*. While it is presumptuous to judge a foreign people based on their customs, one feels certain that natives on the island of **Rhum Boogie** would have been less inclined to roast Curly for supper if only they'd known him better.

Roberta—Stringbean-shaped accomplice to thieves Shemp and Larry in *Cuckoo on the Choo Choo*. See also **Nora**.

"Rock-Caught Sea Bass . . ."—Given the mind-boggling selection of fish offered by the Stooges' fish truck in *Cookoo Cavaliers*, it's a wonder they're not still in business today. The menu was made even more tempting by the jingle Moe rapped out in jiving rhythm to promote the daily specials (as Curly and Larry danced in step):

Moe:

> We have rock-caught
>   sea bass
> Albacore and pickerool
> Sand dab yellowtail
> Tuna fish and mackerel
> Bluefish, sailfish, half-and-
>   half and if you wish
> Swordfish, whitefish, herring,
>   and gefilte fish!

Curly and Larry: And that ain't all!

Rockwood Steel, Ranacoma Copper, Your American Can, Pinpoint Pimple—Stocks that Moe follows on the financial page in *Space Ship Sappy*. When Larry asks about Your American Can,

Moe regretfully informs him that "it's slipping."

Rocky and Mrs. Duggan—She's pretty and needs to borrow a cup of sugar from the Stooges. He makes his living as a strongman who tears telephone books in half. Sugar never cost three men as much as it did the Stooges in *Gents in a Jam*.

Romani Artistic Woodwork—Elegant woodworking studio in *Slippery Silks* that should have had better reason to believe its three workmen were trained in the art of handling priceless antiques.

Room 13—Area in which *K. O. Stradivarius* (Curly) trains—and flirts—in preparation for his big fight against *Killer Kilduff* in *Punch Drunks*.

Room 310—See *"Vacancies Exist."*

Room 810—In the Stooges' day, almost anything was permitted inside a hotel suite. But destructive incidents like the one in Room 810 of the *Hotel Snazzy Plaza* in *Idle Roomers* have made it impossible nowadays to rent rooms to insane wolfmen who dislike bumbling bellhops.

Room 1717—See *Clinton Arms Hotel*.

"Rooms $1 a Month—Free Showers When it Rains"—Irresistible selling point advertised by the *Happy Haven Hotel* in *Loco Boy Makes Good*.

Route 66—Romantic wine served by stately servants Moe, Larry, and Curly Joe on the occasion of *Phileas Fogg III*'s candlelight dinner with *Amelia Carter* in *The Three Stooges Go Around the World in a Daze*.

Routine Number Six—Peppery give-and-take ordered by Moe and dished from the palm of Larry's hand to defeat an enemy henchman in *Hot Stuff*.

"Rubbish Permit 186"—Sign that hangs from the law-abiding Stooges' garbage truck in *Hoi Polloi*.

Ruby Clutch—See *Little Red Book*.

Rue de Schlemiel and **Rue de le Pew**—Parisian hotspots where Shemp's and Joe's torrid romances blossom with *Fifi* in *Love at First Bite* and *Fifi Blows Her Top*, respectively.

Rumsford—Millionaire at wits' end over wife *Sheri*'s carefree derring-do in *Three Sappy People*. Rumsford spares no expense in summoning three brilliant psychiatrists to treat his eccentric wife. One *good* psychiatrist might have been enough.

S

....

St. Patrick's Day—If a detective can be measured by the grittiness of his aliases, Shemp is the modern day Sherlock Holmes. In *Blunder Boys*, he is known variously as St. Patrick's Day, *Independence Day*, *New Year's Day*, *Christmas Day*, *Groundhog Day*, and *Labor Day*. See also *Halliday* and *Tarraday*.

Salve—Socialites, while well-mannered, are often characterized by a distasteful me-only attitude. This is amply demonstrated in *All the World's a Stooge*, where guests at a swank party think only of themselves after Curly mistakenly treats his chest cold with *Limburger cheese spread* instead of salve.

Sam Shovel—Private investigator in *Dopey Dicks* who chooses three office workers less meticulously than he chooses cases.

San Brandon Penitentiary—IMMUTABLE STOOGES LAW #78: The Stooges will tune in radio warnings about impending danger just seconds before that danger shows up on their doorstep. In *Pardon My Backfire*, the Stooges' ears perk up when they hear a radio warning about three cutthroat convicts driving a bum car who escaped from the San Brandon Penitentiary, an institution located precariously close to the Stooges' auto-repair business.

Sandra Sandpile—Star of the radio program "Here's Mud In Your Eye," as concocted by Moe during a broadcast at *Radio KGBY* in *Micro-Phonies*.

Sandwiches—IMMUTABLE STOOGES LAW #79: Sandwiches prepared by the Stooges are more likely than not to bite or otherwise attack them (various films).

SAP 752—Vanity license plate attached to the Stooges' fish truck in *Booby Dupes*.

Sappington—IMMUTABLE STOOGES LAW #80: Butlers featured in Stooge films will be inadequately schooled in the art of discouraging pie fights. In *Half-Wits Holiday* and *Pies and Guys*, stately butler Sappington does well to maintain a regal posture while pastries fly at a society dinner but could not have prevented what is inevitable when a host selects pie as the dinner's featured dessert.

"Say a few syllables! Utter a few adjectives!"—Moe's impassioned plea to the prison warden after Curly mistakenly decks the warden in *Beer Barrel Polecats*.

Schlemiel Number Eight—Fine talcum powder applied—without moderation—by the Stooges in *Hokus Pokus*.

Schmow—Train car where the action unfolds in *Cuckoo on the Choo Choo*.

Schnapps—Joe is a loyal brother in *Horsing Around*, and he does what any loving sibling would do for a sister who was reincarnated as a horse: he saves her mate, Schnapps, from a trip to the glue factory.

Schuyler Davis—A 98-pound weakling inventor who, with the Stooges' constant encouragement, builds himself into Hercules' equal and wins the hand of the beautiful *Diane* in *The Three Stooges Meet Hercules*.

Scowling Scotsman—See *"Are you short of money? . . ."*

Scotland Yard—As detectives with a bloodhound's nose for intrigue in *Hot Scots* and *Hot Ice*, it is only natural that the Stooges' first case comes from Scotland Yard, even if they did arrive there by answering an ad looking for "yard men."

Seabasket—Thoroughbred of dubious bloodline purchased by the Stooges in *Even as I.O.U.*

Seabiscuit Food Corporation—Company that employs the Stooges in *Muscle Up a Little Closer*. Their irresistible motto: "Seabiscuit Gives You an Appetite Like a Horse."

"Secondhand"—How an unimpressed Larry in *Tassels in the Air* describes an antique table when told it belonged to Louis the XVI.

Secretary of the Offense, Secretary of the Inferior, and Toastmaster

General—High-ranking government positions Moe expects for the Stooges after they cast the deciding presidential election votes in *Three Dark Horses*.

Seeress of Roebuck—Clairvoyant consulted by ruthless dictator *Moe Hailstone* in *I'll Never Heil Again*. Roebuck's advice to Hailstone is never fully revealed, but the sight of Hailstone's head hanging in a trophy room at film's end is an unflattering testimonial for psychics everywhere.

Sellwell Advertising Company—Promotional firm with a heart. Sellwell hires the Stooges in *Busy Buddies* without ever suggesting that their recent failure as restaurateurs implied anything about their ability to hang posters for a local cow-milking contest.

Seltzer bottles—IMMUTABLE STOOGES LAW #81: Despite its potential as an effective weapon, a seltzer bottle used by the Stooges will never be aimed correctly (various films).

Semert, anacome, senetoonum, anacanaponner, peenanar, anasinic, cotton, anic, needles, scissors, and more cotton—Precision surgical tools called for by Moe during his delicate surgery on *Dr. Graves* in *Men in Black*. The operation appears successful, but the odds of recovering the tools plummet when the patient walks away with the sound of metal ringing from his body.

Señor Louis Balero Cantino—Debonair baritone in *Pardon My Scotch* who consents to sing at a party, but never agrees to have fruit fired into his mouth by three Scottish distillers who don't fancy opera.

Señorita Cucaracha—Although he is only posing as opera star Señorita Cucaracha in *Micro-Phonies*, Curly's dramatic ability to lip-synch complex classical recordings suggests a lifetime of careful opera training.

Señorita Rita—While Curly's take-no-prisoners approach to flirtation may not be appropriate for all suitors, it works wonders on the lovely Señorita Rita, whose fluttering heart compels her to save the lives of the Stooges—repeatedly—in *Saved by the Belle*.

Señors Mucho and Gusto—Before the Three Tenors there were Señors Mucho and Gusto (Larry and Moe), two virtuoso musicians whose majestic voices and unconventional interpretations in *Micro-Phonies* make it slightly easier to accept that Curly is world-famous opera star *Señorita Cucaracha*.

Serena Flint—Kindly old prune whose wrinkles and snail's pace won't be tolerated by her husband, the hard-hearted *Amos Flint*, in *All Gummed Up* and *Bubble Trouble*. When the Stooges' *Fountain of Youth* serum turns Mrs. Flint into a dazzling blonde, however, Flint sets the

world speed record for a change of heart about a woman.

Sergeant MacGillicuddy—Strong-armed army officer in *Half Shot Shooters* who feels it his duty to beat up three soldiers simply because they slept through World War I.

Señorita Cucaracha (Curly) performs a stirring rendition of "Voices of Spring" while accompanied by Señors Mucho (Larry) and Gusto (Moe) (*Micro-Phonies*, 1945).

Shemp's Fountain of Youth is a success! The proof: ravishing former octogenarian Serena Flint (Christine McIntyre) (*All Gummed Up*, 1947).

Sergeant Mullins—Army officer in *Punchy Cowpunchers* who is demoted to private after an assault he intends for the Stooges lands on the body of his superior, the ill-humored *Captain Daley*.

"Sextetrum Lucia"—Magnificent piece of opera learned quickly by the Stooges in *Micro-Phonies* after the original recording they intended to lip-synch—*"Voices of Spring"*—is broken on Curly's forehead by a frustrated Moe. Also, the melody selected by the Stooges to perform the seductive *"Oh, Elaine"* in *Squareheads of the Round Table* and *Knutzy Knights*.

Shamus O'Brien—Name partner in the talent agency of *Goldberg, Ginsberg, Rosenberg, and O'Brien* in *What's the Matador?* The short-tempered O'Brien might have done well by his other clients, but the Stooges should have been assigned to an agent with a deeper appreciation for three-man comedy bullfight acts.

Shangri-La Upholstering Company—Although the Stooges were known to exercise inconsistent caution with needles, they never gave up on working with fabrics, as evidenced by the Shangri-La Upholstering Company, their thriving business in *Hugs and Mugs*.

"She broke it off"—Larry's explanation in *Tricky Dicks* to describe what became of his sister's engagement to a man with a broken leg.

"She loves me, she loves me not . . ."—Moe is a romantic at heart, and uses an age-old method to determine his lover's true intentions in *I'm a Monkey's Uncle* and *Stone Age Romeos*: he pulls out tufts of Larry's hair, repeating with each yank, "She loves me, she loves me not . . ."

"She Was Bred in Old Kentucky"—Curly was certainly not the first great cook to sing while preparing a recipe, but his rendition of "She Was Bred in Old Kentucky" in *I Can Hardly Wait* remains an inspiration to every chef who knows the joys of fixing a first-rate ham:

> She was bred in old Kentucky
> But she's only a crumb up here
> She's knock-kneed and double jointed
> With a cauliflower ear
> Someday we shall be married
> And if vegetables get too dear
> I'll cut myself a nice big slice
> Of her cauliflower ear
> ('Cause that ain't rationed!)

(Note to music historians: The Stooges also used "Bred" as their signature theme while performing as nightclub singers *Nill, Null, and Void* in *Loco Boy Makes Good*, but Moe is barely able to begin before the tomatoes fly.)

Shempetta—Knee-weakening portrait model in *Self Made Maids* who might have made her mark as one of cinema's great sex symbols had it not been for her uncanny resemblance to Shemp. See also *Moella* and *Larraine*.

Sheri Rumsford—Thrill-seeking millionairess bored by society life and a stodgy husband in *Three Sappy People*. Sheri discovers that while money is no cure for tedium, three phone repairmen posing as psychiatrists might be.

Shickelgruber—The term Moe uses to refer to a well-known German dictator in *They Stooge to Conga* and *Higher Than a Kite*.

Shingled roof—Delicious drink ordered by Larry in *A Merry Mix-Up*. When the waiter looks puzzled by the name of the drink, Larry explains, "It's on the house!"

Shmow—Treacherous stronghold ruled by the cutthroat **Emir of Shmow** in *Malice in the Palace*. The Stooges' trip to Shmow is testament not only to their iron wills but to the confidence they had in their Santa Claus disguises.

Shock Absorber for Earthquakes—Although Curly was known for brilliant inventions (his **Gold Collar Button Retriever** comes quickly to mind) perhaps none was as gracefully simple as the Shock Absorber for Earthquakes. Sold with great success in *Saved by the Belle*, the Absorber consisted of a pillow tied to the rear end of its owner, a truly affordable solution to a life-threatening hazard.

Shtunk Manufacturing Company—Shtunk, the makers of *Vitamins A.P.U.*, which Moe takes for nerves in *Idiots Deluxe* and *Guns A Poppin*, will never use Moe as a celebrity spokesman.

Signor—Menacing tenor who will stop at nothing to halt the virtuoso performance of *Señorita Cucaracha* (Curly) and her accompanists *Señors Mucho and Gusto* (Larry and Moe) in *Micro-Phonies*.

Silver—A cowboy is nothing without his horse, even if that horse happens to be a bicycle. In *Yes, We Have No Bonanza*, Curly rides into a sleepy Western town on a bike he calls, simply, Silver.

Silverware—Immutable Stooges Law #82: Fine silverware will find its way into the Stooges' pockets during high-society parties (various films).

"Simple Simon"—As royal minstrels in *Fiddlers Three*, the Stooges pay tribute to the timeless power of the nursery rhyme with this interpretation of the classic:

> *Simple Simon met a pie man going to the fair*
> *Said Simple Simon to the pie man,*
> * "Lemme taste your ware!"*
> *Said the pie man to Simple Simon, "Show*
> * me first your penny"*
> *Said Simple Simon to the pie man, "Scram,*
> * you don't get any!"*

The Stooges also recite *"Jack and Jill"* and *"Little Miss Muffet,"* though regrettably without quite the same verve and wit.

Simplex Rodent Exterminator—Engineering marvel invented by Moe to eradicate mice in *Termites of 1938*. While the use of a cannon to end a mouse's life was revolutionary, Moe took insufficient care to prevent the device from firing at its inventor.

Sing Sing, Alcatraz, Leavenworth, Joliet—Prisons represented by pennants hung on a wall during a jailhouse party in *Three Smart Saps*.

Singapore Joe's Palace Hotel—Hotel in *Saved by the Belle* that does not look kindly upon guests who run up unpayable beer tabs.

Sir Moeington—See *Lord Larryington and Sir Moeington*.

Sir Satchel—Right-hand man to the wicked **Black Prince** in *Squareheads of the Round Table* and *Knutzy Knights*.

6⅞—Insulting prison uniform number issued to ideal inmate Larry in *So Long Mr. Chumps* and *Beer Barrel Polecats*. Larry's hard work inside the penitentiary should have earned him a solid integer, if not early parole itself. See also **A.A.M. Local 6⅞**. Also, 6⅞ is Larry's affiliation number with the **Needlock Appliance Corp.** in *I Can Hardly Wait*.

"Six lions were tearing me apart bit by bit!"—IMMUTABLE STOOGES LAW #83: Minor injuries will always seem major to the Stooges. In *The Ghost Talks* and *Creeps*, a slithery frog slips down the back of Shemp's workman's uniform, causing him to report to Moe that "Six lions were tearing me apart bit by bit!" Moe's unsympathetic reply: "Quit lyin'."

67 Cents Net—Paltry sum left to **Curly Q. Link** by uncle Bob O. Link in *If a Body Meets a Body*.

"Six Tetrum Lucy"—Posing as opera star **Señorita Cucaracha** in *Micro-Phonies*, Curly is forced to lip-synch to a recording of *"Voices of Spring."* When Moe shatters the platter on Curly's head, the Stooges must find another record. Luckily, Larry discovers a disc called "Six Tetrum Lucy,"

prompting Moe to ask Curly, "Can you sing it?" Curly's confession: "I can't even say it!" See also *"Sextetrum Lucia."*

Skagway, Alaska—See *Edam Neckties*.

Skeleton fish—See *"Tuna fish . . ."*

Skin—Joe's hair color, as described by Moe to police in *Quiz Whizz*. See also *"About five-foot-five by five-foot-five."*

Skin and Flint Finance Corporation—By any standards, the name Skin and Flint Finance Corporation inspires a limited measure of confidence. But the Stooges should have been tipped off to the company's questionable reputation when they dealt with its president, the shady-sounding **I. Fleecem**, in *Sing a Song of Six Pants* and *Rip, Sew and Stitch*.

Skullbone Pass—IMMUTABLE STOOGES LAW #84: Nothing transports the Stooges faster than the bicycle built for three. In *The Three Troubledoers*, Sheriff Curly and his two deputies must reach Skullbone Pass before sunset to bust up a lawless marriage, and they aren't taking any chances traveling by horse.

Sky Aircraft Company—Aviation firm in *Dizzy Pilots* that sends two representatives to evaluate the Stooges' experimental aircraft, **The Buzzard**. They seem like a couple of swell guys, but even the most forgiving observer would have been compelled to report that the Stooges fell out of the *Buzzard* during one of the plane's tricky rollover maneuvers.

Skyscrapers—IMMUTABLE STOOGES LAW #85: The Stooges will lose their sense of balance when in, on, or around the top of a tall building (various films).

Slap-Happy Gym—Site where blood, sweat, and tears flow for the Stooge-trained boxer **Chopper Kane** in *Fling in the Ring*.

Slick Chick—Detective Shemp in *Tricky Dicks* should have kept an eagle's eye fixed on a pretty suspect with a name like Slick Chick. Instead, he is charmed . . . and pickpocketed.

Slipp, Tripp, and Skipp—Investment brokerage firm in *Hold That Lion!* and *Loose Loot*. It may be that Tripp and Skipp are fine fellows, but partner **Icabod Slipp**—who punches out three rightful heirs to an estate he is handling—casts a disreputable shadow over the entire firm.

"Slippery Fingers"—You don't acquire a tough-as-nails nickname like "Slippery Fingers" until you've pulled the kind of big-time bank capers **Terry Hargen** has in *Sing a Song of Six Pants* and *Rip, Sew and Stitch*.

Slug McGurk—Homicide victim in *Tricky Dicks* who surely would have killed the Stooges for botching his murder investigation if he weren't already dead.

"A small kingdom . . ."—In *Fiddlers Three* and *Musty Musketeers*, the action takes place in **Coleslawvania**, "a small kingdom in ye old country where ye men are men and ye women are glad of it."

"Smells like somebody's frying onions!"—Curly's keen sense of smell was never more focused than in *Three Little Sew and Sews*, when after sitting on a burning cigar he remarks, "Smells like somebody's frying onions!"

The Smiling Egyptians—Used chariot dealership owned by the Stooges in *Mummy's Dummies*. A likely improvement over other ancient Egyptian used chariot establishments, The Smiling Egyptians gave customers a two-out-of-three chance of getting a square deal when buying from salesmen **Honest Moe, Honest Shemp, and Larry**.

Let's hope Shemp is wearing asbestos knickers (**Fiddlers Three**, 1948).

Smiling Sam McGann—Maybe Smiling Sam McGann got his friendly moniker earlier in life, perhaps when he was more patient and forgiving. He most certainly did not earn the "smiling" nickname, however, while overseeing the Stooges' repair work in *Monkey Businessmen*.

Smithers—In *The Yoke's on Me*, Smithers thinks he's getting the best of it when he sells his farm to the Stooges for $1,000 cash and their car. The cash, at least, will come in handy.

Smitty—Gritty newshound in *Commotion on the Ocean* who frantically phones the *Daily Gazette* newspaper with a hot tip about stolen atomic documents.

Smorgasbord Castle—It is castles like Smorgasbord—haunted by talking suits of armor, chess-playing skeletons, and

mischievous owls in *The Ghost Talks* and *Creeps*—that give a bad name to legitimate castles everywhere.

Snow White—Lovely and pure as the driven snow, she falls for **Prince Charming**—and develops a soft spot for the Stooges, too—in *Snow White and the Three Stooges*.

"So it shouldn't be a total loss, I'm taking a bath!"—In *Gents Without Cents*, Curly tumbles accidentally into a bathtub, but pulls out a soap and a brush, telling Moe and Larry, "So it shouldn't be a total loss, I'm taking a bath!"

"So We Stuck Our Little Tootsies in the Water"—Most royal troubadours would be insulted by a guard who challenges their qualifications. But in *Squareheads of the Round Table* and *Knutzy Knights*, the Stooges are happy to per-

With such sweet music in the air, it is impossible for Snow White (Carol Heiss) to resist the charms of debonair ventriloquist Quatro the Magnificent (Edson Stroll) (*Snow White and the Three Stooges*, 1961).

form a short medieval favorite to prove they are of noble voice:

> (A-one, a-two, a-three . . .)
> *So we stuck our little tootsies in the water*
> *And we ducked under the waves we did*
> *Ha ha!*

Sodium bicarbonate and popcorn— Key ingredients the Stooges use in *Have Rocket, Will Travel* to inject "fizz" and "bounce" into the rocket fuel recipe they are devising.

"Somebody's roasting a ham!"— Shemp's opinion after he sits on a sizzling iron in *Hugs and Mugs.*

"Somewhere in the Orient"— Mesmerizing opening title for *Malice in the Palace,* which captures the exotic sights, sounds, and intrigue of the Far East. The dramatic full screen reads, "Somewhere in the Orient—Café Casbahbah—Meeting Place of Black Sheep—Bah-Bah-Bah."

South Starv-Vania—Any military general worth his stripes knows that if you master the geography of South Starv-Vania, you have taken your first step toward ruling the world. This lesson was not lost on ruthless dictator **Moe Hailstone** in *You Nazty Spy,* who studies a map showing the South Starv-Vanian countries and waterways listed below:

> *Countries:* Asperin, Hang Gover, Bath, Hotcha, Gin Rickia, Bolonia, Nux Vomica, Double Crossia, Moronika, Mikey Finlen, Shonzi, Chin Chin, Kotchke, Oomphola.
>
> *Waterways:* Razzle Lake, Dazzle Lake, Look Sea, See Sea, Bay of Window, Sea of Biscuit, Bay of Rum.

Southern Comforter—When Judith, enchanting daughter of **Colonel Buttz** in *Uncivil Warriors,* unknowingly bakes a cake containing feathers, she tells the Stooges that the cake is called Southern Comfort. Moe, in between laborious chews and in a moment of culinary insight, replies that the cake tastes more like "Southern Comforter."

"Speak for yourself, rodent!"—Moe's independent-minded response in *Nutty but Nice* after Larry declares that the Stooges are trapped like rats.

Spectus-on-the-floorus—Although the Stooges are janitors in *A Gem of a Jam,* their diagnosis of a dirty floor rings like something straight from *Gray's Anatomy:*

Curly:	*I think it's a bad case of Spectus-on-the-floorus.*
Moe:	*Then we should use plenty of sulpha thya-soap.*
Larry:	*I wouldn't say yes, but I couldn't say no.*
Curly:	*Would you say maybe?*
Larry:	*I might.*
Moe:	*Soap be it.*

Speedy Termite Exterminators— Stooge-run outfit summoned to eliminate pests at Hollywood film studio **B.O. Pictures** in *Studio Stoops.*

Spiffingham—Skittish butler hired by flimflam artists Moe and Larry in *Heavenly Daze.* The presence of Spiffingham is intended to impress the **DePeysters,** but when Shemp's invisible ghost terrifies Spiffingham, Mr. DePeyster remarks that the butler looks as if he's seen a ghost. "Mister," says the spooked Spiffingham, "you don't know the half of it!"

Spike and Butch—No-good kidnappers of *Mr. Williams* in *Nutty but Nice*. Their crime seemed perfect, but Spike and Butch never figured on kidnapping a yodeler—or tangling with three brave singing waiters who could yodel a lick or two themselves.

Spirit of Sir Tom—No one has done more to portray spooky spirits in a positive light than the spirit of Sir Tom, a noble ghost trapped inside an ancient suit of armor in *The Ghost Talks* and *Creeps*. Without resorting to the terror or mayhem favored by other ghosts, Tom relies on sentiment to persuade the Stooges to let him wait for his long-lost love *Lady Godiva*.

Square Deal Swap Shop—Storefront business in *No Census, No Feeling* whose owner does not live up to his shop's name when he discovers the Stooges asleep in his shop's awning.

"Squeak, squeak"—Joe's candid reply in *Sappy Bullfighters* when Moe challenges his honor by demanding to know if he is a man or a mouse.

Squid McGuffey's Café—Notorious hangout of *Dapper Dan* and his thugs in *Crime on Their Hands*.

S.S. Dotty—Rickety ship in *Back from the Front* that harkens back to the days when naval construction standards were lax. Today, no American ship sails unless it can easily withstand the bumblings of *at least* three clumsy merchant mariners.

S.S. Shickelgruber—Nazi warship that is no match for three scrappy American sailors and their dog *Fido* in *Back from the Front*.

Stage 7—Scene of the Stooge-run movie production in *Movie Maniacs*. Moe, Larry, and Curly turn the current romance into something . . . avant-garde.

Stage 19—Dance rehearsal hall where three lovely students learn the finer points of ballet from instructor Shemp in *Hula-La-La*.

Star Cleaning & Pressing Company—Launderers who employ the Stooges to deliver clothing in *Crash Goes the Hash*. Although the company figures only incidentally in the film, the slogans painted on their truck remain a model for dry cleaners of today: "Daily Delivery" and "We Dye For You."

Star Dispatch—Newspaper in *Dutiful but Dumb* that carries the shocking headline, "Percival De Puyster Elopes—Movie Star and Bride Elude Photographers."

Start at Jerkola, go down the Insane River, over the Giva Dam, through Pushover, across Shmowland to the Stronghold of Shmow—The strategic course Moe plots before the Stooges attempt to recover the *King Rootin' Tootin' Diamond* in *Malice in the Palace*.

Starvania—Continent that has fallen to the sword of ruthless dictator *Moe Hailstone* in *I'll Never Heil Again*.

Hailstone proves himself an expert of geography and terrain by nimbly reviewing the maze of Starvanian countries and waterways shown on a sketchy relief map:

Countries: Great Mitten, Cast Toria, Hot Foot, I Ran, He Ran, She Ran, They Ran, Also Ran, Slap Happia, Pushover, Moronica, Bulge-area, Atisket, Atasket, Staywayoff, Jerkola, Rubid-din, Big Zipper, Toot Sweet, Jug O'Saliva.

Waterways: Hot Sea, Tot Sea, Cornychew Straights, Straights of Rye, Cant Sea.

Starvania is also the exotic land to which the Stooges travel to recover the ***King Rootin' Tootin' Diamond*** in *Malice in the Palace*. Moe proves himself to be an expert cartographer by identifying most of the following lands and waterways on a map of Starvania:

Countries: Great Mitten, Rubid-din, Hot Foot, Staywayoff, Woo Woo, Oomphola, Hangover, Snowland, No Land, Shmowland, Stronghold of Shmow, I Ran, He Ran, She Ran, They Ran, Also Ran, Slap Happia, Truck on Down, Pushover, Jerkola, Atisket, Ataskct, Cast Oria, Mickey Finlen.

Waterways: Corneychew Straights, Hot Sea, Tot Sea, Cant Sea, Bay of Window, Bay of Rum, Lake of Lamb, Insane River, Giva Dam.

State of Anemia—Two facts can be gleaned about the State of Anemia by watching *Fuelin' Around* and *Hot Stuff*:

Two seafaring merchant marines doing their duty aboard the S.S. *Shickelgruber* (*Back from the Front*, 1943).

First, Anemian rulers condone kidnapping as a means of forcing a brilliant inventor to reveal his priceless formula; second, Anemian intelligence needs plenty of brush-up work, as they mistake Larry for that brilliant inventor.

Steelia Pumpernickel, Amelia Schwartzbrut, and Celia Schweipak—Alluring German spies with an uncanny ability to sniff out three bumbling imposters in *No Dough Boys*.

Moe teaches an Anemian soldier not to point (*Fuelin' Around,* 1949).

Stella, Nella, and Bella—The Stooges' weeping fiancées in *Three Smart Saps*.

Steve—See *Mr. Jerry Pip and Steve*.

Stincoala, Moronica—Site of the *Wrong Brothers*' experimental test flight in *Dizzy Pilots*. But for an unintended somersault here and an accidental loop-the-loop there, Stincoala would surely have become known as the modern day Kitty Hawk.

Stink—Life wasn't all bad for harem girls in *Ancient Egypt—In the Reign of the Great King Rootentooten*. Sure, they had to cater to the every whim of royal chamberlains like the Stooges in *Mummy's Dummies*, but they were provided with some of life's niceties, too, among them the exotic and aromatic perfume Stink.

Stix Fast Glue—Product that Moe mistakes for maple syrup in *Healthy, Wealthy and Dumb* and *A Missed Fortune*.

Stockyards 1234—See *"When in Chicago . . ."*

Stooge Follies—Variety show commissioned by millionaire *Mr. Boyce* and starring the Stooges and their girls *Hilda, Wilda, and Tilda* in *Rhythm and Weep*.

"The Stooges have landed and have the situation well in hand!"—What a saluting Moe triumphantly tells the U.S. Cavalry upon their arrival at the **Red Dog Saloon** in *Out West*.

"Stop Look and Listen"—Moe drifted from job to job in Stooge films, but he was no loafer. Finding himself unemployed in *Pop Goes the Easel*, Moe enthusiastically offers his services to anyone within reading distance of his sign: "Stop Look and Listen—Social Secretary Seeks Situation—Wages No Objection."

Storey's Saloon—Speakeasy favored by the trigger-happy, Stooge-hating **Noonan Brothers** in *Shot in the Frontier*.

Story Pictures of Farm Animals—Illustrated children's book used by Professor Quackenbush (see **Professors Rich and Nichols, Quackenbush and Sedletz**) to teach the Stooges to read in *Half-Wits Holiday*. See also *"Tar ytrid eeth say . . ."*

Mr. Stutz—Keenly suspicious doorman at the Stooges' apartment in *Mutts to You*. Stutz seems bent on enforcing the building's policy, *"No Dogs or Babies Allowed,"* an unfortunate break for three tenants who work as dog washers and happen upon an abandoned baby.

"Suitors in Third Week of Sit Down Strike"—Newspaper headline from the *Gazette Journal* that announces that the Stooges mean business in their demand to marry sweethearts **Corabell, Dorabell, and Florabell**. The headline reads, "Suitors in Third Week of Sit Down Strike—Persistent Lovers Win Nation's Sympathy as Gifts Pour In."

Sultan of Abadaba—Cheapskate spear thrower in *Three Little Twirps*. A man of Abadaba's talents should hire his own human targets and not take advantage of three reluctant amateurs unaccustomed to the terror such a position inevitably creates.

Sultan of Pish Posh—Although never seen, Pish Posh's influence is colossal in *Rumpus in the Harem*. While his ransom demand for the freedom of the Stooges' sweethearts was a common practice among sultans, his exhorbitant asking price (***1,000 Shilbleenas***) must have made the Stooges wonder whether **Heebah, Reebah, and Sheebah** were all that pretty under those alluring veils.

Sunev—Wondrous planetary destination for the Stooges in *Space Ship Sappy* and *Outer Space Jitters*. The opening title in *Outer Space Jitters* reads, "The Planet of Sunev—Somewhere in Outer Space—Sunev is Venus Spelled Backwards."

"Sunny-side down and don't turn 'em over"—Just because the general population likes its eggs scrambled does not mean that free-thinking Moe must order his that way. In *Idiots Deluxe* and *Guns A Poppin*, Moe orders his eggs "sunny-side down and don't turn 'em over," a variation with which chef Larry proves to be wholly unfamiliar.

Super Service—See *Acme Service Station*.

Super Slueth Detective Agency— Stooge-owned business in *Spooks* that tackles a tricky missing person/haunted mansion case. Effort is everything, but the Stooges probably should have stuck to the specialty advertised on their office door: "Divorce Evidence Manufactured to Your Order."

Super Terrific Productions—Visionary movie production company that casts Curly alongside another non-Method actor, a gorilla, in *Three Missing Links*.

Superior Warehouse and Storage Company—Dreary shipping company in *Three Arabian Nuts* made livelier by Shemp's discovery of a genie in a lamp.

Susquehana 2222—Telephone number of eccentric psychiatrists Drs. *Ziller, Zeller, and Zoller* in *Three Sappy People*. Also, phone number of the first dame Shemp dials in his hurry-up attempt to marry in *Brideless Groom*.

Swamp soup—One of two dinner choices offered to island natives in *Some More of Samoa*. Native or not, the other choice—*Roast Stooge*—just didn't look appetizing.

Swinehardt—Hot-tempered movie director who fails to appreciate the Stooges' avant-garde methods in *Movie Maniacs*.

"Swing it!"—See *"Swingeroo Joe."*

"Swingeroo Joe"—Audition song performed with oomph by the Stooges for eccentric millionaire **Mr. Boyce** in *Rhythm and Weep*. When Boyce asks if the Stooges know "Swingeroo Joe," Curly answers the way only a jazz man can: "Swing it!"

"Swinging the Alphabet"—There is not a Stooge fan today who cannot flawlessly recite the alphabet, an invaluable gift they owe directly to Moe, Larry, and Curly. In *Violent is the Word for Curly*, the Stooges use a college classroom to demonstrate their song "Swinging the Alphabet," a catchy little number that packs an educational wallop (to illustrate the letter "B"):

> *B–A —"Bay"*
> *B–E —"Bee"*
> *B–I —"Bickee Bye"*
> *B–O —"Boe"*
> *Bicky Bye Boe B–U —"Boo"*
> *Bicky Bye Boe Boo!*

(Note to readers still shaky with their ABCs: to learn the rest of the alphabet, make substitutions for the letter "B" above.)

"A swiss cheese"—What Moe says he feels like after Larry and Joe remove the carpenter's tacks they fired into his rear end from a machine gun.

T.B.—Although Moe is no doctor, he makes an accurate diagnosis in *Three Smart Saps*. While trying to fit a belt around Curly's waist, he remarks that things would work more smoothly if Curly didn't suffer from "T.B." When Curly questions the assessment, Moe explains: "Two Bellies."

T. E. Higgins—Sheriff of Lobo City in *Whoops, I'm an Indian!* Higgins's enthusiasm for law enforcement is admirable, but he might have gone overboard by offering a reward for the Stooges' capture ***"Dead or in Bad Shape."***

T.H.—Never has command of the alphabet been so crucial as in *Sing a Song of Six Pants* and *Rip, Sew and Stitch*. At their tailor shop the Stooges find a suit jacket with the initials "T.H." embroidered inside. Never nimble with their ABCs, Larry and Shemp theorize that the jacket belongs to either "Teddy Hoosevelt" or "Thomas Hedison." But Moe's steel-trap mind uncovers a more sinister connection: "T.H." could also stand for ***Terry Hargen***, a notorious holdup man capable of busting more than bank safes were he to find the three tailors holding his lucky jacket.

T.S.—Debilitating disease Curly claims he suffers from in *Three Sappy People*. Further explanation reveals his sad condition: Two Stomachs.

"Tar ytrid eeth say. Glug zap snorglots ramitz. Ronassonce kibertz."—Passage read by Moe from a children's book in *Half-Wits Holiday*. Some doctors might have labeled Moe a dyslexic for his unusual recitation, but the observant Professor Quackenbush (see **Professors Rich and Nichols, Quackenbush and Sedletz**) diagnoses a more basic problem: the book is upside-down.

Tarantula—Curly's term for the succulent-looking crab he finds at the buffet table in *Matri-Phony*.

Tarraday—Larry's role as a crafty gumshoe in *Blunder Boys*. See also **Halliday** and *St. Patrick's Day*.

"Tastes more like marshmallow gumbo"—Larry's opinion of a cake baked by **Serena Flint** in *All Gummed Up* and *Bubble Trouble*. Serena meant to use marshmallows but instead used bubble gum to decorate the cake she calls "marshmallow jumbo."

"Teatro Internacional"—Majestic bullfighting arena in *Sappy Bullfighters* whose billboards trumpet a marvelous overseas arrival: "Teatro Internacional Presenta The Three Stooges—Comicos

1010 Tobacco Road— Address of the Coffin Nail Cigarette Company, sponsors of a $50,000 slogan contest won by Curly in *Healthy, Wealthy and Dumb.*

$10,000—Eye-popping amount wagered by Professor Nichols (see **Professors Rich and Nichols, Quackenbush and Sedletz**) in *Hoi Polloi* on the proposition that he could transform the Stooges into gentlemen with three months' proper training. Sadly for Nichols, the three-month investment was even harder to endure than the loss of $10,000.

Serena Flint (Christine McIntyre) presents her trademark dessert, the delicious (and sticky) marshmallow jumbo (All Gummed Up, 1947).

Americanos." Had the Teatro's owners any class, they would have renamed the joint "Joe Besser Arena" in honor of the only bullfighter in the stadium's history to challenge a bull to a head-on collision—and win.

Telephone calls—IMMUTABLE STOOGES LAW #86: When chased by a bloodthirsty crook, the Stooges' most effective method of escape will be to pick up the nearest telephone and inform the crook that he has a call (various films).

"Tell him to dial inflammation"— Moe's recommendation to a patient in *Dizzy Doctors* who calls the hospital for advice on inflammation.

10 degrees below zero—Reading shown on a thermometer used to take the dying Shemp's temperature in *Bedlam in Paradise.*

A Tenth-Century Ras Bañas Ya-tee Benafucci a Timi Nicaronjee—The vase Curly tries to sell a palace guard in *Matri-Phony,* and sad proof that artisans peddled junk in the tenth century, too.

Terry Hargen—Holdup man nonpareil who is captured by the Stooges in their tailor shop in *Sing a Song of Six Pants* and *Rip, Sew and Stitch.* If Hargen had understood the debilitating effect of a blazing iron to the buttocks as well as he understood bank robbing, he might have avoided capture by the three brave tailors.

Tessie—See *Little Red Book.*

Thaddeus and Maggie Smirch— Nouveau riche couple who commission snooty French designer **Omay** to redecorate their house in *Tassels in the Air.*

Maggie is so keen on impressing new society friends that she neglects to check the credentials of the man who answers to the name of Omay—a man who turns out to be fond of pig latin and goes by the real name Moe.

"Thank you, Mr. Personally"—Gentlemanly reply by Moe, Larry, and Shemp in *A Missed Fortune* after a hotel manager tells them, "If I can be of further service, please call me personally."

"That babe sure can cook!"—Larry's joyous declaration after finding jailbreak tools baked into a loaf of bread by *Princess Elaine* in *Squareheads of the Round Table*.

"That's almost a million!"—Curly always kept a level head about money, but even he is shocked in *Cash and Carry* to hear that *Little Jimmy*'s leg operation will cost $500, declaring, "That's almost a million!"

"That's good; I never could dance before."—When Moe promises Shemp in *Booty and the Beast* that his severed leg will heal so well that he'll be dancing in six months, Shemp gratefully declares, "That's good; I never could dance before."

"That's in case you do and I'm not around"—Moe's startling explanation for hitting Larry and Curly even though they claim to have done nothing to deserve it in *Hoi Polloi*.

"That's nothin'. We had a bed that went back to Sears Roebuck the Third."—Curly and Shemp's worldly

reply to the manager of the *Hotel Costa Plente* in *Healthy, Wealthy and Dumb* (Curly) and *A Missed Fortune* (Shemp) upon being informed that the antique bed in their swank suite goes back to Henry the Eighth.

"That's too permanent!"—What a terrified Larry tells a gangster who has promised to kill him in *Pardon My Backfire*.

"Theatre Chit Chat"—Snooty newspaper column written by drama critic *Nick Barker* in *Three Hams on Rye*. Before he sees the show, Barker writes, "Another Broadway Turkey All Set to Lay an Egg—B.K. Doaks, Producer of Ten Flop Shows, To Open Latest Can of Corn Tonight—'The Bride Wore Spurs'."

"There must be a way to get that ring without getting into trouble with the censor."—Shemp's musing after his former sweetheart refuses to return the ring she has hidden down the front of her dress in *Gypped in the Penthouse*.

"There's no future in it."—Indisputable reason Curly gives for not wanting to die in *Dizzy Detectives*.

Thesus, King of Rhodes—Daffy monarch in *The Three Stooges Meet Hercules* who vows to free *Schuyler Davis* and the Stooges from the galleys if they defeat his annoying enemy, the gargantuan Siamese Cyclops.

"They don't show!"—Moe is concerned that Larry is leaving the ends of

cactus needles in Curly's behind by cutting the tips off with a scissors. Larry,
however, calms Moe's fears by telling
him, "They don't show!"

**"They generally hang out on the
gallows!"**—Prisons are filled with harsh
realities, and Curly doesn't run from
them in *So Long Mr. Chumps*. After Larry
wonders aloud where the prisoners hang
out, Curly remarks, "They generally
hang out on the gallows!"

13—Prison uniform number drawn by
an unlucky horse in *So Long Mr. Chumps*
and *Beer Barrel Polecats*. The horse had to
feel bad enough when guards painted
inmate's stripes over its body, but receiving uniform number 13 only added
insult to injury. Also, 13 is Moe's affiliation number with the **Needlock
Appliance Corp.** in *I Can Hardly Wait*.

1313 Hysteria Terrace—Bone-chilling
address to which detectives Moe, Larry,
and Shemp travel to protect their client,
Old Man Goodrich, in *For Crimin' Out
Loud*. The Stooges' dedication can be
measured by their willingness to continue
the job after being given these directions:

> *Drive up Murder Mulch Highway, along
> Bloody Creek until you come to Dead Man's
> Curve. Turn right on Poison Bend Road until
> you come to the cemetery. Pass the cemetery
> to Skeleton Flats and up Hysteria Terrace.*

30—Larry's football uniform number in
No Census, No Feeling.

35 cents—Budget-friendly price charged
by the Stooges' **Flounder Inn** for their

special of the day, **Lobster with Frog
Legs**, in *Playing the Ponies*.

"This End Up"—Packing label that
ends up glued across Moe's mouth in *Idle
Roomers*.

"This fish looks like Moe!"—Curly's
stunning declaration in *Rockin' Thru the
Rockies*, after realizing that the fish Larry
has brained with an iron rod looks
strangely familiar.

**"This is the hottest June we've
had since last July!"**—Fireman
Moe's lament as the Stooges travel to
another scorching summer blaze in
Soup to Nuts.

**"This Lot Presented to the Three
Sitdown Suitors—Upland Realty
Co."**—Sign marking the site of the
vacant lot gifted to the Stooges and their
new brides in *The Sitter Downers*.

**"This Place Unfair to Union
Suitors"**—Picket sign carried defiantly
by Curly in *The Sitter Downers* to protest
Mr. Bell's refusal to allow his daughters
to marry the Stooges.

**"Thou hath made me shoe the
wrong mule."**—Moe's unsympathetic
observation in *Fiddlers Three* and *Musty
Musketeers* upon mistakenly nailing a
horseshoe into the tender foot of fellow
fiddler Shemp.

**"Three Hams That Lay Their Own
Eggs"**—Glitzy signature line of the
Stooges' nightclub act, **Nill, Null, and
Void**, in *Loco Boy Makes Good*.

The Three Horsemen—Immutable Stooges Law #87: Opponents on the sporting field will make little allowance for the Stooges' lack of athletic training. In *Three Little Pigskins*, Moe, Larry, and Curly are mistaken for gridiron legends The Three Horsemen, causing many in the crowd to revise their opinion of that celebrated trio.

"Three of the best salesmen who ever sailed."—Moe's confident assessment of the Stooges' credentials when applying to sell **Brighto** in *Dizzy Doctors*.

"Three of the best riveters who ever riveted."—Curly's opinion of the Stooges' capabilities when asked by an interviewer in *How High Is Up?* whether they can rivet.

"The Three Stooges Scrapbook"—The Stooges' children's TV show on the verge of cancellation in *The Three Stooges in Orbit*.

3,000 guineas, two geese, and a duck—Amount Moe proposes to wager on a wrestling match in *Restless Knights* but which Larry declares to be a "fowl bet."

Thunderbolt—Man O' War. Citation. Secretariat. Every so often an equine legend is born, a thoroughbred so sleek, so swift, so determined that other horses appear to be standing still on the track beside him. In *Playing the Ponies*, the Stooges thought they were getting such a horse in trade for their restaurant, the **Flounder Inn**. They got Thunderbolt instead.

"Thunderbolt Manager"—Moe's role in training racehorse *Thunderbolt* in *Playing the Ponies*.

"Thunderbolt Nursemaid"—Curly's job in training racehorse *Thunderbolt* in *Playing the Ponies*. By mixing an expert ration of red-hot **chili pepperinos** into Thunderbolt's feed, Curly became the first thoroughbred trainer ever to use a horse's tongue to make him a champion.

"Thunderbolt Pilot"—Larry as jockey atop the racehorse *Thunderbolt* in *Playing the Ponies*.

"Tick-Tick-Tick-Tick-Tick"—Shemp's reply when asked by Moe in *Fright Night* and *Fling in the Ring* what his watch says.

Tillyeth, Millyeth, and Lillyeth—Lovely royal handmaidens in *Musty Musketeers*. The girls find in the Stooges the one timeless quality no woman can resist: the willingness to engage in a swordfight with an evil magician.

The Times—Newspaper in *Spook Louder* that sends cub reporter **Mr. Wallace** to cover the breakup of the Master Spy Ring and the case of the mysterious flying pies.

The Times Press—Newspaper in *No Dough Boys* that should have been more responsible about publishing this headline on a day the Stooges posed as Japanese soldiers for photographers: "Jap Sub Blown Up Off Shore—U.S. Coast Guard Deals Death Blow—3 Japanese Soldiers Escape—Citizens Warned to Keep a Sharp Lookout."

Tiny Landers—Pleasantly rotund nightclub singer whose stage fright is miraculously cured by psychiatrist *Hugo Gansamacher* in *Sweet and Hot*.

Tiny—Joe's fiancée in *Muscle Up a Little Closer*. She's adoring, but she's not tiny.

"Tired of being beautiful and alone . . ."—Candid introduction to the personal ad answered by Larry in *Gypped in the Penthouse*. The entire ad reads, "Tired of being beautiful and alone. Would like to meet clean, well-dressed, handsome man about 35. Object: Matrimony. Address, Box 41144." Larry views the ad realistically, musing, "A handsome man . . . that might be a problem."

Tiska, Taska, and Baska—It's one thing for beautiful Tiska, Taska, and Baska to marry the Stooges—who are condemned to hang in prison—in order to collect an inheritance in *In the Sweet Pie and Pie*. It is quite another, however, to make no effort to love them once they are miraculously spared the hangman's noose.

Tizzy, Lizzy, and Dizzy—The Stooges' girls in *Back from the Front*.

"To say the least if not less."—Unfortunate confirmation provided by veterinarian Curly after Larry asks in *Calling All Curs* whether a dog's condition is serious.

"To your last breath . . ."—The amount of time Moe valiantly pledges to Shemp that he is prepared to battle the gunslinging *Noonan Brothers* in *Shot in the Frontier*.

Tomb of Old King Putentakeit—Top-secret hiding place chosen by palace guard *Radames* to stash stolen tax revenues in *Mummy's Dummies*.

Tommy—Moe's character in *Woman Haters*.

Tongues—IMMUTABLE STOOGES LAW #88: Any Stooge who dares to stick his tongue out at Moe will soon find that tongue covered in layers of salt, dirt, or burning cigar ashes (various films).

Tony—Puny but tough gambler who bets the ranch on wrestler *Ivan Bustoff* in *Grips, Grunts and Groans*. He promises the Stooges 100 bucks if Bustoff wins, 100 slugs from his revolver if not.

Tools—IMMUTABLE STOOGES LAW #89: Whether made of iron, steel, or alloy, tools such as hammers and saws will always bend when used by Moe on Curly's skull (various films).

Toupées—IMMUTABLE STOOGES LAW #90: No toupée lasts long on the head of anyone who comes into contact with the Stooges (various films).

Tractohomolactometer, hammadeemaceemafaren—Intimidating surgical instruments demanded by Moe before he will make the first incision on patient Curly in *Monkey Businessmen*. Curiously, an assistant at the hospital produces the tools immediately.

Tree branches—IMMUTABLE STOOGES LAW #91: When outdoors and in need of a weapon, the Stooges will convert the nearest tree branch into a catapult capable of firing deadly weapons such as mud packs, eggs, beehives, and poison gas (skunks) (various films).

Trigger Mortis—Gunslinging right-hand man to Western land grabber *Rance Roden* in *The Outlaws Is Coming.*

"Try Dr. Belcher's Compound For Gas on the Stomach"—Promising advertisement worn by Moe on his service station attendant's uniform in *Slaphappy Sleuths.*

Tsimiss—IMMUTABLE STOOGES LAW #92: When life and limb depend on avoiding detection, the Stooges will turn to a Santa Claus suit as their disguise of choice. In *Wee Wee Monsieur*, the Stooges are shipped to inhospitable Tsimiss as members of the Foreign Legion. The enemy there is rough and ruthless, yet sufficiently untrained to recognize the stealthy use of the Santa Claus suit by undercover operatives Moe, Larry, and Curly. (*Tsimiss* is a Yiddish word meaning "a big mess" or "a big pile of ingredients" and is often associated with food.)

"Tuna fish . . ."—Anyone who has driven a fish truck knows how difficult it can be to let customers know what types of fish are for sale. The Stooges solve this problem in *Booby Dupes* by using the universal language of music, reciting in joyous rhythms the catches of the day:

> *Tuna fish, cod fish, smelt fish, swordfish*
> *First tuna, second tuna, barracuda bass!*

The Stooges left out skeleton fish, one of which is found underneath a pile of cats living in their truck. But that is

Fresh fish! (*Booby Dupes*, 1945)

Let this scene be a lesson to municipalities everywhere about the dangers of constructing confusing road signs (*We Want Our Mummy*, 1939).

"Turn around, I'll kiss her behind your back!"—Joe is enjoying a kiss with ravishing **Greta** in *Sappy Bullfighters*, so naturally he does not see her jealous husband **José** enter the room. Infuriated at the sight of this infidelity, José demands to know how Joe could dare kiss his wife in front of him, to which Joe boldly replies, "Turn around, I'll kiss her behind your back!"

Turpentine—Only when chemical manufacturers learn to put their products in distinctive containers will innocent chefs like Moe in *Husbands Beware* stop confusing turpentine for salad oil. Also, the active ingredient in the drink pawnbroker Larry fixes for **Molly the Glamour Girl** in *Three Loan Wolves*.

"2 Hr. Parking—8 A.M. to 6 P.M.—Except Sundays, Holidays, & Hangings"—Sobering sign near the horse troughs in *The Outlaws Is Coming*.

probably because the word "skeleton" just doesn't swing.

Tunis—Though the lonely desert sign in *We Want Our Mummy* indicates that Tunis is 1,500 miles away, Curly is delighted nonetheless at the prospect of traveling there to enjoy a "Tunis sandwich."

"Twenty minutes to a pound; we'll be here a month!"—Although Moe is not a trained chef, he makes an admirable estimation while defrosting frozen-to-the-bone Curly in *Violent is the Word for Curly*. His assessment: "Twenty minutes to a pound; we'll be here a month!"

"20 Easy Lessons"—See *Wide Awake Detective School*.

22—Moe's football uniform number in *No Census, No Feeling.*

22 Laredo Street—Address of the lovely Dolores in *What's the Matador?* Unfortunately for the Stooges, Dolores's wildly jealous husband *José* lives there, too.

"26 Rooms—2 Bath Tubs—Rates $4.00 Per Week Up—Mostly Up"—See *Mrs. Hammond Eggerley's Theatrical Apts.*

200 percent wool—Material Shemp claims was used to make a snazzy sportcoat in *Sing a Song of Six Pants* and *Rip, Sew and Stitch*. When a wary customer questions him about the fabric, Shemp replies, "These sheep led a double life."

200 Vapor Blvd., Zircon—Stellar address of spaceship sellers *A.B. Cloud & Company* in *Flying Saucer Daffy.*

217 Linden Drive—Address of the leaky Norfleet residence in *Vagabond Loafers.*

275 Mortuary Road—Bone-chilling address to which the gumshoe Stooges trail a lovely blonde who is kidnapped from under their noses in *Dopey Dicks.*

"Two Souls and a Heel"—Dynamic billing given to the Stooges' stage act in *Gents Without Cents*. The name, while a bit glitzy, does justice to the Stooges' virtuoso performance of their legendary routine, *"Niagara Falls."*

$2,000—Shameless ransom demanded by kidnappers for the return of prize-winning canine *Garçon* in *Calling All Curs.*

$2,198.55—Relatively reasonable fare paid by the Stooges for a cab ride to Egypt in *We Want Our Mummy.*

Tyra and Electra—IMMUTABLE STOOGES LAW #93: Smoke will billow from the Stooges' lips after they are kissed by beautiful women. In *Flying Saucer Daffy*, lovely aliens Tyra and Electra plant some doozies on Joe's kisser, a thrill that produces smoke from his mouth . . . and from his amorous ears, as well.

"U.S. Army Join Now"—Alluring recruiting poster in *Half Shot Shooters* that reveals little about how uncomfortable the army might be for men who sign up accidentally.

U.S. Treasury—Government department that employs humorless guards to protect Vault 3 in *Cash and Carry*. Sure, there's a lot of money lying around Treasury vaults, but shouldn't the department's trigger-happy protectors know the difference between a genuine break-in and three innocent men attempting to discover *Captain Kidd's Kid's Treasure*?

Ulysses—Former king of Ithaca imprisoned by dastardly new ruler *Odius* in *The Three Stooges Meet Hercules*.

Umpchay—See *Amscray, Ixnay, and Umpchay*.

"Unaccusstomed Tailors"—Modest billing the Stooges confer upon themselves while working as clothiers in *Sing a Song of Six Pants* and *Rip, Sew and Stitch*. Their shop window promises a range of services at fair prices: "Unaccusstomed Tailors—Men's Furnishings—New and 2nd Hand Clothes Cheep—Cleaning Pressing Altercations."

Uncle Caleb—Supremely generous uncle from *Brideless Groom* who wills nephew Shemp $500,000 upon his death—provided Shemp marries by 6 P.M. Although Caleb is never seen on-screen, one gets the sense that he was an altruistic man, the kind of man, as Shemp says, who would "give you the shirt off his back and throw in the buttons, too."

Uncle Mortimer—Guardian angel with a decidedly pro-consumer bent in *Heavenly Daze* and *Bedlam in Paradise*. Mortimer orders the recently deceased Shemp to return to earth for one reason: to stop Moe and Larry from peddling their worthless invention, a ***fountain pen that writes under whipped cream***.

Uncle Pete—Well-intentioned uncle who bequeaths to his three nephews the swank fashion boutique ***Madame de France*** in *Slippery Silks*.

Uncle Phineas Bowman—Fabulously wealthy uncle to Moe, Larry, and Shemp in *Gents in a Jam*. It is the rumor about Bowman's money that persuades the Stooges' battle-ax landlady ***Mrs. Magruder*** to allow her three deadbeat boarders to stay, but it is Bowman's uncommon charm that wins her heart.

Uncle Tim—Justice of the peace who, in accordance with Curly's uncanny ability to get whatever he wishes, appears from nowhere to marry the Stooges to three beautiful sisters, ***April, May, and June***, in *Oily to Bed, Oily to Rise*.

"Under the spreading chestnut tree, around the corner, by the pawnshop at Pittsville and Tonsilvania"—Directions to *Cedric the Blacksmith*'s quarters, as provided by *Princess Elaine* in *Knutzy Knights*.

"Unfair to Union Husbands"—See *"No Honeymoon No Work."*

Unitarians—When Larry assures a baby-sitting client in *Baby Sitters Jitters* that the Stooges work as a unit, Shemp confirms as much by telling her the Stooges are "Unitarians."

Upland Realty Company—Real estate firm with a soft spot for romance in *The Sitter Downers*. The Upland Realty Company had high hopes for the newly-wed Stooges when it presented them with a vacant lot upon which to build a dream home, never realizing that a gift requiring the Stooges to work would do little to nurture marital harmony.

Urania—Home country to brilliant inventor of a super-rocket fuel, *Professor Snead*, in *Fuelin' Around* and *Hot Stuff*.

Urania Daily Bladder—Newspaper that publishes this indiscreet headline: "Urania to Have Air Supremacy—Professor Snead's Super-Rocket Fuel Nears Completion—Will Power World's Fastest Aircraft."

V

"Vacancies Exist"—IMMUTABLE STOOGES LAW #94: When enlisting in the army, the Stooges will be assigned to a commanding officer who is the insensitive, unforgiving type. In *Half Shot Shooters*, the Stooges reenlist in an army that never appreciated them the first time around, a situation that might have been avoided were it not for tempting recruiting posters like this: "Vacancies Exist—Enlist Now—U.S. Army—Apply Capt. Burke Room 310."

Vacancy of the Cranium—Discouraging diagnosis arrived at by Professor Quackenbush (see **Professors Rich and Nichols, Quackenbush and Sedletz**) after careful examination of Curly's skull in *Half-Wits Holiday* and Larry's skull in *Pies and Guys*.

Valeska—Known as a "thriving kingdom in the tropics," Valeska is where the Stooges peddle hefty winter clothing in *Saved by the Belle*.

The Van Brocklin Painting—Priceless masterpiece that is the intended target of thieves in *Vagabond Loafers* and *Scheming Schemers*. The Van Brocklin might still be missing had the crooks been able to avoid detection by three bumbling plumbers.

Vandy Legs, Bride's Biscuit, Muddy Water, Turtle Neck, and Hailstorm—Championship-caliber horses that cannot overcome the blazing speed of the Stooge-owned **Thunderbolt** in *Playing the Ponies*. The race certainly would have been closer had these horses also been fed scorchingly hot **chili pepperinos**.

Varunu—IMMUTABLE STOOGES LAW #95: Witch doctors and violent island natives will be deeply offended by the strange customs of the Stooges. In *Hula-La-La*, witch doctor Varunu assigns little value to the Stooges' remaining productive years as dance instructors when he decides to add theirs to his collection of shrunken heads.

Vault 3—See *U.S. Treasury*.

"Ver G'harget," "Over the River," and "Skip the Gutter"—Exuberant toasts offered by the Stooges to a drugstore customer who has ordered a swig of moonshine in *Pardon My Scotch*. Had the customer spoken Yiddish, he might have been less inclined to drink; *Ver G'harget* means "Drop dead."

Venetian Bath—Animal rights groups never gripe about the Stooges, a testament to the trio's long-standing ability to relate well to animals. This quality is nobly demonstrated in *Flat Foot Stooges*, in which Moe, Larry, and Curly take two hardworking fire department horses to relax at a soothing Venetian bath.

Vesuvius Restaurant—Snobbish spaghetti joint that ejects the Stooges in *The Tooth Will Out*. No record of the Vesuvius exists today, a lesson to restaurateurs in the consequences of removing customers who might not measure up to some arbitrarily lofty standard of decorum.

"Vice? I have no vice. I'm as pure as the driven snow."—Curly's moving response in *Dizzy Pilots* to Moe's query: "Where's your vice?"

Vickers Cavendish—Fiendish con man in *The Three Stooges Go Around the World in a Daze* who devises a scheme to wrench 20,000 pounds from English gentleman **Phileas Fogg III**. See also **Randolph Stuart III**.

Vitamin P.D.Q.—IMMUTABLE STOOGES LAW #96: The Stooges will place sharp objects like syringes and bear traps only where people are likely to sit. In *Some More of Samoa*, tree doctor Curly does not properly dispose of a syringe containing a tree-growth concoction known as Vitamin P.D.Q., causing him to grow to an awkward height of ten feet upon being jabbed by the exposed needle.

"Vitamins A, B, C, D, E, F; Gee, I like food!"—Curly's proclamation in *Matri-Phony* after spotting a luscious buffet in the Emperor's palace.

Vitamins A.P.U.—Natural remedy that does nothing to help Moe's case of shat-tered nerves in *Idiots Deluxe* and *Guns A Poppin*.

"Viva Vulgaria!"—Jubilant cheer recited by the Stooges in *Dutiful but Dumb* upon learning they will be sent to Vulgaria. Sung with machine-gun rapidity and with a dramatic solo by Moe, the ditty goes like this:

Together:	*Vulgaria! Vulgaria! Viva Vulgaria! A-veevo! A-vyevoe! A-veevo-vyevoe-vum!*
Moe:	*Bum kitta ratkat, pitta patta kat kat*
Together:	*Rah rah rah rah Vulgaria!*

"Voices of Spring"—Lilting song that launched the short career of **Señorita Cucaracha** (Curly) in *Micro-Phonies*. While Señorita Cucaracha was able to hit the high notes in "Voices of Spring" by use of fascinating facial expressions and bodily contortions, the song proved too much for **Miss Dinkelmeyer**, the tone-deaf but amorous student of renowned singing coach **"Professor Shemp Howard—Teacher of Voice,"** in *Brideless Groom* and *Husbands Beware*.

"Vote For Honest Icabod Slipp"—Slogan on the self-promoting poster of the decidedly dishonest **Icabod Slipp** in *Hold That Lion!* and *Loose Loot*.

Vulgaria—Country that imposes the death penalty upon photographers—even inept photographers—in *Dutiful but Dumb*.

WGN—Far-reaching radio station tuned in by Curly as he turns tumblers on what he thinks is a safe in *Horses' Collars*.

W.H.—Initials emblazoned on a button worn by the Stooges in *Woman Haters*. Moe, Larry, and Curly have just joined the Woman Haters Club, a regrettable decision given the bevy of beauties that routinely cross the Stooges' paths.

WX21—Call letters of the television station broadcasting live from Niagara Falls in *A Plumbing We Will Go*.

"Wake up and go to sleep!"—Moe's angry reprimand to the slumbering Larry in *A Pain in the Pullman, Booty and the Beast*, and *Hold That Lion!*

Waldo Twitchell—Nightlife reviewer whose opinion of the Stooges' stage act, **Nill, Null, and Void**, will make or break the new **Chisel Inn Hotel** in *Loco Boy Makes Good*. Twitchell laughs uproariously, although not for reasons the Stooges would prefer.

Walker—Devious mastermind of the plot to frame the father of **Stella, Nella, and Bella** in *Three Smart Saps*.

Walla Walla—Location on a map of the state of Washington thought by the Stooges to show the site of buried treasure in *Cash and Carry*.

"Wanted for Vagrancy"—In *Phony Express* and *Merry Mavericks*, the wanted poster that bears the mugs of the Stooges and practically guarantees their capture. It reads: "Wanted for Vagrancy—Reward 50 Cents or 3 for $1."

Washington Chronicle—Newspaper that published the still-startling headline, "Flying Saucer Photo Alerts Capitol" in *Flying Saucer Daffy*.

Watts D. Matter—Dean of the school of criminology attended by the Stooges in *Blunder Boys*, and also father to the school's registrar and star instructor, **Alma Matter**.

"Way Down South in New York City"—Uplifting traditional song sung by the Stooges to the tune of "Dixie" in *Uncivil War Birds*:

> *Oh, way down south in New York City*
> *The cotton grows on the trees so pretty*
> *On the trees? On the trees!*
> *In the south? South Brooklyn!*

> *Oh, south of the Bronx where I was born*
> *The songs are rotten and the jokes are corn*
> *Look away, get away*
> *Get a waitress; we're hungry!*

"We Baked You a Birthday Cake"—IMMUTABLE STOOGES LAW #95: The Stooges will arrive at the homes of wealthy socialites just before a big party is to commence and just after the cook, butlers, and maids have quit. In *An Ache in Every Stake*, the Stooges fill in admirably for a cook and maid who have just stormed off, even preparing a luscious-looking birthday cake served with a song of heartfelt celebration and sung to the tune of London Bridge:

> We baked you a birthday cake
> If you get a tummy ache
> And you moan and groan and woe
> Don't forget we told you so!

"We Dye For You"—Slick slogan painted on the side of the Stooges' laundry truck in *Crash Goes the Hash*.

"We graduated with the highest temperatures in our class!"—Braggadocious claim made by Larry to a colleague who dares to question the Stooges' medical credentials in *Men in Black*.

"We Just Dropped in to Say Hello"—Irresistible ditty sung by the Stooges in ringing three-part harmony while auditioning for *Manny Weeks Theatrical Enterprises* in *Gents Without Cents*:

> We didn't come to borrow any money
> We didn't come to borrow any dough
> We didn't come to borrow any trouble
> We just dropped in to say hello
>
> Hello to you, Mr. Manny
> Please don't think that we are hammy
> We just dropped in from Alabamy
> We just dropped in to say hello

"We Make Everything From Beds to Bustles"—Lofty claim made by the Stooge-owned *Shangri-La Upholstering Company* in *Hugs and Mugs*.

"We need the eggs."—Ironclad explanation Larry provides to a judge in *Listen, Judge* when asked why he and Moe don't institutionalize Shemp, who is convinced he is a chicken.

"We Never Sleep"—Well-intentioned slogan used by the Stooges as *Day and Nite Plumbers* in *Vagabond Loafers* and *Scheming Schemers*.

"We Repare Enything"—See *Jiffy Fixers*.

"The Wedding Bells"—Young love causes the exuberant soul to sing, and the Stooges know the feeling in *Three Smart Saps* when they chant this ode to their upcoming marriage to *Stella, Nella, and Bella*:

> The wedding bells will start to ring
> Ding dong ding!
> The birdies, they will start to swing
> Ding dong ding!
> The bride and groom will start to swing
> Oh, swing
> So swing it!

"A week back"—The date Larry tells an officer in *Uncivil Warriors* that he began suffering from a weak back.

"Welcome to Cucaracha"—See *Cucaracha*.

"We'll be there in a flash in the flesh!"—Repairman Moe's exuberant declaration when told on the phone that a patient will pay any amount for the services of psychiatrists **Ziller, Zeller, and Zoller** in *Three Sappy People*.

"Well, being as there's no other place around the place, I reckon this must be the place, I reckon."—Although stuck in an Egyptian desert in *We Want Our Mummy* and a swamp in *Uncivil Warriors*, Curly still demonstrates a bloodhound's nose for geography. When Moe wonders aloud if the Stooges are near their destination, Curly confirms it by remarking, "Well, being as there's no other place around the place, I reckon this must be the place, I reckon."

"We'll Get That Filthy Lucre . . ."—Facing an inevitable confrontation with the crooked **Icabod Slipp** in *Hold That Lion!* and *Loose Loot*, Larry and Shemp chant this song for inspiration and courage:

Larry: *We'll get that filthy lucre!*

Shemp: *The moolah!*

Larry: *The geedus!*

Together: *No slippery guy named Slipp*
           Is ever gonna cheat us!
           A-zoop! A-zope! A-zoe!

"Well, I'm too young. . . ."—After proclaiming himself too young and handsome to be hanged in *In the Sweet Pie and Pie*, Curly looks in the mirror, then reassesses the situation by proclaiming, "Well, I'm too young. . . ."

"Well, we're not in my country . . ."—When the rough-and-tumble **Icabod Slipp** calls Shemp a dirty crook in *Hold That Lion!* and *Loose Loot*, Shemp declares those to be fighting words in his country. Slipp prepares to fight, but Shemp seems to have reconsidered, sheepishly telling Slipp, "Well, we're not in my country. . . ."

"We're dressed as ballerinas"—Lovely introduction provided by ballerinas Moe, Larry, and Curly for the dancing act of **Hilda, Wilda, and Tilda** in *Rhythm and Weep*:

> *We're dressed as ballerinas*
> *Of course you know we're not*
> *And what you're going to see now folks*
> *Is something we ain't got!*

"We're on our way . . ."—Spirited chant recited by the Stooges in *So Long Mr. Chumps*. It's not every day that three men are paid handsomely to locate an honest man, and the Stooges are not about to let the moment slip by without a jingle:

> *We're on our way for an honest man*
> *We'll bring him back as fast as we can*
> *Excelsior!*

Western surprise—Exotic cocktail deftly mixed by Curly in *Yes, We Have No Bonanza*. When Moe, after careful observation, declares that the drink contains no alcohol, Curly retorts, "That's the surprise!"

Whack Magazine—Photographic periodical for which the Stooges snap pictures in *Dutiful but Dumb*. *Whack*'s motto —"If It's a Good Picture It's Out of *Whack*" —hints at the magazine's willingness to go the extra mile for that one-of-a-kind photo, even if it means sending its less-able photographers to countries that execute photographers on sight.

"What a beautiful messterpiece!"—Shemp has insulted a customer's suit in *Sing a Song of Six Pants* and *Rip, Sew and Stitch* by asking where the man got such a mess. When the customer replies that he bought the suit from the Stooges' tailor shop, the quick-thinking Shemp remarks, "What a beautiful messterpiece!"

"What a hideous, monstrous face!"—Shemp's opinion of a creepy bat that swoops down on the Stooges in *Spooks*. Sadly, the bat is the spitting image of Shemp himself.

"What's a matter with my eyes; do they look like halvah?"—Jealousy can be an unattractive quality in a man, even one as dapper as Shemp. When a luscious-looking woman in *Hugs and Mugs* tells Moe how beautiful his eyes are, Shemp asks enviously, "What's a matter with my eyes; do they look like halvah?"

"What size, madam? We have some lovely ground-grippers!"—Although Moe has impolitely ordered Shemp to shoe a nearby horse in *Punchy Cowpunchers*, Shemp does not let the ill humor of the moment stop him from treating the horse with dignity and respect. His first question to the beast: "What size, madam? We have some lovely ground-grippers!"

"When in Chicago . . ."—Even cut-throat bandits have a soft spot for romance, as proven by this note found in the wallet of bloodthirsty outlaw **Double Deal Decker** in *Horses' Collars*. It reads, "When in Chicago call Stockyards 1234, Ask for Ruby."

"When You Get Back . . ."—Appetizing advertisement worn on the back of Curly's army uniform in *Boobs in Arms*. It reads: "When You Get Back Eat at **O'Brien's Kosher Restaurant**—Soup, Salad, Entrée, Coffee, Desert—All This and Herring, Too—40 (Cents)."

"Whereas I, Shemp the Stooge . . ."—Tear-jerking first passage from Shemp's will in *Heavenly Daze* and *Bedlam in Paradise*. It reads, "Whereas I, Shemp the Stooge, being of unsound mind, do hereby prove it by leaving all my worldly possessions to my cousins, Moe and Larry, to share and share alike."

"Which one?"—Although Shemp is slapped for asking "Which one?" Moe probably should have been more specific when he asked for a hand in *Pardon My Clutch*.

"Which one is Will?"—Curly's question after Moe orders him to "Fire at will" at a flock of turkeys.

White on rye—Bread of choice ordered by Larry for his ham and corned beef sandwich in *Soup to Nuts*.

"Who came in?"—Larry's reply in *Space Ship Sappy* when **Professor A. K. Rimple** addresses the Stooges as "gentlemen."

"Why don't you sing 'Mame'?"—Request made by Larry after Moe's face is blackened with automobile soot in *Slaphappy Sleuths*. Although he never says so directly, Moe uses his fists to make it clear that he doesn't take requests.

Wide Awake Detective School—Training grounds for detectives Moe, Larry, and Shemp in *Scotched in Scotland*.

Widow Jenkins—Usually, kindness is its own reward, and in the case of the Widow Jenkins it paid off in spades. Happy to share her homemade dinner of roast chicken and dumplings and hot apple pie with the Stooges in *Oily to Bed, Oily to Rise*, Moe, Larry, and Curly express their gratitude by recovering the deed to her oil-rich property from swindlers. And as a bonus, the Stooges marry her three beautiful daughters, *April, May, and June*.

Wienerschnitzel Straza—Romantic hideaway where Moe finds love with the braided *Katrina* in *Fifi Blows Her Top*.

Wild Bill Hicup—Moe in *Goofs and Saddles*. See also **Buffalow Billious** and **Just Plain Bill**.

"Wild Bill Hicup Due In"—Ingenious fib written by a frustrated sheriff to frighten bandits away in *Phony Express*. The writing appears in a newspaper featuring the befuddled faces of the Stooges, who are in actuality **"Wanted for Vagrancy."**

One more pinch and the Widow Jenkins (Eva McKenzie) will be forever smitten with debonair Curly (*Oily to Bed, Oily to Rise, 1939*).

Wild Hyacinth—Boxers would sell their souls for even a drop of Wild Hyacinth, the perfume in *Grips, Grunts and Groans* that enabled Curly to lose his sanity and use a whirlwind of punches to knock out everyone in the ring.

Wilkes—Genteel butler who summons the **Day and Nite Plumbers** (the Stooges) to fix a problem at the **Norfleet Mansion** in *Vagabond Loafers*. To his credit, Wilkes later seems to feel a measure of responsibility for his choice.

Will Idge—Conscientious blacksmith in *Fiddlers Three* and *Musty Musketeers* who leaves this polite note: **"Gone to Rest Under the Spreading Chestnut Tree."**

William—Creepy butler in *The Three Stooges in Orbit* whom **Professor Danforth**

promises will show the Stooges "to your tombs . . . I mean *rooms*."

Williams—Scheming butler in *In the Sweet Pie and Pie* who purposely slips and spills a cake into Moe's face, thereby disrupting the Stooges' entrée into high society. Also, the butler in *Three Sappy People* who places a fateful call to the three famous psychiatrists *Ziller, Zeller, and Zoller*.

Winkelburg—Fun-filled town that is home to circus horse *Schnapps* in *Horsing Around*.

Wm. "Bill Wick"—Shady campaign manager for crooked presidential candidate *Hammond Egger* in *Three Dark Horses*.

Woman Haters Club 87—Gathering place for victims of infidelity like Larry and Shemp in *Gypped in the Penthouse*.

Wong Hi Lee Hand Laundry—Conveniently located Chinese laundry into which the Stooges make a quick getaway while dodging the incensed *Officer O'Halloran* in *Mutts to You*.

Wrong Brothers—Moe, Larry, and Curly as visionary inventors of the revolutionary airplane *The Buzzard* in *Dizzy Pilots*. The Wrong Brothers might have made a go of the *Buzzard* had they stuck to basic design and left the test flying to more seasoned pilots.

Lucy Wykoff—IMMUTABLE STOOGES LAW #97: When on business, the Stooges will visit the homes of women married to insanely jealous and violent husbands who are due back any minute. In *Don't Throw That Knife*, Lucy Wykoff is kind enough to allow the Stooges inside her apartment to take the census, a government necessity her soon-to-arrive husband does not appreciate.

X-Ray Fluoroscope—It is a sad day when the technological marvels of the twentieth century are utilized for evil purposes. But such was the fate of the astonishing X-Ray Fluoroscope in *A Bird in the Head*, a machine capable of determining whether Curly's brain could be successfully transplanted into a wild ape without causing harm to the ape.

Y

Yankee Noodle Soup—After seeing the Stooges serve delicious Yankee Noodle Soup with an equally appetizing song (sung to the tune of "Yankee Doodle Dandy") in *Nutty but Nice*, one wonders why most restaurants in the country still haven't hired singing waiters:

> Our Yankee Noodle Soup is good
> You'll find it is no phony
> If you don't care for noodle soup
> We'll serve you macaroni!

"Yanks Win World Series"—When a roughneck thief finds a newspaper tucked under the bandages of Curly's mummy disguise in *We Want Our Mummy*, one only hopes the crook isn't a Cubs fan. The paper's headline: "Yanks Win World Series."

Ye Colonial Inn—Restaurant that caters to music lovers in *Nutty but Nice*. Ye Colonial features three singing waiters billed as the *"Hilarious Hash Slingers."* Their motto: "America's Gift to Indigestion."

Ye Olde Furniture Shoppe—Stooge-owned business in *A Snitch in Time* that made antique collecting more accessible to everyone. Their motto: "Antiques Made While-U-Waite."

Ye Olde Pilgrim Hotel—Ramshackle hotel remodeled by the Stooges into a nightclub in *Loco Boy Makes Good*.

"Ye Olde Tilt"—Modern pinball players should be thankful that today's machines simply switch off when tilted. In *Three Little Pirates*, Larry's ancient pinball machine not only responds to his aggressive play by lighting a sign that reads, "Ye Olde Tilt," it also releases a gigantic mallet onto his head to remind him to play more gently in the future.

Ye Stooges Three—Sole Purveyors of Yuk—Stooge-owned business that peddles miracle elixir *Yuk* in *Snow White and the Three Stooges*.

"Yeah, but I don't like the stuffing."—Larry's reply to Moe when asked in *A Pain in the Pullman* if he likes crab.

"Yeah, but I'm goin' anyhow."—Larry's brave reply in *Three Dark Horses* after Moe asks if he has worms for their upcoming fishing trip.

"Yeah, it reminds me of the reform school."—Larry is no interior designer, but his analysis of the rarified decor in the Bixby home in *Micro-Phonies* suggests an eye for art uncommon outside Paris.

"Yeah, two bucks!"—Curly's interjection in *Hoi Polloi* as Moe learns to read the sentence, "Oh, see the deer; has the deer a little doe?"

Yorrick—Hardworking pack mule who carries more than his fair share in *Yes, We Have No Bonanza*. Moe exposes a tender side when he thinks Yorrick has been blown to smithereens by a stick of dynamite. Says the grieving Moe, "Alas! Poor Yorrick; I knew him well."

"You burnt my little bugle!"—Larry's assessment of his injuries after Moe pushes his face into boiling water in *I Can Hardly Wait*.

"You know I'm not normal!"—Poignant warning Curly provides Moe to explain why he shouldn't be hit in the head in *Dizzy Pilots* and *Loco Boy Makes Good*.

"You know, you should fish for a whale."—Moe's opinion after Larry remarks in *Pardon My Clutch* and *Wham-Bam-Slam!* that fish is great brain food.

"You need another strike."—Moe's opinion—expressed first verbally, then physically—of Curly's bowling skills in *An Ache in Every Stake*.

"You see-eth, it's like this-eth . . ."—Larry's brief but regal-sounding explanation to an English judge in *Back to the Woods*. The impatient judge, unconvinced by Larry's persuasive opening, issues an immediate guilty verdict and sentences the Stooges to fifty-five years of hard labor.

"You told me to drop what I was doing, so I did."—Hard-to-argue-with explanation provided by Larry as he stands amid a pile of broken dishes in *Three Loan Wolves*.

"You were delivered by a buzzard."—Crushing news broken by Moe to Curly in *Sock-A-Bye Baby* after Curly wonders aloud whether he looked cute when he was delivered by the stork.

"You'll Never Know"—Song of melancholy sung by the Stooges in mournful three-part harmony in *Half Shot Shooters* and *A Ducking They Did Go*:

> You'll never know
> Just what tears are
> 'Til you cry
> Like you made me cry.

"Your mother and my mother are both mothers."—Curly's plea for mercy to a Foreign Legion officer who intends to execute the Stooges in *Wee Wee Monsieur*.

"You're a very intelligent imbecile."—High compliment paid by Moe to Shemp in *Vagabond Loafers* after Shemp declares that a leak in the basement must be coming from higher up.

"You're getting no place fast!"—Moe's impatient assessment of Shemp's jailbreak technique in *Out West*.

"You're not even married."—Interesting issue raised by Curly in *Flat Foot Stooges* after Moe declares a brilliant idea to be his "brainchild."

"You're tearing my heart out!"—Moe's diagnosis in *Corny Casanovas* as Larry yanks dozens of carpenter's tacks from his rear end. See also *"I'm losing my mind!"*

"You're telling me!"—After beautiful sisters Aggie and Maggie have introduced themselves to a delighted Moe and Larry in *I'm a Monkey's Uncle* and *Stone Age Romeos*, Shemp can't wait to hit the jackpot with the third sister. But when she reveals her frightening mug to Shemp and introduces herself by saying, "I'm Baggie," Shemp can only declare the truth by replying, "You're telling me!"

Yuk—Dubious elixir peddled by *Ye Stooges Three* in *Snow White and the Three Stooges*. Although pitch man Moe claims that Yuk "cures all known afflictions that confound mankind, reduces weight, kills moths, and restores the hair," he is unwelcome by townfolk who have purchased Yuk before.

Yukon Ice Cream—Ice cream truck used by the quick-thinking Stooges to make a speedy getaway in *Violent is the Word for Curly*.

Z

"Zee Lollipop"—Joyous ditty recited by the Stooges to celebrate their lives as Parisian artists in *Wee Wee Monsieur*. Sung in three-part harmony (with Curly taking the "woo-woo" lines), it goes like this:

> *Zee lollipop, zee lollipop*
> *Zee la-la-la lollipop*
> *Woo-woo!*
>
> *Zee lollipop, zee lollipop*
> *Zee la-la-la lollipop*
> *Woo-woo!*
>
> *Zee Frenchman knows just what to eat*
> *He eats something so nice and sweet!*
> *Zee lollipop, zee lollipop*
> *Zee la-la-la lollipop*
>
> *Woo-woo!*

Zendayfus, mishegas, pyareecon, cotton—Never-before-published formula for the **Fountain of Youth** serum

invented by the Stooges in *All Gummed Up* and *Bubble Trouble*. (This formula, it goes without saying, is for informational purposes only.)

Zero Ice & Coal Co.—Although civilians no longer need ice and coal delivered for home use, the motto of the Stooge-owned Zero Ice & Coal Co. in *An Ache in Every Stake* makes one yearn for those bygone days when necessities were brought to the door with a smile and panache: ***"Ice with Personality—Coal with Oomph."***

Ziller, Zeller, and Zoller—Renowned psychiatrists whose reputations are altered after the Stooges assume their identities in *Three Sappy People*.

Zircon—Home planet to hourglass-shaped aliens **Tyra and Electra** in *Flying Saucer Daffy*. Not much is known about life on Zircon, but Tyra and Electra's lovey-dovey treatment of Joe on their visit to Earth suggests that the Zircon's male prototype was short, stout, and bald.

PART III

Entries Listed by Category

Addresses

1010 Tobacco Road

111 Riverside Drive

1122 Lillyflower Terrace

118 6th Street, San Francisco, California

1313 Hysteria Terrace

1410 South America Way

1414 Bleecker Street

200 Vapor Blvd., Zircon

217 Linden Drive

22 Laredo Street

275 Mortuary Road

418 Meshugena Avenue

919 Circle Avenue

Box 41144

"Prof. A. K. Rimple No. 60"

Advertisements, Slogans, and Boastful Claims

"Amazing! Incredible! Horrific! . . ."

"America's Gift to Indigestion"

"Antiques Made While-U-Waite . . ."

"Are you short of money? . . ."

"At Your Service . . ."

"Brightens Old Bodies"

"Cards for All Occasions"

"A Chicken in Every Pot with Egger"

"Cuddle Up a Little Closer with Hammond Egger"

"Cures Every Ailment Known to Man"

"Dice, Dancing, Dames, Drinking, and Dunking"

"Direct from Three Hot Weeks in Kansas"

"Distilled Monday"

"Distilled Yesterday"

"Divorce Evidence Manufactured . . ."

"Dogs Washed While U Wate . . ."

"Dollar Day"

"Don't Be a Muttonhead—Vote For Abel Lamb Stewer for President"

"Feel Tired? . . ."

"Got Ants in Your Plants? We'll Kill 'Em!"

"Gritto spelled sideways is 'Ottri-guh-guh'"

"Hammond Egger Wants Your Vote"

"Have You Sore Feet? Try Tic-Tac. Good for the Toe"

"He'll Steal Your Breath Away!"

"Here This Week—The Great Hypnotist Svengarlic . . ."

"Here Today, Pawn Tomorrow"

"High altitude, low prices . . ."

"Ice with Personality—Coal with Oomph"

"If It's a Good Picture, It's Out of Whack!"

"If We Solve Your Crime It's a Miracle!"

"If You Buy a Home Like This It's a Miracle"

"If You Got 'Em—We'll Get 'Em!"

"If you have a knick knack with a nick in it . . ."

"In Onion There Is Strength"

"Invest with Honest Icabod Slipp"

"It was nothing, Mademoiselle . . ."

"Joe Stack's Tigers to Meet Cubs . . ."

"Join the Army and See the World—or What's Left of It"

"Little America"

"Moronika for Morons"

"Never in the history of motion pictures . . ."

"No qualms or trepidations . . ."

"Old Holland Cheese . . ."

"Our Leader—President Ward Robey—the People's Friend"

"Rooms $1 a Month—Free Showers
    When it Rains"
"Super Service"
"Three Hams That Lay Their Own Eggs"
"Three of the best salesmen who ever
    sailed"
"Three of the best riveters who ever
    riveted"
"Try Dr. Belcher's Compound for Gas on
    the Stomach"
"20 Easy Lessons"
"26 Rooms—2 Bath Tubs—Rates $4.00
    Per Week Up—Mostly Up"
"Unaccusstomed Tailors"
"We Dye For You"
"We Make Everything From Beds to
    Bustles"
"We Never Sleep"
"We Repare Enything"

Aliases
5736 and Mr. No One
Mr. No One
Mr. Zero
Slippery Fingers

Bars, Taverns, and Saloons
Black Louie's Pirate Den
Double Deal's Five "D" Delight
Felix Stout's Bar
Longhorn Saloon
Maxey's Place
Peaceful Gulch Saloon
Red Dog Saloon
Rite Bar
Storey's Saloon

Beautiful Babes, Dames, and Heroines
Alice Bixby
Alma Matter
Amelia Carter
Annie Oakley

Belle and Zell
Carol Danforth
Diane
Dr. Ingrid
Dolly Devore
Dolores
Gail Tempest
Greta
Helen Blazes
Juanita, Conchita, Pepita, and Rosita
Judith
Kitty
Lady Godiva
Leiloni Baggiagaloupe
Lorna Doone
Lucy Wykoff
Lulu
Mirabel Mirabel
Miss Beebee
Miss Bopper
Miss Hopkins
Miss Janie Bell
Miss Jones
Miss Kelly
Miss Lapdale
Miss Scudder
Miss Shapely
Mrs. Duggan
Nora
Nell
Rita
Snow White
Señorita Rita
Serena Flint
Tyra and Electra

Beer, Wine, and Spirits
Amarillo Beer
Breath O' Heather Vat 106 Plus
Eenar fraapini
Giggle water
Gin smothered in bourbon
Nip and Tuck

Old Homicide
Old Panther
Panther Pilsner Beer
Route 66
Shingled roof
Western surprise
185

Birds and Fish

Bill
Carey
Cedric the Clam
Dogfish
Jake
Polly

Blue Bloods, Tycoons, Socialites, and Millionaires

Mrs. Smythe Smythe
Ajax
Arthur van Twitchett
George Morton
Miss Gottrocks
Mr. and Mrs. Manning
Mr. Boyce
Mr. Morgan
Mr. Norfleet
Mr. Winthrop
Mrs. Bedford
Mrs. Bixby
Mrs. Burlap
Mrs. Castor
Mrs. Catsby
Mrs. Henderson
Mrs. Morgan
Mrs. Pendall
Mrs. Van Bustle
Muriel van Twitchett
Rumsford
Sheri Rumsford
Thaddeus and Maggie Smirch

Boats, Ships, and Vessels

Admiral Hawkins's Flagship
Garbage Scow #188 N.Y.C.
The Good Ship Pfifernill
S.S. *Dotty*
S.S. *Shickelgruber*

Books, Magazines, and Pamphlets

A.P. Willis Co.
Elementary Chemistry
Facts and Figures Magazine
How to Be a Plumber
How to Become a Babysitter
How to Make Panther Pilsner Beer
Little Red Book
Love Tales
Practical Dentistry
Story Pictures of Farm Animals
The Amateur Carpenter
"Theatre Chit Chat"
Whack Magazine

Bosses and Supervisors

A. Mouser
A. Panther
Amscray, Ixnay, and Onay
B. K. Doaks
B. O. Botswaddle
City Assessor
Dainty Dolly Dish Company
Fuller Bull
Fuller Grime
Fuller Rath
George B. Bopper
I. M. Greecy
Ixnay
J. B. Fletcher
J. L. Cameron
J. P. Morse
Joe Strubachincoscow
John Bradley

Maxey
Mr. Baines
Mr. Beedle
Mr. Graves
Mr. Herbert
Mr. Jones
Mr. Romani
Mr. Smellington
Mr. Wilson
President of the United States
Ralph Dimsal
Señor Pedro Alvarez
Shamus O'Brien
Smiling Sam McGann

Boxers, Wrestlers, and Fighters

Chopper Kane
Gorilla Watson
Ironhead
Ivan Bustoff
Kid Pinky
Killer Kilduff
Mighty Itchy-Kitchy
Oscar the Dummy

Businesses, Miscellaneous

A.B. Cloud & Co.
Acme Escort Bureau
Acme Service Station
Brighto Medical Company
Calamity Insurance Company
Carnation Pictures
Cheatham Investment Company
Colossal Insurance Company
Columbia Uniform Supply Company
Diggs, Graves, and Berry Undertakers
Dr. Abdul's Medicine Show
First National Bank
General Motorcycle: 17½ . . .
Gottrox Jewelry Company
Gypsom Good Inc., Antiques

Hendrix Jewelry Store
Miracle Homebuilders, Inc.
Mrs. Throttlebottom's Chicken Coop
National Express and Storage Co.
Noazark Shipbuilding Co.
Panther Brewing Co.
Pedro Ruiz Business Opportunities
Perfect Underwear Company
Pinch Penny Market
Rockwood Steel, Ranacoma Copper . . .
Shtunk Manufacturing Company
Skin and Flint Finance Corporation
Sky Aircraft Company
Slipp, Tripp, and Skipp
Super Terrific Productions
Goldberg, Ginsberg, Rosenberg, and
    O'Brien
Goldstein, Goldberg, Goldblatt, and
    O'Brien
Cess, Poole, and Drayne
Ginsberg, Rosenburg, Goldstein, and
    O'Brien
Investors Inc.
Upland Realty Company
Wong Hi Lee Hand Laundry

Businesses, Stooge-Owned

A to Z Express Co.
Acme Exterminating Company
Cantina de Rosa
Cut Throat Drug Store
Day and Nite Plumbers
Fix-All Fixers, Ink.
Jiffy Fixers
K-9 Dog Laundry
Larry's Pet Shop
Lightning Pest Control Company
Madame De France
Minute Menders, Inc.
Pip Boys Lary Moe & Shemp
Shangri-La Upholstering Co.
Speedy Termite Exterminators

Super Slueth Detective Agency
The Smiling Egyptians
Ye Olde Furniture Shoppe
Ye Stooges Three—Sole Purveyors of Yuk
Zero Ice & Coal Co.

Butlers, Maids, and Servants

Barters
Clayhammer
Fifi
Flint
Gawkins
Jerkington
Mandy
Meadows
Sappington
Spiffingham
Wilkes
William
Williams

Castles and Mansions

Glenheather Castle
Norfleet Mansion
Smorgasbord Castle

Chants

"Gold, gold, we want gold . . . zoot!"
"We'll Get That Filthy Lucre . . ."
"We're on our way . . ."

Children

Egbert
Jimmy Collins
Junior
Little Betty Williams
Little Jimmy
Mergatroyd

Clothes

Asbestos suit
Mink, skunk, and porcupine

Clubs and Organizations

A.A.M. (Amalgamated Association of
    Morons) Local 6⅞
Canvas Back Duck Club
Liar's Club 27th Annual Convention
Rancho Golf Club
The Inventors Association
Woman Haters Club 87

Codes and Initials

C-A-N-D-Y
L-R-L-R-L-R-L 1-1-2-3-2-2-1
T.H.
W.H.

Colleges, Universities, and Trade Schools

A-1 Correspondence School of Detecting
Blue Point University
Boulder Dam University
Kraft's College of Arts
Mildew College
Wide Awake Detective School

Contests

Carrot County Fair Champion Milking
    Contest
Coffin Nail Cigarette Contest

Criminology

Mushroom Murders
Intent to Commit Mayhem

Crooks, Thieves, Con Men, and Swindlers

Angus and McPherson
B. O. Davis
Badlands Blackie
Blackie and Doyle
Blackjack and Lefty
Buck Wing
Cliff

Clipper
Daisy
Dandy Dawson
Dapper Dan
Diggins
Doc Barker
Double Deal Decker
The Eel
Elmo Drake
Filch
G. Y. Prince
Ghinna Rumma
Gyp the People
Haffa Dalla
Hassan Ben Sober
I. Cheatham
I. Fleecem
Icabod Slipp
Lefty Loomis
Lone Wolf Louie
Longhorn Pete
Mad Bill Hookup
Dr. Mallard
Mary
Miss Daisy Flowers
Molly the Glamour Girl
Montgomery M. Montgomery
Mr. and Mrs. Allen
Mr. Dill
Mr. Jerry Pip and Steve
Muscles
R. O. Broad
Ralph
Rance Roden
Randolph Stuart III
Reardon
Red Morgan
Sir Satchel
Slick Chick
Spike and Butch
Terry Hargen
Trigger Mortis

Vickers Cavendish
Walker

Curly

Characters
Coney Island Curly
Baron of Brains
Baron of Gray Matter
Buffalow Billious
Curleycue
Curly Q. Link
Curlylocks
Field Marshal Herring
Gallstone
Jackie
K. O. Bossy
K. O. Stradivarius
Maharajah of Canazzi
Major Hyde
McSnort
Mrs. Dennis O'Toole
Operator 15
Señorita Cucaracha
"Thunderbolt Nursemaid"
Tommy

Jokes, Phrases, and Sayings
"A frozen dainty"
"Are you casting asparagus on my
    cooking?"
"Are you married or happy?"
"Boxcars!"
"Canned Corn"
"Certainly; we're all incompetent!"
"Every man for himself!"
"He don't smoke, drink, nor chew."
"He drew twenty years with one stroke
    of the pen."
"Hello ma, hello pa. It wasn't much of
    a fight . . ."
"Hot stake is better than a cold chop."

"How I shall gobble this gobbler!"

"I can do very nicely with a highball!"

"I didn't know it was Monday!"

"I got my eyes closed."

"I got Stetson; which one is she?"

"I shot a seven, but they wouldn't give me the money!"

"I'll be back in a quack with a quack . . . and I do mean quack!"

"I'll make a note of it!"

"I'll take a ham sandwich."

"I'm a pedestrian!"

"I'm a victim of circumstance!"

"I'm glad he can't smell them any closer."

"I'm too pleasingly plump as it is."

"I'm trying to think, but nothing happens."

"Knights of Columbus"

"Look at the grouse!"

"The morbid the merrier!"

"No, but I get a little attack there every time I eat too much."

"No, but I know a big fence in Chicago."

"Oh, I don't know; I've been around!"

"On the end of a rope"

"Only when I take bicarbonate!"

"Smells like somebody's frying onions!"

"So it shouldn't be a total loss, I'm taking a bath!"

"Swing it!"

"That's almost a million!"

"The back of the drapes"

"There's no future in it"

"They generally hang out on the gallows!"

"This fish looks like Moe!"

"To say the least if not less"

"Vice? I have no vice. I'm as pure as the driven snow."

"Well, being as there's no other place . . ."

"Well, I'm too young . . ."

"Which one is Will?"

"Yeah, two bucks!"

"You know I'm not normal!"

"Your mother and my mother are both mothers."

"You're not even married."

Doctors and Dentists

Dr. A. Yank

Dr. Ba Loni Sulami

Dr. Belcher

Dr. Bright

Dr. D. Lerious

Dr. Gezundheidt

Dr. Graves

Dr. Howard, Dr. Fine, Dr. Howard

Dr. I. Yankum

Dr. Y. Tug

Dr. York

Drs. Hart, Burns, and Belcher

Drs. Lyman and Walters

Hugo Gansamacher

Ziller, Zeller, and Zoller

Dogs

Butch

Fido

Garçon

Pepé

Employers and Places of Work

Alert Detective Agency

Apex Construction Company

B.O. Pictures Corporation

Foreign Legion Headquarters

Hyden Zeke Detective Agency

Ithaca Pharmacy

Jones' Drugstore

Midland Fire Department

Miracle Detective Agency

National Space Foundation
Onion Oil Company
Police Station Section 13 Detective Bureau
Recruiting Headquarters
Romani Artistic Woodwork
Room 310
Scotland Yard
Seabiscuit Food Corp.
Sellwell Advertising Company
Stage 19
Star Cleaning & Pressing Company
Superior Warehouse and Storage Co.

Enemies

Amscray, Ixnay, and Umpchay
Black Louie
Black Prince
Blackie
Chizzilini
Dungen
George Lloyd
Hordred the Huntsman
Hugo
Johnson
José
Manuel
Marshal Bommell
Marshal Boring
Mattie Herring
Mergatroyd the Magician
Mr. Bell
Mr. Heller
Oga
Ogg and Zogg
Pierre
Radames
Rocky Duggan
Seeress of Roebuck
Shickelgruber
Signor
Steelia Pumpernickel, Amelia
    Schwartzbrut, and Celia Schweipak

Swinehardt
The High Mucky Muck
Umpchay
Varunu

Food

Adam and Eve on a Raft
Another turkey
Burned toast and a rotten egg
Bologna and whipped cream
Cackle fruit
Cackle soup
Chili pepperinos
Collision mats
Creampuffs
Filet of sole and heel
Flipper's Fluffy Fablongent Flapjacks
Four slices of burned toast and a
    rotten egg
(I'll take) A milkshake with sour milk
"Jive Dinners . . ."
Ketchup
Limburger cheese
Limburger cheese spread
"Liver and milk . . . and a banana split"
Lobster with frog legs
Maskazino cherry
Matzohs
Mrs. Flipper's Fluffy Pancake Mix
Nice cold hotcakes smothered in vinegar
A nice salami sandwich
Nice soup from a nice, juicy bone
Paté D'Fagua
Pig's feet smothered in lubricating oil . . .
Puppo Dog Biscuits
Roast Stooge
Southern Comforter
Sunny-side down and don't turn
    'em over
Swamp soup
Tarantula
White on rye

Gangs

Dillon Gang
The Killer Dillons
Mickey Finn Gang
Moose and Chuck
Noonan Brothers
Phantom Gang

Girlfriends, Fiancées, and Wives

Aggie, Maggie, and Baggie
April, May, and June
Bell
Betty, Hettie, and Nettie
Corabell, Dorabell, and Florabell
Dora and Flora
Effie
Ella, Bella, and Stella
Faith, Hope, and Charity
Flo, Mary, and Shirley
Heebah, Reebah, and Sheebah
Hilda, Wilda, and Tilda
Jane
Jessie, Bessie, and Tessie
Katrina
Lulu Belle, Mary Belle, and Ringa Belle
Mabel
Maisy, Mimi, and Minnie
Maria
Marigold, Narcissus, and Petunia
Mary
Millie
Miss Dinkelmeyer
Roberta
Stella, Nella, and Bella
Tillyeth, Millyeth, and Lillyeth
Tiny
Tiska, Taska, and Baska
Tizzy, Lizzy, and Dizzy

Goodguys and Partners

Arizona Kid

Axis Partners
Captain Andrews
Cedric the Blacksmith
Clarence Cassidy
Elmer
Kenneth Cabot
Mr. Williams
Old Man Goodrich
Percy Pomeroy
Prince Charming
Quatro the Magnificent
Quinto
Schuyler Davis
Will Idge

Gorillas, Apes, and Monkeys

Bonzo
Congo
Darwin
Harold the Ape
Igor the Ape
Joe

Gymnasiums and Health Spas

Hangover Athletic Club
Muscle Manor
Room 13
Slap-Happy Gym
Venetian Bath

Hideouts

Blackie's Place
Clark's Warehouse
Tomb of Old King Putentakeit

Homes and Residences

City Dump
Folger Apartments
Maintenance Men's Quarters
Mrs. Hammond Eggerley's
    Theatrical Apts.

Horses and Mules

Annie and Fannie
Bearded Lady
Birdie
Charger
Piggy
Schnapps
Seabasket
Silver
Thunderbolt
Vandy Legs, Bride's Biscuit . . .
Gladys
Yorrick

Hospitals

Bellevue Hospital
Croakers Sanitarium
Dr. Dippy's Retreat
Los Arms Hospital
Mallard's Rest Home and Clinic

Hotels

Biltless Hotel
Chisel Inn Hotel
Clinton Arms Hotel
Frontier Inn
Ghost Town Hotel
Happy Haven Hotel
Hotel Costa Plente
Hotel Snazzy Plaza
Room 1717
Room 810
Singapore Joe's Palace Hotel
Ye Olde Pilgrim Hotel

Indians

Chief Growling Bear
Chief Leaping Lizard
Chief Rain in the Puss

Ingredients

Anacanapanasan, eenar, anasana-
    pacarscram
Anacanapon and piddledictatar
Anapanacag, cedascram falsyeth,
    anacanapon, and eenots
Bretta, croomithistle, papeeptoomin,
    pickle juice
Eenginzoemen, anacanapanasan
Enchiladas, spaghetti, artichokes . . .
Fine powdered alum
A gallon of gasoline, two tumblers of
    bicarbonate . . .
Half a pint of ectowhozis (may substitute
    with ectowhatsis) . . .
Jumbo Mexican Jumping Beans
Molasses, Tabasco, seltzer
Popping corn
Sodium bicarbonate and popcorn
Turpentine
200 percent wool
"Vitamins A, B, C, D, E, F; Gee . . ."
Zendayfus, mishegas, pyareecon, cotton

Innocent Bystanders

Cousin Basil
The DePeysters
Miss Emma Blake
Philip Black

Inventions

"A Maid on a Night Out Winding . . ."
The Buzzard
Fountain of Youth
Fountain pen that writes under whipped
    cream
Gold Collar Button Retriever
Modes Modernistique
Poison Gas
Shock Absorber for Earthquakes
Simplex Rodent Exterminator

Jails and Prisons

City Pound
Hangemall Prison
Lobo Jail
San Brandon Penitentiary
Sing Sing, Alcatraz, Leavenworth, Joliet

Joe

Jokes, Phrases, and Sayings

"Nobody lives here, either!"
"Squeak, squeak"
"Turn around, I'll kiss her behind your back!"

Judges

J. M. Benton
Judge Henderson
Judge Woodcock R. Strinker
Nick Barker
Uncle Tim

Landlords

Amos Flint
Mr. Dinkelspiel
Mr. Gingy
Mr. Scroggins
Mr. Singapore
Mr. Stutz
Mrs. Magruder

Larry

Characters

Duke of Durham
Duke of Mixture
Jim
Just Plain Bill
Larraine
Larrycus
Lieutenant Duck

McSniff
Minister of Propaganda
Moronica (Larry)
Operator 12
Pebble
Tarraday
Thunderbolt Pilot

Jokes, Phrases, and Sayings

"The bag left me holding the babe!"
"Eighteen blondes and twelve redheads"
"Dububb, zedubb, wubbub, dewubb dee dub wub"
"Gezundheidt"
"He'll feblonger him."
"Henna color at all."
"Huck mir nisht a chynick, and I don't mean efsher."
"I can't die; I haven't seen *The Jolson Story!*"
"I'm going to get myself a cheap lawyer."
"Isn't he quisn't!"
"It ain't spring yet!"
"It's our duty to posterior."
"Listen to that exhaust!"
"The mortar the merrier!"
"No, I'll wait; maybe I'll get potatoes"
"No, Milwaukee"
"Oh, thank you. I couldn't dance a step last year."
"Oh, woe is Moe!"
"Secondhand"
"She broke it off"
"Tastes more like marshmallow gumbo."
"That babe sure can cook!"
"That's too permanent!"
"They don't show!"
"We graduated with the highest temperatures in our class!"
"We need the eggs."

"Who came in?"
"Why don't you sing 'Mame'?"
"Yeah, but I don't like the stuffing."
"Yeah, but I'm goin' anyhow."
"You burnt my little bugle."
"You see-eth, it's like this-eth."
"You told me to drop what I was doing, so I did."
"A week back."

Letters and Notes

"Darling Husband . . ."
"Dear General Muster . . ."
"Dear Hatchet Face . . ."
"Giveth Them the Works"
"Gone to Rest Under the Spreading Chestnut Tree"
"Merry X-Mas, Your Pet Man Larry"
"Tired of being beautiful and alone . . ."
"When in Chicago . . ."
"Whereas I, Shemp the Stooge . . ."

Maps

Cow
Map of Unknown Lands . . .
Walla Walla

Medicines, Prognoses, and Diagnoses

Abdul's Cactus Remedy
Botanical offshoot
Brighto
Cerebrum decapitation
"Completely illogical, preponderantly impracticable . . ."
Crushed eyebrows
Executive clemency
G.C.M.
Goiter
"Incomprehensible and utterly impractical"
Nerve tonic

90 Proof
95 percent temper; 5 percent mental
Potomac poisoning
Practically unoccupied
Pungfauthadrednock with the bicuspid canafran
Salve
Skin
Spectus-on-the-floorus
T.B.
T.S.
10 degrees below zero
Vacancy of the cranium
Vitamins A.P.U.
Vitamins P.D.Q.
X-Ray fluoroscope
Yuk
106$^{7}/_{8}$

Military Personnel

Admiral H. S. Taylor
Captain Burke
Captain Daley
Captain Gorgonzola
Captain Roarke
Colonel Buttz
Colonel Henderson
General Muster
Kelly
Major Filbert
Republic of Televania Naval Base
Sergeant MacGillicuddy
Sergeant Mullins

Miscellaneous

Elvis
"Go two miles north and make a left-hand turn at the pool room"
"I want a good dirty fight . . ."
"Is it true that the time and space . . ."
M. Balmer
N.U.T.Z.

Mobsters

Big Mike
Butch McGee
Gashouse Protective Association
Mugsy
Tony

Moe

Characters

Halliday
Captain Dodge
Count of Five
Fife of Drum
McSnuff
Mickey Moe the Murderin' Masseur
Mike Lipincranz
Moe Hailstone
Moella
Mohicus
Omay
Operator 14
The Gin of Rummy
"Thunderbolt Manager"
Wild Bill Hicup

Jokes, Phrases, and Sayings

"About five-foot-five by five-foot-five"
"At a loss for adjectives"
"Breaker-uppers of the peanut brittle foundry"
"Don't let 'em kill you till we get there!"
"Don't worry; you smell . . . good!"
"Gevalt!"
"Highly polished mahogany and termites with big blue eyes"
"I hope it didn't hit the pool room"
"If you were over here I'd give you this!"
"I got it for my bar mitzvah!"
"I'm losing my mind!"
"I'm poisoned!"
"Impossible"

"It must be something else"
"Just straight salary"
"Last year"
"Look in these shoes for some toes!"
"Mademoiselle"
"Meet my bare hand"
"Mingle or I'll mangle!"
"The mouth is in the front!"
"Not since I was a baby"
"Parasites"
"Pump in four more slices"
"Quit bragging"
"Say a few syllables! Utter a few adjectives!"
"Speak for yourself, rodent!"
"The Stooges have landed and have the situation well in hand!"
"A swiss cheese"
"Tar ytrid eeth say . . ."
"Tell him to dial inflammation"
"That's in case you do and I'm not around"
"This is the hottest June we've had since last July!"
"Thou hath made me shoe the wrong mule"
"To your last breath . . ."
"Twenty minutes to a pound; we'll be here a month!"
"Wake up and go to sleep!"
"We'll be there in a flash in the flesh!"
"You know, you should fish for a whale"
"You were delivered by a buzzard"
"You're a very intelligent imbecile"
"You're getting no place fast!"
"You're tearing my heart out!"

Money, Moolah, Rewards, and Loot

$4.95/$4.85
400 Shekels
489 Shekels

$97
$100
$140
$1,000
1,000 Shilbleenas
1,000 Shilbleenas Virgin Tax
67 Cents Net
$10,000
35 cents
3,000 guineas, two geese, and a duck
$2,000
$2,198.55

Monsters

Angel
Desmond of the Outer Sanctorum
Dr. Jekyll and Mr. Hyde
The Goon
Lupe the Wolf Man
Nikko

Museums

Museum of Ancient History
Museum of Natural History

Newspaper Headlines

"Candid Cameraman . . ."
"Actual Photo of Flying Saucer Sets
    Country Ablaze"
"Another Broadway Turkey . . ."
"Armored Car Robbers Identified . . ."
"Atomic Documents Missing"
"Councilman Goodrich Threatened with
    Death . . ."
"Curly Q. Link Sought . . ."
"Earthmen Return Home . . ."
"Flying Saucer Photo Alerts Capitol"
"Flying Saucer Photographer Awarded
    City's Highest Honor"
"Jap Sub Blown Up . . ."
"Law Officers on the Way . . ."

"Madcap Wins Ten Thousand Dollar
    Sweepstakes"
"Manning Baby Disappears!"
"Mysterious Burglaries Panic City . . ."
"Prince Shaam of Ubeedarn Engaged . . ."
"Punjab Diamond Stolen"
"Rich Oil Man Gets Divorce Yesterday . . ."
"Suitors in Third Week of Sit Down Strike"
"Yanks Win World Series"

Newspapers

Daily Chronicle
Daily Gazette
Daily News
The Daily Press Post
The Daily Record Post
Daily Star Press
Daily Star-News
Gazette Journal
New York Gazette
New York Globe
Star Dispatch
The Times
The Times Press
Urania Daily Bladder
Washington Chronicle

Pals

Claude A. Quacker
Gladys Harmon
J.T.
Jerry
Smithers
Spirit of Sir Tom
Tiny Landers
Widow Jenkins
Bill and Rosebud

Patients

Anna Conda
Puckerless Persimmon Tree

Perfumes and Colognes

Fleur de Polecat
Fleur de Skunk
Fleur de Stinkun
Lily of the Alley
Schlemiel Number Eight
Stink
Wild Hyacinth

Places, Destinations, Kingdoms, and Faraway Lands

Anesthesia
Ancient Erysipelas
Anemia
Bay of Rum
Below the McMason McDixon line
Bonny Banks
Bravuria
Cloud 49
Coleslawvania
Coyote Creek
Coyote Pass
Cucaracha
Dead Man's Gulch
Dead Man's Island
Erysipelas
Ever Rest Pet Cemetery
Hill 303
Hollywood Storage Company
Isle of Stromboli
Ithaca
Kingdom of Anesthesia
Lake Winapasakee
Little America
Lobo City
Moronica
Pago Pago
Peaceful Gulch
Pier 7
Raribonga

Red Dog Canyon
Rhum Boogie
Rue de Schlemiel and Rue de le Pew
Shmow
Skagway, Alaska
Skullbone Pass
South Starv-Vania
Start at Jerkola
Starvania
State of Anemia
Stincoala, Moronica
Sunev
The Brooklyn Building
Tsimiss
Tunis
"Under the spreading chestnut tree . . ."
Urania
Valeska
Vault 3 U.S. Treasury
Vulgaria
Wienerschnitzel Straza
Winkelburg
Zircon

Plays, Movies, Attractions, and Show-Biz Skits

"At the Front"
"The Bride Wore Spurs"
Brooks Circus
Herman's Great Combined Shows
Jilted in the Jungle
Joe's Minstrels Songs and Dances
Kiss the Moonbeams Off My Elbow
Kokonuts Grove
Leander's Carnival
Mlle. Zora
"Mystery Motor Jackpot" show
Nell's Belles
"The Panics of 1936"
"Stooge Follies"
"Two Souls and a Heel"

Poems

"Dear Old Mexico"
"I shoot an arrow into the air . . ."
"I Was Born in Brazil"
"Jack and Jill"
"Little Fly Upon the Wall"
"Little Miss Muffet"
"Mame"
"Mary, Mary, Quite Contrary"
"My Beautiful Jane"
"Number 22"
"She loves me, she loves me not . . ."
"Simple Simon"
"We Baked You a Birthday Cake"
"We're dressed as ballerinas"

Police, Sheriffs, and Other Lawmen

B. A. Copper
Captain Casey and Brown
Captain Mullins
Chief Kelly
F. B. Eye
F.B.I.
I. Doolittle
Inspector McCormick
J. J. Figbee
Officer O'Halloran
Sam Shovel
T. E. Higgins

Politicians

Abel Lamb Stewer
Hammond Egger
Wm. "Bill Wick"

Proclamations and Declarations

"For Duty and Humanity!"
"Give me that fillum!"
"Mazel Tov!" and "L'Chaim!"
"Thank you, Mr. Personally"
"Ver G'harget," "Over the River," and
    "Skip the Gutter"

Products for Sale

Becky
Consolidated Fujiyama California
    Smog Bags
Clux Dog Soap
Crumb's Pies
Dopey Dan's Daily Double
Edam Neckties
Felix Famous Concentrated Soap
Hazel
Instant Glue
Krispy Krunchies
La Stinkadora
Last in Kadora
Latherneck Shaving Cream
Miracle Massage Reducing Machine
Mother's Pies
No Burpoline
N'Yuk-N'Yuks
Pamo Hair Remover
Skeleton Fish
Stix Fast Glue
A tenth-century Ras Bañas . . .

Professors and Instructors

B. Bopper
Davenport Seats
Dr. Powell
O. U. Gonga
Professor A. K. Rimple
Professor Bilbo
Professor Bob O. Link
Professor Danforth
Professor Fuller
Professor Hicks
Professor Jones
Professor Panzer

Professor Repulso
"Professor Shemp Howard—Teacher of Voice"
Professor Snead
Professor Tuttle
Professors Feinstein, Frankfurter, and Von Stueben
Professors Rich and Nichols, Quackenbush and Sedletz
Watts D. Matter

Promoters

Manny Weeks Theatrical Enterprises
Mr. and Mrs. Leander

Radio and TV Stations

B-U-R-P
Radio KGBY
WGN
WX21

Relatives

Fifty Generations
Louie, Max, and Jack
Luke, Morris, and Jeff
Mr. Stevens
Popsie
Uncle Caleb
Uncle Mortimer
Uncle Pete
Uncle Phineas Bowman

Reporters

Brown
Mr. Wallace
Smitty
Waldo Twitchell

Restaurants

Black Bottom Café
Café Casbahbah

Café La-Mer-Essen
Elite Café
Flounder Inn
Jive Café
Joe's Beanery
O'Brien's Kosher Restaurant
Squid McGuffey's Café
Vesuvius Restaurant
Ye Colonial Inn

Routines

81C
Maha
"Niagara Falls"
Number Four in the Blue Book
Routine Number Six

Royalty

Countess Schpritzwasser
The Earl of Glenheather
Emir of Shmow
Gilda
King Cole
King Herman $6\frac{7}{8}$
King Putentakeit
King Rootentooten
King Rootin' Tootin' Diamond
King Rutentuten
King Winter Outfitting Co.
Lord Larryington and Sir Moeington
Luana
Octopus Grabus
Odius
Prince Boris
Prince Gallant III of Rhododendron
Prince Shaam
Princess Alicia
Princess Elaine
Queen Anne of Anesthesia
Queen Hotsytotsy
Sir Moeington

Sultan of Abadaba
Sultan of Pish Posh
Thesus
Ulysses

Rulers

Emir of Shmow
Governor of Dead Man's Island
Government of Urania—Department
   of Inferior
Grand Zilch of Sunev
Omagosh
President Ward Robey
Republic of Cannabeer

Screen Titles

"According to Darwin . . ."
"All Parts in this Picture Are Played by
   the Three Stooges"
"Ancient Egypt. In the Reign of the Great
   King Rootentooten"
"Any Resemblance . . ."
"Any Similarity . . ."
"The Characters in this Picture . . ."
"Dead Man's Island 1672"
"Filmed in Glorious Black and White"
"A Flying Field Somewhere in Somewhere"
"Fort Scott, Kansas, 1868—The Heroic
   Men of the U.S. Cavalry"
"In Days of Old . . ."
"In the Spring . . ."
"Merrie Olde England"
"Mexico—Where Men Are Men and
   Women Are Glad of It"
"The Orient . . ."
"Paris—Somewhere in France"
"A Small Kingdom . . ."
"Somewhere in the Orient"

Shemp

Characters

Christmas Day

Groundhog Day
Independence Day
Labor Day
New Year's Day
Painless Papyrus
Shempetta
St. Patrick's Day

Jokes, Phrases, and Sayings

"A barking dog never bites . . ."
"Come to Papa!"
"A couple a pip pips, a little barbecue,
   and what have you!"
"Don't look at me when you say that!"
"Eureka!"
"Gee, Moe, I'm sorry, Moe, what Moe
   can a fella say? . . ."
"The genius!"
"A gorg goggle yata . . ."
"Hi, Lorna; how ya doone?"
"Hospital"
"I know how!"
"I mean business!"
"I used to play in five flats . . ."
"I've had it ever since I was a little kid."
"Is my slip showing?"
"It don't say anything, you gotta look
   at it."
"It's putrid!"
"It's sharp medicine, but it's a sure cure
   for all diseases."
"Me, three!"
"My ex-wife and ten bartenders"
"1,000"
"And the rest of the day for myself!"
"Six lions were tearing me apart bit
   by bit"
"Somebody's roasting a ham!"
"That's good; I never could dance before"
"That's nothin'. We had a bed that went
   back to Sears Roebuck the Third"
"There must be a way to get
   that ring . . ."

"Tick-Tick-Tick-Tick-Tick"

"Unitarians"

"Well, we're not in my country . . ."

"What a beautiful messterpiece!"

"What a hideous, monstrous face!"

"What size, madam? We have some
      lovely ground-grippers!"

"What's a matter with my eyes; do they
      look like halvah?"

"Which one?"

"You're telling me!"

Show-Biz Stars and Acts

Ali Ben Woodman and His Swinging
      Bedouins

Balbo the Magician

Bill Stein

Castor and Earle Revue

The Fishmarket Duet

The Great Svengarlic

Hilarious Hash Slingers

J. O. Dunkfeather

The Original Two-Man Quartet

Paul Pain

Percival DePuyster

Mr. Philander

Sandra Sandpile

Señor Louis Balero Cantino

Scowling Scotsman

The Three Stooges Scrapbook

Signs, Insignias, and Emblems

"All Unmarried Redheaded Maidens . . ."

"Bad Lands"

"Beneath This . . ."

"The Biggest Chiselers in Town"

"The Biggest Grafters in Town"

"Blacksmith Shop"

"The Busiest Spot on the Map"

"Cairo City Limits—Tunis 1500 mi."

"CA MERAS PROH IBITED O NPENAL
      TYOF DEATH"

"Can U Take It? Try Our Mush"

"Casey the Plumber"

"Census Takers Report Here"

"Cry in This"

"Danger Dynamite Caps . . ."

"Dangerous—Keep Away . . ."

"Dead or in Bad Shape"

"Decker 117, Opponents 0"

"Delegates Welcome to Convention City"

"Deposit Dogs Here"

"Do Not Disturb"

"Double Featur"

"Dump No Rubbish Here"

"Engine 1 M.F.D."

"Everything From a Needle to a
      Battleship . . ."

"Examination Room"

"Exit Tunnel 12"

"Fairport Theatre"

"Finders Keepers"

"Football To-day. Tigers Vs. Cubs.
      Positively No Admittance"

"Free Auto"

"Friday the 13th"

"General Handiwork Our Speshalty"

"Gone to Lunch—Moe, Larry, Curly"

"Happy 10th Anniversary"

"Here Lies a Father of 28 . . ."

"Hey You No Smoking"

"Home Sweet Home"

"Horseradish"

"Hours 2 to 5 or by Appointment"

"I Am Starving . . ."

"I Must Not Eat Out of Garbage Cans"

"Inspector"

"It's In His Left Pocket"

"Joe's Traveling Store General
      Merchandise"

"Keep Our City Clean"

"Laughing Gas"

"Mama Loved Papa . . ."

"The Management Reserves the Right to
      Refuse $1,000 Bills"

"Men at Work"
"Must Have a Job . . ."
"No Dogs or Babies Allowed"
"No Honeymoon No Work . . ."
"No Hunting, Fishing, or Swimming"
"No Peddlers"
"No Sale"
"No Smoking—No Hunting—No Fishing—No Nothing Go Home"
"No Use—You're Doomed"
"Not Responsible for Hats and Coats"
"Nothing to Buy, Nothing to Sell . . ."
"Open 10 to 3"
"Opportunities in Mexico . . ."
"Patents Bought and Sold"
"Players Only"
"Plymouth City Limits . . ."
"Post No Bills"
"Press-Press-Pull"
"Proclamation . . ."
"Quiet—Do Not Disturb"
"Rubbish Permit 186"
"SAP 752"
"Stop Look and Listen"
"This End Up"
"This Lot Presented to the Three Sitdown Suitors . . ."
"This Place Unfair to Union Suitors"
"2 Hr. Parking . . ."
"U.S. Army Join Now"
"Unfair to Union Husbands"
"Vacancies Exist"
"Wanted for Vagrancy"
"Welcome to Cucaracha"
"When You Get Back . . ."
"Wild Bill Hicup Due In"
"Ye Olde Tilt"

Songs

"A-Calling We Do Come"
"Adirondack . . ."
"Boo-hoo"

"Don't Chop the Wood . . ."
"The Elevator Dance"
"Home on the Farm"
"Home on the Range"
"Let's Fall in Love"
"Oh, Elaine"
"Old King Cole"
"Pop Goes the Weasel"
"Ramonones Sequidimes, by Fleeacrons"
"Rock Caught Sea Bass . . ."
"Sextetrum Lucia"
"She Was Bred in Old Kentucky"
"Six Tetrum Lucy"
"So We Stuck Our Little Tootsies in the Water"
"Swingeroo Joe"
"Swinging the Alphabet"
"The Farmer in the Dell"
"The Heat Is On"
"The Wedding Bells"
"Tuna Fish . . ."
"Viva Vulgaria!"
"Voices of Spring"
"Way Down South in New York City"
"We Just Stopped In To Say Hello"
"Yankee Noodle Soup"
"You'll Never Know"
"Zee Lollipop"

Spies

Bortch
Count Alfred Gehrol
Mr. Cash
Operator 13

Spinsters

Mrs. Crump
Mrs. Magruder

Stadiums and Arenas

Gilmore Stadium
Majestic Fight Arena

Platt Field
Plaza D'Toros
Teatro Internacional

Stooges

Characters
Click, Clack, and Cluck
Honest Moe, Honest Shemp, and Larry
Hook, Line, and Sinker
Horsethieves!
Howard, Fine, and Besser—Stage, Screen, and Radar
Inky, Binky, and Dinky
Johnny, Frankie, and Mabel
Link, Mink, and Pink
Naki, Saki, and Waki
Nill, Null, and Void
Señors Mucho and Gusto
Secretary of the Offense . . .
The Three Horsemen
Wrong Brothers

Stores and Shops
Ajax Sportswear
Complete Outfitters
Crosby Building
Metropole Flower Shop
Square Deal Swap Shop
The Doggy Pet Shop

Suspects and Shady Characters
Antonio Zucchini Salami Gorgonzola de Pizza
Chopper
Gilbraith Q. Tiddledewadder
Joe Stack

Telephone Numbers
Bleep Bluep Blop
Main 2468
Stockyard 1234
Susquehana 2222

Theatres
Circle Follies Theatre
Eagon's Rehearsal Hall Theatre
Garden Theatre

Tools
Derstick, anacanapooner
Hemoglober, sulfademus
Lubazac, whozica, pashcunyakas, cotton
Semert, anacome, senetoonum . . .
Tractohomolactometer, hammadeemaceemafaren

Trains and Railroads
Cannonball Express
Car 314
C.M. & St. P. R.R.
Heavenly Express
Penciltucky Railroad Co.
Penciltucky Railroad Co. No. 428
Schmow

Treasures, Riches, and Priceless Artifacts
Ambrose Rose Estate
Captain Kidd's Kid's Treasure
$5,000 Benson County Sweepstakes
The Lost Mine
The most beautiful cave in Mesopotamia
Punjab Diamond
The Van Brocklin Painting
U.S. Treasury

Uniform Numbers
A-K-70
B-K-68
18
41144
H_2O

H^2O^2
O-K-67
$1/2$
+4
?
$6^7/8$
13
30
22

Vehicles

Bronx Taxi Cab
Bunion Eight
Columbus
Yukon Ice Cream

Victims

Kirk Robbin
Slug McGurk

PART IV

Entries Listed
by Film

An Ache in Every Stake

"Are you married or happy?"

"A frozen dainty"

"Ice with Personality—Coal with Oomph"

"On the end of a rope"

"Pump in four more slices!"

"We Baked You a Birthday Cake"

"You need another strike"

Zero Ice & Coal Co.

A Ducking They Did Go

Blackie and Doyle

Canvas Back Duck Club

Crosby Building

"I'll be back in a quack with a quack . . . and I do mean quack!"

"You'll Never Know"

All Gummed Up

Amos Flint

Cackle fruit

Cut Throat Drug Store

Eenginzoemen, anacanapanasan

"Everything from a Needle to a Battleship . . ."

Fountain of Youth

"Horseradish"

"It's putrid!"

Jumbo Mexican Jumping Beans

"The mortar the merrier!"

Pinch Penny Market

Serena Flint

"Tastes more like marshmallow gumbo"

Zendayfus, mishegas, pyareecon, cotton

All the World's a Stooge

Ajax

Barters

Dr. I. Yankum

Johnny, Frankie, and Mabel

Limburger cheese spread

"Little Fly upon the Wall"

"Mame"

Paté D'Fagua

Salve

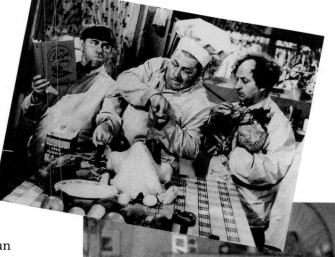

Chef Curly has always been delightfully liberal in deciding which ingredients to add to a turkey (*An Ache in Every Stake*, 1941).

You can always get a second helping of cake when Moe's around (*All Gummed Up*, 1947).

Ants in the Pantry

A. Mouser
Gawkins
"Got Ants in Your Plants? We'll Kill 'Em!"
Lightning Pest Control Company
"Meet my bare hand"
Mrs. Burlap
Professor Repulso

A Plumbing We Will Go

"Casey the Plumber"
Columbia Uniform Supply Company
The Doggy Pet Shop
Mrs. Throttlebottom's Chicken Coop
Professor Bilbo
WX21

Baby Sitters Jitters

Davenport Seats
"Eureka!"
Felix Famous Concentrated Soap
Folger Apartments
George Lloyd
"Gezundheidt"
How to Become a Babysitter
Junior
Mrs. Crump
1,000
Unitarians

Back from the Front

"Any Resemblance . . ."
Dungen
Fido
"Hang Hitler!"
Inky, Blinky, and Dinky
Minister of Propaganda
"No Hunting, Fishing, or Swimming"
S. S. *Dotty*
S. S. *Shickelgruber*
Tizzy, Lizzy, and Dizzy

Back to the Woods

Chief Rain in the Puss
Faith, Hope, and Charity
"Giveth them the works"
The Good Ship Pfifernill
"How I shall gobble this gobbler!"
"I'll take a ham sandwich"
"Merrie Olde England"
"Plymouth City Limits . . ."
"You see-eth, it's like this-eth . . ."

Bedlam in Paradise

Asbestos suit
Cloud 49
The DePeysters
Fountain pen that writes under whipped
   cream
Heavenly Express
Helen Blazes
I. Fleecem
Miss Jones
Mr. Heller
$140
10 degrees below zero
Uncle Mortimer
"Whereas I, Shemp the Stooge . . ."

Beer Barrel Polecats

A-K-70
B-K-68
Burned toast and a rotten egg
H_2O
How to Make Panther Pilsner Beer
O-K-67
185
Percy Pomeroy
+4
"Say a few syllables! Utter a few
   adjectives!"
13

A Bird in the Head

Igor the Ape
Mr. Beedle
Nikko
"Practically unoccupied"
Professor Panzer
X-Ray Fluoroscope

Blunder Boys

Alma Matter
Biltless Hotel
Christmas Day
The Eel
81C
F. B. Eye
Groundhog Day
Halliday
Independence Day
La Stinkadora
Labor Day
Last in Kadora
New Year's Day
St. Patrick's Day
Tarraday
Watts D. Matter

Boobs in Arms

"Adirondack . . ."
"Cards for All Occasions"
"Join the Army and See the World—or
    What's Left of It"
"Laughing Gas"
Number 22
O'Brien's Kosher Restaurant
Recruiting Headquarters
"When You Get Back . . ."

Booby Dupes

"Don't Chop the Wood . . ."
"My, what a beautiful head of bone
    you have!"

SAP 752
Skeleton Fish
"Tuna Fish . . ."

Booty and the Beast

"That's good; I never could dance
    before."
"Wake up and go to sleep!"

Brideless Groom

Cousin Basil
"Impossible"
J. M. Benton
Miss Dinkelmeyer
Miss Hopkins
"Professor Shemp Howard—Teacher
    of Voice"
Susquehana 2222
Uncle Caleb
"Voices of Spring"

Bubble Trouble

Amos Flint
Cut Throat Drug Store
Eenginzoemen, anacanapanasan
"Everything from a Needle to a
    Battleship . . ."
Fountain of Youth
"Horseradish"
"It's putrid!"
"The mortar the merrier!"
Pinch Penny Market
Serena Flint
"Tastes more like marshmallow gumbo"
Zendayfus, mishegas, pyareecon, cotton

Busy Buddies

"Are you casting asparagus on my
    cooking?"
Cackle soup
"Can U Take It? Try Our Mush"

Carrot County Fair Champion Milking
    Contest
Collision mats
Cow
Jive Café
"Jive Dinners—4 Bits—Bloop Soup, Reat
    Meat, Jake Cake, Hava Java"
K. O. Bossy
$97
"No Sale"
Sellwell Advertising Company

Cactus Makes Perfect

"Finders Keepers"
Ghost Town Hotel
Gold Collar Button Retriever
"Gold, gold, we want gold . . . zoot!"
"I shoot an arrow into the air, where it
    lands I do not care; I get my arrows
    wholesale!"
"Incomprehensible and utterly
    impractical"
The Inventors Association
"It's In His Left Pocket"
The Lost Mine
Mother's Pies

Calling All Curs

Anacanapon and piddledictatar
Botanical offshoot
Dr. Howard, Dr. Fine, and Dr. Howard
G.C.M.
Garçon
"I got my eyes closed"
"I Must Not Eat Out of Garbage
    Cans"
"I'm trying to think, but nothing
    happens!"
"Mazel Tov!"
Mrs. Bedford
"To say the least if not less"
$2,000

Cash and Carry

Boxcars
Canned Corn
Captain Kidd's Kid's Treasure
City Dump
Executive clemency
"I'll make a note of it!"
Little Jimmy
President of the United States
"That's almost a million!"
U.S. Treasury
Vault 3
Walla Walla

Commotion on the Ocean

Bortch
J. L. Cameron
Daily Gazette
"Give me that fillum!"
Miss Emma Blake
Pier 7
Smitty

Cookoo Cavaliers

"The Busiest Spot on the Map"
Cantina de Rosa
Cucaracha
"Double Featur"
Fleur de Skunk
1410 South America Way
A gallon of gasoline, two tumblers of
    bicarbonate of soda, an ounce of
    iodine, and a pinch of mustard
"Henna color at all"
Hook, Line, and Sinker
Juanita, Conchita, Pepita, and Rosita
Manuel
"No, but I get a little attack there every
    time I eat too much"
"Opportunities in Mexico . . ."
Pamo Hair Remover
Pedro Ruiz Business Opportunities

"Rock Caught Sea Bass . . ."
"Welcome to Cucaracha"

Corny Casanovas

"Gee, Moe, I'm sorry, Moe . . ."
"I'm losing my mind!"
"You're tearing my heart out!"

Crash Goes the Hash

Daily News
Daily Star Press
Flint
Fuller Bull
Mrs. van Bustle
Prince Shaam
Puppo Dog Biscuits
Star Cleaning & Pressing Company
"We Dye for You"

Creeps

A to Z Express Co.
Desmond of the Outer
    Sanctorum
"Six lions were tearing me
    apart bit by bit"
Smorgasbord Castle
Spirit of Sir Tom

Crime on Their Hands

Daily Gazette
Dapper Dan
Harold the Ape
J. L. Cameron
Muscles
Punjab Diamond
"Punjab Diamond Stolen"
Squid McGuffey's Café

Cuckoo on the Choo Choo

Carey
"Do Not Disturb"
Limburger cheese

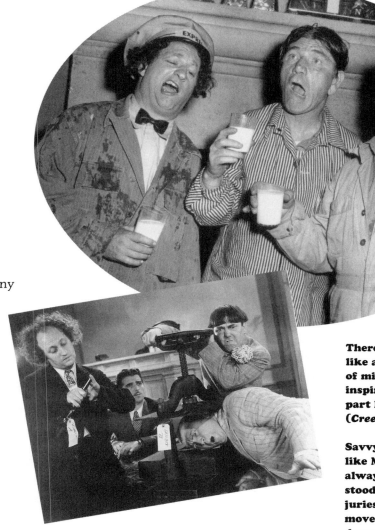

There's nothing like a cold glass of milk to inspire three-part harmony (*Creeps,* 1956).

Savvy witnesses like Moe have always understood that juries are moved by dramatic courtroom demonstrations (*Disorder in the Court,* 1936).

Nora
Penciltucky Railroad Co.
Penciltucky Railroad Co. No. 428
Roberta
Schmow

Disorder in the Court

Black Bottom Café
Buck Wing
Gail Tempest
"Gone to Lunch—Moe, Larry, Curly"

"I'm a victim of circumstance!"
Kirk Robbin
Polly

Dizzy Detectives
Bonzo
The Brooklyn Building
Daily Chronicle
Gypsom Good Inc., Antiques
I. Doolittle
"I'm poisoned!"
Mr. Dill
"Mysterious Burglaries Panic City—Police Shakeup as Ape Man Strikes Again"
"There's no future in it"

Dizzy Doctors
"Brightens Old Bodies"
Brighto
Brighto Medical Company
Doctor Bright
"Hello ma, hello pa. It wasn't much of a fight. I stood like that . . . but not for long"
"If you have a knick knack with a nick in it, we'll knock the nick out of the knick knack with Brighto"
Los Arms Hospital
"Quiet—Do Not Disturb"
"Tell him to dial inflammation"
"Three of the best salesmen who ever sailed"

Dizzy Pilots
The Buzzard
Hydrogen gas
Joe Strubachincoscow
Republic of Cannabeer, P.U.
Sky Aircraft Company
Stincoala, Moronica
"Vice? I have no vice. I'm as pure as the driven snow."
Wrong Brothers

Don't Throw That Knife
"Any Resemblance . . ."
"Cry in This"
Earysyphillus
Hospital
Lucy Wykoff

Dopey Dicks
Main 2468
Ralph
Sam Shovel
275 Mortuary Road

Dunked in the Deep
Bortch
"Danger Dynamite Caps . . ."
The Fishmarket Duet
"Give me that fillum!"
"Number Four in the Blue Book"
"Old Holland Cheese . . ."
Pier 7

Dutiful but Dumb
"CA MERAS PROH IBITED O NPENAL TYOF DEATH"
Click, Clack, and Cluck
"If it's a Good Picture, it's out of Whack!"
Mr. Wilson
Percival DePuyster
Star Dispatch
"Viva Vulgaria!"
Vulgaria
Whack Magazine

Even as I.O.U.
Bearded Lady
Dopey Dan's Daily Double
"If You Buy a Home Like This It's a Miracle"
Miracle Homebuilders, Inc.
Press-Press-Pull
Seabasket

False Alarms

Maisy, Mimi, and Minnie

Fiddlers Three

Coleslawvania
F.B.I.
"Gone to Rest
Under the
Spreading
Chestnut Tree"
"Jack and Jill"
King Cole
"Little Miss Muffet"
Mergatroyd the
Magician
"Old King Cole"
Prince Gallant III of
Rhododendron
Princess Alicia
"Simple Simon"
"A Small Kingdom . . ."
"Thou hath made me shoe
the wrong mule"
Will Idge

Fifi Blows Her Top

Café La-Mer-Essen
Fifi
"Howard, Fine and Besser—Stage Screen
and Radar"
Katrina
Leiloni Baggiagaloupe
Maria
Parasites
Rue de Schlemiel and Rue de le Pew
Wienerschnitzel Straza

Flagpole Jitters

Calamity Insurance Company
Garden Theatre
Gottrox Jewelry Company
The Great Svengarlic

Too many chefs . . . (*Flagpole Jitters*, 1956)

"He'll Steal Your Breath Away!"
"Here This Week—The Great Hypnotist
Svengarlic—He'll Steal Your Breath
Away—A Stellar Attraction—
Scientific—Educational—2
Performances Daily"
Mary
Nice cold hotcakes smothered in vinegar

Flat Foot Stooges

Annie and Fannie
Butch
Chief Kelly
"Engine 1 M.F.D."
"I'm too pleasingly plump as it is"
Midland Fire Department
Miss Kelly
Reardon
"You're not even married"

Fling in the Ring

Big Mike
Chopper Kane
Creampuffs
Crushed eyebrows
Gorilla Watson
"He'll feblonger him"
Kitty
Majestic Fight Arena
Moose and Chuck
Oscar the Dummy
Slap-Happy Gym
"Tick-Tick-Tick-Tick-Tick"

Flying Saucer Daffy

A.B. Cloud & Co.
"Actual Photo of Flying Saucer Sets
    Country Ablaze"
Bleep Bluep Blop
Daily Star-News
Facts and Figures Magazine
"Flying Saucer Photo Alerts Capitol"
"Flying Saucer Photographer Awarded
    City's Highest Honor"
Giggle water
New York Gazette
200 Vapor Blvd., Zircon
Tyra and Electra
Washington Chronicle
Zircon

For Crimin' Out Loud

"Councilman Goodrich Threatened with
    Death—Promise to Clean Up Vice and
    Corruption Brings Threat from
    Racketeers"
"A couple a pip pips, a little barbecue,
    and what have you!"
"Don't let 'em kill you till we get there!"
"Highly polished mahogany and
    termites with big blue eyes"
"I mean business!"

"If We Solve Your Crime It's a Miracle!"
"It don't say anything, you gotta look
    at it"
Miracle Detective Agency
Nikko
Old Man Goodrich
1313 Hysteria Terrace

Fright Night

Big Mike
Chopper Kane
Clark's Warehouse
Creampuffs
Crushed eyebrows
Gorilla Watson
Kitty
"Love Tales"
Majestic Fight Arena
Muscle Manor
Oscar the Dummy
"Tick-Tick-Tick-Tick-Tick"

From Nurse to Worse

Bellevue Hospital
Cerebrum decapitation
City Pound
Colossal Insurance Company
Dr. D. Lerious
"I raised it from a cent"
Jerry

Fuelin' Around

"And the rest of the day for myself!"
Captain Roarke
Elementary Chemistry
Half a pint of ectowhozis (may substi-
    tute with ectowhatsis), 4 grams of
    alkabob, shishkabob, jigger of
    sastrophonia, carbolic acid, squirt
    of haratang
"It's our duty to posterior"
Professor Snead

State of Anemia

Urania

A Gem of a Jam

Drs. Hart, Burns, and Belcher

Hemoglober, sulfademus

Spectus-on-the-floorus

Gents in a Jam

Mrs. Magruder

Rocky and Mrs. Duggan

Uncle Phineas Bowman

Gents Without Cents

At the Front

Bay of Rum

Castor and Earle Revue

Flo, Mary, and Shirley

Hill 303

Manny Weeks Theatrical Enterprises

"Niagara Falls"

Noazark Shipbuilding Co.

"So it shouldn't be a total loss, I'm taking a bath!"

"Two Souls and a Heel"

"We Just Stopped In to Say Hello"

The Ghost Talks

A to Z Express Co.

Charger

Desmond of the Outer Sanctorum

Lady Godiva

"Six lions were tearing me apart bit by bit"

Smorgasbord Castle

Spirit of Sir Tom

G.I. Wanna Go Home

418 Meshugena Avenue

Ginsberg, Rosenburg, Goldstein, and O'Brien

Jake

Jessie, Bessie, and Tessie

"Nothing to Buy, Nothing to Sell, We've Gone Fishing, You Can Go . . . Fishing Too"

Goof on the Roof

Bill and Rosebud

Goofs and Saddles

"Bad Lands"

Bill

Buffalow Billious

"Dear General Muster . . ."

General Muster

"Go two miles north and make a left-hand turn at the pool room"

Joe's Traveling Store General Merchandise

A grim reminder to anyone contemplating home electronic repair (*Goof on the Roof*, 1953)

Just Plain Bill
Longhorn Pete
Longhorn Saloon
Wild Bill Hicup

Grips, Grunts and Groans

Another turkey
Hangover Athletic Club
Ironhead
Ivan Bustoff
Kid Pinky
Tony
Wild Hyacinth

Guns A Poppin

"I got it for my bar mitzvah!"
Intent to Commit Mayhem
Mad Bill Hookup
Nerve tonic
"Not since I was a baby"
106⅞

"The Original Two-Man Quartet"
"Shtunk Mfg. Co.
"Sunny-side down and don't turn 'em over"
Vitamins A.P.U.

Gypped in the Penthouse

Box 41144
"Distilled Yesterday"
"Home on the Farm"
"I know how!"
"I used to play in five flats but I got kicked out of the last one"
Jane
"My Beautiful Jane"
Old Panther
"There must be a way to get that ring without getting into trouble with the censor"
"Tired of being beautiful and alone . . ."
Woman Haters Club 87

Good soldiers use their ears as well as their eyes to avoid danger on the gun range (*Half Shot Shooters*, 1936).

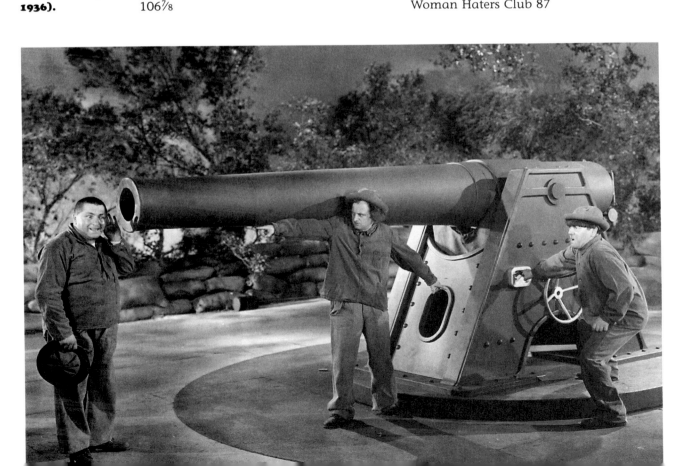

Half Shot Shooters

Admiral Hawkins' Flagship
Captain Burke
"I hope it didn't hit the pool room"
"I'm a pedestrian!"
"Mazel Tov!"and "L'Chaim!"
"No, Milwaukee"
Sergeant MacGillicuddy
"U.S. Army Join Now"
"Vacancies Exist"
"You'll Never Know"

Half-Wits Holiday

A.A.M. (Amalgamated Association of
    Morons), Local 6⁷⁄₈
"Completely illogical, preponderantly
    impracticable, and moreover, it stinks"
Countess Schpritzwasser
Fifty generations
Jerkington
Lulu
Mink, skunk, and porcupine
Miss Gottrocks
Mrs. Smythe Smythe
"No qualms or trepidations . . ."
$1,000
Petty larceny Stooge
Professors Quackenbush and Sedletz
    (see **Professors Rich and Nichols . . .**)
"Quit bragging"
Sappington
"Story Pictures of Farm Animals"
"Tar ytrid eeth say. Glug zap snorglots
    ramitz. Ronassonce kibertz."
Vacancy of the cranium

Have Rocket, Will Travel

Dr. Ingrid
"Earthmen Return Home . . ."
"Isn't he quisn't!"
"It was nothing, Mademoiselle . . ."
J. P. Morse
Knucklehead

Maintenance Men's Quarters
National Space Foundation
New York Globe
Sodium bicarbonate and popcorn

He Cooked His Goose

Bell
Cedric the Clam
Larry's Pet Shop
"Merry X-Mas, Your Pet Man Larry"
Millie
Miss Lapdale
Perfect Underwear Company

Healthy, Wealthy and Dumb

Coffin Nail Cigarette Contest
Darwin
1122 Lillyflower Terrace
$4.95
Hotel Costa Plente
Stix Fast Glue
1010 Tobacco Road
"That's nothin'. We had a bed that went
    back to Sears Roebuck the Third"

Heavenly Daze

Asbestos suit
Fountain pen that writes under whipped
    cream
Heavenly Express
I. Fleecem
Lord Larryington and Sir Moeington
Miss Jones
$140
Spiffingham
Uncle Mortimer
"Whereas I, Shemp the Stooge . . ."

Higher Than a Kite

Colonel Henderson
"A Flying Field Somewhere in Somewhere"
Kelly
Marshal Bommell

Marshal Boring

Moronica (Larry)

Shickelgruber

Hoi Polloi

Maskazino cherry

"Oh, thank you. I couldn't dance a step last year"

Professors Rich and Nichols, Quackenbush and Sedletz

"Rubbish Permit 186"

$10,000

"That's in case you do and I'm not around"

"Yeah, two bucks!"

Hokus Pokus

Calamity Insurance Company

Cliff

The Great Svengarlic

"He'll Steal Your Breath Away!"

"Here This Week—the Great Hypnotist Svengarlic—He'll Steal Your Breath Away—A Stellar Attraction—Scientific—Educational—2 Performances Daily"

Mary

Nice cold hotcakes smothered in vinegar

Schlemiel Number Eight

Hold That Lion!

Ambrose Rose Estate

Cannonball Express

Cess, Poole, and Drayne

"Dububb, zedubb, wubbub, dewubb dee-dub-wub"

Icabod Slipp

Judge Woodcock R. Strinker

Slipp, Tripp, and Skipp

"Vote For Honest Icabod Slipp"
"Wake up and go to sleep!"
"We'll Get That Filthy Lucre . . ."
"Well, we're not in my country . . ."

Hoofs and Goofs
Birdie
Mr. Dinkelspiel

Horses' Collars
"Decker 117, Opponents 0"
"Dice, Dancing, Dames, Drinking, and
    Dunking"
Double Deal Decker
Double Deal's Five "D" Delight
Hyden Zeke Detective Agency
Nell
Stockyards 1234
WGN
"When in Chicago . . ."

Horsing Around
Birdie
Brooks Circus
Piggy
Schnapps
Winkelburg

Hot Ice
A-1 Correspondence School of Detecting
Dapper Dan
Harold the Ape
Inspector McCormick
Muscles
Punjab Diamond
Scotland Yard

Hot Scots
A-1 Correspondence School of Detecting
Angus and McPherson
Below the McMason McDixon line
The Earl of Glenheather

Glenheather Castle
"Hi, Lorna; how ya doone?"
Inspector McCormick
"Is my slip showing?"
Lorna Doone
Scotland Yard

Hot Stuff
"And the rest of the day for myself!"
Captain Roarke
Elementary Chemistry
Government of Urania—Department of
    Inferior
Half a pint of ectowhozis (may substitute
    with ectowhatsis), 4 grams of alkabob,
    shishkabob, jigger of sastrophonia,
    carbolic acid, squirt of haratang
"It's our duty to posterior"
Pig's feet smothered in lubricating oil,
    raw potatoes boiled in pure varnish,
    and head cheese garnished with
    rusty nails
Professor Snead
Routine Number Six
State of Anemia
Urania
Urania Daily Bladder

How High Is Up?
Apex Construction Company
"Men at Work"
Minute Menders, Inc.
"Three of the best riveters who ever
    riveted"

Hugs and Mugs
"The Management Reserves the Right to
    Refuse $1,000 Bills"
Mugsy
National Express and Storage Co.
Shangri-La Upholstering Co.
"Somebody's roasting a ham!"

"We Make Everything from Beds to
    Bustles"
"What's a matter with my eyes; do they
    look like halvah?"

Hula-La-La

B.O. Pictures Corp.
Luana
Mr. Baines
Raribonga
Stage 19
Varunu

Husbands Beware

Cousin Basil
Dora and Flora
J. M. Benton
Miss Hopkins
"Professor Shemp Howard—Teacher of
    Voice"
Turpentine
"Voices of Spring"

I Can Hardly Wait

Doctor A. Yank
Doctor Y. Tug
H_2O
"She Was Bred in Old Kentucky"
$6\frac{7}{8}$
13
"You burnt my little bugle!"

Idiots Deluxe

Intent to commit mayhem
Nerve tonic
"No Smoking—No Hunting—No
    Fishing—No Nothing Go Home"
"Not since I was a baby"
"Oh, woe is Moe"
$106\frac{7}{8}$
"The Original Two-Man Quartet"
Shtunk Manufacturing Company

Sunny-side down and don't turn 'em over
Vitamins A.P.U.

Idle Roomers

"Amazing! Incredible! Horrific! . . ."
Hotel Snazzy Plaza
Leander's Carnival
Lupe the Wolf Man
Mr. and Mrs. Leander
Room 810
"This End Up"

If a Body Meets a Body

Curly Q. Link
"Curly Q. Link Sought . . ."
Jerkington
Link, Mink, and Pink
"The morbid the merrier!"
Nice soup from a nice, juicy bone
Professor Bob O. Link
67 Cents Net

I'll Never Heil Again

Amscray, Ixnay, and Umpchay
Axis Partners
Bay of Rum
"The Characters in this Picture . . ."
Chizzilini
Field Marshal Herring
Gilda
King Herman $6\frac{7}{8}$
Minister of Rum
Moe Hailstone
Moronica
"Moronica for Morons"
Seeress of Roebuck
Starvania

I'm a Monkey's Uncle

"According to Darwin . . ."
Aggie, Maggie, and Baggie
"Any Similarity . . ."

Dogfish
"Don't worry; you smell . . . good!"
"Horsethieves!"
Lily of the Alley
"Me, three!"
The most beautiful cave in Mesopotamia
Poison gas
"She loves me, she loves me not . . ."
"You're telling me!"

In the Sweet Pie and Pie

A-K-70
B-K-68
Bill Stein
Diggins
Edam Neckties
Fleur de Stinkun
Hangemall Prison
Little America
Mickey Finn Gang
Mushroom Murders
"No, but I know a big fence in Chicago"
O-K-67
Pago Pago
Skagway, Alaska
Tiska, Taska, and Baska
"Well, I'm too young . . ."
Williams

Income Tax Sappy

Instant Glue
Mr. Cash
"My ex-wife and ten bartenders"

Knutzy Knights

Black Prince
Cedric the Blacksmith
"In Days of Old . . ."
"Oh, Elaine"
Princess Elaine
Sextetrum Lucia
Sir Satchel

"So We Stuck Our Little Tootsies in the
    Water"
"Under the spreading chestnut tree . . ."

Listen, Judge

C-A-N-D-Y
George Morton
Jiffy Fixers
Judge Henderson
"Men at Work"
Mrs. Henderson
"We need the eggs"
"We Repare Enything"

Loco Boy Makes Good

Balbo the Magician
Chisel Inn Hotel
Happy Haven Hotel
Kokonuts Grove
"Mingle or I'll mangle!"
Mr. Scroggins
Nill, Null, and Void
Paté D'Fagua
"Rooms $1 a Month—Free Showers
    When it Rains"
"She Was Bred in Old Kentucky"
"Three Hams That Lay Their Own Eggs"
Waldo Twitchell
Ye Olde Pilgrim Hotel
"You know I'm not normal!"

Loose Loot

Ambrose Rose Estate
Cess, Poole, and Drayne
Circle Follies Theatre
Icabod Slipp
"Invest with Honest Icabod Slipp"
Judge Woodcock R. Strinker
919 Circle Avenue
Slipp, Tripp, and Skipp
"We'll Get That Filthy Lucre . . ."
"Well, we're not in my country . . ."

Love at First Bite
Café La-Mer-Essen
"Distilled Yesterday"
Fifi
Katrina
Maria
Old Panther
Rue de Schlemiel and Rue de le Pew

Malice in the Palace
Café Casbahbah
Emir of Shmow
Ghinna Rumma
Haffa Dalla
Hassan Ben Sober
King Rootin' Tootin' Diamond
Omagosh
1,000 Shilbleenas
Shmow
"Somewhere in the Orient"
Start at Jerkola . . .

Matri-Phony
"All Unmarried Redheaded Maidens . . ."
Ancient Erysipelas
The back of the drapes
"The Biggest Chiselers in Town"
Curleycue
Diana
Dollar Day
Larrycus
Mohicus
Octopus Grabus
"Proclamation . . ."
Tarantula
A Tenth-Century Ras Bañas Ya-tee
    Benafucci
"Vitamins A, B, C, D, E, F; Gee, I like
    food!"

Men in Black
Anapanacag, cedascram falsyeth,
    anacanapon, and eenots

Anna Conda
Dr. Graves
Dr. Howard, Dr. Fine, Dr. Howard
"For Duty and Humanity!"
Los Arms Hospital
Semert, anacome, senetoonum,
    anacanaponner, peenanar, anasinic,
    cotton, anic, needles, scissors, and
    more cotton
"We graduated with the highest tempera-
    tures in our class!"

Merry Mavericks
Clarence Cassidy
"Law Officers on the Way . . ."
Red Morgan
Peaceful Gulch
Peaceful Gulch Saloon
"Wanted for Vagrancy"

A Merry Mix-Up
Louie, Max, and Jack
Luke, Morris, and Jeff
Shingled roof

Micro-Phonies
Alice Bixby
"Gritto spelled sideways is 'Ottri-guh-guh'"
Krispy Krunchies
Radio KGBY
Mrs. Bixby
Sandra Sandpile
Señorita Cucaracha
Señors Mucho and Gusto
Sextetrum Lucia
Signor
Six Tetrum Lucy
Skin
"Voices of Spring"
"Yeah, it reminds me of the reform school"

A Missed Fortune
Bunion Eight

B-U-R-P
Darwin
$4.85
Hotel Costa Plente
"It ain't spring yet!"
Mystery Motor Jackpot Show
Stix Fast Glue
"Thank you, Mr. Personally"
"That's nothin'. We had a bed that went
    back to Sears Roebuck the Third"

Monkey Businessmen

Breaker-uppers of the peanut brittle
    foundry
Dr. Mallard
"High altitude, low prices. No matter what
    you got you'll lose it at Mallard's."
Mallard's Rest Home and Clinic
Miss Shapely
90 Proof
Smiling Sam McGann
Tractohomolactometer,
    hammadeemaceemafaren

Movie Maniacs

C.M. & St. P. R.R.
Carnation Pictures
Fuller Rath
Hollywood Storage Company
Stage 7
Swinehardt

Mummy's Dummies

"Ancient Egypt. In the Reign of the Great
    King Rootentooten."
489 Shekels
400 Shekels
Honest Moe, Honest Shemp, and Larry
King Putentakeit
King Rootentooten
Painless Papyrus
Radames
The Smiling Egyptians

Stink
Tomb of Old King Putentakeit

Muscle Up a Little Closer

Elmo Drake
Matzohs
Seabiscuit Food Corp.
Tiny

Musty Musketeers

"A-Calling We Do Come"
Coleslawvania
F.B.I.
"Gone to Rest Under the Spreading
    Chestnut Tree"
King Cole
Mergatroyd the Magician
Prince Gallant III of Rhododendron
Princess Alicia
"A Small Kingdom . . ."
"Thou hath made me shoe the wrong
    mule"
Tillyeth, Millyeth, and Lillyeth
Will Idge

Muffs to You

Butch
Clux Dog Soap
"Deposit Dogs Here"
"Dogs Washed While U Wate . . ."
"He don't smoke, drink, nor chew"
"Huck mir nisht a chynick, and I don't
    mean efsher!"
"If you were over here I'd give you
    this!"
"Inspector"
K-9 Dog Laundry
"Listen to that exhaust!"
"Manning Baby Disappears"
Mrs. Dennis O'Toole
Mr. and Mrs. Manning
Mr. Stutz
"No Dogs or Babies Allowed"

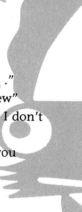

Few men demonstrate more courage at gunpoint than the Stooges (*Nutty but Nice*, 1940).

Officer O'Halloran
Wong Hi Lee Hand Laundry

No Census, No Feeling
"Census Takers Report Here"
City Assessor
18
"Exit Tunnel 12"
Fifi
Fine powdered alum
Lake Winapasakee
"Players Only"
Square Deal Swap Shop
30
22

No Dough, Boys
"Hey You No Smoking"
Hugo
"Jap Sub Blown Up . . ."

Joe's Beanery
Latherneck Shaving Cream
Naki, Saki, and Waki
Steelia Pumpernickel, Amelia
    Schwartzbrut, and Celia Schweipak
The Times Press

Nutty but Nice
America's Gift to Indigestion
Drs. Lyman and Walters
Felix Stout's Bar
Hilarious Hash Slingers
"Home on the Range"
Little Betty Williams
"Mary, Mary, Quite Contrary"
Mr. Williams
"Speak for yourself, rodent!"
Spike and Butch
Yankee Noodle Soup
Ye Colonial Inn

Of Cash and Hash

Angel
"Armored Car Robbers Identified—Café
    Workers Name Loomis Gang"
Captain Mullins
Elite Café
Gladys Harmon
Lefty Loomis

Oil's Well That Ends Well

Red Dog Canyon

Oily to Bed, Oily to Rise

April, May, and June
Clipper
Fairport Theatre
"Free Auto"
Uncle Tim
Unitarians
Widow Jenkins

Out West

Arizona Kid
"Come to Papa!"
"Distilled Monday"
Doc Barker
"I'm going to get myself a cheap lawyer"
"I've had it ever since I was a little kid"
Molasses, Tabasco, seltzer . . .
Nell
"Never in the history of motion
    pictures . . ."
Old Homicide
Red Dog Saloon
"The Stooges have landed and have the
    situation well in hand!"
"You're getting no place fast!"

Outer Space Jitters

"General Motorcycle: 17½,
    Anacanapana Steel: 25¼, Tsimmis
    Incorporated: 17"

The Goon
Grand Zilch of Sunev
The High Mucky Muck
A nice salami sandwich smothered in
    sour cream with cherry jelly . . .
Professor Jones
Sunev

The Outlaws Is Coming

Annie Oakley
Elvis
Kenneth Cabot
Rance Roden
Trigger Mortis
"2 Hr. Parking—8 A.M. to 6 P.M.—
    Except Sundays, Holidays &
    Hangings"

Though Moe
looks fetching,
he does not
appreciate
kisses intended
for someone else
(*Oily to Bed, Oily
to Rise*, 1939).

A Pain in the Pullman

Goldstein, Goldberg, Goldblatt, and
    O'Brien
Joe
Johnson
Mrs. Hammond Eggerley's
    Theatrical Apts.
"The Panics of 1936"
Paul Pain
"Wake up and go to sleep!"

Pals and Gals

Belle and Zell
"Come to Papa!"
Doc Barker
"I'm going to get myself a cheap lawyer"
"I've had it ever since I was a little kid"
Joe's Minstrels Songs and Dances
Joe's Traveling Store General
    Merchandise
Molasses, Tabasco, seltzer, eggs, paint,
    and paint remover
Nell
Old Homicide
Red Dog Saloon

Pardon My Backfire

Betty, Hettie, and Nettie
"Happy 10th Anniversary"
San Brandon Penitentiary
"That's too permanent!"

Pardon My Clutch

Claude A. Quacker
Columbus
"It must be something else"
"Look in these shoes for some toes!"
Marigold, Narcissus, and Petunia
"Which one?"
"You know, you should fish for a whale"

Pardon My Scotch

Breath O' Heather Vat 106 Plus

J.T.
Jones' Drugstore
McSniff
McSnort
McSnuff
Mr. Jones
Señor Louis Balero Cantino
"Ver G'harget," "Over the River," and
    "Skip the Gutter"

Pest Man Wins

"A barking dog never bites . . ."
Fifi
"Got Ants in Your Plants? We'll
    Kill 'Em!"
Lightning Pest Control Company
Meadows
Mrs. Castor
Mr. Philander

Phony Express

Abdul's Cactus Remedy
Dr. Abdul's Medicine Show
50 cents or 3 for $1
First National Bank
Hayfever, spotted fever . . .
"And lay you right down, too!"
"Open 10 to 3"
Peaceful Gulch
Peaceful Gulch Saloon
Red Morgan
"Wanted for Vagrancy"
"Wild Bill Hicup Due In"

Pies and Guys

"Completely illogical, preponderantly
    impracticable, and moreover, it stinks"
Countess Schpritzwasser
Lulu
Mink, skunk, and porcupine
Miss Gottrocks
Professors Quackenbush and Sedletz (see
    Professors Rich and Nichols . . .)

On-the-job accidents are often nobody's fault, a fact Moe isn't always ready to accept (*Pardon My Scotch*, 1935).

Curly, in a serious moment between takes on the set of *Phony Express*, 1943

Sappington
Vacancy of the cranium

Playing the Ponies
"Adam and Eve on a Raft"
"At a loss for adjectives"
Chili pepperinos
$5,000 Benson County Sweepstakes
Flounder Inn
H_2O
Lobster with frog legs
"Madcap Wins Ten Thousand Dollar Sweepstakes"
35 cents
Thunderbolt
"Thunderbolt Manager"

"Thunderbolt Nursemaid"
"Thunderbolt Pilot"
Vandy Legs, Bride's Biscuit, Muddy Water, Turtle Neck, and Hailstorm

Pop Goes the Easel
Anacanapanasan, eenar, anasanapacarscram
"He drew twenty years with one stroke of the pen"
"I Am Starving . . ."
Kraft's College of Arts
"Look at the grouse!"
"Must Have a Job . . ."
Professor Fuller
"Stop Look and Listen"

Punch Drunks

"Four slices of burned toast and a
 rotten egg"
Killer Kilduff
K. O. Stradivarius
"Pop Goes the Weasel"
Room 13

Punchy Cowpunchers

Blackjack and Lefty
Captain Daley
Coyote Creek
Dillon Gang
Elmer
"Fort Scott, Kansas, 1868—the Heroic
 Men of the U.S. Cavalry"
"I'll take a milkshake . . . with
 sour milk!"
"The Killer Dillons"
Nell
Red Dog Saloon
Sergeant Mullins
"What size, madam? We have some
 lovely ground-grippers!"

Quiz Whizz

"About five-foot-five by five-foot-five"
Consolidated Fujiyama California
 Smog Bags
Daily Gazette
G. Y. Prince
Investors Inc.
J. J. Figbee
Montgomery M. Montgomery
R. O. Broad
Skin

Restless Knights

Baron of Brains
Baron of Gray Matter
Count of Five
Duke of Durham

Duke of Mixture
"Every man for himself!"
Fife of Drum
Kingdom of Anesthesia
Parasites
Prince Boris
3,000 guineas, two geese, and a duck

Rhythm and Weep

"Doctor Dippy's Retreat"
Eagon's Rehearsal Hall Theatre
Garden Theatre
Hilda, Wilda, and Tilda
Mike Lipincranz
Mr. Boyce
Mr. Smellington
Stooge Follies
"Swing it!"
"Swingeroo Joe"
"We're dressed as ballerinas"

Rip, Sew and Stitch

I. Fleecem
L-R-L-R-L-R-L 1-1-2-3-2-2-1
No Burpoline
Pip Boys Lary Moe & Shemp
Skin and Flint Finance Corporation
"Slippery Fingers"
T.H.
Terry Hargen
200 percent wool
"Unaccusstomed Tailors"
"What a beautiful messterpiece!"

Rockin' Thru the Rockies

Chief Growling Bear
"Direct From Three Hot Weeks in
 Kansas"
Frontier Inn
Nell
Nell's Belles
"This fish looks like Moe!"

Rumpus in the Harem

Café Casbahbah
Emir of Shmow
Ghinna Rumma
Haffa Dalla
Hassan Ben Sober
Heebah, Reebah, and Sheebah
King Rootin' Tootin' Diamond
1,000 Shilbleenas
Omagosh
"The Orient . . ."
Sultan of Pish Posh

Rusty Romeos

Flipper's Fluffy Fablongent Flapjacks
Mabel
Mrs. Flipper's Fluffy Pancake Mix

Sappy Bullfighters

"Boo-hoo"
Greta
José
"Mexico—Where Men are Men and
    Women are Glad of It"
Pepé
"Squeak, squeak"
"Teatro Internacional"
"Turn around, I'll kiss her behind
    your back!"

Saved by the Belle

Amarillo Beer
King Winter Outfitting Co.
Mr. Singapore
95% temper; 5% mental
"Oh, I don't know; I've been around!"
"Our Leader—President Ward Robey—
    The People's Friend"
President Ward Robey
Señorita Rita
Shock Absorber for Earthquakes

Singapore Joe's Palace Hotel
Valeska

Scheming Schemers

Day and Nite Plumbers
1414 Bleecker Street
How to Be a Plumber
Mr. Norfleet
Norfleet Mansion
The Van Brocklin Painting
"We Never Sleep"

Scotched in Scotland

Angus and McPherson
Below the McMason McDixon line
The Earl of Glenheather
Glenheather Castle
"Hi, Lorna; how ya doone?"
"Is my slip showing?"
Lorna Doone
O. U. Gonga
Wide Awake Detective School

Scrambled Brains

Croakers Sanitarium
Dr. Gezundheidt
Drs. Hart, Burns, and Belcher
Isle of Stromboli
Nora

Self Made Maids

"All Parts in this Picture Are Played By
    the Three Stooges"
Derstick, Anacanapooner
Larraine
Mergatroyd
Moella
Shempetta

Shivering Sherlocks

Angel

"Armored Car Robbers Identified—Café
    Workers Name Loomis Gang"
Captain Mullins
Daily Record Post
Elite Café
Gladys Harmon
Lefty Loomis

Shot in the Frontier

"Beneath This . . ."
Diggs, Graves, and Berry Undertakers
"Distilled Yesterday"
Ella, Bella, and Stella
"Friday the 13th"
"Here Lies A Father of 28, He Might Have
    Had More But Now It's Too Late"
M. Balmer
"Mama Loved Papa . . ."
"No Use—You're Doomed"
Noonan Brothers
Old Panther
Storey's Saloon
"To your last breath . . ."

Sing a Song of Six Pants

I. Fleecem
L-R-L-R-L-R-L 1-1-2-3-2-2-1
No Burpoline
Pip Boys Lary Moe & Shemp
Skin and Flint Finance Corporation
"Slippery Fingers"
T.H.
Terry Hargen
200 percent wool
"Unaccusstomed Tailors"
"What a beautiful messterpiece!"

The Sitter Downers

Corabell, Dorabell, and Florabell
Gazette Journal
"I got Stetson; which one is she?"
"In the Spring . . ."

Metropole Flower Shop
Mr. Bell
"No Honeymoon No Work/Unfair to
    Union Husbands"
"This Lot Presented to the Three Sitdown
    Suitors—Upland Realty Co."
"This Place Unfair to Union Suitors"
Upland Realty Company

Slaphappy Sleuths

Becky
"Feel Tired? . . ."
Fuller Grime
"Have You Sore Feet? Try Tic-Tac. Good
    for the Toe"
Hazel
I. M. Greecy
"In Onion There Is Strength"
Just straight salary
Onion Oil Company
Popping Corn
"Try Dr. Belcher's Compound for Gas on
    the Stomach"
"Why don't you sing 'Mame'?"

Slippery Silks

Madame De France
Mrs. Morgan
Mr. Morgan
Mr. Romani
"Modes Modernistique"
Romani Artistic Woodwork
Uncle Pete

A Snitch in Time

"Antiques Made While-U-Waite . . ."
Hendrix Jewelry Store
Miss Scudder
Mr. Jerry Pip and Steve
Steve
Ye Olde Furniture Shoppe

Snow White and the Three Stooges

Bravuria
Hordred the Huntsman
Oga
Prince Charming
Quatro the Magnificent
Quinto
Snow White
Ye Stooges Three—Sole Purveyors of Yuk
Yuk

So Long Mr. Chumps

B. O. Davis
41144
Gyp the People
H_2O
"Keep Our City Clean"
Lone Wolf Louie
118 6th Street, San Francisco, California

Percy Pomeroy
+4
$6\frac{7}{8}$
"They generally hang out on the
    gallows!"
13
"We're on our way . . ."

Sock-A-Bye Baby

Enchiladas, spaghetti, artichokes, onions,
    celery, olives, radishes, pigs feet,
    and herring
"I Was Born in Brazil"
Jimmy Collins
"You were delivered by a buzzard"

Some More of Samoa

"The Biggest Grafters in Town"
Dr. Howard, Dr. Fine, Dr. Howard
Lubazac, whozica, pashcunyakas, cotton

A momentary setback during a daring jail-break (*So Long Mr. Chumps*, 1941)

Mr. Winthrop
Puckerless persimmon tree
Rhum Boogie
Roast Stooge
Swamp soup
Vitamin P.D.Q.

Soup to Nuts

"This is the hottest June we've had since
　last July!"
White on rye
Bologna and whipped cream
"Liver and milk . . . and a banana split"
"The Elevator Dance"

Space Ship Sappy

Filet of sole and heel
"Flying Saucer Photographer Awarded
　City's Highest Honor"
"Gevalt!"
Liar's Club 27th Annual Convention
"Nobody lives here, either!"
"Prof. A. K. Rimple No. 60"
Professor A. K. Rimple
Rockwood Steel, Ranacoma Copper, Your
　American Can, Pinpoint Pimple
Sunev
"Who came in?"

Spook Louder

J. O. Dunkfeather
Miracle Massage Reducing Machine
Mr. Graves
Mr. Wallace
"No Peddlers"
The Times

Spooks

Congo
Crumb's Pies
"Divorce Evidence Manufactured . . ."
Dr. Jekyll and Mr. Hyde

George B. Bopper
Mary Bopper
Super Slueth Detective Agency
"What a hideous, monstrous face!"

Squareheads of the Round Table

"Are you short of money? . . ."
Black Prince
Cedric the Blacksmith
"I can't die; I haven't seen *The Jolson
　Story*!"
"In Days of Old . . ."
"It's sharp medicine, but it's a sure cure
　for all diseases"
"Oh, Elaine"
Princess Elaine
Scowling Scotsman
Sextetrum Lucia
Sir Satchel
"So We Stuck Our Little Tootsies in the
　Water"
"That babe sure can cook!"

Stone Age Romeos

Aggie, Maggie, and Baggie
B. Bopper
Dogfish
"Horsethieves!"
Map of Unknown Lands Where Cavemen
　Are Still Supposed to Exist
"Me, three!"
The most beautiful cave in
　Mesopotamia
Museum of Natural History
Poison gas
"She loves me, she loves me not . . ."
"You're telling me!"

Studio Stoops

B.O. Pictures Corp.
Captain Casey and Brown

Clinton Arms Hotel
Dandy Dawson
Dolly Devore
"A gorg goggle yata benefucci . . ."
"I'm Brown from the *Sun*"
J. B. Fletcher
Kiss the Moonbeams Off My Elbow
Room 1717
Speedy Termite Exterminators

Sweet and Hot

"The Heat Is On"
Hugo Gansamacher
"Let's Fall in Love"
Tiny Landers

Tassels in the Air

"Mademoiselle"
"Men at Work"
Mrs. Pendall
"Not Responsible for Hats and Coats"
Omay
Secondhand
Thaddeus and Maggie Smirch

Termites of 1938

Acme Escort Bureau
Acme Exterminating Company
At Your Service . . .
Clayhammer
"If You Got 'Em—We'll Get 'Em!"
Mandy
Ramonones Sequidimes, by Fleeacrons
Simplex Rodent Exterminator
Arthur van Twitchett
Muriel van Twitchett

They Stooge to Conga

Fix-All Fixers, Ink.
"General Handiwork Our Speshalty"
Mlle. Zora
Shickelgruber

Three Arabian Nuts

"The genius!"
John Bradley
Superior Warehouse and Storage Co.

Three Dark Horses

Abel Lamb Stewer
"A Chicken in Every Pot with Egger"
"Cuddle Up a Little Closer With
    Hammond Egger"
"Delegates Welcome to Convention City"
"Don't Be a Muttonhead—Vote for Abel
    Lamb Stewer for President"
"Don't look at me!"
Hammond Egger
"Hammond Egger Wants Your Vote"
Secretary of the Offense, Secretary of the
    Inferior, and Toastmaster General
Wm. "Bill Wick"
"Yeah, but I'm goin' anyhow"

3 Dumb Clucks

Complete Outfitters
Daisy
"Home Sweet Home"
"Men at Work"
Popsie

Three Hams on Rye

"Another Broadway Turkey . . ."
B. K. Doaks
"The Bride Wore Spurs"
"Dangerous—Keep Away . . ."
Miss Janie Bell
Nick Barker
"Theatre Chit Chat"

Three Little Beers

A. Panther
"I shot a seven, but they wouldn't give
    me the money!"
Panther Brewing Co.

Panther Pilsner Beer
Press-Press-Pull
Rancho Golf Club

Three Little Pigskins

Blue Point University
Boulder Dam University
Daisy Simms
"Football To-day. Tigers Vs. Cubs.
    Positively No Admittance"
Gilmore Stadium
H^2O^2
Joe Stack
"Joe Stack's Tigers to Meet Cubs in
    Professional Football Classic"
Lucille Ball
$\frac{1}{2}$
Platt Field
?
The Three Horsemen

Three Little Pirates

Black Louie
Black Louie's Pirate Den
Dead Man's Island
Dead Man's Island 1672
Garbage Scow #188 N.Y.C.
The Gin of Rummy
Governor of Dead Man's Island
"A hot stake is better than a cold chop"
Maha
Maharajah of Canazzi
Rita
"Ye Olde Tilt"

Three Little Sew and Sews

Admiral H. S. Taylor
Count Alfred Gehrol
Eighteen blondes and twelve redheads
Republic of Televania Naval Base
"Smells like somebody's frying onions!"

Three Little Twirps

Effie
Herman's Great Combined Shows
Last Year
Sultan of Abadaba

Three Loan Wolves

"The bag left me holding the babe!"
Butch McGee
Egbert
Gashouse Protective Association
"Here Today, Pawn Tomorrow"
Mickey Moe the Murderin' Masseur
Molly the Glamour Girl
Turpentine
"You told me to drop what I was doing,
    so I did."

Three Missing Links

B. O. Botswaddle
Dr. Ba Loni Sulami
"Hours 2 to 5 or by Appointment"
Jilted in the Jungle
Mirabel Mirabel
Mr. Herbert
Super Terrific Productions

Three Pests in a Mess

Ajax Sportswear
Cheatham Investment Company
"Dump No Rubbish Here"
Ever Rest Pet Cemetery
I. Cheatham
"Patents Bought and Sold"
Philip Black

Three Sappy People

Burned toast and a rotten egg
Dr. York
Gin smothered in bourbon
"Post No Bills"

Rumsford
Sheri Rumsford
Susquehana 2222
T.S.
"We'll be there in a flash in the flesh!"
Williams
Ziller, Zeller, and Zoller

Three Smart Saps

"Candid Cameraman . . ."
"5736" and "Mr. No One"
Mr. Stevens
On the end of a rope
"Only when I take bicarbonate"
Sing Sing, Alcatraz, Leavenworth,
    Joliet
Stella, Nella, and Bella
T.B.
Walker
"The Wedding Bells"

The Three Stooges Go Around the World in a Daze

Amelia Carter
Filch
"I want a good dirty fight; now shake
    hands and come out gouging"
Mighty Itchy-Kitchy
Phileas Fogg III
Randolph Stuart III
Route 66
Vickers Cavendish

The Three Stooges in Orbit

Captain Andrews
Carol Danforth
N'Yuk-N'Yuks
Ogg and Zogg
Professor Danforth
"The Three Stooges Scrapbook"
William

The Three Stooges Meet Hercules

Diane
"Filmed in Glorious Black and White"
"I haven't eaten in 3,000 years!"
Ithaca
Ithaca Pharmacy
Odius
Ralph Dimsal
Schuyler Davis
Thesus, King of Rhodes
Ulysses

The Three Troubledoers

A.P. Willis Co.
Badlands Blackie
Blackie's Place
"Blacksmith Shop"
Coney Island Curly
Dead Man's Gulch
Gladys
Nell
Skullbone Pass

The Tooth Will Out

The Amateur Carpenter
Coyote Pass
Dainty Dolly Dish Company
Miss Beebee
"The mouth is in the front!"
Practical Dentistry
Pungfauthadrednock with the bicuspid
    canafran
Vesuvius Restaurant

Tricky Dicks

Antonio Zucchini Salami Gorgonzola
    de Pizza
B. A. Copper
Chopper
Gilbraith Q. Tiddledewadder

Old Panther
Police Station Section 13 Detective
    Bureau
"She broke it off"
Slick Chick
Slug McGurk

Triple Crossed

Bell
Larry's Pet Shop
"Merry X-Mas, Your Pet Man Larry"
Millie
Miss Lapdale

Uncivil War Birds

Curlylocks
Lulu Belle, Mary Belle, and Ringa Belle
"Way Down South in New York City"

Uncivil Warriors

Captain Dodge
Colonel Buttz
"I got sick of the dough and thought I'd
    go on the loaf"
"I'm glad he can't smell them any
    closer!"
Judith
Lieutenant Duck
Major Filbert
Major Hyde
Nip and Tuck
Operator 12
Operator 13
Operator 14
Operator 15
Southern Comforter
A week back
"Well, being as there's no other place
    around the place . . ."

Up in Daisy's Penthouse

Bretta, croomithistle, papeeptoomin,
    pickle juice

Daisy Flowers
Eenar fraapini
Popsie
"Rich Oil Man Gets Divorce Yesterday—
    Gets New Bride Today"

Vagabond Loafers

Day and Nite Plumbers
How to Be a Plumber
Mr. and Mrs. Allen
Norfleet Mansion
217 Linden Drive
The Van Brocklin Painting
"We Never Sleep"
Wilkes
"You're a very intelligent imbecile"

Violent is the Word for Curly

Acme Service Station
"A frozen dainty"
"I can do very nicely with a highball!"
"Is it true that the time and space are
    calculated by the interplanetary mag-
    netism to solar radiation?"
"Men at Work"
Mildew College
Mrs. Catsby
Professor Hicks
Professors Feinstein, Frankfurter, and
    Von Stueben
Super Service
"Swinging the Alphabet"
"Twenty minutes to a pound; we'll be
    here a month!"
Yukon Ice Cream

We Want Our Mummy

Ali Ben Woodman and His Swinging
    Bedouins
"At Your Service . . ."
Bronx Taxi Cab
"Cairo City Limits—Tunis 1500 mi."
Dr. Powell

King Rutentuten
Museum of Ancient History
Professor Tuttle
Queen Hotsytotsy
Tunis
$2,198.55
"Well, being as there's no other place
    around the place . . ."
"Yanks Win World Series"

Wee Wee Monsieur

Captain Gorgonzola
Foreign Legion Headquarters
"A Maid on a Night Out Winding a
    Grandfather Clock with Her
    Left Hand"
Mr. Gingy
"Paris—Somewhere in France"
Tsimiss
"Your mother and my mother are
    both mothers"
"Zee Lollipop"

Wham-Bam-Slam!

Claude A. Quacker
Columbus
"It must be something else"
L.B.S., F.O.B., N.U.T.Z.
"Look in these shoes for some toes!"
Marigold, Narcissus, and Petunia
"You know, you should fish for a whale"

What's the Matador?

"Dear Old Mexico"
Dolores
Goldberg, Ginsberg, Rosenberg, and
    O'Brien
José
Plaza D'Toros
Pedro Alvarez
Shamus O'Brien
22 Laredo Street

Who Done It?

Alert Detective Agency
"A couple o' pip pips, a little barbecue,
    and what have you!"
Highly polished mahogany and termites
    with big blue eyes
"I mean business!"
Nikko
Old Man Goodrich
Phantom Gang

Whoops, I'm an Indian!

Chief Leaping Lizard
"Darling Husband . . ."
"Dead or in Bad Shape"
Knights of Columbus
Lobo City
Lobo Jail
Pierre
T. E. Higgins

Woman Haters

Jackie
Jim
Mary
Mr. Zero
Tommy
W.H.

Yes, We Have No Bonanza

Maxey
Maxey's Place
Silver
Western surprise
Yorrick

The Yoke's On Me

The Farmer in the Dell
Smithers

You Nazty Spy

Amscray, Ixnay, and Onay
"Any Resemblance . . ."

Bay of Rum
Fleur de Skunk
Gallstone
June East
King Herman $6\frac{7}{8}$
Little Red Book
Mattie Herring
Minister of Propaganda

Moe Hailstone
Moronica
"Moronika for Morons"
$\frac{1}{2}$
Pebble
Ruby Clutch
South Starv-Vania
Tessie

PART V

Film Synopses and Key Gags

An Ache in Every Stake (1941)

Third Stooge: Curly

Stooge Occupation(s): Ice men; cooks; waiters

Nemesis: The heat; a rich man carrying a birthday cake; a temperamental chef

Synopsis: With temperatures blazing, the Stooges could have made a fortune with their ice business—if only they hadn't fallen asleep in the truck. After dislodging Curly's head from a block of ice and then knocking over a man carrying a birthday cake, the Stooges duck into a fancy house, where they manage to drive a knife-throwing chef into quitting. The lady of the house, desperate for domestic help, hires the Stooges to prepare lunch for an afternoon party. Although their inventive recipes fail miserably, the Stooges do manage to make a cake look fluffy by inflating it with gas. The cake, however, explodes when its candles are blown out by the man of the house . . . the same man, it turns out, whose previous cake was demolished by the Stooges outside.

Key Gag: Although he demonstrates admirable hustle, Curly cannot deliver a block of ice up several flights of stairs before the ice melts. Moe and Larry determine to use a pony express method, whereby each Stooge carries the ice part of the way. The system is an immediate success, inspiring Curly to hoist the block of ice triumphantly for all to see. His grip, however, isn't as sure as his joy, and the ice shatters into a thousand tiny pieces.

A Ducking They Did Go (1939)

Third Stooge: Curly

Stooge Occupation(s): High pressure salesmen of memberships in duck hunting clubs

Nemesis: Police; governor; mayor; local duck breeder

Synopsis: Having pulled off a daring watermelon heist in broad daylight, the Stooges take cover inside an office building, where they find slightly more honest work selling memberships to the Canvas Back Duck Club. Not realizing that the club is a sham, the Stooges succeed in recruiting the police chief, governor, and mayor, all of whom lick their chops at the bountiful paradise of ducks the Stooges guarantee. At the cabin, when a passing local informs the Stooges that there are no ducks in the area, the quick-thinking Moe decides to use inflatable decoys instead, an idea that works beautifully—until the ducks burst in midair. Curly, who always seems to have a way with animals, musically saves the day for the Stooges in a way that would turn even Dr. Dolittle green with envy.

Key Gag: With no ducks in sight and a twenty-year prison term looming, the Stooges turn nervously to Curly, who sets out into the woods with grim determination at his side. He soon returns, playing a flute and leading an orderly procession of prize ducks to the delighted hunters. Moe and Larry are flabbergasted and ask Curly to explain the miracle he has worked, to which Curly replies, "You've heard of the pie-eyed piper of Hamelin, ain't ya? Well, I figured if he could pipe rats pie-eyed, then I could pipe ducks sober!"

All Gummed Up (1947)

Third Stooge: Shemp
Stooge Occupation(s): Druggists; inventors
Nemesis: Crotchety octogenarian landlord Amos Flint

Synopsis: The Stooges run the Cut Throat Drug Store, a neighborhood establishment much friendlier than its name implies. Shemp decides to make the Stooges rich by inventing a fountain of youth potion, and tests it on Mrs. Flint, their landlord's old and decrepit wife. In no time, Mrs. Flint is transformed into a curvaceous young blonde; the fountain of youth is a success! Seeing the miracle, old man Flint demands a dose for himself, greedily trading the drug store as payment. The effect, however, is more pronounced with Mr. Flint, turning the old coot into a whining infant.

Key Gag: To celebrate the wondrous success of their fountain of youth potion, the Stooges sit down with a now-sprightly Mrs. Flint to enjoy a cake she has baked. But instead of adding marshmallows, as Mrs. Flint requested, the Stooges mistakenly add bubble gum. At first the cake is delicious, but chewing soon becomes difficult, with full bubbles popping from the Stooges' mouths. After Mrs. Flint remarks that her cake is called marshmallow jumbo, Larry whispers to Moe, "Tastes more like marshmallow gumbo."

All the World's a Stooge (1941)

Third Stooge: Curly
Stooge Occupation(s): Window washers; dentists; adorable children
Nemesis: The scheming millionaire who adopts them

Synopsis: After being mistaken for dentists (the patient should have realized that real dentists don't use gunpowder), the Stooges bump into a local millionaire who makes them an offer they can't refuse: come to his house dressed as children, play games, and eat. This, thinks the man, will sober up his flighty wife, who has been hankering to adopt a child. Once inside, however, the precious little Stooges behave in naughty ways, smoking cigars, playing craps with the butler, and flirting with houseguests. Though the millionaire finally grabs an ax in frustration, it appears certain that his wife no longer wants children, either.

Key Gag: Three refugee children (the Stooges in disguise) are about to make their debut in society, but cute little Frankie (Curly) has a cold. Luckily, Moe spots a jar of salve and orders Curly to use it. Curly doesn't read well, however, and reaches for a jar of limburger cheese spread instead, which he applies liberally to his chest, creating a social handicap his childlike charms cannot overcome.

Ants in the Pantry (1936)

Third Stooge: Curly
Stooge Occupation(s): Exterminators
Nemesis: The world of pests

Synopsis: The Lightning Pest Control Company is desperate for business, but manager A. Mouser has a plan. If people don't have ants, mice, and moths, he'll *give* them ants, mice, and moths. His three exterminators, the Stooges, get the message and, loaded with jars of pests, infest the nearest fancy mansion. With the guests sufficiently panicked, the Stooges announce themselves at the door and offer their services. "Heaven must have sent you!" declares Gawkins, the butler. The Stooges—dressed in riding outfits so as not to be noticed—use hammers, poison, and squealing cats to conquer the pests and are noticed, after all.

Key Gag: Exterminator Larry has strategically placed several mouse-chasing cats inside a piano, never considering the musical implications of his pest-fighting act. When a distinguished guest sits at the instrument to give a short recital, the squealing felines do nothing to cement the man's reputation as a virtuoso pianist.

A Plumbing We Will Go (1941)

Third Stooge: Curly
Stooge Occupation(s): Chicken thieves; plumbers
Nemesis: The legal system; water

Synopsis: On trial for stealing chickens, the Stooges impress the judge with their honesty and integrity and are acquitted. The judge might have been too lenient, however, as feathers fly from Curly's hat as he celebrates the verdict. On the run and desperate for work, the Stooges land inside a mansion that is in dire need of plumbing repair. It turns out that plumbing is not a skill that comes naturally to the Stooges, and before long water flows from everywhere except where it should. Curly becomes trapped in a maze of

pipes, Larry digs a trench in the backyard, and Moe causes the kitchen sink to turn upside down. With the entire mansion in danger of drowning, the Stooges attempt a hasty getaway that is wetter than it is successful.

Key Gag: Guests at a ritzy party are unaware of the plumbing problems being worked on behind the scenes by the Stooges. Downstairs, a hostess has gathered a crowd to demonstrate the wonders of her new television set, which is transmitting pictures live from Niagara Falls. "Are you ready, Niagara Falls? Let her go!" commands the TV announcer, whereupon a flood of water bursts forth from the set, dousing the stunned hostess and her distinguished guests.

Baby Sitters Jitters (1951)

Third Stooge: Shemp
Stooge Occupation(s): Baby-sitters
Nemesis: Babies

Synopsis: Battle-ax landlady Mrs. Crump has just about had it with the Stooges, who are months behind on the rent and show no visible means of support. The Stooges calm her, however, by promising that their new baby-sitting business will generate stupendous revenues. On their first job, the Stooges manage to entertain a baby named Junior (though not entirely by design). But when the baby's mother returns, she finds the Stooges fast asleep and Junior kidnapped by her jealous husband. The Stooges track the culprit to the Folger

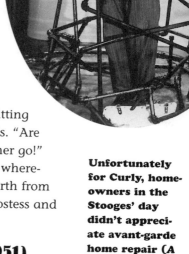

Unfortunately for Curly, homeowners in the Stooges' day didn't appreciate avant-garde home repair (*A Plumbing We Will Go*, 1940).

Apartments, where Shemp's dazzling display of shadowboxing nearly leads to fisticuffs before Junior's mother shows up and reconciles with her husband.

Key Gag: Baby-sitter Shemp shows an uncanny instinct for quieting children; he simply stands on his head to make a baby stop crying. Shemp's performance is so compelling, in fact, that it works wonders when later used on the baby's weeping mother, and better still on Shemp himself when the baby stands on its head to stop Shemp's pitiful sobs.

Back from the Front (1943)

Third Stooge: Curly
Stooge Occupation(s): Merchant mariners
Nemesis: Dungen, a German naval spy; the German navy

Synopsis: Mean-spirited German spy Dungen takes extra pleasure in ordering a torpedo strike against the ship on which merchant mariners Moe, Larry, and Curly have caused him untold annoyance. When the bomb fails to explode, the Stooges mistake it for a whale and attack it, causing a colossal explosion that destroys the boat. Cast adrift at sea in a tiny lifeboat pulled by their dog, Fido, the Stooges find and climb aboard a Nazi warship and soon disguise themselves as Hitler (Moe, with trademark minimustache) and his two henchmen. In a stroke of military genius, Moe orders the ship's top officers to shoot themselves, but an untimely sneeze dislodges his mustache and blows his cover. With furious German naval officers in pursuit, the Stooges grease the ship's deck, causing all pursuing enemies to slip and slide into an unforgiving sea.

Key Gag: Trapped on an enemy ship, sailors Moe, Larry, and Curly don't cower from the grim reality of their predicament; they must knock out every German crewman in order to survive. Working with clocklike precision and a brilliant plan, Moe and Larry taunt German seamen until they emerge from their quarters, leaving them easy marks for Curly's knockout blows. As the soldiers are felled, Larry keeps morale high by making a chalk mark on the wall to commemorate each knockout, a practice Moe refines by making five chalk marks all at once after Curly crowns a 400-pound sailor.

Back to the Woods (1937)

Third Stooge: Curly
Stooge Occupation(s): Common criminals; protectors of American colonists
Nemesis: English common law; Indians

Synopsis: Sentenced to fifty-five years in ball and chain, life looks all but over for Englishmen Moe, Larry, and Curly. But a bailiff, who has taken a long look at Curly's girth, reminds the judge that it would be immensely expensive to feed the Stooges for so long. His suggestion: send the ruffians to America to defend the colonists from savages. Storming the American shores in full colonist garb, the Stooges are soon cornered by Indians who look frighteningly adept at warfare. With little choice but to resort to guerrilla tactics, the Stooges use a nearby tree branch to fire mud packs, fish, and a beehive at the scalp-hungry natives. But only after they launch their secret weapon—a skunk—does the angry tribe retreat, an obvious illustration of why even small armies should be trained in poison gas warfare.

Key Gag: Larry is captured and tied to a tree by vengeful Indians, who commence a bloodcurdling war dance to celebrate his imminent scalping. To add insult to injury, a woodpecker thoughtlessly lands on Larry's head and starts an agonizing pecking routine. When it looks like Larry is about to take his last breath, Curly and Moe appear disguised as Indians and join the whooping scalp dance, clubbing each Indian unconscious and saving their terrified comrade, who is none the worse for wear and tear on his woodpecked head.

Bedlam in Paradise (1955)

Third Stooge: Shemp
Stooge Occupation(s): Angel (Shemp); swindlers (Moe and Larry)
Nemesis: Each other

Synopsis: A remake of *Heavenly Daze*. New footage includes Shemp dying, Satan trying to coax Shemp to the wrong side, and Satan making a pact with Moe and Larry.

Key Gag: See *Heavenly Daze*.

Beer Barrel Polecats (1946)

Third Stooge: Curly
Stooge Occupation(s): Home brewers; prisoners
Nemesis: Prohibition; the prison system; yeast

Synopsis: Parched, the Stooges have scoured every corner of town for a bottle of beer, but Prohibition has made the drink as rare as gold. Faced with the terri-

fying prospect of sobriety, Curly comes through in the clutch with an ingenious plan: the Stooges will brew their own beer. Basic chemistry interferes, however, when each of the Stooges takes it upon himself to add the yeast, causing an avalanche of suds in their kitchen and a red alert to the authorities. In jail for their crimes against clean living, the Stooges do not establish themselves as model prisoners and spend the next forty years behind bars. Finally free, the old and bushy-bearded Stooges emerge from prison, but first Curly has a wish: for a tall, beautiful . . . bottle of beer.

Key Gag: In prison for bootlegging beer, Curly has managed to sneak in a full keg under his coat. All looks well until the prison photographer fixes hot lights on the Stooges while posing them for a mug shot. The heat causes the beer to boil and explode, providing sudsy evidence that

Wardens are supposed to believe in rehabilitation, but Vernon Dent's thumb points clearly toward the gallows (*Beer Barrel Polecats*, 1946).

causes the teetotalling warden to reserve space on the gallows for the Stooges.

A Bird in the Head (1946)

Third Stooge: Curly
Stooge Occupation(s): Paperhangers; guinea pigs
Nemesis: Mad scientist Professor Panzer

Synopsis: Normally, paperhangers face little danger from mad professors who desire to perform lobotomies. But it is the Stooges' misfortune to be working across the hall from Professor Panzer, a diabolical scientist who is determined to transplant a human brain into his pet gorilla, Igor. The only problem is that Panzer cannot find a brain puny enough to fit Igor's skull. One look at Curly, however, and Panzer becomes convinced that he has found his donor. All looks lost until Igor takes a special shining to Curly, a man who seems naturally to understand the ape's inner pain.

Key Gag: Mad Professor Panzer engages his ingenious X-Ray Fluoroscope to deter-mine whether Curly's brain is puny enough to transplant into a wild ape. The machine confirms that it is, showing a cuckoo clock chiming noisily inside Curly's skull. But even the cuckoo is not grade-A; when the professor taps Curly's head with a blunt instrument, the bird falls dead off its perch.

Blunder Boys (1955)

Third Stooge: Shemp
Stooge Occupation(s): Detectives
Nemesis: The Eel

Synopsis: Detectives Halliday (Moe), Tarraday (Larry), and St. Patrick's Day (Shemp) are faced with the kind of case that would make Sherlock Holmes turn and flee. After The Eel, a burglar who masquerades as a woman and smokes cigars, robs the Biltless Hotel from under their noses, the Stooges take decisive action. Matching the crook wit-for-wit, Moe, Larry, and Shemp disguise themselves as women and go deep undercover

The literal meaning of "about face" (*Blunder Boys,* 1955)

to effect his capture. But The Eel is too slippery even for the instincts of the Stooges, and flees the Biltless to remain at large, possibly to this day (a spoof of the *Dragnet* television series).

Key Gag: The Stooges are in training at detective school when they apprehend and pummel a man with his hand in the school's coffers. When they discover that the man is none other than the dean of criminology, Moe makes amends by ordering Shemp and Larry to prepare for "81C." The two beg for mercy and plead hard against the dreaded 81C, but Moe won't relent, extending two fingers on each hand while Shemp and Larry run forward and poke their own eyes onto the menacing digits.

Boobs in Arms (1940)

Third Stooge: Curly

Stooge Occupation(s): Greeting card salesmen; army recruits

Nemesis: A jealous husband/army sergeant

Synopsis: A red-faced jealous husband chases the Stooges into army recruiting headquarters, where they emerge ten minutes later, enlisted and assigned to a platoon commanded by a snorting, nasty sergeant . . . who happens to be the jealous husband. This unfortunate coincidence makes for much unpleasant basic training, although the Stooges do score some geese when their rifles discharge wildly into the air. Regrettably, the Stooges' poor showing in boot camp is reflected in their sloppy handling of battlefield weaponry and their ultimate undoing at the hands of the enemy.

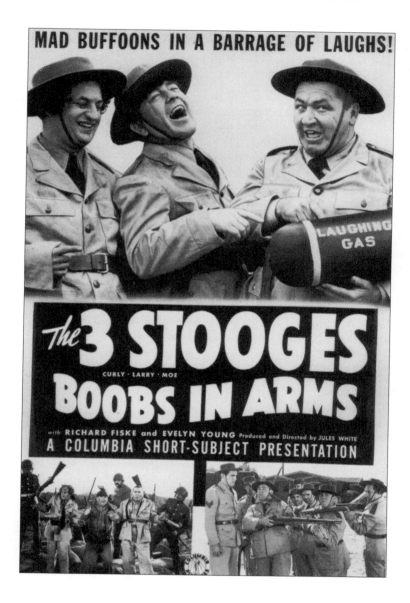

Lobby poster from *Boobs in Arms* (1940)

Key Gag: During a wartime battle, the Stooges use substandard care while firing a canister of laughing gas, and are struck by the weapon themselves. Overcome with laughter and unable to defend themselves, the Stooges nonetheless manage to dodge enemy bombs and projectiles until one guided missile speeds between their legs and carries them—horseback-style—into outer space.

Booby Dupes (1945)

Third Stooge: Curly
Stooge Occupation(s): Fish salesmen; fishermen
Nemesis: A navy captain; a con man; American fighter pilots

Synopsis: Demonstrating acumen in finance usually reserved for top business school graduates, the Stooges decide to boost the profits of their fish truck by catching the fish themselves. Once at sea, an ornery fish infuriates Curly, ultimately causing the Stooges' boat to sink. Thinking quickly, Moe hoists a white flag to signal airplanes overhead, but the pilots mistake the signal for a Japanese flag and drop their bombs. Sadly, not even Moe's brave cry, "Hey, it's the Stooges!" can stop the ferocious attack.

Key Gag: The Stooges' new fishing boat is seaworthy—until Curly chops a hole in the bottom with an ax while trying to kill a fish. With the boat sinking rapidly, Captain Moe orders Curly to get the water out of the vessel. Lucky for everyone, Curly has brought a giant hand-cranked drill, which he uses as "water letter-outter" to drill holes in the boat's other end.

Booty and the Beast (1953)

Third Stooge: Shemp
Stooge Occupation(s): Good neighbors; safecrackers; amateur detectives
Nemesis: A gentlemanly but disloyal burglar

Synopsis: A wily safecracker cannot seem to pry open the door to the house he intends to victimize, but this is his lucky day. The Stooges have run out of gas nearby and, believing the crook to be the man of the house, volunteer to climb into a second floor window to allow him inside. The gentlemanly thief accepts the offer, and soon persuades the Stooges to blast open a stubborn safe inside. The dynamite shakes the neighborhood, and

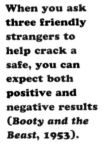

When you ask three friendly strangers to help crack a safe, you can expect both positive and negative results (*Booty and the Beast*, 1953).

the neighbors call the cops. Only then do the Stooges realize that they'll be going to jail unless they apprehend the now-departed crook. Proving themselves as adept at detective work as they are at safecracking, the Stooges track the burglar to a train, where a ferocious and fair-minded lion assists them in capturing the no-good robber. (Scenes on the train are taken from *Hold That Lion!*)

Key Gag: See *Hold That Lion!*

Brideless Groom (1947)

Third Stooge: Shemp

Stooge Occupation(s): Voice instructor (Shemp); pianist (Larry); matchmaker (Moe)

Nemesis: Greedy women who want to marry Shemp for money, not love

Synopsis: Professor of Voice Shemp is informed that his Uncle Caleb has passed away and has left him $500,000 . . . if he gets married by 6 P.M. Shemp calls every woman he knows and is rejected outright, including by an exquisite blonde down the hall who temporarily mistakes him for her treasured Cousin Basil. Miss Dinkelmeyer, his tone deaf but adoring student, arrives in the nick of time and is delighted to discover that Shemp is looking for a wife. But word has leaked out that Shemp is about to become rich, and every woman who had rejected him has now fallen in love and demands his hand in marriage. Punches fly across the room as various beauties vie for Shemp's hand, but a determined justice of the peace finally marries Shemp to Miss Dinkelmeyer in the nick of time.

Key Gag: With mayhem in the air and Shemp's 6 P.M. marriage deadline closing

in, Justice of the Peace J. M. Benton knows he must hitch Shemp and Miss Dinkelmeyer soon. But Benton is a romanticist and, despite being injured by flying purses and kicks to the shin, will not be pressured to give up his trademark slogan, "Hold hands, you lovebirds!"

Bubble Trouble (1953)

Third Stooge: Shemp

Stooge Occupation(s): Druggists; inventors

Nemesis: Crotchety octogenarian landlord Amos Flint

Synopsis: A remake of *All Gummed Up.* New footage includes Amos Flint turning into a destructive gorilla with superhuman strength after ingesting the Stooges' fountain of youth formula.

Key Gag: See *All Gummed Up.*

Busy Buddies (1944)

Third Stooge: Curly

Stooge Occupation(s): Restaurateurs; poster hangers; cow-milkers

Nemesis: A pastry delivery man; the local cow-milking champion; a stubborn cow

Synopsis: As owners of the avant-garde Jive Café, the Stooges specialize in such house specialties as collision mats (pancakes) and cackle (chicken) soup. Although most customers seem displeased with both the service and the food at the Jive Café, it is an impatient delivery man who ultimately forces the Stooges to find work elsewhere. A job hanging posters leads Moe to a brilliant idea: the Stooges will enter—and win—a local cow-milking contest as a shortcut to riches. Curly, however, lacks finesse with the cow, and it's up to Moe and Larry—and a patchwork bovine disguise—to save the day.

Key Gag: Curly's chances to win a cow-milking tournament increase greatly when Moe and Larry hide inside a cow costume armed with a bottle of milk. But Moe and Larry did not invest in the finest disguise, and the gallon they pour while Curly milks the "cow" breaks through the flimsy material and douses any hope the Stooges had for collecting the championship prize.

Cactus Makes Perfect (1942)

Third Stooge: Curly
Stooge Occupation(s): Inventors; gold prospectors
Nemesis: Scruffy claim jumpers

Synopsis: Curly has invented a gold finder that The Inventors Association has deemed "incomprehensible and utterly impractical." Delighted with the news, the Stooges set out for the Old West, ready to make their fortunes. Two scruffy claim jumpers, however, don't take kindly to the success of strangers, and while they don't resort to using their six-shooters, they do utilize a stick of dynamite to express their desire for the Stooges' gold and their personal dislike for Moe, Larry, and Curly.

Key Gag: A local con man observes the Stooges' excitement as they prepare to use Curly's gold finding invention to strike it rich. Sensing an easy mark, the swindler offers to sell the Stooges a map to The Lost Mine, a secret location that holds 100,000 tons of pure gold valued at $35 an ounce. Sensing a colossal pay-off, Moe orders Curly to calculate how

much money the Stooges would realize upon such a discovery. Curly presses various buttons on his jacket, each of which makes the sound of an adding machine, then pulls a lengthy tape from his mouth that reveals the whopping sum total: "80 billion, 16 million, and 51 cents . . . and a fraction."

Calling All Curs (1939)

Third Stooge: Curly
Stooge Occupation(s): Veterinarians
Nemesis: Dog-nappers

Synopsis: Blue-blooded Mrs. Bedford is positively sick with worry about her priceless dog, Garçon. But veterinarians Moe, Larry, and Curly are world-renowned, and their treatment of the pooch is a success. Two crooks, however, manage to kidnap Garçon from under the Stooges' noses, demanding $2,000 for the dog's safe return. After an ill-conceived attempt to substitute another dog for Garçon, the Stooges track the dog-nappers to their hideout and prove that veterinarians, if provided the proper motivation, can use their fists as well as pharmaceuticals to preserve the health of a needy animal.

Key Gag: In a panic after allowing priceless prize pooch Garçon to be kidnapped from their dog hospital, the Stooges fashion a brilliant plan to replace the missing hound: they glue stuffing from a mattress onto a mutt until it looks enough like Garçon so that its owner will never know the difference. The Stooges return the dog and for a time their plan works, until a maid's vacuum cleaner brushes against the Garçon impersonator, pulling most of the stuffing off the mutt and causing Garçon's owner to fall dead away in a faint.

Cash and Carry (1937)

Third Stooge: Curly

Stooge Occupation(s): Good Samaritans; treasure hunters

Nemesis: Con men; the humorless guardians of the U.S. Treasury

Synopsis: It's not much, but to the Stooges, the city dump is home. A young lady and her little brother, however, have moved into the modest quarters while the Stooges were away, and there's not enough room for both families. The Stooges stand firm . . . until they realize that little Jimmy is handicapped and can walk only with a crutch. Vowing to raise enough money for the boy's medical care, Moe, Larry, and Curly set out to invest the meager sum Jimmy and his sister have managed to save. The Stooges, who never possessed sharp instincts for finance, use the money to buy a treasure map, and succeed in blasting their way into Vault 3 of the U.S. Treasury. What looks like a jackpot turns into life in prison for the Stooges until a very powerful man intervenes, pays for Jimmy's operation, and grants the Stooges a well-deserved executive clemency.

Key Gag: The Stooges, believing they possess a map showing the location of a buried treasure, blast their way into Vault 3 of the U.S. Treasury. Only minutes into cramming every pocket with the newfound loot, the Stooges are startled by Treasury agents who burst in with loaded shotguns. Moe, not about to give up what's rightfully his, boldly accuses the agents of being "claim jumpers," a charge that none of the rifle-pointing lawmen seem to appreciate.

One privilege of being a patient at a Stooge-owned animal hospital (*Calling All Curs*, 1939)

Commotion on the Ocean (1956)

Third Stooge: Shemp

Stooge Occupation(s): Janitors; undercover reporters; neighbors; stowaways

Nemesis: Foreign spy Bortch; the high seas

Synopsis: A remake of *Dunked in the Deep,* with stock footage of the Stooges as would-be reporters (from *Crime on Their Hands*). New footage includes a hungry Moe and Larry stealing what turns out to be a wooden fish from a woman passenger on board the boat, then coughing up sawdust after digesting the fish.

Key Gag: See *Dunked in the Deep.*

Cookoo Cavaliers (1940)

Third Stooge: Curly

Stooge Occupation(s): Fish salesmen; designer hairstylists

Nemesis: Smelly fish; angry showgirls

Synopsis: It is not a good sign for the Stooges' fish business—or any fish business—when the proprietors must wear gas masks to handle the merchandise. Fed up with fish, the Stooges try to buy a saloon in Mexico, but a language barrier makes them owners of a salon instead. Showing great confidence in their ability to work with hair, the Stooges assure their first customers—three beautiful showgirls—that it will be a cinch to dye their long hair blond. The girls, however, are displeased with the end result, not so much because their hair isn't blond, but because their hair isn't, period.

Key Gag: Still new to the hairstyling profession, the Stooges get a complicated first assignment: bleach the hair of three gorgeous showgirls. A bit insecure with the bleaching solution they have concocted, the Stooges add an additional ingredient with no hair coloring properties whatsoever—quick-acting hair remover.

Corny Casanovas (1952)

Third Stooge: Shemp

Stooge Occupation(s): Spurned lovers

Nemesis: A three-timing blond gold digger

Synopsis: What a coincidence! The Stooges are about to be married, and discover that in each of their cases, it was the *woman* who proposed. Moreover, Moe, Larry, and Shemp have dates planned for

Salon patrons should never rely solely on the judgment of their stylists (*Cookoo Cavaliers,* 1940).

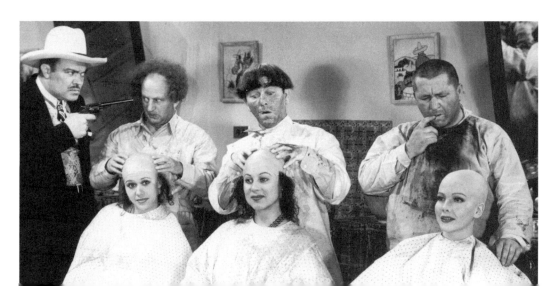

the same evening and at the same time, and shave and primp to look their best for romance. They are not pleased, however, to find each other at the same woman's apartment, and administer near lethal doses of punishment to the other, all in the name of love.

Key Gag: Handyman Moe puts a handful of tacks into his mouth while preparing to tack fabric to a couch. During a disagreement with Larry, Shemp bumps Moe, causing Moe to swallow the tacks. Larry and Shemp try obvious methods of tack removal, such as shaking and beating Moe, but only after Larry forces a foot-long magnet down Moe's throat are the tacks finally yanked back out.

Crash Goes the Hash (1944)

Third Stooge: Curly
Stooge Occupation(s): Laundry delivery men; newspaper reporters; cook (Moe) and butlers (Larry and Curly)
Nemesis: The crooked Prince Shaam

Synopsis: Fuller Bull, managing editor of the *Daily News*, is fed up with reporters who can't get the scoop on Prince Shaam's engagement to heiress Mrs. van Bustle. Mistaking the Stooges for rival reporters, Bull offers laundrymen Moe, Larry, and Curly a big bonus to bring back the story. In a remarkable stroke of luck, Mrs. van Bustle happens to be looking for a cook and two butlers at precisely the moment the Stooges arrive. This places the Stooges in perfect position to snap enough undercover photos to foil Prince Shaam's plans to rob Mrs. van Bustle's safe, a result that causes the grateful heiress to declare that she now intends to marry a man even more charming than Prince Shaam: Curly.

Key Gag: Chef Moe has prepared a magnificent turkey for guests at a posh society dinner, but doesn't notice that a parrot has crawled into the turkey. Stately butler Curly is chosen to carve the turkey, but when he tries to slice it, the bird lets out a startling yelp, causing Curly to pronounce that the turkey is haunted. The turkey then jumps off the table and does what all carving-ready turkeys wish they could: it walks away.

Creeps (1956)

Third Stooge: Shemp
Stooge Occupation(s): Storytelling fathers; movers
Nemesis: The spirit of Sir Peeping Tom

Synopsis: A remake of *The Ghost Talks*. New footage includes the Stooges' triplets demanding a spooky bedtime story and the spirit of Sir Tom engaging the Stooges in a swordfight.

Key Gag: See *The Ghost Talks*.

Crime on Their Hands (1948)

Third Stooge: Shemp
Stooge Occupation(s): Janitors; newspaper reporters
Nemesis: Notorious jewel thief Dapper Dan and his roughneck crew

Synopsis: Dapper Dan and his gang have stolen the priceless Punjab Diamond, and might have gotten away scot-free if not for the gumshoe instincts of would-be detectives Moe, Larry, and Shemp. The Stooges trace Dapper to his hideout, where Shemp mistakes the diamond for a breath mint and swallows the rock. Dapper, an impatient sort, decides to perform immediate stomach surgery on Shemp to extract the diamond—without pity, remorse, or benefit of anesthetic.

Key Gag: Shemp has accidentally swallowed the priceless Punjab Diamond, but jewel thief Dapper Dan and his mean-spirited assistant Muscles prefer not to wait for Shemp to pass the rock in a natural manner. Their solution: perform immediate surgery on the stomach of the trembling Shemp. With Dan clutching an unsterilized knife and Shemp's last breath drawing near, a gorilla bursts into the room, observes the injustice about to transpire, and fixes Dan the way the criminal justice system should have long before.

Cuckoo on a Choo Choo (1952)

Third Stooge: Shemp
Stooge Occupation(s): Train car thieves (Larry and Shemp); detective (Moe)
Nemesis: Alcohol; Carey, a giant canary

Synopsis: Aboard the stolen train car Schmow, thieves Shemp and Larry attempt to stay one step ahead of detective Moe, who is hot on their trail. Shemp, however, is extremely drunk and continues to hallucinate about Carey, a giant canary with whom he dances and falls deeply in love. Aboard the train, Moe's sleuthing is derailed by his love for the lovely Roberta, but she is waiting for Shemp to propose . . . an unlikely event with Carey in the picture.

Key Gag: While the Stooges are enjoying luscious limburger cheese sandwiches for lunch, a skunk creeps on top of Shemp's head. Not realizing the source of the resulting foul odor, Moe tries to dissipate the smell by dousing Larry's sandwich with perfume. When the stink fails to clear, however, Moe relies on a more familiar method of problem solving: he turns a hammer upon the skunk.

Disorder in the Court (1936)

Third Stooge: Curly
Stooge Occupation(s): Expert witnesses
Nemesis: Jurisprudence

Synopsis: Statuesque dancer Gail Tempest insists on the witness stand that she is innocent of the murder of Kirk Robbin, but the evidence suggests otherwise. Her only hope is three star witnesses—who happen to be playing jacks on the floor outside the courtroom. The Stooges, hearing that Gail is in trouble, rush in to give testimony, and dramatize the struggle they saw between Kirk Robbin and villain Buck Wing. But the case cracks when Polly, a parrot who was present at the murder, pleads with someone to read a letter tied to her foot. The Stooges leap to the occasion, and after much difficulty catching the mischievous Polly, obtain Buck Wing's confession from the bird's troublemaking toe.

Key Gag: During a critical stage in the murder trial of Gail Tempest, the Stooges use a piece of chalk to play a game of tic-tac-toe on an empty chair. After a humorless defense attorney uses the seat, his backside becomes a permanent testament to the progress of the game.

Dizzy Detectives (1943)

Third Stooge: Curly
Stooge Occupation(s): Carpenters; detectives
Nemesis: Mr. Dill and his crew of light-fingered burglars; Bonzo the Gorilla

Synopsis: No rookie detectives should be assigned a case so complex, but the Stooges are ordered to solve a series of burglaries committed by a daring and greedy gorilla. The crime trail leads to a spooky antiques shop, where stray cats screech without concern for the fragile nerves of new gumshoes. The Stooges stick it out, however, and discover human crooks behind the ape's larcenous behavior. Gleeful that they have cracked the case, the Stooges celebrate, not noticing that the ape has swallowed a bottle of nitroglycerin. Curly's subsequent decision to head-butt the gorilla's stomach, therefore, proves to be exceedingly unwise.

Key Gag: As door installers, it is essential that the Stooges be able to follow these precise instructions: *The door goes on the right.* But when Moe consults Curly on just which way is "right," each points in the opposite direction. Faced with this dilemma, Moe summons Larry to settle the argument: Just which way is to the right? Larry points to his right—a different direction altogether.

Dizzy Doctors (1937)

Third Stooge: Curly

Stooge Occupation(s): Brighto salesmen; physicians

Nemesis: The police; Dr. Bright; the staff at Los Arms Hospital

Synopsis: The Stooges awaken at 11 A.M. every morning, shave, then go back to bed at 11:05 A.M. Their wives, who seem not to understand that some men need more sleep than others, insist that their husbands get a job selling Brighto, a cure-all medicine. Sales fall flat (although this can be attributed to the Stooges' initial belief that Brighto is car polish) but skyrocket once the Stooges infiltrate the Los Arms Hospital, where

Moe proves that the great crooners can sing despite distractions (*Dizzy Doctors*, 1937).

patients appear interested in the three new doctors—but don't seem to get much healthier using Brighto.

Key Gag: Desperate to sell even a single bottle of the miracle medicine Brighto, Larry attempts to garner pity by putting his leg through a hole in a nearby fence and posing as an amputee. A sympathetic cop remarks that it's a shame Larry's leg is gone, to which Larry mournfully replies, "Gone, but not forgotten."

Dizzy Pilots (1943)

Third Stooge: Curly

Stooge Occupation(s): Aviators; army recruits

Nemesis: The United States Army

Synopsis: The Wrong Brothers—Moe, Larry, and Curly—are given thirty days to prove to the military that their magnificent flying machine, the *Buzzard*, is airworthy. Otherwise, they'll be drafted. Once airborne, it is apparent that the Stooges should have spent more time on research and development; the *Buzzard* flips, flops, and sputters, probably due to the decision by Curly to discard crucial equipment from the plane after Moe orders him to "throw out the clutch." Life in the army is painful and unsatisfing for the creative Wrong Brothers, who one senses could make the *Buzzard* hum if only given another thirty days.

Key Gag: Covered in self-sealing rubber (the result of an unfortunate chasing incident with Curly), Moe orders Larry and Curly to inflate him with nitrogen gas, and then to cut the rubber away as it is forced from his body. Larry and Curly add a bit too much gas, however, turning Moe into a human balloon that floats through a hole in the roof. Curly and Larry use a shotgun to retrieve Moe, dropping him thousands of feet to what would have been a certain death had he not fallen into a divinely placed well.

Don't Throw That Knife (1951)

Third Stooge: Shemp
Stooge Occupation(s): Census takers
Nemesis: A jealous, knife-throwing husband

Synopsis: A weeping woman confides in three census takers—Moe, Larry, and Shemp—that her marriage is being wrecked by a husband so insanely jealous he will kill a man just for speaking to her. Bravely, the Stooges stick around to complete their interview, but when the

woman's husband arrives, the Stooges make only limited use of the apartment's available hiding places.

Key Gag: Restricted to a single bedroom in which to hide from an insanely jealous husband, the Stooges improvise brilliantly using only household items. Moe kneels down, extends his arms, and drapes fabric over himself to pose as a chair. Larry hides under the bed, and Shemp hides under the bed's covers. The plan seems foolproof until the husband tries to sit in the chair, which collapses; lies on the bed, which presses an exposed nail into Larry's behind; and flirts with the strangely unfeminine woman under the covers who answers his love calls in a less romantic fashion than that to which he is accustomed.

Dopey Dicks (1950)

Third Stooge: Shemp
Stooge Occupation(s): Janitors; detectives
Nemesis: A mad professor who desires their brains

Synopsis: While cleaning the office of private eye Sam Shovel, the Stooges are startled by the hasty arrival of a beautiful blonde, who claims that she is being followed. But before the Stooges can gather more information, she is abducted from beneath their noses, leaving only her bracelet and an address: 275 Mortuary Road. The Stooges bravely set out for the spooky address, where, it turns out, a mad professor is seeking human brains for transplant into an army of evil robots. The Stooges battle mightily to save their necks and, after freeing the dame, hitch a ride to safety with a most unlikely driver.

Key Gag: Finally and gloriously free from the clutches of a headhunting mad professor, the Stooges hitch a ride with a kindhearted driver who passes them on the road. Breathing a sigh of relief as they climb into the car, the Stooges take a moment to look at their driver, a headless monster from the professor's laboratory who proceeds to drive away at an unsafe rate of speed.

Dunked in the Deep (1949)

Third Stooge: Shemp
Stooge Occupation(s): Handbill distributors; neighbors; stowaways
Nemesis: Foreign spy Bortch; the high seas

Synopsis: The three juicy watermelons on Bortch's table look delicious, but inside they contain secret documents the sinister spy has stolen from the American government. Unable to lug the cumbersome fruit to a waiting getaway boat, Bortch persuades his neighbors, Moe, Larry, and Shemp, to haul the watermelons to the vessel. The Stooges panic when the boat suddenly sets sail but are helpless to do anything but overeat and get seasick while Bortch looks like he'll get away scot-free. Hungry again, the Stooges dig into Bortch's watermelons, causing the furious spy to repeatedly demand, "Give me that fillum!" until knocked out by the seafaring Stooges.

Key Gag: Though he is a stowaway on a ship bound for faraway lands, Shemp seems to be a true seafaring soul, a man raised on the rhythms of the waves and tales of the oceans. But whenever he opens a porthole for a breath of fresh air, he is struck with a mighty burst of salt water, a situation Shemp does not abide

patiently. Determined not to be doused yet again, Shemp ducks under the porthole, then waves a hand above to test conditions. His hand moves with impunity, giving Shemp the confidence to take a safe breath of ocean air. The reward for his optimism: a face full of ocean mud.

Dutiful but Dumb (1941)

Third Stooge: Curly
Stooge Occupation(s): Photographers; spies
Nemesis: The editor of *Whack Magazine*; the Vulgarian government; an oyster

Synopsis: The editor of *Whack Magazine* assigns photographers Moe, Larry, and Curly to travel to Vulgaria, where cameras are prohibited "on penalty of death." Moments after their arrival, they shoot hundreds of photos and are immediately placed before a firing squad. Luckily, Curly is granted his request for a final smoke and produces a cigar the size of a baseball bat, which he heartily enjoys until the executioners fall asleep. The Stooges seize the opportunity and duck into an office, where Moe ingeniously disguises himself as a lamp and Curly hides inside a radio console from which he delivers newscasts. Strangely, their identities are discovered shortly thereafter, resulting in their capture on the ends of three Vulgarian bayonets.

Key Gag: Concerned always to eat the finest foods, Curly asks a waiter if a restaurant's oyster soup is fresh. When the waiter assures him the oysters were just dropped in, Curly's palette is whetted. The soup arrives, and naturally Curly adds a cracker. The oyster in the soup, however, is also hungry, and immediately swallows the cracker whole. At first, Curly chalks up the missing cracker to fate, but when three more crackers disappear Curly senses that something unusual is living at bowl's bottom. Sensing a showdown, he holds another cracker tantalizingly near soup level and the oyster bites—both the cracker and the finger. It isn't until Curly unloads his revolver into the bowl that his ordeal with the ornery oyster comes to a deadly close.

Even as I.O.U. (1942)

Third Stooge: Curly
Stooge Occupation(s): Kindly vagrants
Nemesis: Poverty; swindlers at the horse track

Synopsis: Homeless, the Stooges hole up in a vacant lot populated by a young woman and her daughter. The pair, it turns out, have been dispossessed and are hungry, a situation the warmhearted Stooges will not abide. Curly attempts to get milk from some ornery goats, with mixed results, but the Stooges manage to turn the vacant lot into a delightful and loving abode. Still, the ladies need funds, so the Stooges travel to the racetrack determined to win them a better life. Two swindlers at the track sell the Stooges a nag named Seabasket, a horse that soon gives birth to a youngster who, we can only hope, the Stooges sell for a healthy profit.

Key Gag: Not necessarily up to date on the latest veterinary techniques, Curly tries to use a gigantic straw to blow a medicine tablet down the throat of a newly purchased racehorse. But Seabasket has no appetite for medicine, and takes the initiative by blowing the pill down Curly's throat, causing the

Stooge to whinny and neigh magnificently, and to give Moe a ride worthy of the best Kentucky thoroughbreds.

False Alarms (1936)

Third Stooge: Curly
Stooge Occupation(s): Firemen
Nemesis: The fire captain; a rotund woman who desperately wants a boyfriend; fire

Synopsis: The Stooges have missed another big fire. But how can the captain of the department be angry after Curly explains that the Stooges were "out shakin' our tootsies with the girls last night"? Furious, the captain asks why the Stooges became firemen in the first place, to which Curly replies, "So we wouldn't have to buy any tickets for the fireman's ball!" The captain fires the Stooges, but relents when begged for another chance. Curly handles the reprieve by departing for a date, but Moe locks himself and Larry in a janitor's closet to resist temptation. Curly's honey, however, has a couple of friends and they, too, insist on dates. Still, Moe and Larry won't budge. Left with no alternative, Curly pulls a nearby fire alarm, forcing Moe and Larry to take the chief's soon-to-be-ruined new car to the scene.

Key Gag: Curly has telephoned pals Moe and Larry to invite them to a swell party. When Moe tells him that they are still on duty at the firehouse, Curly calls Moe a coward, confident that Moe cannot retaliate at such a distance. Moe, however, doesn't let geography interfere with punishment, and pokes the telephone receiver with two fingers, whereupon Curly feels that familiar and distinctive stinging that comes only from eyes poked by Moe.

Pumpeth not your bellows, Shempeth! (*Fiddlers Three*, 1948)

Fiddlers Three (1948)

Third Stooge: Shemp
Stooge Occupation(s): Fiddlers in the kingdom of Coleslawvania
Nemesis: Power-hungry Mergatroyd the Magician

Synopsis: Moeth, Larryeth, and Shempeth are the consummate royal fiddlers: they sing, dance, and make mirth worthy of their noble ruler, King Cole of Coleslawvania. The king is so fond of his fiddlers, in fact, that he allows them to wed their sweethearts . . . but only after his daughter, Princess Alicia, marries. Evil Mergatroyd the Magician, however, has his own designs on the princess, and abducts her forthwith. The Stooges boldly volunteer to rescue Alicia, even venturing inside Mergatroyd's conjuring box—without any formal training in magic—to brave the razor-tipped swords and jagged-toothed saws the treasonous magician plunges most painfully into the wood.

Key Gag: Hiding precariously inside an evil magician's magic box, the Stooges' survival depends on their ability to remain silent as various swords are jammed and hammered into their skulls, stomachs, and rear ends. When the magician yanks a particularly stubborn sword from the box to reveal a pair of loud boxer shorts, the Stooges succumb to their discomfort and spring ingloriously from the magic box.

Fifi Blows Her Top (1958)

Third Stooge: Joe
Stooge Occupation(s): Suitors
Nemesis: A jealous husband

Synopsis: Melancholy Joe can't shake the memory of his darling Fifi, with whom he fell in love on the Rue de Schlemiel in Paris. Miraculously, Fifi moves next door to the Stooges, but Joe is despondent to learn that she is married . . . and to a jealous and mean-spirited bully. After Fifi visits to borrow a cup of sugar, Larry manages to drench her in a cocktail he had been brewing, forcing her to slip into a pair of Joe's dry and cuddly pajamas. When Fifi's husband arrives, she ducks for cover, but soon bursts forth—with a baseball bat—after the man brags of his plans to dump her. Joe, always a gentleman, takes the bat away from Fifi . . . and allows her to use a bowling ball on the ungrateful cad instead.

Key Gag: Joe, wooing the lovely Fifi in a fine Parisian restaurant, bombards her with an irresistible arsenal of batted eyelashes and sweet nothings. When Joe feels a light caress on his shin underneath the table, his confidence soars. When Fifi feels a wet tongue on her leg underneath the table, she doesn't take it well. Both regroup happily after discovering that a little dog was responsible for all that love under the table.

Flagpole Jitters (1956)

Third Stooge: Shemp
Stooge Occupation(s): Sympathetic neighbors; poster hangers
Nemesis: Crooked hypnotist/bank robber The Great Svengarlic

Synopsis: A partial remake of *Hokus Pokus*. In this version, it is never established that wheelchair-bound Mary is scheming to defraud the Calamity Insurance Company. Instead, the bad guy is hypnotist The Great Svengarlic, who is in cahoots with a crew of bank robbers. The Stooges still fall off a skyscraper flag-pole, but instead of foiling Mary's insurance scam, they break up a robbery in progress at the Gottrox Jewelry Company.

Key Gag: See *Hokus Pokus*.

Flat Foot Stooges (1938)

Third Stooge: Curly
Stooge Occupation(s): Firemen
Nemesis: An unethical fire truck salesman; fire

Synopsis: Reardon is a crooked fire truck salesman who will stop at nothing to sell modern, gasoline-powered vehicles to Fire Chief Kelly. Kelly, however, prizes the horses that pull his fire trucks, and uses three of his firemen—Moe, Larry, and Curly—to groom the majestic Annie and Fannie. But while the Stooges pamper the horses with a rubdown and manicure at a Turkish bath, Reardon sabotages a company truck. He is confronted by Chief Kelly's beautiful daughter, who lands a perfect haymaker before they both are knocked out. A fire breaks out and it looks like curtains for both Reardon and Miss Kelly, but Moe smells smoke and, after tangling with a pesky firehouse mouse, the Stooges battle the blaze and save the day.

Key Gag: A hungry duck gobbles up gunpowder spilled at the Stooges' firehouse, then lays an exploding egg that tests the Stooges' mettle as firefighters—and duck lovers.

Fling in the Ring (1955)

Third Stooge: Shemp
Stooge Occupation(s): Fight trainers
Nemesis: Gangster Big Mike and his henchmen

Synopsis: A remake of *Fright Night*. New footage includes the Stooges trading exploding cigars with gangster Big Mike.

Key Gag: Moe and Larry are mixing it up with Mafia toughguys, but the fight is being heavily dominated by the enemy. Shemp wisely realizes that if the battle is to be won, it must be won by using ingenuity and brains. To that end, he spills thousands of mothballs across an empty room, then waits for the action to arrive. As Moe, Larry, and the crooks slide across the balls, Shemp crashes an ax across the craniums of the thugs, brilliantly avoiding Moe and Larry in the process. With the fight won, there is nothing left for Shemp to do but celebrate, which he does by tossing the ax into the air. His joy, however, lasts only until the ax makes its way back to his unfortunate skull.

Flying Saucer Daffy (1958)

Third Stooge: Joe
Stooge Occupation(s): Ne'er-do-well horse players (Moe and Larry); hard-working mechanic (Joe)
Nemesis: A blowing paper plate

Synopsis: It's Joe's camera, the picnic was his idea, and the photograph he took of a blowing paper plate belongs to him. But lazy cousins Moe and Larry interpret the photo as a snapshot of a flying saucer, and use it to win $10,000 in a magazine's candid camera photo contest. The magazine, however, gets wise to the fraud and throws Moe and Larry into jail. Lonely, Joe returns to the woods hoping to get a picture of a real flying saucer so that his family might be reunited. Moments later, two hourglass-shaped aliens swoop down in a spaceship to grant the kindhearted Joe his photograph . . . along with two steamy kisses. Moe and Larry, however, don't believe his story . . . until they watch

Joe's ticker-tape parade—in straitjackets—from their jail cell window.

Key Gag: Only Joe has faith in the reality of flying saucers, a confidence that pays off when the stupendously curvaceous Tyra and Elektra decide to land their spaceship and plant two stratospheric kisses on Joe's nervous lips. The proof that these ladies pack an interplanetary punch: smoke billows not only from Joe's mouth after the kiss, but from his grateful ears, as well.

For Crimin' Out Loud (1956)

Third Stooge: Shemp
Stooge Occupation(s): Detectives
Nemesis: The Phantom Gang and Nikko, the hideous monster who does their dirty work

Synopsis: A remake of *Who Done It?* New footage includes the Stooges hard at work at the Miracle Detective Agency (motto: "If We Solve Your Crime It's a Miracle!").

Key Gag: See *Who Done It?*

Fright Night (1947)

Third Stooge: Shemp
Stooge Occupation(s): Fight trainers
Nemesis: Gangster Big Mike and his henchmen

Synopsis: The Stooges run Muscle Manor, a testosterone-laden gymnasium where they train boxer Chopper Kane into tip-top shape. Gangster Big Mike, however, has word sent to the Stooges that Chopper had better lose his upcoming fight against Gorilla Watson . . . or else. Terrified, the Stooges ply Chopper with cream puffs and the affections of Kitty, a winsome blonde, until he can't fathom hurting anyone. But on the night of the fight, Chopper shows up furious; Kitty has dumped him for Watson and worse, Gorilla has broken his hand and can't fight. Big Mike is not pleased, and takes the Stooges for what he chillingly calls a "one-way ride." But Big Mike and his thugs never counted on Shemp's facility with mothballs and an ax, and the Stooges survive to train another day. (*Fright Night* marks Shemp's first short as a member of the Three Stooges.)

Key Gag: Cornered by angry mobster Big Mike and his gun-toting gang, it looks like curtains for the double-crossing Stooges. But Shemp tugs at the gangsters' heartstrings, telling them he's too young and good-looking to die ("Well," Shemp confesses, "I'm too young . . ."). The thugs aren't convinced, so Shemp regales them with details about his mother, father, and little brother, who, Shemp says as he holds his hand near the floor for illustration, is only *this* high. With the gangsters fully invested emotionally, Shemp then tells about his great big brother who is *THIS* high, shooting his hand upward and heroically knocking a thug's gun into the air. Later, when Shemp tries to pull the same trick, gangster Big Mike won't hear of it, telling Shemp, "I met your family before!"

From Nurse to Worse (1940)

Third Stooge: Curly
Stooge Occupation(s): Wallpaper hangers; insurance fraud perpetrators
Nemesis: Jerry, an insurance man; Dr. D. Lerious, the insurance examiner

Synopsis: The Stooges are tutored by an acquaintance in the art of defrauding an insurance company by feigning mental

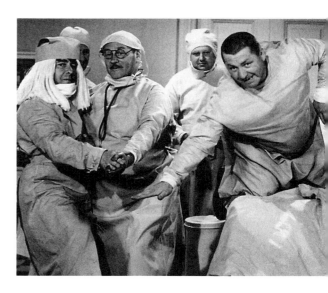

illness. With policy secured, Moe and Larry show up at the office of Dr. D. Lerious, pulling a barking and growling Curly on a leash; if they can convince Dr. Lerious that Curly thinks he's a dog, the Stooges figure they'll be rich. Stunned when Curly takes a ferocious bite out of the leg of a table, Lerious orders an immediate "cerebrum decapitation." The bad news sends the Stooges fleeing before being recaptured by Dr. Lerious and taken to Bellevue Hospital, where the high-strung physician prepares to lobotomize Curly. Using lightning-quick instincts, Moe and Larry disguise themselves as nurses, free Curly, and make their escape on a windblown stretcher.

Key Gag: As part of an insurance scam, Moe and Larry instruct Curly to act like a dog so that an insurance examiner will declare him nuts and award the Stooges big money. At first Curly is brilliant in his role, looking well-trained on his leash and panting adorably at the feet of attractive women. But on the examining table Curly turns rabid, growling and barking

The Stooges enjoy the days when physicians and patients were on friendlier terms (*From Nurse to Worse*, 1940).

and even taking a ferocious bite out of a wooden table. When the doctor orders a lobotomy, the Stooges take flight, prompting Moe to tell Curly, "If you had played your part like a Pekinese instead of a wolfhound, our plan woulda worked!"

Fuelin' Around (1949)

Third Stooge: Shemp
Stooge Occupation(s): Carpenters; chemists
Nemesis: Anemian spies; chemistry

Synopsis: Three fiendish spies from the State of Anemia determine to abduct Professor Snead and force him to reveal the formula to his secret rocket fuel. Like Larry, Snead has a marvelous head of hair, so it is not surprising that the spies mistakenly kidnap the Stooges. Back in Anemia, Moe, Larry, and Shemp struggle to invent the fuel, but their facility with chemistry is far below Ph.D. levels. They do manage, however, to brew a bubbling cauldron of random chemicals that allows them to make the most explosive getaway in Anemian history.

Key Gag: With guards closing in and ready to kill, Larry uses a supercharged rocket fuel to burn a hole in the floor, allowing him and Moe to escape to a room below. Shemp tries to drop, too, but his neck is grabbed by the guards, who stretch it to a length of nearly three feet before they finally lose out to Moe and Larry, who have stretched Shemp's legs an equal amount from the room below.

A Gem of a Jam (1943)

Third Stooge: Curly
Stooge Occupation(s): Janitors; surgeons
Nemesis: Three angry bank robbers

Synopsis: Three desperate bank robbers, one nursing a bullet wound, burst into the offices of Drs. Hart, Burns, and Belcher and demand treatment. The Stooges, who are cleaning the office, try to explain that the doctors are not in, but the crooks aren't listening to explanations; the Stooges will operate . . . or else. Curly successfully uses a mallet to apply "anesthetic," but the rest of the surgery is a dismal failure, resulting in the patient being dumped out an open window. Acting as most new doctors would, the Stooges replace the lost bank robber with a skeleton, causing the two healthy crooks to mistake the results of the operation. A wild chase ensues, with the Stooges emerging victorious on the strength of a spilled vat of plaster and Curly's remarkable resemblance to a chubby ghost.

Key Gag: After an unfortunate accident that caused a goldfish bowl to lodge on Curly's head, Moe and Larry successfully extricate Curly from his predicament. But something still feels strange. An x-ray administered by Moe reveals that

Curly has swallowed a goldfish that is swimming blissfully around in his stomach. Using the instincts of a champion angler, Moe fashions fishing tackle out of a needle, string, and some bait, then shoves the package down Curly's throat. The goldfish goes for the bait hook, line, and sinker, and after giving fisherman Moe a fight worthy of a Hemingway novel, pops out of Curly's throat and into Moe's waiting hand.

Gents in a Jam (1952)

Third Stooge: Shemp
Stooge Occupation(s): Deadbeat tenants
Nemesis: Battle-ax landlady Mrs. Magruder; the world's strongest man, Rocky Duggan

Synopsis: Landlady Mrs. Magruder has a heart. Not only does she allow the Stooges to work off their rent, she allows them to do so by renovating an apartment that contains many priceless furnishings. After seeing the results, a furious Mrs. Magruder evicts the Stooges. But Shemp's wealthy Uncle Phineas Bowman is due to visit soon, and Moe convinces Mrs. Magruder to allow them to stay until Phineas arrives. In the meantime, a pretty neighbor loses her skirt in a freakish accident while borrowing a cup of sugar from Shemp. Her husband, who happens to be the world's strongest man, assumes the worst when he sees his wife so scantily clad in the Stooges' apartment. It looks like curtains for the Stooges until Mrs. Magruder saves the day in a knockout command performance that leads to a reconciliation with her childhood sweetheart, Shemp's dear old Uncle Phineas.

Key Gag: Shemp has angered his neighbor, a hulking giant who performs a stage act as the world's strongest man. Incorporating a crunching display of headlocks, backbreakers, bearhugs, and helicopter spins, the tough man teaches Shemp an excruciating lesson about messing around with married women. Shemp's pleas for leniency fall on deaf ears, and when the building's elderly landlady orders the beating to cease, the brute tells her, "Beat it, lady; no dame's going to tell me what to do!" The landlady, however, is not as accommodating as Shemp, and delivers a blistering right cross to the strongman's jaw, knocking out his "choppers" and saving the day for the wheezing Shemp.

Gents Without Cents (1944)

Third Stooge: Curly
Stooge Occupation(s): Vaudevillians
Nemesis: Niagara Falls

Synopsis: How can the Stooges rehearse their brilliant "Niagara Falls" stage routine with such noisy upstairs neighbors? With fists poised for confrontation, Moe, Larry, and Curly storm into their neighbors' apartment to find three stunning dancers—Flo, Mary, and Shirley—practicing their own song-and-dance act. Deciding to combine their talents, the Stooges and the girls land a job in the blockbuster Castor and Earle Revue, where they slay audiences that delight in their vaudeville style. With an offer to join Manny Weeks's Broadway show, the Stooges marry Flo, Mary, and Shirley and take a honeymoon to that most unlikely of spots . . . Niagara Falls.

Key Gag: The Stooges are on the verge of stardom with their stage routine, "Niagara Falls," a bit in which Moe and Larry become enraged at Curly's mention of the name "Niagara Falls," and methodically stalk Curly "step-by-step" and "inch-by-inch" before bombarding him with physical abuse. After debuting to roaring success, the Stooges marry three lovely dancers and use their honeymoon to get away from the stage for a few days. After driving for several miles, Moe pulls the car over and asks Curly to find a road sign to clarify their location. When Curly reports back that they are only a few miles from Niagara Falls, Moe and Larry rise to the occasion, turning the car upon a terrified Curly and using the gas and brakes to chase him step-by-step and inch-by-inch for miles down the road.

The Ghost Talks (1949)

Third Stooge: Shemp
Stooge Occupation(s): Movers
Nemesis: The spirit of Sir Peeping Tom

Synopsis: Cowardly movers would have turned back the moment the first door creaked at spooky Smorgasbord Castle. But the Stooges have a job to do and they plan to do it right, especially when it comes to removing a talking suit of armor that doesn't want to cooperate. The rusty spirit of Sir Tom tries to explain things rationally, beseeching the Stooges to leave him alone until the ghost of Lady Godiva returns for a rendezvous. And while the Stooges manage to warm up to Tom (even enjoying a glass of milk with the haunted suit of armor), various other castle spooks and spirits aren't nearly so genteel.

Key Gag: Already struggling with the natural pitfalls of being stuck inside a spooky castle, the Stooges have an especially difficult time removing a talking suit of armor. Shemp warms to the armor, however, when it returns his lost

coin by paying back a jackpot of coins. Moe decides he would like to hit the jackpot, too, but the armor is less generous with him, dropping only its weighty metal arm on Moe's delicate cranium.

G.I. Wanna Home (1946)

Third Stooge: Curly
Stooge Occupation(s): Transients
Nemesis: The current housing shortage

Synopsis: No soldier should return to an empty home, but the recently discharged Stooges have it even worse. While Moe, Larry, and Curly were away, their fiancées were dispossessed; without a home, the girls tell them, there will be no wedding. The Stooges search high and low for an apartment, but not a vacancy exists anywhere. With belongings packed in their rickety car, the couples move into a vacant lot and try to make the best of things. Curly vacuums the grass, Larry searches for eggs in a tree, and Moe tries to figure a better way. After a farmer flattens their home with a tractor and chases them away, the Stooges finally find a tiny flat that seems custom-made to their specifications: the place, it turns out, is equipped with matching triple bunkbeds.

Key Gag: Curly would be happy to honor Moe's request that he peel some potatoes—if he knew how. Moe insists, so Curly adapts by drawing upon other peeling experiences in his life. Using shaving cream and a brush, Curly works up a healthy lather and applies it gingerly to the chin of the potato. With the precision touch of a veteran barber, he maneuvers the razor to shave skin from the potato, even politely asking the spud if there is any shaving cream in its eye. A brisk towel-off and some talcum powder finish the job, leaving Curly concerned only with which potato is next.

Goof on the Roof (1953)

Third Stooge: Shemp
Stooge Occupation(s): Tenants
Nemesis: A television set

Synopsis: The Stooges' landlord, Bill, has wonderful news: he has just gotten married. Even better, he has ordered a television to be installed that very day. Larry, frugal as always, suggests that the Stooges install a TV antenna for Bill in lieu of spending valuable dollars on a wedding present. Unfortunately, Shemp has lost the ring his best girl gave him from a Cracker Jack box, and it seems to have slipped into the back of the TV. Never proficient with wires, Shemp soon has the set discombobulated and in decidedly nonworking condition. The rest of the house fares no better, a result that Bill's darling Rosebud won't abide, and that the Stooges pay for—literally—out of their hides.

Key Gag: Moe demonstrates his shaky grasp of the principles of electricity when he sticks a large screwdriver into an exposed power socket. With sparks and yelps flying from the sizzling Moe, Larry attempts to save the day, but he, too, is electrically undereducated, as proven by his decision to toss a bucket of water on his suffering pal.

Goofs and Saddles (1937)

Third Stooge: Curly
Stooge Occupation(s): Civil War scouts; crooked card sharks
Nemesis: Cattle rustler Longhorn Pete; a traitorous homing pigeon

Synopsis: With the fate of a nation in the balance, Civil War General Muster calls upon his three finest scouts to stop the encroachment of notorious cattle rustler Longhorn Pete. Wild Bill Hicup (Moe), Buffalow Billious (Curly), and Just Plain Bill (Larry) make their way to the Longhorn Saloon, where they pose as high rollers in order to muscle in on a high-stakes poker game with Pete. Spotting a homing pigeon, Curly scribbles a detailed intelligence report and instructs the bird to carry the note to General Muster. The pigeon, however, belongs to Pete and flies a direct route into its owner's arms. Furious, Pete and his henchmen chase the Stooges into a cabin, where a frantic gun battle is won by the Stooges on the firing power of a meat grinder Curly converts into a machine gun.

Even in the Old West, a proper military salute was essential to a regiment's well-being (*Goofs and Saddles*, 1937).

Key Gag: Although Larry claims not to play cards, he stealthily positions himself behind Longhorn Pete, who is engaged in a high-stakes poker game against Moe and Curly. When Larry sees that Pete holds a nearly unbeatable hand containing four kings, he clutches his back and cries out that he is suffering from "four kinks" in his back. Curly and Moe get the message, and pass cards underneath the table until Curly holds the winning hand. Curly bets everything the Stooges own, but is distracted when three dead men are carried past the table. Moe inquires as to their fates, and Pete casually informs him that they were three crooks he shot for cheating at cards. Suddenly less intent on winning, Curly tosses his cards in, telling Pete he was "only bluffing."

Grips, Grunts and Groans (1937)

Third Stooge: Curly
Stooge Occupation(s): Vagrants; wrestling trainers
Nemesis: The thugs who manage wrestler Ivan Bustoff; alcohol

Synopsis: Curly is a pacifist. But the Stooges are hungry, so when the mugs at the Hangover Athletic Club offer him five bucks to spar with Kid Pinky, Curly is in no position to be peaceful. Curly spars poorly, but world champion Ivan Bustoff takes a liking to the Stooges and invites them out for a night of merriment. Bustoff's handlers don't want their prize-fighter drunk, and warn the Stooges to keep him sober. But Bustoff can't quench his thirst and soon passes out. With their backs to the wall, the Stooges disguise Curly as the bearded Bustoff and pray for the best. In the ring, Curly is soundly

thrashed until he breathes a whiff of Wild Hyacinth perfume, a scent that drives him berserk and turns the match—and everyone in the vicinity—around for good.

Key Gag: Curly gets the upper hand in a championship wrestling match when his overeager opponent is knocked cold on a ring post. Sensing victory, Moe and Larry tell Curly to pin his opponent, whereupon Curly obediently borrows a hat pin from a ringside lady and attempts to pin the wrestler's trunks to the mat. When Moe pleads with Curly to pin the wrestler's shoulders, Curly jabs the hat pin into his opponent's shoulder, promptly reviving him and changing the entire complexion of the match.

Guns A Poppin (1957)

Third Stooge: Joe
Stooge Occupation(s): Roommates
Nemesis: Moe's nerves; a grizzly bear; escaped noisy bandit Mad Bill Hookup

Synopsis: A remake of *Idiots Deluxe.* New footage includes the Stooges' noisy standoff with escaped gunslinger Mad Bill Hookup outside the cabin Moe is supposed to be using to calm his frazzled nerves, and Hookup's tip-toe escape as the Stooges thank the sheriff profusely for the reward money for his capture.

Key Gag: See *Idiots Deluxe.*

Gypped in the Penthouse (1955)

Third Stooge: Shemp
Stooge Occupation(s): Spurned lovers
Nemesis: Women

Synopsis: Larry and Shemp are delighted to bump into each other at the Woman Haters Club 87, where they trade sorrowful tales to explain their memberships. Larry, it turns out, answered a classified ad from a beautiful woman who fell hard for his good looks until a jealous Moe violently intervened and claimed the dame as his own. Shemp's story is equally melancholy. After digesting a wonderful meal with his honey (who, strangely, looks just like Larry's girl), he became mortified to discover that the woman was married to the insanely possessive Moe. Swearing off women forever, Larry and Shemp celebrate their newfound brotherhood . . . until they're introduced to the newest member of the Woman Haters Club: Moe.

Key Gag: Larry is giddy after deciding to answer an enticing personal ad, but suspects that the ad's "handsome" requirement might be problematic. His suspicion is given credence when a nearby clock stops upon his gaze, and is confirmed by the full-length mirror that shatters after Larry asks coyly, "Who is the fairest one of all?"

Half Shot Shooters (1936)

Third Stooge: Curly
Stooge Occupation(s): Soldiers; vagrants
Nemesis: The U.S. Army; the long-term memory of Sergeant MacGillicuddy

Synopsis: Asleep in a bunker as World War I rages around them, the Stooges are rudely awakened by their sergeant's boot—and word that the war has ended. After being decorated for their wartime injuries, the Stooges return the sergeant's shabby treatment by plucking his underarm hair and administering various other jarring punishments. But the subsequent years aren't kind to the Stooges, who find themselves ducking into an

office after being chased by a man for stealing his chicken dinner. The office, it turns out, belongs to a recruiting officer, who not only enlists the Stooges, but assigns them to their old sergeant, a man with the memory of an elephant. The years, it turns out, have done little for the Stooges' battlefield abilities, their relationship with superiors, or their ability to resist firing live ammunition at Admiral Hawkins's flagship.

Key Gag: Not knowing that target practice has been canceled, soldiers Moe, Larry, and Curly dutifully man one of the army's most powerful cannons. Using unorthodox loading and aiming procedures, the Stooges manage to inflict direct hits upon a tower, a bridge, a barracks, and Admiral Hawkins's flagship.

Half-Wits Holiday (1947)

Third Stooge: Curly
Stooge Occupation(s): Plumbers; gentlemen
Nemesis: Heredity; environment; society; evolution

Synopsis: A remake of *Hoi Polloi*, with the Stooges playing plumbers about to be rehabilitated as gentlemen and introduced to high society. *Half-Wits Holiday* was Curly's last starring role with the Stooges (he later made cameo

appearances in *Hold That Lion!* and *Malice in the Palace*), and the first for legendary bit player Emil Sitka, who played the role of the stately butler.

Key Gag: The Stooges' debut into high society is greeted with great anticipation, but their formal repartée suggests that their recent etiquette training might have been incomplete. To Mrs. Gottrocks, Larry bows and says, "Delighted." Moe bows and says, "Devastated." Curly bows and says, "Dilapidated!" To the countess, Larry bows and says, "Enchanted." Moe bows and says, "Enraptured." Curly bows and says, "Embalmed!"

On their way to becoming gentlemen (*Half-Wits Holiday*, 1947)

Have Rocket, Will Travel (1959—feature-length film)

Third Stooge: Curly Joe

Stooge Occupation(s): Maintenance men at the National Space Foundation; the first men in outer space

Nemesis: Rocket science; a gigantic fire-breathing tarantula; three evil robots who bear an uncanny resemblance to the Stooges

Synopsis: Dr. Ingrid is brilliant, gorgeous, and intense. But the blond rocket scientist just can't seem to invent a safe rocket fuel. Her boss at the National Space Foundation is not the type who rewards effort, and threatens to fire her—and her three favorite maintenance men—unless she perfects the formula immediately. Crazy about Ingrid and not desiring to lose their own jobs, the Stooges determine to brew the fuel themselves, using a laboratory full of volatile chemicals to whip up a whopper of a tank of gas that they funnel into a nearby spaceship. The craft soon blasts off and, because the Stooges happen to be hiding from their boss inside, Moe, Larry, and Curly Joe are rocketed on a collision course with Venus. Once on the planet, the Stooges cross paths with a fire-breathing tarantula (that seems only to aim for rear ends), a friendly talking unicorn, and an evil robot with unpleasant plans for earthly visitors. Making a narrow escape back into the spaceship, the Stooges return to a hero's welcome on Earth, enjoying the good life of wine, women, and song until three familiar-looking—and robotic—visitors pay them a visit they never counted on.

Key Gag: The Stooges have made a career of escaping from the world's deadliest crooks, goons, and goblins. But never have they been chased by villains who seem to know their every move like the robots in *Have Rocket, Will Travel.* And why not? The evil mastermind who created them used the Stooges' brains and bodies as models, fashioning a three-member diabolical army comprised of a robotic Moe, Larry, and Curly Joe capable of matching the human Stooges poke-for-poke and smash-for-smash.

He Cooked His Goose (1952)

Third Stooge: Shemp
Stooge Occupation(s): Jealous lovers (Moe and Shemp); underwear salesman (Shemp)
Nemesis: Homewrecker and pet shop owner Larry

Synopsis: Does Larry's libido know no bounds? First, the pet shop owner makes a play for Shemp's fiancée, the beautiful Millie. Next, he sends a suggestive Christmas card to Moe's wife signed, "Your pet man, Larry." But worse, he schemes to turn Moe and Shemp against each other by sending Shemp to model underwear at Moe's home, knowing full well that Moe carries a short fuse, an awful temper . . . and a revolver.

Key Gag: Underwear salesman Shemp climbs up a chimney to escape jealous husband Moe. While Shemp had the advantage of being dressed in a Santa Claus suit, he is unable to make a complete escape after Moe fires his pistol directly up the chimney and into parts unknown.

Healthy, Wealthy and Dumb (1938)

Third Stooge: Curly
Stooge Occupation(s): Contest winners; nouveau riche
Nemesis: Hotel management; gold-digging beauties; taxes

Synopsis: Curly writes jingles like Shakespeare, so it's no wonder that he is declared the winner of the $50,000 Coffin Nail Cigarette Contest. Finally able to live as they should, like gentlemen, the Stooges check into the swank Hotel Costa Plente wrapped in tuxedos, donning top hats, and smoking colossal-sized cigars. Although the hotel has many priceless furnishings that break easily and often, the Stooges enjoy the high life provided by rivers of flowing champagne and the lovey-dovey affections of three gold-digging dames and their mischievous monkey. But a telegram delivered by furious hotel management is not nearly as poetic as was Curly's winning entry; the Stooges' after-tax prize money, it seems, amounts to a paltry $4.85.

Key Gag: Curly has sipped a bit too much champagne and is not emotionally prepared to see a neighbor's pet monkey climb into a pair of neatly folded pants. Convinced that he is seeing gorillas, Curly persuades Moe to kill the wriggling pair of pants, which everyone is convinced is haunted. Never one to duck a tough problem, Moe takes a swing at the pants with a two-by-four, breaking a $5,000 vase in the process and causing Moe to criticize Larry for not supplying him with "a softer board."

Heavenly Daze (1948)

Third Stooge: Shemp
Stooge Occupation(s): Angel (Shemp); swindlers (Moe and Larry)
Nemesis: Each other

Synopsis: Uncle Mortimer guards the gates of heaven, but cannot decide whether to admit the recently deceased Shemp. As a test, Mortimer sends Shemp back to earth—invisible—to reform the dishonest ways of his cousins Moe and Larry. Shemp arrives and immediately teaches his cousins a series of painful lessons. But they still intend to sell their phony invention—a fountain pen that writes under whipped cream—to innocent millionaires the DePeysters. Shemp, of course, cannot abide such a fraud, and intercedes in the Stooges' sales demonstration in a very messy but convincing manner.

Key Gag: Returning to earth as an invisible angel, Shemp is on a mission to reform Moe and Larry, who are in the process of selling a worthless invention to a wealthy but gullible couple. Moe and Larry demonstrate their $50,000 fountain pen that writes under whipped cream by turning a blender containing the pen on the "low" setting. Shemp, however, sets the machine to "high," causing whipped cream to fly everywhere, the fountain pen to fly into Larry's forehead, and the deal to fly out the window.

One more lie from the Stooges and attorney I. Fleecem (Vernon Dent) will charge them triple, not double (*Heavenly Daze*, 1948).

Higher Than a Kite (1943)

Third Stooge: Curly
Stooge Occupation(s): Mechanics; spies
Nemesis: Automobile engines; Axis military leadership

Synopsis: Colonel Henderson's shiny new car is squeaking and he wants it fixed this instant. Military mechanics Moe, Larry, and Curly are on duty in the airbase garage, but don't yet seem adept at handling jacks, wrenches, or other complex tools. Still, they set to work on the colonel's auto with passion and determination, rearranging much of what used to be under the hood into a maze of modern sculpture. Furious, the colonel's assistant vows to have the Stooges' heads, causing them to escape into what they think is a sewer pipe but is actually a bomb. Dropped from a terrifying height directly into a meeting of German officers, the Stooges manage to overthrow the enemy on the strength of Larry's disguise as Moronica, a fetching seductress with a fruit basket hat.

Key Gag: Mechanic Moe is hard at work under the jacked-up tire of a problem automobile. Mechanic Curly carelessly puts the car in gear and steps on the gas, catapulting Moe headfirst into a hunk of pipe. Unable to remove Moe's head from the pipe with everyday tools like a crowbar and sledgehammer, Curly and Larry put the hunk of pipe containing Moe's head over a welding flame, hoping the intense heat will loosen the pipe's hold. Broiling, Moe is secured in a giant vice while Curly pulls on his ankles, stretching Moe's neck a good three feet before his head pops free.

Hoi Polloi (1935)

Third Stooge: Curly
Stooge Occupation(s): Garbagemen; gentlemen
Nemesis: Heredity; environment; society; evolution

Synopsis: A brilliant professor wagers a colleague $10,000 that he can take three men from the lowest strata of life and, by exposure to the proper environment, transform them into gentlemen. Moments later, the scholars come upon the Stooges, who are having difficulty cooperating with each other while working as garbagemen. The Stooges, the professors agree, will be perfect subjects for the bet. Through sheer will and determination, the professor trains the Stooges in etiquette and presentation, and for a moment their debut at a black tie society party is splendid. But the challenge soon overwhelms them, as the Stooges' difficulties with their clothes, their instinct to steal, and especially with each other cost the professor $10,000 and his optimistic view of human nature.

Key Gag: Professor Nichols's lovely daughter intends to do her part to transform the Stooges into gentlemen, and to that end has agreed to teach them to dance. The Stooges' initial steps are rather graceless, but Nichols proceeds patiently, instructing the Stooges to watch carefully and "do *exactly* as I do." A nearby bee, however, has chosen the moment to fly down the back of Miss Nichols's dress, causing her understandable distress and producing a wild display of screaming and wriggling, all of which the Stooges dutifully mimic in every detail.

Hokus Pokus (1949)

Third Stooge: Shemp
Stooge Occupation(s): Sympathetic neighbors; poster hangers
Nemesis: Insurance scam artist Mary; shaky hypnotist The Great Svengarlic

Synopsis: Flimflam artist Mary is scheming to defraud the Calamity Insurance Company: by pretending to be a wheelchair-bound invalid and using her unwitting neighbors, the Stooges, as character references, she'll be on easy street in no time. The Stooges, in the meantime, have been hypnotized by The Great Svengarlic, who sends them—in full trance—onto a skyscraper's flagpole. "You will now start dancing!" Svengarlic commands, but the flagpole soon breaks and the Stooges are hurtled into the offices of the Calamity Insurance Company. Inside, a startled Mary jumps from her wheelchair . . . and forfeits what looks to be a whopper of a settlement check.

Key Gag: Shemp is convinced that famed hypnotist The Great Svengarlic has no unique powers. Using Moe as his guinea pig, Shemp casts a mesmerizing spell that seems to put Moe into a hypnotic trance. "You are now in Los Angeles!" Shemp declares, and the hypnotized Moe confirms, "I am now in Los Angeles." "You are now in New York!" Shemp commands, and again Moe confirms, "I am now in New York." "You are now in Sing Sing!" cries Shemp, and sure enough, Moe lifts the back of his chair in front of his face, giving the appearance of prison bars, and confirms, "I am now in Sing Sing." Shemp then tells Moe that he is in Boston, but Moe continues to hold the chair and declare that he is in Sing Sing. Larry observes that Shemp can't get Moe out of Sing Sing, to which Shemp replies, "Good, that's just where he belongs!" Moe, however, does not think he belongs there, and expresses his displeasure by crashing the chair on the head of ex-hypnotist Shemp.

Hold That Lion! (1947)

Third Stooge: Shemp
Stooge Occupation(s): Heirs
Nemesis: Honest Icabod Slipp

Synopsis: Honest Icabod Slipp has bamboozled the Stooges out of their inheritance, but Moe, Larry, and Shemp are determined as bloodhounds to track the crook and serve him with a subpoena. At Slipp's office, however, each of the Stooges is knocked unconscious by the leaden-fisted crook, who escapes to the safety of an express train headed straight out of town. The Stooges pick up his trail and manage to board the train, although they create several undue invasions of privacy before releasing a ferocious lion from a cargo car. The lion, it turns out, loves justice, too, and flushes Slipp out of his berth and into the vengeful hands of the Stooges.

Key Gag: On the prowl for swindler Icabod Slipp, the Stooges search a train berth for the slippery crook. A sleeping passenger with a derby covering his face looks sure to be Slipp, but when Moe, Larry, and Shemp remove the hat and a clothespin from the man's face, he lets out a very familiar cry: "Woo woo woo woo woo . . . ruff! ruff! ruff!" The Stooges know it's not Slipp and move on to the next suspect. (Eagle-eyed viewers will recognize the slumbering man as Curly Howard, who had recently retired from the Stooges due to failing health.)

Hoofs and Goofs (1957)

Third Stooge: Joe

Stooge Occupation(s): Brothers who mourn the passing of their sister, Birdie

Nemesis: Mr. Dinkelspiel, a landlord who does not permit horses in his apartments

Synopsis: Although the Stooges' sister, Birdie, has been dead for more than a year, Joe will not allow her memory to fade. He makes a careful study of reincarnation, trusting that someday Birdie might return. While walking the street with high hopes and an empty heart, Joe hears Birdie's pleasant voice . . . coming from a horse. The Stooges are delighted to have found their reincarnated sister and take her home to celebrate. Mr. Dinkelspiel, their landlord, is not favorably disposed toward keeping horses in the apartment, forcing the Stooges to spend so much time hiding Birdie that they don't realize she's about to turn the Stooges into uncles.

Key Gag: Birdie, the Stooges' deceased sister, has been

reincarnated as a horse. Gleeful to find her on a city street, Moe, Larry, and Joe attempt to take Birdie home, but she is reluctant, biting Joe and swishing her tail in Moe's face. Determined to succeed, Moe ties a brick to Birdie's tail, but the horse swishes anyway, swatting Moe in the face with a brick until Moe's horse sense returns.

Horses' Collars (1935)

Third Stooge: Curly

Stooge Occupation(s): Detectives; gunslingers

Nemesis: Homicidal bandit Double Deal Decker

Synopsis: As new gumshoes at the Hyden Zeke Detective Agency, Moe, Larry, and Curly are sent to recover a stolen IOU from murderous gunslinger Double Deal Decker. The Stooges mosey into Decker's saloon, where they engage in a discouraging display of marksmanship, but are able nonetheless to pluck the IOU from Decker's pocket. The heist is a success, but Decker's henchmen are wise to the Stooges and prepare them for the hang-

Even the roughest Western bandits break into song when the mood is right (*Horses' Collars*, 1935).

man's noose. Curly breaks free and, although Moe and Larry hang by the neck for a most uncomfortable duration, they, too, escape and finally triumph by nabbing the IOU for good.

Key Gag: Fists and pokes don't phase him, but the sight of a mouse turns Curly into a whirlwind of sound and fury capable of annihilating everything in his path. Cheese is the only known antidote, and Moe and Larry carry a ready supply of Roquefort, Camembert, and Limburger for those dramatic occasions when Curly screams, "Moe, Larry, the cheese! Moe, Larry, the cheese!"

Horsing Around (1957)

Third Stooge: Joe
Stooge Occupation(s): Brothers to Birdie, their deceased sister who has come back to life as a horse
Nemesis: Hasty circus trainers

Synopsis: The Stooges' apartment is not the ideal home for their deceased sister, who has been reincarnated as a horse. Nonetheless, Birdie makes the best of Moe, Larry, and Joe's housekeeping while raising her baby and searching for her long-lost mate, the legendary circus horse Schnapps. But there is terrible news in the day's newspaper: Schnapps has been injured and might be destroyed. The Stooges, knowing that Schnapps's demise would crush their sister, travel valiantly to the circus, determined to rescue the famed horse. Although their journey is marred by poor cooperation, the Stooges benefit from the nearsightedness of the old coot assigned to shoot Schnapps; his bad aim allows Birdie to reach her ailing mate and revive him with a big, old-

fashioned kiss. (*Horsing Around* is the sequel to *Hoofs and Goofs*, 1957.)

Key Gag: The Stooges' recently deceased sister Birdie has been reincarnated as a horse, but even she gets tired pulling the Stooges in a rickety covered wagon. Always the gentlemen, the Stooges switch places with Birdie, hitching themselves to the front of the wagon and pulling their now-comfortable sister.

Hot Ice (1955)

Third Stooge: Shemp
Stooge Occupation(s): Graduates of mail-order detective school
Nemesis: Notorious jewel thief Dapper Dan and his roughneck crew

Synopsis: A remake of *Crime on Their Hands*, using stock footage of the Stooges at Scotland Yard from *Hot Scots* to segue into the Dapper Dan/Punjab Diamond plotline. New footage includes the Stooges searching the pocketbook of a curvy brunette for the stolen diamond, but finding only a blackjack, a bottle of nitroglycerin, two sticks of dynamite, a hatchet, and a crowbar.

Key Gag: See *Crime on Their Hands*.

Hot Scots (1948)

Third Stooge: Shemp
Stooge Occupation(s): Landscapers; Scottish detectives
Nemesis: Angus, McPherson, and Lorna Doone, three Scotch crooks

Synopsis: Fresh out of the A-1 Correspondence School of Detecting, the Stooges answer an ad for "yard work" at Scotland Yard. The outdoor cleaning duties they are assigned, however, don't

sufficiently challenge their gumshoe instincts, so the Stooges take it upon themselves to respond to a note they find seeking detectives at Glenheather Castle in Scotland. Dressed in kilts and armed with full Scottish brogues, the Stooges are commissioned by The Earl of Glenheather to guard his valuables overnight. Only moments after the Earl departs, crooks dressed as hideous ghouls and goblins begin to make off with the castle loot while scaring the Stooges nearly out of their kilts. Only the Stooges' persistence in the face of sheer terror reveals the larceny to be an inside job, a bittersweet ending considering Moe's affection for lovely blond burglar Lorna Doone.

Key Gag: The Earl of Glenheather wants desperately to reward the Stooges for spending a terrifying night in his spooky castle. To that end, he opens a special liquor cabinet for a drink of rare scotch, but the Stooges need a double after a talking skeleton pops out and greets them.

Hot Stuff (1956)

Third Stooge: Shemp
Stooge Occupation(s): Carpenters; chemists
Nemesis: Anemian spies; chemistry

Synopsis: A remake of *Fuelin' Around*. New footage includes Anemian officials scheming to kidnap Professor Snead, the Stooges disguised in phony stomach-length beards, Moe and Larry flirting with shapely—and tough—Anemian secretaries, and Moe and Larry perpetrating "Routine Number Six" on a soldier who delivers them their last meal before execution.

Key Gag: See *Fuelin' Around*.

How High Is Up? (1940)

Third Stooge: Curly

Stooge Occupation(s): Fix-it men; high-rise welders

Nemesis: A construction supervisor; heights

Synopsis: A new day has dawned for fix-it men the Stooges, and Moe perks things up by ordering Curly to fix the flat tire on their truck. Curly does a masterful job, though the tire surely would have lasted longer had he not patched it with a slice of salami from Moe's sandwich. Now desperate for work and without a truck, the Stooges gravitate toward a construction site and are given jobs after Curly brags that he, Moe, and Larry are "three of the best riveters who ever riveted." Assigned to the 97th floor, the Stooges work in distressingly unsafe fashion until they're forced to make a dramatic getaway from a supervisor who values on-the-job safety more than they do.

Key Gag: The Stooges do not exercise textbook caution while working as riveters on the 97th floor of a skyscraper. Among their violations: the barbecuing of hot dogs over an open welding flame, the careless manipulation of a pail of grease, the use of a jackhammer in an unsafe manner upon each other's heads, and the imprecise hurling of red-hot rivets. Curly, however, proves to be the safety-minded man of the trio, deploying a parachute built for three after the Stooges carelessly plummet from the skyscraper.

Hugs and Mugs (1950)

Third Stooge: Shemp

Stooge Occupation(s): Upholsterers

Nemesis: Three flirtatious jewel thieves; gangster Mugsy and his felonious crew

Synopsis: Freed from the slammer after serving twelve months for larceny, three dazzling dames set out in search of the priceless pearl necklace they stole and stashed a year before. But the jewelry, it turns out, has been sold at auction to Moe, Larry, and Shemp, three businessmen who run the nearby Shangri-La Upholstering Company. Determined to reclaim the necklace by hook, crook—or especially by looks—the gorgeous trio turn on the charm and soon have the smitten Stooges eating out of their hands. But the girls aren't the only ones with an appetite for pearls. A gangster named Mugsy and his strong-armed outfit turn up with fists flying, determined to pilfer the pearls themselves. The Stooges, now filled with romance, use hammers, a birdcage, and a blazing hot iron to fight for the honor of their newfound sweethearts.

Key Gag: Through an unusual set of circumstances, the Stooges and three murderous thugs end up at the bottom of a crate full of stuffing. Only Shemp can get to a weapon, a red-hot iron, which he uses expertly on the behinds of friend and foe alike. So grateful is Shemp to his trusty iron that he confesses, "Baby, I love ya," whereupon he plants a blistering kiss on the still-steaming appliance.

Hula-La-La (1951)

Third Stooge: Shemp

Stooge Occupation(s): Dance instructors; shrunken head candidates

Nemesis: Raribongan tribal chief and shrunken-head aficionado, Varunu

Synopsis: One look at Shemp's pirouettes makes it obvious that the dance instructor is among the finest ballerinas in the land. That is welcome news to movie mogul Mr. Baines, who cannot seem to get the natives on the island of Raribonga to dance for the blockbuster film he's shooting there. With his studio's survival hanging in the balance, Baines implores Moe, Larry, and Shemp to teach the natives to dance, and soon the Stooges are headed for Raribongan soil. The natives, however, are not only restless, they are hungry—to shrink the Stooges' heads. Moe and Larry think better of this tiny fate, and use a case of dynamite to teach the Raribongans that to dance is better than to shrink.

Key Gag: If the Stooges can reach a nearby box of hand grenades, they stand a fighting chance against a savage witch doctor who desires to shrink their heads. The grenades, however, are guarded by a mesmerizingly pretty four-handed hydra, a creature who slaps Moe and Larry silly whenever they try to snatch the explosives. Drawing upon decades of eye-poking experience, Moe forces two fingers expertly through the hydra's four-armed defense and into her peepers, leaving the creature wincing and the grenades free for the taking.

Husbands Beware (1956)

Third Stooge: Shemp
Stooge Occupation(s): Voice instructor (Shemp); pianist (Larry); matchmaker (Moe)
Nemesis: Greedy women who want to marry Shemp for money, not love

Synopsis: A partial remake of *Brideless Groom*. New footage includes Moe and Larry marrying Shemp's cuckolding sisters, the sisters knocking Moe and Larry down "just to show you who's going to

be boss around here," and Moe "shaving" a turkey and basting it with turpentine.

Key Gag: See *Brideless Groom*.

I Can Hardly Wait (1943)

Third Stooge: Curly
Stooge Occupation(s): Handymen; amateur dentists
Nemesis: Curly's tooth

Synopsis: Moe has finally done it. By serving Curly a bone for dinner, he virtually guaranteed that his hungry friend would crack a tooth. Faced with the prospect of having to pull the aching molar (or be kept awake by Curly's constant moaning), Moe improvises, using a variety of tactics still not approved by the American Dental Association. Nothing, not even a giant firecracker, can dislodge the tooth (although the explosive might have worked better had Curly not tossed it into Moe's pajamas). Only after Moe uses a homegrown remedy—a sock to the jaw—does the stubborn tooth come loose.

Key Gag: After Moe's homemade remedies fail to remove Curly's aching molar, the Stooges visit dentist Dr. Y. Tug for a more professional extraction. Like many, Curly is terrified at the sight of dental picks and drills, so Moe demonstrates how to sit calmly in the dental chair. But Dr. Tug has previously handed the case off to partner Dr. A. Yank, leading to a case of mistaken identity and some toothless consequences for Moe.

Idiots Deluxe (1945)

Third Stooge: Curly
Stooge Occupation(s): Roommates
Nemesis: Moe's nerves; a grizzly bear

Synopsis: Moe tells a tale of woe from the witness stand to make even lumberjacks weep. Suffering from frazzled nerves, he tells the judge, he tried to follow his doctor's orders for strict peace and quiet. Larry and Curly, however, continued to rehearse their Original Two-Man Quartet, even allowing a trombone slide to become wrapped around Moe's neck. With Moe on the verge of a nervous breakdown, his concerned roommates took him to relax at a cabin in the woods, where a hungry bear made quick work of Moe's breakfast . . . and his sanity. The sad story is too much even for the judge, who pronounces Moe innocent and releases him—with his ax—to the custody of his roommates.

Key Gag: On vacation in a country log cabin, Moe cooks a scrumptious breakfast of scrambled eggs and fried potatoes. All he asks is that Larry and Curly wait for him to join them. This request is honored by the two, but not by a hungry grizzly bear who pokes his nose through an open window and makes quick work of Moe's culinary delights—a crime for which an innocent Larry and Curly pay dearly.

Idle Roomers (1944)

Third Stooge: Curly
Stooge Occupation(s): Hotel bellhops
Nemesis: Lupe the Wolf Man

Synopsis: Hotel bellboys are taught never to flirt with guests. But when the ravishing Mrs. Leander checks into the Hotel Snazzy Plaza, all bets are off as bellhops Moe, Larry,

and Curly unleash a flurry of irresistible charm. Unfortunately, there exists a Mr. Leander, and worse, he has brought a wolf man from the carnival into the couple's room. The beast, it turns out, is tame so long as he hears no music, and Mr. Leander is careful to warn his wife of the ghastly consequences should the sharps and flats sound. The Stooges, however, have received no such warning, and try to tame the beast in the manner they think best: with a musical concert from Curly's trombone.

Key Gag: Things don't look right to Curly when he gazes into the mirror; his reflection has a hairy face, unruly eyebrows, and hideous fangs. Curly tests his reflection by moving around and is relieved when the reflection does exactly as he does. Only after Curly spits in the mirror to clean the glass does he realize that his reflection really is Lupe the Wolf Man, a beast who takes a particular disliking to people who spit in his eye.

One of the perils of being a bellhop (*Idle Roomers*, 1944)

If a Body Meets a Body (1945)

Third Stooge: Curly

Stooge Occupation(s): Hobos; heirs to a fortune

Nemesis: An evil maid; the good intentions of Curly's uncle, Professor Bob O. Link

Synopsis: You know the Stooges are broke when Curly, who has prepared so many scrumptious delicacies in the past, is reduced to cooking "nice soup from a nice, juicy bone." But the day's newspaper delivers wonderful news: Curly's uncle, Professor Bob O. Link, has died and Curly is in line for a $3 million inheritance. With dollar signs dancing in their eyes, the Stooges make their way to a spooky mansion where Bob O. Link's will is to be read. But a detective springs gruesome news on those assembled: Bob O. Link, it turns out, was murdered. Forced to spend the night in the very room in which the ghastly crime occurred, the Stooges brave a parade of hideous spooks and horrors until the crime is solved and the will is read. The reward for their bravery from Uncle Bob O. Link's will: 67 cents net.

Key Gag: A parrot with a macabre sense of humor crawls into a skull carelessly left near the foot of the Stooges' bed. Not content to use his hideous cackling laugh to scare the Stooges (who are already on edge as guests in a haunted mansion), the parrot picks up a ghostly white sheet and swoops about the room, leaving no doubt in the Stooges' minds that the world can be a truly terrifying place.

I'll Never Heil Again (1941)

Third Stooge: Curly

Stooge Occupation(s): Dictators

Nemesis: The Free World

Synopsis: A sequel to *You Nazty Spy*. The deposed ruler of Moronica, King Herman $6^7/_8$, determines to regain the rule wrestled from him by ruthless dictator Moe Hailstone. (Note: The Stooges continue their indictment of Hitler and the Axis powers, portraying the dictator as buffoonish, cruel, and insecure. The satire, as in *You Nazty Spy,* cuts sharply, as in Field Marshal Herring's (Curly) military report to Moe: "We bombed 56 hospitals, 85 schools, 42 kindergartens, 4 cemeteries, and other vital military objects.")

Key Gag: Few dictators in history have been undone by an exploding billiard ball, but that was the fate of Moronica's Moe Hailstone. Another lesson in why balls were meant to be thrown outdoors only, the explosion caused by Curly's wild throw landed the Stooges' heads on the trophy wall of King Herman $6^7/_8$.

I'm a Monkey's Uncle (1948)

Third Stooge: Shemp

Stooge Occupation(s): Cavemen

Nemesis: Rival cavemen

Synopsis: Dressed in their finest bearskins, cavemen Moe, Larry, and Shemp go about the usual caveman chores of fishing, churning butter, and fighting with mischievous ducks. But Moe has something special planned: a date with Aggie, a beautiful cavewoman. Even better, he promises to introduce Shemp and Larry to her two sisters. Aggie and Maggie turn out to be gorgeous, but Shemp's date, Baggie, is precisely that. Three nearby cavemen, in the meantime, don't take kindly to the Stooges' theft of their girlfriends, and start a war that the Stooges win by using fearsome ancient weapons such as spears, eggs, mud pies, and a skunk.

Key Gag: Caveman Moe spots a mouth-watering duck sitting innocently in a nearby pond. Moe intends to make dinner of the duck, but the bird doesn't cooperate, spraying Moe with a torrent of water from its bill. Infuriated, Moe chases the duck about the pond, but each time is bitten by the duck on his leg or nose. Finally, Moe gets close. So close, in fact, that the duck sits atop his back without Moe knowing it. Larry and Shemp spot the duck but do not see Moe, who is concealed in the pond's underbrush. Thrilled, they fire their bows and arrows with near-marksman accuracy, hitting Moe square in the backside for a bull's-eye of sorts.

In the Sweet Pie and Pie (1941)

Third Stooge: Curly
Stooge Occupation(s): Condemned prisoners; resented husbands
Nemesis: Capital punishment; their scheming wives Tiska, Taska, and Baska

Synopsis: Beautiful Tiska, Taska, and Baska must get married by midnight or they will lose a $10 million inheritance. So their shady lawyer, Diggins, concocts a scheme: the girls will marry three con-victs—the Stooges—who are scheduled to hang; after the executions, the girls will be free to collect the dough. An unro-mantic wedding takes place behind bars, after which the Stooges are marched to the gallows. The nooses break, however, and the Stooges are freed. Naturally, they rush to their brides, none of whom is

pleased to see them. The girls determine to drive the Stooges away by forcing them to become society gentlemen, but Moe, Larry, and Curly show great resolve in retaining their innate natures, even during a pie fight that would have hum-bled lesser men.

Key Gag: Moments away from hanging for a murder they did not commit, the Stooges wave graciously to a crowd that has assembled at the gallows. Suddenly sensing their impending doom, Larry remarks to the warden that strawberries might cure a cough Curly seems to have just developed. When the impatient war-den barks that strawberries won't be in season for six months, the quick-thinking trio attempt to walk away, responding in unison, "We'll wait!"

Income Tax Sappy (1954)

Third Stooge: Shemp
Stooge Occupation(s): Tax cheats
Nemesis: The tax collector

Synopsis: Moe is skeptical, but Shemp and Larry seem to know every loophole in the tax laws, including deductions for Shemp's "ex-wife and ten bartenders." Soon, the Stooges are in business as tax advisors, vowing to keep half of all monies they will save clients by cheating the tax collector. The Stooges prosper into the stratosphere of six-figure salaries, enjoying the good life by eating grandly and lighting cigars with $100 bills. But at a swank dinner thrown for their client Mr. Cash, the tax scheme comes undone when Cash removes his phony beard and announces his true identity as a tax collector. The Stooges respond as would any criminals caught red-handed: by throwing a bowl of mashed potatoes at their pursuer and making a run for it.

Key Gag: Moe prepares to dine on a wonderful hot dog, but his sandwich isn't eager to cooperate, opening its "jaws" and biting Moe flush on the nose. Moe initially approaches the problem nonviolently, trying to tame the angry hot dog by applying liberal portions of mustard to its front and back. The dog, however, bites Moe's finger, and from that point forward all gentlemanly methods of problem solving go out the window. Determined to kill his sandwich, Moe raises his knife in an effort to assassinate, but the hot dog jumps out of the bun, starts squealing in fear, and flips onto the floor. Stunned, Moe can only cry out to his lost lunch, "Hey, Fido, come back!"

Knutzy Knights (1954)

Third Stooge: Shemp
Stooge Occupation(s): Royal troubadours
Nemesis: The Black Prince

Synopsis: A remake of *Squareheads of the Round Table*. New footage includes the Stooges' attempt to cheer the forlorn Princess Elaine with their vaudeville routine, and the princess imploring the Stooges for their help in breaking her engagement to the wicked Black Prince.

Key Gag: See *Squareheads of the Round Table*.

Listen, Judge (1952)

Third Stooge: Shemp
Stooge Occupation(s): Fix-it men; domestic help

Nemesis: Electricity; food; high society; a (formerly) nonhanging judge

Synopsis: Most men narrowly acquitted of chicken stealing might take a day off after leaving the courtroom . . . especially after a chicken flies out of their coats. Not the Stooges, who return immediately to their fix-it business, tending to a broken doorbell at a nearby ritzy home. Soon, however, the home is in deeper disrepair than the doorbell, and worse, a snooty chef has quit on the spot. Staying true to their motto that they fix anything, the Stooges volunteer to prepare dinner for a high society party being thrown that evening by the lady of the house. The man of the house, however, turns out to be the judge that freed the Stooges, so it is imperative that Moe, Larry, and Shemp keep a low profile while serving dinner . . . not an easy task when dessert is a gas-filled cake that explodes when its candles are blown out.

Key Gag: Shemp's repair work on a broken doorbell is not electrically sound, and he pays the price by absorbing thousands of volts directly into his convulsing body. Always the technician, Moe tests the voltage by placing a lightbulb in Shemp's ear, and becomes convinced the problem is a serious one when the bulb burns bright. Only Larry is of a mind to remedy the shocking situation, and does so by sticking a large screwdriver into Shemp's other ear, thereby short-circuiting the voltage and causing the lightbulb to shatter instantly.

Loco Boy Makes Good (1942)

Third Stooge: Curly
Stooge Occupation(s): Carpenters; nightclub owners; entertainers

Nemesis: A Scrooge-like landlord

Synopsis: Just eight months behind on their rent, the Stooges are evicted by the impatient proprietor of the Happy Haven Hotel without so much as a handshake. At another hotel, the Stooges witness the shakedown of the kindly hotel owner by a Scrooge-like lender. Mortified, the Stooges determine to use their own hands to remodel the woman's hotel into a grand palace of dining and entertainment. Although construction does not go smoothly, the Stooges open to a full house and, hopefully, many years of rave reviews.

Key Gag: The Stooges have formulated a can't-miss scam to collect a big insurance payoff. All Curly has to do is enter a hotel, slip on a bar of soap, and the lawsuit begins. On his first attempt, Curly flails backward but is caught in the nick of time by a good Samaritan. On his next attempt, Curly takes the bar of soap into his confidence, promising, "You work with me and I'll see that you're put in a tub and nobody uses you!" This time, however, he crashes into and injures Moe, who is beginning to see the holes in the scheme. Finally, Curly spots a dog who is eating some of the soap, so he eats his soap, too, ending the Stooges' hopes of personal injury riches.

Revenge (*Loco Boy Makes Good,* 1942)

Loose Loot (1953)

Third Stooge: Shemp
Stooge Occupation(s): Heirs
Nemesis: Honest Icabod Slipp

Synopsis: A remake of *Hold That Lion!* New footage includes the Stooges tracking Icabod Slipp to the Circle Follies Theatre, Shemp's attempted getaway in a phony beard, and the Stooges' escape into a crate full of straw.

Key Gag: Crooked estate executor Icabod Slipp knows the Stooges are tracking him with subpoenas in hand, but turns the tables by accusing each Stooge of being the villainous Slipp. Slipp has no trouble knocking out Larry and Moe, but is thrown temporarily by Shemp's unorthodox boxing style, a whirlwind of phantom jabs, spins, bobs, and weaves. Shemp doesn't last long, however, going down for the count from Slipp's first punch as a fishbowl tips over and lodges securely onto his head.

Love at First Bite (1950)

Third Stooge: Shemp
Stooge Occupation(s): Gentlemen suitors
Nemesis: Old Panther whiskey

Synopsis: Before nightfall, the Stooges will be married to their sweethearts. Jubilant, they prepare their home in the grandest fashion for the girls' arrival, and even Shemp's unsanitary habit of leaving old chewing gum in places Moe cannot avoid doesn't dampen the Stooges' spirit of celebration. To pass the time, Moe, Larry, and Shemp each recounts with great fanfare how he met his dreamboat overseas. Larry charmed an Italian waitress, Moe fell for a Viennese maid, and Shemp wooed a French socialite. With such lovely memories revisited, the Stooges drink a toast of Old Panther, which knocks them drunk, unconscious, and in less than glamorous shape to greet their sweethearts' arrival.

Key Gag: Still drunk on the round of Old Panther they gulped to celebrate their upcoming weddings, Moe and Larry think that the still-unconscious Shemp has died. Deciding that the body must be disposed of, Moe and Larry cement Shemp's feet into a cast-iron pot so that Shemp will sink when tossed into the ocean. Later, when sober, they realize their mistake and decide to use dynamite to liberate Shemp

from the cement. The blast launches all three—including Shemp still stuck to the pot—directly to the pier where their loving sweethearts await.

Malice in the Palace (1949)

Third Stooge: Shemp
Stooge Occupation(s): Restaurant owners; diamond thieves
Nemesis: The Emir of Shmow

Synopsis: Arabian thief Hassan Ben Sober wants nothing more than to steal the King Rootin' Tootin' Diamond. But his wise partner Haffa Dalla reminds him that the stone is cursed. Ben Sober's idea: send three waiters—the Stooges—to do his bidding, then slit their throats after they return with the diamond. The Stooges travel to the land of Shmow, where they stealthily disguise themselves in Santa Claus suits and recover the diamond from the terrified Emir of Shmow. The coast looks clear, but the Stooges must use fruit and swords to battle a muscle-bound palace guard before their escape is complete.

Key Gag: Chef Larry prepares hot dogs with the joie de vivre and panache of the great cooks of France. But when his customers see him chasing a cat and dog from his kitchen with a cleaver, they get the wrong idea about Larry's choice of ingredients. Although his customers lose their appetites, Larry doesn't hesitate to eat the meal he has prepared, proudly declaring, "Hot dog! When it comes to cooking I'm the cat's meow!" (Note: Curly Howard made a cameo appearance in *Malice in the Palace* as a hot-blooded, hatchet-wielding chef, but the scene was inexplicably cut from television prints. It was the second and final cameo for the ailing Curly after his retirement from the team. See *Hold That Lion!*)

Matri-Phony (1942)

Third Stooge: Curly
Stooge Occupation(s): Potters
Nemesis: Redhead-loving and near-sighted Emperor Octopus Grabus

Synopsis: Mohicus, Larrycus, and Curlycue run Ye Olde Pottery and Stone Works in Ancient Erysipelas, and might have stuck to ceramics had not Diana, a stunning redhead, sought refuge in their shop. She is on the run from Emperor Octopus Grabus, who demands a redhead for his bride. The Stooges are promptly arrested for girl-hoarding and sentenced by Grabus to be thrown to the lions, but make a hasty escape and disguise Curlycue—in lovely robes and veil—as Diana. The bifocaled emperor enters "Diana's" chamber, where he becomes immediately enraptured by the dainty Curlycue, chasing "her" around the room with mad passion in his eyes. Only a dive out the palace window—and onto the spears of waiting soldiers—annuls the near-marriage.

Key Gag: Hidden behind a curtain and with mighty club in hand, the Stooges knock out a palace guard who is seated on a bench. Although unconscious, the guard never slumps over, giving Curly a perfect opportunity to manipulate the man like a puppet from behind the curtain. When the guard's pal comes along asking about the fugitive Stooges, Curly shrugs the unconscious guard's shoulders, nods his head, and remains entirely convincing as a puppeteer until he tells the guard not to hurt those "three nice fellas." Suddenly on to Curly's ruse, the guard takes careful aim with his imposing fist and delivers a devastating punch through the curtain directly to Moe's jaw.

Men in Black (1934)

Third Stooge: Curly
Stooge Occupation(s): Medical interns
Nemesis: Human physiology; a relentless intercom system

Synopsis: The Stooges have not graduated at the top of their medical school class. However, their love of medicine shines through in their energized work at the Los Arms Hospital, where even Dr. Graves's glass office door can't contain them. The Stooges make the rounds at the hospital, dispensing unorthodox medical advice and even finding time to flirt with the nurses. But their surgical technique on the unwilling Dr. Graves proves, unfortunately, that at least another year in medical school is appropriate.

Key Gag: The Stooges show saintly patience with a hospital intercom system that demands constant attention. "Doctor Howard, Doctor Fine, Doctor Howard!" cries the intercom incessantly, and the three new physicians jump to respond, first by bicycle, next by horse, and finally by miniature race cars. But even doctors have limits (and sometimes guns), and the Stooges use their pistols to teach the babbling intercom a lesson about nagging. Its dramatic dying words: "Oh, they got me!"

Merry Mavericks (1951)

Third Stooge: Shemp
Stooge Occupation(s): Vagrants; lawmen
Nemesis: Bank robber Red Morgan and his gang

Synopsis: A reworking of *Phony Express.* New plot twists include the Stooges guarding stolen money at a spooky mansion and doing battle with a headless Indian chief.

Key Gag: Things look bad for the Stooges in their battle with bank bandit Red Morgan and his gang of cutthroat thugs until Shemp dons a headless Indian costume and knocks out the bunch of them. Faced with a decision as to the fate of the gang's shapely blond cohort, Moe declares that they should throw her to the dogs, whereupon Larry and Shemp begin to bark and howl deliriously.

A Merry Mix-Up (1957)

Third Stooge: Joe
Stooge Occupation(s): Triplets
Nemesis: Assorted wives and girlfriends

Synopsis: Moe, Larry, and Joe are but one set of triplets trying to make sense of love and women. Unbeknownst to them, their long-lost brothers are living in the same city . . . and everyone seems to arrive where somebody else's women are waiting. So many cases of mistaken identity cause so much havoc that anyone sitting through *A Merry Mix-Up* will soon be seeing triple.

Key Gag: Already infuriated at the Stooges, the suspicious wives of Moe, Larry, and Joe do not know that the Stooges are discussing a chicken dinner when they overhear these disturbing words coming from behind the kitchen door: "Are they beautiful, and what beautiful legs they have!" and "Yum, there's something I could really go for!"

Micro-Phonies (1945)

Third Stooge: Curly
Stooge Occupation(s): Handymen; opera stars
Nemesis: Ornery tenor Signor

Synopsis: Unable to resist the sounds of opera in a nearby recording studio, handyman Curly dons women's clothing and lip-synchs a lovely rendition of "Voices of Spring." A nearby socialite, convinced that she is witnessing the dawning of a new diva, insists that the Stooges perform at her party that evening. At the event, however, a menacing tenor unplugs the Stooges' phonograph and fires a banana into Curly's mouth, thereby exposing the Stooges' musicianship as something less than virtuoso. The socialite is scandalized, and it looks like jail for the Stooges until the real singer steps forth to claim responsibility . . . and congratulations for possessing such a beautiful voice.

Key Gag: Threatened by a tenor who is muscling in on their territory, opera singer Señorita Cucaracha (Curly) and accompanists Señors Mucho and Gusto (Larry and Moe) use a marksman's aim to fire cherries into the flabbergasted singer's mouth until he gags, chokes, and coughs his way out of the Stooges' path to stardom.

A Missed Fortune (1952)

Third Stooge: Shemp
Stooge Occupation(s): Contest winners; nouveau riche
Nemesis: Hotel Costa Plente management; gold-digging beauties; taxes

Synopsis: Never has a foot-stomping been so rewarding. On the telephone with radio station B-U-R-P, Shemp stands to win $50,000 if he can identify a car by the sound of its engine. Moe, who is frustrated with Shemp, stomps on his foot, causing Shemp to cry in pain, "My bunion aches! Bunion aches!" Because the name of the car in the contest is the Bunion Eight, Shemp is declared the winner and the Stooges celebrate what is certain to be a life of high style and fancy living. But the priceless furnishings at their new home—the posh Hotel Costa Plente—break easily and often, and the hotel seems to attract its share of gold-digging dames. But it is a much bigger enemy, the tax man, who puts the biggest damper on the Stooges' lofty plans.

Key Gag: Even Moe cannot deny the deliciousness of Shemp's pancakes as he prepares to smother them in scrumptious maple syrup. But Shemp has carelessly left a can of glue on the dining room table, and in his haste to pour the syrup Moe isn't careful to read the labels. Suffering from a dreadful case of glue mouth, Moe panics and furiously motions Larry and Shemp to unstick his lips. Brute force proves unsuccessful, but Larry shows great creativity by pouring a pot of boiling water onto Moe's face, freeing Moe to express his extreme dissatisfaction with the situation.

Monkey Businessmen (1946)

Third Stooge: Curly

Stooge Occupation(s): Electricians; rest home patients

Nemesis: Electricity; Dr. Mallard, the crooked proprietor of Mallard's Rest Home and Clinic

Synopsis: Tired of being electrocuted, electricians Moe, Larry, and Curly decide

People today forget the bravery of early electricians (*Monkey Businessmen,* 1946).

they need a vacation, and travel to Mallard's Rest Home and Clinic to recharge their batteries. But Mallard is no doctor and his henchmen aren't nurses; the entire clinic exists to defraud vulnerable patients of their hard-earned money. After being put through a murderous workout regimen designed to break their spirits, the Stooges get wise to Mallard's game and struggle mightily to escape the grueling world of rest and relaxation.

Key Gag: It is 5 A.M. and time for the Stooges to face the day. Climbing wearily from bed, Moe, Larry, and Curly undo their long sleeping gowns to reveal spiffy suits, ties, and suspenders. Not the most wrinkle-free way to dress, but effective and efficient in a pinch.

Movie Maniacs (1936)

Third Stooge: Curly
Stooge Occupation(s): Aspiring actors; movie directors
Nemesis: Movie studio head Fuller Rath; snooty film director Swinehardt

Synopsis: As aspiring actors, everything about the Stooges screams stardom. Sadly, ornery studio guards fail to see their potential, and deny them admission to the Hollywood lot. But timing is everything, and the Stooges are soon mistaken for three high-powered movie executives who have been sent to turn the studio around. Given free rein and absolute power, director Moe and actors Curly and Larry proceed to make what must be deemed an avant-garde film until their true identities are discovered.

Key Gag: Mistaken for new chiefs of a Hollywood motion picture studio, the Stooges waste no time in taking over a movie currently in production. The acting, declares director Moe, is lifeless and boring, and he instructs Curly and Larry to demonstrate true drama to the cast and crew. Positioning themselves behind the film's two stars, Curly and Larry thrust their own arms under the stars' arms, using them to make melodramatic gestures and gesticulations until the real director and stars stomp off the set.

Mummy's Dummies (1948)

Third Stooge: Shemp
Stooge Occupation(s): Used chariot dealers; royal chamberlains
Nemesis: Radames, the crooked chief of the palace guard

Synopsis: Honest Moe, Honest Shemp . . . and Larry operate The Smiling Egyptians, a used-chariot lot doing bang-up business in ancient Egypt. They make the mistake, however, of selling a lemon to Radames, chief of the palace guard. Dragged before the great King Rootentooten—who is especially ornery because of a toothache—the Stooges are sentenced to die in a pit full of crocodiles. Thinking fast, Moe

How can she be expected to choose? (*Mummy's Dummies,* 1948)

presents Shemp as "Painless Papyrus," a specialist in ailments of the tooth. Donning pop bottle bifocals, Shemp approaches the king warily and, after pulling Moe's tooth accidentally, manages to extract Rootentooten's molar. As a reward, the king invests the Stooges as royal chamberlains, and they soon stumble onto and foil Radames's plan to steal tax money from the king.

Key Gag: As a reward for recovering his stolen tax revenues, King Rootentooten offers the Stooges a king's greatest gift: the hand of his fair daughter, the princess. Blond and mysterious behind her veil, the flirtatious princess causes the Stooges to push and shove for the right to marry her. But when the princess removes her veil to reveal the face of a bloodhound, the Stooges have a quick change of heart. "Let the lucky man take one pace forward!" declares the joyous king, whereupon Moe and Larry take one pace backward, leaving Shemp the lucky groom-to-be.

Muscle Up a Little Closer (1957)

Third Stooge: Joe
Stooge Occupation(s): Fiancés; shipping clerks
Nemesis: Tough-guy jewelry thief Elmo Drake

Synopsis: Joe's gargantuan fiancée, Tiny, is devastated after discovering that her five-carat engagement ring has been stolen. The Stooges suspect Elmo Drake, the trucking foreman at the Seabiscuit Food Corp., where they and the girls work, and even catch the crook in possession of Tiny's locker key. But Drake is in tip-top physical condition, and han-

dles the Stooges' flying fists with casual abandon. Tiny, however, is a different breed of fighter; when she takes a running leap and allows the full weight of her fury to land on Drake's chest, the ring—and her adoring Joe—are hers to love forever.

Key Gag: Poor Joe has dropped hundreds of eggs on the floor and Moe is not about to help him with the cleanup job. But what Joe lacks in a sure grip he makes up for with ingenuity; sprinkling oil over the broken eggs, he proceeds to fry them with a gigantic blowtorch.

Musty Musketeers (1954)

Third Stooge: Shemp
Stooge Occupation(s): Fiddlers in the kingdom of Coleslawvania
Nemesis: Power-hungry Mergatroyd the Magician

Synopsis: A remake of *Fiddlers Three*. New footage includes the Stooges wooing three lovely damsels, a grueling swordfight with Mergatroyd the Magician, and a happy reunion with sweethearts Tillyeth, Millyeth, and Lillyeth.

Key Gag: See *Fiddlers Three*.

Mutts to You (1938)

Third Stooge: Curly
Stooge Occupation(s): Dog laundry operators
Nemesis: Eagle-eyed police officer O'Halloran; a suspicious landlord

Synopsis: The Stooges operate the K-9 Dog Laundry, a state-of-the-art facility that relies on a baffling assembly line system powered by Curly and his bicycle. During lunch, the Stooges find an abandoned baby and gingerly sneak it past their busybody landlord. They struggle to adapt to the rigors of raising a child, but it's not long before a newspaper headline announces that the baby they found is believed to have been kidnapped. Moe, sensing the Stooges' predicament, dresses Curly to look like the baby's mother and the Stooges attempt to escape town undetected. But Officer O'Halloran smells a rat and gives chase, making an arrest that spells certain jail time until the baby's parents arrive on the scene and announce the entire affair to have been a mistake.

Key Gag: The Stooge-owned K-9 Dog Laundry is a marvel of technology, where dogs ride a conveyor belt and are lathered, rinsed, and dried by a myriad of mechanical implements. Larry monitors the dogs' progress, Curly rides a bicycle that keeps water flowing, and Moe oversees the operation from inside a control room of intricate gears and levers, including a special lever that causes a mechanical hand to spank Curly when his peddling slows to an unacceptable pace.

No Census, No Feeling (1940)

Third Stooge: Curly
Stooge Occupation(s): Census takers; football stars
Nemesis: A jittery shop owner; police; opposing football players

Synopsis: After an insensitive shop owner dumps them from the storefront awning in which they sleep, the Stooges take refuge in City Hall, where they unwittingly emerge as census takers. Inside the fancy home of a local socialite, Moe and Larry gather information while Curly romances an exquisite French maid named Fifi. As often hap-

pens at society events, patience for the Stooges wears thin, and they leave to take the census in a bigger and better location. At a packed football stadium, the Stooges stay focused on their work, never allowing the perils of an ongoing game to deter them from requesting census information from players between bone-crushing tackles.

Key Gag: Curly thinks the fruit punch at a society bridge party needs sweetening but uses powdered alum instead of powdered sugar, and in great amounts. The guests immediately sense that this is a flavor they haven't tasted before, and might even have mentioned it to Curly were they able to pry open their lips.

No Dough Boys (1944)

Third Stooge: Curly
Stooge Occupation(s): Models; Japanese spies
Nemesis: German spies

Synopsis: Painted to look like Japanese soldiers for a magazine ad, models Moe, Larry, and Curly are consummate professionals, never removing their makeup and costumes even during a much-needed lunch break. But when they lean against a secret trapdoor, the Stooges stumble into the hideout of top-ranking German spies, and suddenly the Free World hangs in the balance. Deciding bravely to stay undercover (there are three gorgeous enemy spies that need to be dealt with), the Stooges baffle the Germans with demonstrations of ju jitsu and other proofs of their Japanese heritage until the real spies arrive to face a barrage of pies, seltzer bottles, and other Stooge artillery.

Key Gag: Mistaken for Japanese saboteurs, the Stooges find themselves pressed to demonstrate the ancient fighting art of ju jitsu for three lovely German spies. Moe and Larry improvise brilliantly, tossing their German counterparts in the manner of true martial arts masters. Curly, however, is manhandled by the most delicate of the three lady spies, who picks him up, whirls him around several times, and then catapults him at breakneck speed across the room.

Nutty but Nice (1940)

Third Stooge: Curly

Stooge Occupation(s): Singing waiters; detectives

Nemesis: A fiendish kidnapping crew who don't like yodelers

Synopsis: Two doctors believe the Stooges are just the medicine for a heartbroken girl whose father has been kidnapped. But even Moe, Larry, and Curly can't make the forlorn child laugh. The Stooges agree to search for the girl's father, who, they are informed, always answers when his daughter yodels. With the Stooges on the lookout, it is the kidnappers' bad luck to turn on a radio station playing an air-piercing yodel. The Stooges track the music to a nearby apartment, where they burst in and bust up one of the thugs. (It is interesting to observe that even under such dire circumstances, Larry and Curly still find time to clap and dance as Moe hops in pain after being injured by a falling bed frame.) The Stooges ultimately win a nail-

biter of a fight against the rest of the thugs and return the grateful father to his yodel-loving daughter.

Key Gag: A neighborhood man emerges from his local tavern carrying many wonderful pails of beer on two wooden poles. His thoughts are of cool refreshment and quiet relaxation, but the Stooges have violated that golden rule of grade school: Look where you run. The man, his beer, and his visions of rejuvenation are toppled—four times—by the onrushing trio.

Of Cash and Hash (1955)

Third Stooge: Shemp

Stooge Occupation(s): Café workers; detectives

Nemesis: Bloodthirsty armored car robber Lefty Loomis and his hideous hatchet man, Angel

Synopsis: A remake of *Shivering Sherlocks*. New footage includes the Stooges caught in the middle of a shoot-out, the Stooges

When you cook like the great chefs of Paris, what's not to sing about? (*Of Cash and Hash*, 1955)

chasing an armored car robber to the hideout of Lefty Loomis, and Shemp's hailstorm of celebratory kisses to the delicate face of Gladys Harmon.

Key Gag: See *Shivering Sherlocks*.

Oil's Well That Ends Well (1958)

Third Stooge: Joe
Stooge Occupation(s): Loyal sons; uranium miners
Nemesis: A stubborn uranium mine

Synopsis: The Stooges' poor papá needs a lifesaving operation, but neither he nor his sons have any money. The only glimmer of hope, it seems, is to be found in the hills: the old man has a uranium mine in Red Dog Canyon that might yield enough of the valuable metal to make everyone rich. None of the Stooges, however, is adept at handling dynamite or pickax, and it looks like curtains for Pa without any uranium to sell. Thirsty and downtrodden, the Stooges stop at a well to take a drink, but tap instead into an oil geyser, a slippery but still profitable means to save dear old Dad's life. (This film is a partial reworking of *Oily to Bed, Oily to Rise,* with Joe reprising Curly's uncanny knack for realizing his every wish and his willingness to serve as a human cork on the oil well.)

Key Gag: Joe has done his part to quench the Stooges' thirst by finding a cow; now it's Larry's job to milk it. When Larry places a bottle directly under its udders, the cow remains uncooperative even though Larry issues the unmistakable order, "Give!" Deciding to use a take-charge, hands-on approach, Larry

pumps the cow's tail, this time getting a devastating hoof in the face for his unorthodox milking methods.

Oily to Bed, Oily to Rise (1939)

Third Stooge: Curly
Stooge Occupation(s): Vagrants; farmhands; vigilantes
Nemesis: Three swindlers who take advantage of defenseless widows

Synopsis: Curly seems always to get his wish: a car, roast chicken and dumplings, even the love of three beautiful girls named April, May, and June. But swindlers have conned the girls' mother, the kindly Widow Jenkins, and the Stooges won't sit still for such injustice. Furious, they take off in hot pursuit of the crooks, but seem lost until Curly wishes to get his hands on the thieves. Moments later, they find the crooks walking on the road and fisticuffs ensue, with the Stooges emerging victorious on the strength of a perfectly executed triple handshake flip. With the deed to Mrs. Jenkins's oil-rich land recovered, Curly has a final wish: for a justice of the peace . . . who appears out of nowhere to marry the Stooges to their adoring loves.

Key Gag: When a thick black liquid erupts from a water well they are cleaning, the Stooges realize they've struck oil. But the uncontrolled gusher is costing them dough, so Curly sits atop the well, temporarily halting the eruption and proclaiming himself a "successful cork." Soon, however, the oil pressure is too much, and blasts Curly into the air, bobbing him fifty feet aboveground. Now, he yells to Moe and Larry below, he has become an "unsuccessful cork," a situation Moe remedies quickly by expert use of a lasso and a healthy tug.

Out West (1947)

Third Stooge: Shemp
Stooge Occupation(s): Convalescents; vacationers; cowboys
Nemesis: Hard-hearted gunslinger Doc Barker

Synopsis: The doctor draws a sobering diagram: Shemp's leg—especially the vein—is in bad shape. So the Stooges head west for a therapeutic vacation. Trouble brews, however, when the Stooges mosey into a speakeasy and Shemp begins to brag about his gigantic vein. Dirty-dealing Doc Barker, believing Shemp to be referring to a gold mine, determines to muscle in on Shemp's millions. The lovely Nell, in the meantime, begs the Stooges to help spring her boyfriend, the Arizona Kid, who has been unjustly imprisoned. Moe fixes a Mickey Finn that knocks Barker for a loop, and the Stooges take advantage of the commotion to grab Barker's keys and free the Arizona Kid, who summons the U.S. Cavalry to save the day.

Key Gag: Dressed in his finest Western duds, Shemp finds himself mixed up in a high-stakes poker game with Doc Barker and his shifty gang. When Shemp feels a tickle on his toe, he reaches under the card table to discover an ace being passed by a confederate to Barker, and smoothly takes the card for himself, substituting a worthless one in its place. Three tickles later, Shemp reveals four aces to a stunned Barker and collects one of the biggest pots the Old West has ever

seen. Shemp's victory declaration: "Come to Papa!"

Outer Space Jitters (1957)

Third Stooge: Joe
Stooge Occupation(s): Interplanetary travelers
Nemesis: Celestial madman the Grand Zilch of Sunev

Synopsis: Space travelers Moe, Larry, and Joe are grateful to have traveled with Professor Jones to the planet Sunev, where priceless gems, fine foods, and curvaceous blondes are in unlimited supply. But the planet's leader, the Grand Zilch of Sunev, is engaged in a shocking set of experiments designed to create an army of killer zombies, and he intends to waste little time disposing of the meddlesome visitors before continuing with his deadly plan. The Sunevians, however, have never dealt with Stoogian war tactics, and soon succumb to the kind of frenetic confusion that works so well for the Stooges on Earth.

Key Gag: Bewitched by three shapely aliens from the planet Sunev who look like they love to kiss, the Stooges turn on the charm and pucker up. But these ladies are electrocharged, as Larry finds out after a red-hot kiss transforms his pockets of unpopped corn into mounds of fluffy and ready-to-eat popcorn.

The Outlaws Is Coming (1965—feature-length film)

Third Stooge: Curly Joe
Stooge Occupation(s): Printers; deputies; buffalo conservationists
Nemesis: Wild West power monger Rance Roden and his gunslinging enforcer Trigger Mortis

Synopsis: If frontier megalomaniac Rance Roden has his way, every buffalo in the Wild West will be slaughtered. His bloody purpose: to infuriate the Indians, sell them weapons, and turn them against his enemy, the U.S. Cavalry. And with bullet-happy gunslinger Trigger Mortis to enforce his greedy policies, it looks like the only place buffalo will survive is on the nickel. Back in Boston, a conservationist magazine publisher gets word of the slaughters and sends his editor, Kenneth Cabot, and three bumbling printers—the Stooges—to Wyoming to investigate. Desperately in need of lawmen (who seem to die daily in Wyoming), the townsfolk hire Cabot as sheriff and deputize the Stooges for good measure. Soon, the four easterners drive Roden and Mortis to distraction, and would certainly have been filled full of lead but for the bull's-eye assistance of beautiful blond sharpshooter Annie Oakley, who develops a crush on Cabot and won't allow a single bullet to muss his dreamy head. Even a posse of the Wild West's great desperadoes cannot seem to defeat Cabot and the Stooges, and it's only a matter of time before the good guys use a hidden camera, a wobbly stagecoach, and crates of delicious cream pies to defeat Roden and Mortis and return the frontier to its rightful owner, the buffalo.

Key Gag: The Stooges have always been scrupulous about wiping Moe clean after spilling ink, desserts, or other staining items onto his face. But when printers Larry and Curly Joe send him sprawling into a printing press, they demonstrate a more scholarly side by reading the day's headlines imprinted on Moe's face and then wrenching his head to the side in order to continue perusing the story as it continues onto his neck.

A Pain in the Pullman (1936)

Third Stooge: Curly
Stooge Occupation(s): Song-and-dance men
Nemesis: Melodramatic heartthrob actor Paul Pain; the Stooges' pet monkey, Joe

Synopsis: Despite the huffy protests of their neighbor, heartthrob actor Paul Pain, the Stooges use every square inch of their apartment to rehearse a noisy song-and-dance act that they hope will make them famous. A big break follows when they're hired—along with their monkey, Joe—to perform in "The Panics of 1936," a blockbuster production certain to make them stars. Boarding a locomotive bound for Hollywood, Joe soon demonstrates why most trains have a no-monkeys policy—and why it's best not to monkey with the Stooges.

Key Gag: The Stooges' pet monkey, Joe, has twice removed the toupee of sniffy stage star Paul Pain, so Pain takes pains to ensure that Joe is locked inside the baggage compartment of a train on which he and the Stooges are traveling. Joe, however, is partial to traveling first class and makes his way into Pain's berth and then into Pain's pajama leg, and finally onto the train's emergency brake, which cannot quite support the weight of a mischievous monkey.

Pals and Gals (1954)

Third Stooge: Shemp
Stooge Occupation(s): Convalescents; vacationers; cowboys
Nemesis: Hard-hearted gunslinger Doc Barker

Synopsis: A remake of *Out West,* minus the involvement of the U.S. Cavalry. New footage includes Nell's imprisoned sisters, Belle and Zell, the Stooges disguising themselves as Southern gentlemen, their escape in a covered wagon, and an amorous rendezvous with Nell, Belle, and Zell.

Key Gag: See *Out West*.

Pardon My Backfire (1953)

Third Stooge: Shemp
Stooge Occupation(s): Mechanics; ·
   suitors
Nemesis: An impatient and grumpy father-in-law to be; a band of deadly escaped convicts with a bum car

Synopsis: It's been just ten years since the Stooges got engaged to beauties Betty, Hettie, and Nettie, but the girls' impatient father insists that the wedding occur soon . . . or else. Vowing to keep their garage open until they earn enough to pay for the nuptials, mechanics Moe, Larry, and Shemp demonstrate the kind of proficiency with tools that will keep them bachelors for life. To make matters worse, their first customers seem to match detailed descriptions of recently escaped convicts. Soon, the Stooges are wise to the crooks, utilizing a monkey wrench, power sander, and even a blowtorch in ways never intended on the human behind, and finally capturing the escapees and collecting enough reward money to marry their sweethearts. (Along with *Spooks*, this is one of two Three Stooges shorts filmed in thrilling 3-D.)

Key Gag: Using improper care with a welding torch, Larry directs an unwieldy four-foot flame directly onto Moe's trouser seat. Larry's keen sense of smell causes him to comment that he smells rubbish burning, an observation with

which even Moe agrees until he realizes precisely what is on fire.

Pardon My Clutch (1948)

Third Stooge: Shemp
Stooge Occupation(s): Caretakers to an ailing Shemp
Nemesis: A flimflam friend named Claude A. Quacker; Shemp's frazzled nerves

Synopsis: Shemp should see a physician for his shattered nerves. But the Stooges' pal, Claude A. Quacker, has read lots of "doctor books" and saves the Stooges a fee by prescribing a camping vacation— and selling them his dubious car for the privilege. The car breaks down immediately, but a nearby Hollywood talent scout offers the Stooges big bucks for the beater, saying it would be perfect for his motion picture. Quacker, seeing the opportunity for bigger profits, hastily refunds the Stooges' money and greedily claims that the car belongs to him. But after two men in white jackets come to take the "talent scout" back to the asylum, the frustrated Quacker loses his marbles, too.

Key Gag: Moe and Larry have been given explicit instructions: give the ailing Shemp one dose of medicine and then skip an hour. They faithfully deliver the pill, but then force Shemp to take a jump rope . . . and skip an hour.

Pardon My Scotch (1935)

Third Stooge: Curly
Stooge Occupation(s): Handymen;
   bootleggers
Nemesis: Prohibition; basic chemistry

Synopsis: Jones' Drugstore is in a pickle. With supplies of bootleg scotch drying up, its customers will surely find another place to quench their thirsts. Determined to find a new supply of hooch, Mr. Jones asks his three handymen, Moe, Larry, and Curly, to mind the store while he scours the area for a new distributor. When a thirsty customer requests "some of the prescription stuff," the customer service–oriented Stooges mix a bubbling and smoking cauldron of chemicals that packs a mighty wallop. Convinced that he has just tasted the finest scotch on the black market, the customer invites the Stooges to debut their "Breath O' Heather" at a swank party. The Stooges arrive with much fanfare, dressed in kilts and wielding mean Scottish brogues, but show little skill in tapping their potent product, causing an explosion of suds not even the government could repeal.

Key Gag: Posing in full regalia as three Scottish distillers, the Stooges are the toast of a swank party thrown in their honor by wealthy bootleggers. When snooty baritone Señor Louis Balero Cantino rises to perform for the guests, it is only fitting that the Stooges fire grapes into the wiseguy singer's mouth. Undaunted, Cantino continues the opera, forcing Curly to take deadly aim with a peeled banana. His shot is true and the music stops, causing Cantino to declare indignantly, "What you try to make for me, a fruit salad?"

Pest Man Wins (1951)

Third Stooge: Shemp
Stooge Occupation(s): Exterminators
Nemesis: The world of pests

Synopsis: Mrs. Castor's magnificent display of pies and cakes is certain to impress her society guests, who are due for luncheon at any moment. The Stooges, working in the neighborhood as exterminators, have had no luck finding a home that requires their services. In a moment of inspiration, Larry devises a surefire plot: the Stooges will plant moths, ants, mice, and bedbugs in the Castor home, then ring the doorbell and announce themselves to the owner. "Heaven must have sent you!" exclaims Mrs. Castor, who then hires the Stooges to work incognito. Although dressed dashingly in tuxedos and tails, the Stooges are not entirely discreet, losing cats in the piano and pests everywhere else before the pies and cakes become used for a purpose for which they never were intended.

Key Gag: The Stooges are having a tough time controlling the mice they have unleashed at a party, even losing one down the jacket of a dignified guest. Naturally, the guest is startled at the sudden wiggling down his back, and yelps and jumps in an effort to undo the distressing situation. The Stooges, however, are inspired by the man's gyrations, and begin to clap and join the man in his unorthodox but lively dance.

Phony Express (1943)

Third Stooge: Curly
Stooge Occupation(s): Vagrants; lawmen
Nemesis: Bank robber Red Morgan and his gang

Synopsis: Trigger-happy bandit Red Morgan is turning Peaceful Gulch into a war zone. Desperate for help, town officials decide to intimidate Morgan by announcing the fictitious arrival of three famous marshals hired to clean up the town. The officials even print flyers—

using a photo of the Stooges from a recent "Wanted for Vagrancy" poster—to lend credence to the threat. Soon, the Stooges mosey into the Peaceful Gulch Saloon, where the nervous Morgan shows them the respect due three notorious law enforcers. But when Morgan picks up on clues that the Stooges are more vagrant than vigilante (Curly uses a slingshot in a shooting contest), he goes back to robbing banks and causing mayhem, succumbing only to a barrage of bullets Curly manages to fire in a most revolutionary fashion.

Key Gag: It's Curly and notorious gunslinger Red Morgan in a good old-fashioned shooting contest. Suspecting Curly to be an unsteady shot, Larry lines up five whiskey bottles from behind the bar, smashing one each time Curly fires his gun. Morgan is astonished at Curly's mastery of the six-shooter until the gun jams and Larry bursts the bottle anyway. Moe's explanation to the suddenly suspicious Morgan: "He scared it to death!"

Pies and Guys (1958)

Third Stooge: Joe
Stooge Occupation(s): Plumbers; gentlemen
Nemesis: Heredity; environment; society; evolution

Synopsis: A remake of *Half-Wits Holiday*, although Joe is no more able to learn to become a gentleman than was Curly.

Key Gag: Although he is making a valiant attempt to become a gentleman, Joe cannot resist the lures dangled before him at a trendy society party. While gallantly kissing the hand of a woman to whom he is introduced, Joe bites and

removes the diamond from her ring finger. Scandalized at this petty act of larceny, Moe drags Joe behind a doorway and unleashes a fist to his head, producing an avalanche of silverware and other finery stored in the pockets of the robbery-minded Joe.

Playing the Ponies (1937)

Third Stooge: Curly
Stooge Occupation(s): Restaurateurs; racehorse trainers
Nemesis: Con men; the easy-does-it instincts of their horse Thunderbolt

Synopsis: As proprietors of the Flounder Inn, the Stooges serve delicious dishes like lobster with frog legs and filet of sole and heel. But artistry in the kitchen isn't always enough to pay the bills, so the Stooges eagerly accept a proposition by two swindlers that they trade the restaurant for a champion racehorse named Thunderbolt. At the track, however, Thunderbolt runs more like a donkey than a thoroughbred . . . until he tastes a handful of chili pepperinos, a blazing hot snack that turns him into the second coming of Secretariat.

Key Gag: Displaying uncanny horse sense, the Stooges discover that their broken down nag, Thunderbolt, runs like the wind when fed blazing hot chili pepperinos. When the big race starts, Larry feeds Thunderbolt the stuff but guides him in the wrong direction on the track, making victory virtually impossible. But Moe and Curly think fast, hijacking a motorcycle and holding a bucket of water just in front of Thunderbolt while speeding along the track, causing the desperately thirsty horse to blaze past his competition and into the winner's circle.

Pop Goes the Easel (1935)

Third Stooge: Curly
Stooge Occupation(s): Vagrants; artists
Nemesis: Unemployment; the police;
   their own limited artistic abilities

Synopsis: Moe is only trying to earn an honest buck when he and the Stooges voluntarily sweep a store owner's sidewalk, but the crusty shopkeeper calls the cops and the Stooges are forced to make a hasty getaway. Ducking into a nearby building, Moe, Larry, and Curly find themselves among wide-eyed art students at Kraft's College of Arts. Although they have little aesthetic instinct, the Stooges blend in by fashioning art so avant-garde it will still be unappreciated well into the twenty-first century.

Key Gag: On the run from a fleet-footed cop, the Stooges come upon two girls playing hopscotch. Although the cop is closing in, the Stooges uphold the game's tradition by hopscotching in each box before resuming full getaway speed. (Note: the two girls playing hopscotch are Moe's daughter Joan and Larry's daughter Phyllis.)

Punch Drunks (1934)

Third Stooge: Curly
Stooge Occupation(s): Boxing promoter (Moe); violinist (Larry); waiter/boxer (Curly)
Nemesis: Heavyweight boxing champ Killer Kilduff

Synopsis: Virtuoso violinist Larry drops into a restaurant in which boxing promoter Moe is trying to calm the worries of his penniless fighters. But when Larry launches into a jivey rendition of "Pop Goes the Weasel," waiter Curly goes

bananas, knocking out Moe and all his boxers. Moe dubs Curly a born champ and, after recruiting Larry to his cause, becomes Curly's manager. With Larry by his side, "K. O. Stradivarius" is unstoppable, winning all his fights by musical knockout and earning the right to fight Killer Kilduff for the world championship. Stradivarius looks like a cinch until Larry's violin breaks, but the resourceful fiddler has another idea about how to salvage the championship.

Key Gag: As boxer K. O. Stradivarius, Curly depends upon Larry's violin rendition of "Pop Goes the Weasel" to transform him from harmless cream puff to vicious mauler. But during Curly's big bout with Killer Kilduff, Larry's violin breaks, rendering Curly as helpless as a baby. Only Larry's inspired theft of a truck that plays the magic song saves the day after he crashes it into the arena just in time to inspire one of the great boxing comebacks of all time.

Punchy Cowpunchers (1950)

Third Stooge: Shemp
Stooge Occupation(s): Horse groomsmen; undercover desperadoes
Nemesis: Merciless outlaws The Dillon Gang

Synopsis: The Dillon Gang is too much for Coyote Creek and even for statuesque blond cowboy Elmer, who rushes to summon the U.S. Cavalry. The Stooges, who ordinarily groom horses but have recently annoyed a commanding officer, are assigned the unenviable duty to go undercover dressed as desperadoes and confront the bandits . . . a mission from which they are not expected to return. Moe, Larry, and Shemp battle the gang valiantly, and Elmer makes another trip to recruit more cavalry . . . but it is the haymaker right fist of lovely barmaid Nell that ultimately fells the most notorious gang in the Old West.

Key Gag: Shemp thinks he has found the perfect hiding place when he locks himself inside a safe, but it happens to be the same safe the murderous Killer Dillon gang plans to crack. The outlaws turn the safe's tumblers, but Shemp counters by turning the tumblers back. Now dynamite seems the only available means to bust open the stubborn safe. The fuse is lit and dropped through a hole in the safe, but Shemp tosses it back out, blowing the bandits to smithereens and saving the day for the Stooges and lovely barmaid Nell.

Quiz Whizz (1958)
Third Stooge: Joe
Stooge Occupation(s): TV jackpot winners; mischievous little boys
Nemesis: Bunko men G. Y. Prince and R. O. Broad

Synopsis: Most television jackpot winners might squander their winnings on wine, women, and song. But Joe invests his $15,000 in Consolidated Fujiyama California Smog Bags, hoping to realize far greater returns. Moe, however, smells a rat and rushes the Stooges to the office of G. Y. Prince and R. O. Broad, the two curiously initialed smog bag salesmen with whom Joe did business. The crooks, however, slip into disguise and advise Joe to visit the home of an eccentric millionaire who wishes to adopt three nice boys. Dressed in knickers and ruffled cuffs, the Stooges arrive and prance adorably, all the while hoping to relieve the millionaire

of his loot. But the Stooges' new "daddy" is in cahoots with Prince and Broad, and dishes out some homicidal reprimands before the Stooges crown him—and the recently arrived Prince and Broad—before recovering their jackpot wad.

Key Gag: The Stooges are ecstatic after recovering Joe's $15,000 TV jackpot check from swindlers, and it brings out the best in Moe. Determined to split the money evenly and equitably among his partners, Moe rips the check into three perfectly equal pieces.

Restless Knights (1935)
Third Stooge: Curly
Stooge Occupation(s): Palace guards
Nemesis: Kidnap-happy Prince Boris and his no-good henchmen

Synopsis: Summoned to the bed of their dying father, the Stooges receive what must have been a common blessing in medieval times: the triple slap. With father gone, the Stooges make their way into the local palace, where they convince the queen to hire them as bodyguards. Moments later, she is abducted from under their noses. Prince Boris and his no-good henchmen, sensing an opportunity, sentence the Stooges to death, and while Moe, Larry, and Curly battle valiantly to prevent their executions, their swordfighting technique nearly hastens their demise. Luck intervenes and the Stooges stumble onto the kidnappers' hideout, where Curly successfully lures the bad guys past Moe and Larry, who use weighty clubs to administer a series of royal knockout blows.

Key Gag: Moments away from execution, the Stooges are allowed to choose the

Three great wrestlers of the Middle Ages (*Restless Knights*, 1935)

method: they may die either by beheading or by burning at the stake. Larry immediately opts for beheading, but Curly overrules him, choosing to burn because "a hot stake is better than a cold chop!" As the impatient executioners take aim with crossbows, it looks like curtains for the Stooges, but from a palace window the silhouette of a shapely woman distracts the firing squad long enough to facilitate a hasty escape by the Stooges.

Rhythm and Weep (1946)

Third Stooge: Curly

Stooge Occupation(s): Song-and-dance men

Nemesis: The cold shoulder of show business; eccentric millionaire Mr. Boyce

Synopsis: Suicide is the only realistic option for the Stooges after their song-and-dance act is rejected for the twenty-sixth time. But they have company on the ledge of a skyscraper: three lovely dancers named Hilda, Wilda, and Tilda, who themselves are despondent over the cruel hand dealt them by the world of show business. As the couples prepare to jump together, love blossoms and music fills the air; eccentric millionaire Mr. Boyce is practicing piano nearby, and he happens to need six performers for the new musical he is financing. Rehearsals go splendidly and it looks like the show will be a smash . . . until the men in the white jackets arrive from Doctor Dippy's Retreat and return Boyce to the asylum from which he came.

Key Gag: Although the Stooges stand poised to jump from a skyscraper, the prospect of suicide reminds Moe that he is due at the cleaners at two o'clock. Always ready to help, Larry rolls up a coat sleeve to reveal the three wristwatches he uses to tell time. The first, he tells Moe, runs ten minutes fast every two hours. The second runs twenty minutes slow every four hours. The one in the middle, Larry says ruefully, is broken and stopped at two o'clock. Less interested now in death than in Larry's ingenious system, Moe asks for the current time. Taking a pocket watch from beneath his hat, Larry matter-of-factly replies, "It's 3:15; simple, isn't it?"

Rip, Sew and Stitch (1953)

Third Stooge: Shemp
Stooge Occupation(s): Tailors
Nemesis: Shifty bank robber Terry "Slippery Fingers" Hargen

Synopsis: A remake of *Sing a Song of Six Pants.* New footage includes the Stooges using hammer and nail to hunt for bank robber Terry "Slippery Fingers" Hargen in their tailor shop.

Key Gag: See *Sing a Song of Six Pants.*

Rockin' Thru the Rockies (1940)

Third Stooge: Curly
Stooge Occupation(s): Bodyguards
Nemesis: Indians; Nell, their acid-tongued boss

Synopsis: The Stooges are semibrave bodyguards for traveling entertainers Nell's Belles. Nell, however, doesn't appreciate their laid-back approach to security and expresses her discontent by impolitely crashing their heads together before dinner. Later, when Curly fires his noisy rifle into Moe's toe, a tribe of Indians arrives and orders everyone to "twenty-three skidoo." But a snowstorm is closing in, so the Stooges fashion shelter so flimsy that the walls sway in

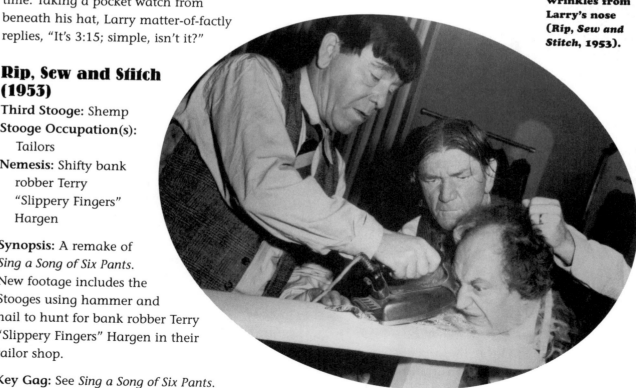

Moe and Shemp valiantly attempt to remove the wrinkles from Larry's nose (*Rip, Sew and Stitch,* 1953).

rhythm to their snoring. Morning is no more comfortable and brings a chill so cold that Larry pumps ice cubes from a nearby well. But with Indians closing in and no horses to pull their wagon, the Stooges are forced to hoist a sail and make a thrilling, windblown getaway.

Key Gag: Curly's thunderous snoring is finally too much for the half-asleep Moe, who angrily orders him out of the Stooges' bed. Worried that he hasn't any covers, Curly takes Moe's suggestion to use a nearby bearskin for warmth. A live grizzly bear, however, has made its way into the Stooges' cabin, and Curly wastes no time in tugging on its thick coat, believing the bear to be his blanket. Faced with an angry bear and a potentially deadly showdown, Curly barks like a bloodhound, terrifying the bear and sending it scampering for its life.

Rumpus in the Harem (1956)

Third Stooge: Shemp
Stooge Occupation(s): Restaurant owners; diamond thieves
Nemesis: The Emir of Shmow

Synopsis: A remake of *Malice in the Palace*. New footage includes the Stooges' weeping girlfriends revealing that unless they pay 1,000 shilbleenas, they will be sold to the Sultan of Pish Posh. *Rumpus in the Harem* is the first of four films shot after Shemp's death, with Shemp doubled by a lookalike in new footage.

Key Gag: See *Malice in the Palace*.

Rusty Romeos (1957)

Third Stooge: Joe
Stooge Occupation(s): Spurned lovers
Nemesis: A three-timing blond gold digger

Synopsis: A remake of *Corny Casanovas*, with Joe masterfully reprising Shemp's role as the third spurned lover.

Key Gag: Moe, Larry, and Joe find that using a hammer to tack fabric to a couch is a painstakingly slow process. Showing a creative spark, Larry uses a machine gun to fire several tacks into the couch, completing half the job quickly and efficiently. Larry reloads for round two, but Joe insists on taking a turn with the gun. A mighty struggle ensues and wayward shots are fired, sending hundreds of tacks into Moe's behind with stinging accuracy and causing the suffering Moe to declare, "I'm losing my mind!"

Sappy Bullfighters (1959)

Third Stooge: Joe
Stooge Occupation(s): Bullfighters
Nemesis: A jealous husband named José; a humorless bull

Synopsis: A remake of *What's the Matador?*, with Joe playing the pivotal role of bullfighter. The plot varies only slightly from *What's the Matador?*, with ravishing blonde Greta booking the Stooges' comedy bullfighting act before switching suitcases. Shot in 1959, *Sappy Bullfighters* was the last Three Stooges short ever filmed.

Key Gag: Joe wants nothing more than a kiss from eye-popping blonde Greta, and she is not the type to disappoint. Greta is married, but manages to find the perfect compromise solution. Telling Joe to pucker up and close his eyes, she lifts her tiny dog Pepe to his lips and allows the pooch to plant a wet one on Joe. The transfixed Joe's opinion: "Boy, what a kiss!"

Saved by the Belle (1939)

Third Stooge: Curly

Stooge Occupation(s): Traveling salesmen; spies

Nemesis: A hotel owner who is stingy with credit; Valeskan soldiers; a loudmouth parrot

Synopsis: Salesman Curly has customers lining up for his ingenious new invention: a shock absorber for earthquakes. So many citizens of the tropical kingdom of Valeska have purchased the item, in fact, that the Stooges are brought into the local general's office for questioning. Inside, Curly's parrot suggests that the general search the Stooges, advice the suspicious officer heeds at once. The general discovers a telegram that instructs the Stooges to get rid of their "present wardrobe" but interprets it to read, "Get rid of President Ward Robey," an act of treason punishable by death. The Stooges depart in haste, using a horse with a sagging middle and even a bicycle built for three to effect a breathtaking Valeskan escape.

Key Gag: The Stooges must bust out of prison or face a grisly execution. Luckily, they are in possession of state-of-the-art jailbreak tools, although to use them would rouse a nearby guard, who is slurping soup just outside the Stooges' cell. Capitalizing on the guard's zest for his lunch, the Stooges turn their tools loose during each of the guard's loud slurps, thereby avoiding detection and making slow progress toward glorious freedom.

Scheming Schemers (1956)

Third Stooge: Shemp

Stooge Occupation(s): Plumbers

Nemesis: Water; cunning art thieves

Synopsis: A remake of *Vagabond Loafers*. New footage includes Moe and Larry trying to retrieve a valuable ring from a wash basin, and the Stooges apprehending art thieves by means of expertly aimed cream pies.

Key Gag: Moe always approaches a problem directly. So when Larry loses a valuable diamond ring down a wash basin, Moe turns him upside down and tries to shove him down the drain to retrieve it. Realizing that Larry won't fit, Moe goes to get some tools, but is horrified when he returns to find that Larry is missing . . . presumably down the pipes. Worse, Moe can see Larry's face in the drain looking up at him! Although Moe is an experienced plumber, it takes even him quite a while to realize that Larry has simply crawled under the sink for a better look.

Scotched in Scotland (1954)

Third Stooge: Shemp

Stooge Occupation(s): Scottish detectives

Nemesis: Angus and McPherson and Lorna Doone, three Scotch crooks

Synopsis: A remake of *Hot Scots*. New footage and storyline include the Stooges receiving their diplomas from the Wide Awake Detective School (where they graduated with the "lowest possible honors" in school history); dean O. U. Gonga sending them to Glenheather Castle in Scotland; Angus, McPherson, and Lorna Doone plotting to terrify the already frightened Stooges; and a mischievous parrot who climbs into a skull.

Key Gag: See *Hot Scots*.

Scrambled Brains (1951)

Third Stooge: Shemp

Stooge Occupation(s): Moe and Larry are caretakers to an ailing Shemp

Nemesis: Shemp's hallucinations; Nurse Nora's father

Synopsis: Croakers Sanitarium has done wonders for Shemp's case of frazzled nerves. And he's met a girlfriend there, too. Although Nora appears to normal eyes to be a hideous hag, Shemp is just delusional enough to see her as a beautiful blonde. At home, Shemp's condition deteriorates, and Moe and Larry decide the only cure is Nora. But on their way back to Croakers, the Stooges tangle with a man over the right to use a phone booth, twisting the poor soul in a web of telephone wire. Later, dressed in tuxedos and ready for Shemp's nuptials, the Stooges make an unhealthy discovery: if there's one man in the world who doesn't appreciate being tangled in telephone wire, it's Nora's father.

Key Gag: Moe and Larry summon Dr. Gezundheidt to examine an ailing and hallucinating Shemp, but even the doctor is confounded by the symptoms he observes. A preliminary inspection of Shemp's head uncovers alarming evidence of cuckoo birds singing inside. But the truly troubling indication occurs when the doctor puts his stethoscope to Shemp's heart and hears a small girl cry out, "Mama!" The doctor is unnerved but steadies himself and leans forward to again hear the child wail, "Mama!" Only after a little girl comes in to retrieve her talking doll from under the doctor's rocking chair does the physician see hope for Shemp's recovery.

Self Made Maids (1950)

Third Stooge: Shemp

Stooge Occupation(s): Dazzling portrait models; painters

Nemesis: The curmudgeonly father of their fiancées Moella, Larraine, and Shempetta

Synopsis: Ravishing beauties Moella, Larraine, and Shempetta (played by the Stooges) commission renowned artists Moe, Larry, and Shemp to paint their portraits. And while an infestation of ants in their dresses makes it difficult for the women to maintain their poses, a sizzling attraction grows between painters and subjects and soon the couples are engaged. The girls' father, however, won't consent to the marriage until meeting the suitors, so the Stooges journey to their fiancées' home determined to make a good impression. In the hallway, they meet an old coot so ornery that they sacrifice their chocolate engagement cake to teach the crusty buzzard a lesson. Only later, when the girls' father arrives wearing that cake, do the Stooges realize that consent will never be granted unless they take even more drastic measures: the tickling of the father's feet until he agrees to give away his daughters.

Key Gag: Three lovely ladies sit majestically while the Stooges paint their portraits, but find it difficult to hold their poses due to an infestation of ants in the studio. Although the ladies bravely try to sit still, the magnitude of the problem becomes clear when even the subjects in a nearby painting scratch themselves before returning to their frozen poses.

Shivering Sherlocks (1948)

Third Stooge: Shemp

Stooge Occupation(s): Café workers; detectives

Nemesis: Bloodthirsty armored car robber Lefty Loomis and his hideous hatchet man Angel

Synopsis: Cutthroat armored car robber Lefty Loomis has pulled a quick one, but it's the Stooges who are rounded up for questioning. Hooked to a lie detector, the police determine little more than that Larry has been in jail and that Shemp is responsible for the quarter missing from Moe's shoe. After Gladys Harmon, owner of the Elite Café, vouches for them, the Stooges are freed and go to work for Gladys, even helping to evaluate an offer to buy the mansion she owns. While inspecting the house, the Stooges stumble upon Loomis and his hideous hatchet man, Angel, an ungodly beast who has been ordered to use his shiny cleaver to dispatch the Stooges. Shemp, however, slows Loomis and his thugs with expertly aimed barrels of flour— and a lot of bravado—until the police arrive.

Key Gag: The Stooges didn't pull that daring armored car heist, but they are brought to police headquarters for intensive interrogation, anyway. After Larry and Shemp flunk their lie detector tests (it turns out Shemp did, in fact, steal a quarter from Moe's shoe the evening before), the police sergeant finds himself attached to the machine and asked by the Stooges where *he* was at 11 P.M. last night. "I was at a lodge meeting," stammers the sergeant, a dubious reply that, the lie detector operator reports, "seems to have broken the machine."

Shot in the Frontier (1954)

Third Stooge: Shemp

Stooge Occupation(s): Lovers, not fighters

Nemesis: Trigger-happy bandits the Noonan Brothers

Synopsis: Now that they've wed stunning cowgirls Ella, Bella, and Stella, the Stooges seem destined for a dreamy life of love and kisses. But you don't marry the three prettiest gals in the West without attracting the attention of the Noonan Brothers, a gang of cutthroat bandits who don't take kindly to strangers moseying in on their dames. As high noon rolls in, the Stooges duck behind the tombstones at the offices of undertakers Diggs, Graves, and Berry and exchange a furious round of gunfire with the Noonans. Although Larry is hit several times in the hindquarters, he manages to draw fire while Shemp uses his suspenders to launch destructive boulders at the enemy. Soon out of ammunition, the Stooges battle the Noonans hand-to-hand in the dusty street, finally triumphing on the strength of Larry's boot spurs and an undying determination to continue loving Ella, Bella, and Stella.

Key Gag: Only a half-hour remains before the Stooges' showdown with deadly gunslingers the Noonan Brothers, and Larry isn't convinced that he wants to die so soon. Taking admirable initiative, Larry attempts to turn back the hands of a nearby clock, but the clock keeps resetting itself—and no wonder— the date on its face reads ominously, "Friday the 13th." A shaken Larry makes one more valiant attempt to tack more time onto the Stooges' lives, but this time the clock's printed message is unmistakable: "It's No Use—You're Doomed."

Sing a Song of Six Pants (1947)

Third Stooge: Shemp
Stooge Occupation(s): Tailors
Nemesis: Shifty bank robber Terry "Slippery Fingers" Hargen

Synopsis: The Stooges' Pip Boys tailor shop is in trouble; if they don't pay their bills soon, the Skin and Flint Finance Corporation will repossess needles, thread, and building. Although Shemp fantasizes about capturing recent fugitive bank robber Terry "Slippery Fingers" Hargen and collecting a huge reward, the odds seem slim that three tailors will ever come across the likes of such a notorious criminal. Hargen, in fact, has ducked into Pip Boys, where he is forced to pose as a motionless dummy while the Stooges remove his clothes for tailoring. He later returns for his coat, which contains the combination to a safe he plans to crack. A colossal battle ensues in which the Stooges make expert use of their steam press and irons, finally recovering enough cash in the unconscious Hargen's pocket to pay Skin and Flint for a hundred tailor shops.

Key Gag: Notorious bank robber Terry Hargen figures he has Shemp

licked when he hitches Shemp to a revolving metal coatrack. But for every punch Hargen delivers, Shemp revolves around at breakneck speed to deliver an unintentional but devastating return punch.

The Sitter Downers (1937)

Third Stooge: Curly
Stooge Occupation(s): Suitors; collectivists; carpenters
Nemesis: A protective father-in-law; their bossy wives

Synopsis: The Stooges emerge from a flower shop with love blooming for Corabell, Florabell, and Dorabell. On bended knees they propose, but the girls remind them that they must have their father's consent, which the grumpy old coot refuses to give. Fed up and desperately in love, the Stooges stage a sit-

Can you blame her? Florabell (Betty Mack) falls heavy for Moe (*The Sitter Downers*, 1937).

down strike in the girls' home that generates nationwide headlines and sympathy. Stymied by the Stooges' staying power, the girls' father gives in, and the happy couples depart to build a new home from the gift of wood and nails given to them by a supporter. The new marriages are blissful . . . until the girls realize that committed romantics don't necessarily make competent carpenters.

Key Gag: Curly soaks his feet a bit too long in wet cement and soon learns that wet cement eventually becomes dry cement. To Moe, a master in the no-nonsense approach to problem solving, there is but one solution: dynamite. Despite Moe's assurances that "dynamite always blows down," Curly views the situation differently from the tall tree he is blasted into.

Slaphappy Sleuths (1950)

Third Stooge: Shemp
Stooge Occupation(s): Detectives; service station attendants
Nemesis: A slippery ring of thieves partial to holding up gas stations

Synopsis: The Onion Oil Company has fallen victim to a series of baffling robberies at its service stations. General manager Fuller Grime, therefore, wants to hire three stupid-looking but brainy detectives to crack the case. Claiming to be flexible on the brainy requirement, he hires gumshoes Moe, Larry, and Shemp to work undercover at the company's gas stations. On the job, the Stooges provide first-class service not typically associated with such establishments (shaves, manicures, and cologne), but manage nonetheless to be robbed the moment their backs are turned. Tracing a trail of

motor oil to the crooks' hideout, the Stooges demonstrate boxing skills far more efficient than their detective skills, saving the day for Onion Oil and again making the purchase of gasoline safe—if a bit less luxurious—for everyone.

Key Gag: Shemp is all business when a customer pulls into the Stooges' service station with an overheating radiator, but mistakenly adds popping corn instead of stop-leak under the hood. Fluffy popcorn soon flows in rivers around the car, which Shemp and his customer enjoy by the handful—especially Shemp, who uses his mechanic's oil can to freshly "butter" his bountiful batch.

Slippery Silks (1936)

Third Stooge: Curly
Stooge Occupation(s): Woodworkers; fashion designers
Nemesis: Mr. Morgan, owner of a priceless Chinese cabinet; the highfalutin world of fashion

Synopsis: Wealthy Mr. Morgan is not the forgiving type. As the owner of a priceless Chinese cabinet, he should understand that woodworkers like the Stooges might not appreciate classic Chinese art the way a millionaire would. After the Stooges saw his cabinet in half, Morgan vows revenge. Luckily for the Stooges, they have inherited their Uncle Pete's chic dress shop, the Madame de France, and begin work at the boutique to create fashion that is truly ahead of its time, even inspiring a woman to order a custom-made dress on the spot. The woman's husband, however, doesn't see the art in the Stooges' wondrous creations, but his temper only fully erupts when he recognizes Moe, Larry, and

Curly as the men who ruined his precious Chinese cabinet.

Key Gag: Although thrilled to be inheriting swank fashion boutique Madame de France, the Stooges reflect their woodworking roots by designing gigantic dresses finely appointed with wood and elegantly adorned with drawers, handles, and working cabinets.

A Snitch in Time (1950)

Third Stooge: Shemp
Stooge Occupation(s): Carpenters
Nemesis: Daring jewel thieves Mr. Jerry Pip and Steve

Synopsis: Always on the cutting edge, the Stooges run Ye Olde Furniture Shoppe, an establishment specializing in "Antiques Made While-U-Waite." The lovely Miss Scudder, Moe's favorite customer, is pleased to have the Stooges deliver the furniture she ordered, but terrified to tell them that her home has been taken over by Mr. Jerry Pip and Steve, two gun-wielding jewel thieves on the prowl for family heirlooms. The Stooges find out soon enough, however, when the crooks discover Larry and Shemp listening to a radio broadcast giving their descriptions. Never the kind to be held at gunpoint indefinitely, the Stooges bust free and give the thugs what for, providing Miss Scudder with ample opportunity to return the heroic Moe's flirtations . . . if only Shemp hadn't celebrated by spilling paint on his flirtatious pal's head.

Key Gag: Repairman Moe has spilled glue on his hands, a problem that causes understandable panic when he becomes stuck to a large board. Larry and Shemp

act quickly to extricate their furious leader, who has identified his co-workers as being responsible for his predicament. A hammer smashed on Moe's hands fails to loosen the board, but Shemp seems to make progress by attempting to use a saw to remove Moe's hands at the wrists. Finally separated from the board, Moe takes little time to enjoy his freedom as he slaps the faces of Larry and Shemp, thereby becoming stuck to two new hard-to-remove surfaces.

Snow White and the Three Stooges (1961—feature-length film)

Third Stooge: Curly Joe
Stooge Occupation(s): Wandering minstrels; stepfathers
Nemesis: A jealous and evil queen; her right-hand man Oga

Synopsis: Unable to tolerate Snow White's radiant beauty, a jealous queen locks the lovely princess in a dungeon for life. But this queen didn't just turn mean. Years earlier, she had commissioned an assassin to murder the young Prince Charming, to whom Snow White was betrothed. Wandering minstrels Moe, Larry, and Curly Joe, however, stumbled upon that crime scene and foiled the killing by punching, poking, and clubbing the would-be killer until he fled in terror. Unable to remember his identity, the young prince went to live with the Stooges, who raised him, renamed him Quatro the Magnificent, and trained him in the subtle arts of ventriloquism and magic. The queen, not satisfied that Snow White lives, commissions her killing, but again the assassin fails (this time from a tender heart) and the princess goes free.

After Quatro and the Stooges meet up with Snow White at the vacant home of the Seven Dwarfs, the young couple fall in love and, with the noble help of Moe, Larry, and Curly Joe, endure swordfights, chases, and black magic on their way to regaining the throne.

Key Gag: Desperate to gain entrance to the palace where Prince Charming and Snow White are being held captive, Moe poses as a vegetable peddler while Larry and Curly Joe hide beneath a cornucopia of squash, corn, and lettuce. But when a suspicious cook gets wind that Moe doesn't know vegetables, Larry and Curly Joe burst forth from the freshness and defeat the cook and his men in a salad bar of fury and vengeance.

So Long Mr. Chumps (1941)

Third Stooge: Curly
Stooge Occupation(s): Street sweepers; jailbirds
Nemesis: Bond swindler B. O. Davis (a.k.a. Lone Wolf Louie)

Synopsis: While cleaning rubbish in the park, the Stooges discover a stack of oil bonds belonging to a Mr. B. O. Davis. Lesser men would have pocketed such a windfall, but the Stooges' ethics are grounded firmly in Aristotelian tradition, and Moe, Larry, and Curly return the loot. The man is so impressed by the gesture that he offers the Stooges $5,000 to bring back an honest man. Their search leads them to Pomeroy, a wrongly accused convict in the local jail. Determined to bust this honest man out of the slammer, the Stooges get themselves incarcerated and nearly pull off a daring escape with Pomeroy . . . until they are met at the gates by jailers admitting Lone Wolf Louie—a.k.a. B. O. Davis—one of America's biggest bond swindlers. (Note: watch the final moments of *So Long Mr. Chumps* closely; after Curly remarks about the rock Larry wants to break on his head, Larry breaks character and flashes a gleaming, Hollywood-caliber smile.)

Key Gag: Inside prison, the Stooges prove themselves to be masters with the simple paint and brushes issued to them by guards. Curly is especially inspired, removing a slice of bologna from a guard's sandwich and expertly painting a substitute slice on the bread. The real masterpiece comes, however, when the Stooges use their raw materials to paint perfect guard uniforms on one another, thereby enabling a stealthy escape from under the noses of real guards.

A tear-jerking scene sadly deleted from the final print of *So Long Mr. Chumps* (1941)

Sock-A-Bye Baby (1942)

Third Stooge: Curly
Stooge Occupation(s): Surrogate parents
Nemesis: The police; nature

Synopsis: A despondent mother depends on the kindness of strangers when she deposits her baby, Jimmy, on a random doorstep. Luckily for the lad, the doorstep belongs to the Stooges, who have a soft spot for youngsters they don't always show for each other. The Stooges soon realize that babies need to eat and treat the tyke to a scrumptious meal of enchiladas, spaghetti, artichokes, onions, celery, olives, radishes, pigs' feet, and herring. The child, however, turns out to be a finicky eater and refuses the banquet. Larry, in the meantime, has made a shocking discovery: according to the newspaper, a baby matching Jimmy's description has been reported kidnapped. Always savvy in matters of the law, the Stooges leap out the window and, without damaging a hair on Jimmy's head, make a daring getaway that would have crushed men unaccustomed to running from the cops.

Key Gag: Suspected of kidnapping and with the cops closing in, the Stooges make a breathtaking getaway by disguising their car as a tent. Two policemen get near but suspect nothing until Curly leans over and forces Moe's face into the steering wheel's horn, blowing their cover and forcing the Stooges to improvise by posing as shrubs to avoid further detection.

Some More of Samoa (1941)

Third Stooge: Curly
Stooge Occupation(s): Tree surgeons
Nemesis: Savage Rhum Boogian island natives; a hungry alligator

Synopsis: Eccentric Mr. Winthrop is worried sick about his ailing Puckerless Persimmon tree, and calls on the Elite Painless Tree Surgeons—Moe, Larry, and Curly—for a cure. Their diagnosis is sobering: the Puckerless Persimmon needs a girlfriend. But, the Stooges warn, such a mate can be found only on the island of Rhum Boogie. The Stooges set sail for the island, where they are immediately surrounded by vicious savages who resolve to cook them for dinner. In the commotion, Curly spots the Puckerless Persimmon, which happens to be guarded by an evil spirit who beats him senseless. After defeating the spirit and retrieving the Persimmon from the mouth of an alligator, the Stooges make a hasty getaway into a boat they should first have inspected for seaworthiness.

Key Gag: Curly is captured by natives of the island of Rhum Boogie and is sched-

Moe and Larry demonstrate perfect parenting technique—except for the beer they use to comfort Curly (*Sock-A-Bye Baby*, 1942).

uled to be the featured dish in the island's evening supper. The natives stuff an apple into his mouth, measure his ribs and calf for steaks, and prepare a boiling cauldron into which he and select vegetables are to be dropped. The island chief's daughter offers Curly freedom if he agrees to marry her, but Curly takes one look at her homely mug and decides that his fate as dinner would be far less painful.

Soup to Nuts (1930)

Third Stooge: Shemp
Stooge Occupation(s): Firemen, women chasers
Nemesis: Ted Healy; fire

Synopsis: The first-ever film appearance by the Three Stooges. *Soup to Nuts* was written by the famous cartoonist Rube Goldberg and starred Ted Healy; the Stooges were billed as bit players (including Moe, who was called "Harry Howard" in the credits). Moe, Larry, and Shemp, however, steal the film, executing many of the hilarious slapstick routines they had perfected over years on vaudeville stages and which would become part of their legendary comic lexicon as star performers in their own films. The Stooges are firemen in *Soup to Nuts* and don't mind a bit that their pal, Ted Healy, is addicted to the camaraderie of the firehouse and the adrenaline rush of chasing blazes. But away from the firehouse, Healy's got problems. He's on the rocks with his girlfriend, and the costume shop owned by his elderly friend is about to be repossessed. Healy manages—unwittingly—to help save the shop, but not before he has several comic run-ins with his three pals, Moe, Larry, and Shemp, who frustrate, infuriate, and exasperate the not-as-smart-as-he-thinks-he-is Healy.

Key Gag: In a sense, nearly all of the gags the Stooges pull in *Soup to Nuts* are key, in that they foretell the modus operandi of the greatest comedy team of all time. The Stooges sing harmonies, gyp Shemp on crooked coin flips, fall off speeding fire engines, huddle together like football players in order to perfect a plan, slap each other silly, and order preposterous meals at restaurants. (Moe orders "liver and milk . . . and a banana split," to which Shemp replies, "There's only one banana left, and it's too old to do the splits.") One of the funniest gags comes when the Stooges and Healy are performing for an appreciative crowd, and Larry promises to do "the Elevator Dance." Delighted, Healy waits with wide eyes, but Larry stands motionless. Healy fidgets a bit, but Larry continues to stay stonestill. Finally, Healy demands an explanation for this befuddling "Elevator Dance," to which Larry replies, "There's no steps to it!" Healy, being the impatient sort, shoves all three Stooges to the ground.

Space Ship Sappy (1957)

Third Stooge: Joe
Stooge Occupation(s): Transients; outer space travelers
Nemesis: Hourglass-shaped space women; a Godzilla-like space lizard

Synopsis: Hungry and out of work, the Stooges are delighted to answer an advertisement seeking three sailors for an adventurous cruise. But "captain" A. K. Rimple has a different kind of journey in mind and traps Moe, Larry, and Joe aboard a spaceship headed for the planet Sunev. The Stooges have little choice but to stay put (although Larry does dangle by his toes from the craft

In the Stooges' day, secret revolving bookcases were built without modern safety features (*Spook Louder*, 1943).

after attempting an escape) until the ship lands with a frightening thud. The planet, it turns out, is populated by curvaceous Amazon women and is therefore judged by the Stooges to be eminently inhabitable. But a gigantic space lizard hungry for a three-course meal forces the Stooges back into the spaceship, panicked and bound for Earth. The trip, however, is not a total loss, as Moe, Larry, and Joe are awarded special honors for their story at the Liar's Club 27th Annual Convention.

Key Gag: Unaccustomed to the romantic or culinary ways of extraterrestrial women, the Stooges are taken aback when three shapely aliens bite instead of kiss them, and tickle their feet to tenderize the Stooges for a delicious stew they are preparing for the evening's supper.

Spook Louder (1943)

Third Stooge: Curly
Stooge Occupation(s): Salesmen; guardians of a haunted house
Nemesis: Cutthroat spies; a mysterious pie thrower

Synopsis: Rarely has there been a traveling sales team as industrious as the Stooges. When a potential customer refuses to buy their Miracle Massage Reducing Machine (perhaps because she is built like a string bean), they succeed in selling her a "No Peddlers" sign for her door. But the Stooges' job gets tougher as they happen upon the spooky home of the great inventor Mr. Graves, who hires them to guard his house against enemy spies while he is away. The Stooges suffer a double dose of bad luck when three spies not only show up, but decide to dress as hideous monsters. Worse, pies fly mysteriously through the air and strike without warning. Things look grim for the Stooges after they are cornered by the spies, but Curly detonates a bomb that blasts the spies to kingdom come and establishes the Stooges as three of history's great spooky-mansion guards.

Key Gag: It is a rare day when the victim of a thrown pie cannot identify the perpetrator, but that is the fate that befalls all who dare poke their noses into Mr. Graves's eerie mansion and meddle in the baffling case of the master spy ring.

Pies fly in Graves's house without rhyme or reason, causing generations who have heard the legend to ask that now famous question, "Who threw those pies?"

Spooks (1953)

Third Stooge: Shemp
Stooge Occupation(s): Detectives
Nemesis: A mad professor and his creepy assistant; Congo the Gorilla

Synopsis: No wonder Mr. B. Bopper has rushed to the Stooges' Super Slueth Detective Agency. His daughter Mary has been kidnapped, and her life depends on the swift response of the ace gumshoes. Proving again that they are masters of disguise, the Stooges pose as pie salesmen and travel to a haunted mansion, where a mad scientist and his creepy assistant are preparing to transfer Mary's brain into the skull of a gorilla. Although many spooks and goblins make a mighty effort to drive the Stooges from the scene, Moe, Larry, and Shemp manage to free Mary . . . and also the gorilla. Naturally, the ape is grateful and assists in knocking out the crooks with a head-clunk and, for fun, the Stooges with some pies.

Key Gag: The Stooges are trapped in a haunted mansion, but this joint has one goblin more hideous than any other: a swooping bat that possesses a horrifyingly familiar face: Shemp's. *Spooks* was filmed in 3-D, making the attacking Shemp bat look even more ominous.

In the Stooges' day, sterile operating rooms were not always available to patients requiring emergency surgery (*Spooks*, 1953).

Squareheads of the Round Table (1948)

Third Stooge: Shemp
Stooge Occupation(s): Royal troubadours
Nemesis: The Black Prince

Synopsis: Dreamy Cedric the Blacksmith is in love with Princess Elaine, but the palace guard has reserved space on the chopping block for the commoner's lovesick head. With his life in danger and his heart still aching, Cedric enlists the help of three royal troubadours—Moe, Larry, and Shemp—who serenade Elaine outside a courtyard window. The Stooges and Cedric are arrested and sentenced to death, but Elaine makes a bargain: she will marry the evil Black Prince if Cedric's life is spared. The Black Prince agrees, but nonetheless instructs his men to murder Cedric when the wedding trumpets blow. The Stooges, who have escaped from their cell, overhear this treasonous plot and, in a master stroke of strategy, design never to allow those trumpets to sound.

Key Gag: The sinister Black Prince has ordered the beheading of valiant Cedric the Blacksmith at the moment the king's trumpeters sound their horns. The Stooges cannot allow this fate to befall their friend, but seem powerless to stop the dastardly deed as the royal musicians prepare to play. "Let the trumpets sound!" declares the king, but the Stooges think quickly, snatching apples, oranges, and melons from a basket and firing the fruit expertly into the horns until they are silenced.

Stone Age Romeos (1955)

Third Stooge: Shemp
Stooge Occupation(s): Explorers; cavemen
Nemesis: Rival cavemen

Synopsis: A remake of *I'm a Monkey's Uncle.* New footage and plot include museum curator B. Bopper sending explorers Moe, Larry, and Shemp to film evidence of the existence of cavemen and Bopper's subsequent discovery that the swindling Stooges starred in the bogus film themselves.

Key Gag: See *I'm a Monkey's Uncle.*

Studio Stoops (1950)

Third Stooge: Shemp
Stooge Occupation(s): Exterminators; Hollywood publicists
Nemesis: Kidnapper Dandy Dawson

Synopsis: Exterminators Moe, Larry, and Shemp defeat pests with style and drama. So it's no wonder that they are mistaken by movie studio head J. B. Fletcher for three bigwig Hollywood publicity agents sent to boost the career of

glamorous starlet Dolly Devore. The Stooges' plan for Dolly is ingenious: fake her kidnapping to make front-page news, then rescue her to the delight of a worried public. The idea sounds foolproof until Dolly actually is kidnapped by crooks, who demand $10,000 for her return. The Stooges trace Dolly to the Clinton Arms Hotel, where they succeed in trouncing the crooks and saving the day for millions of motion-picture fans.

Key Gag: Moe has a brilliant idea and dictates it to Shemp, who sits poised to memorialize it at a typewriter. Moe's first sentence is a long one, but it takes Shemp only a stroke or two on the keyboard to finish it. Moe's next dictation is but a single word, but this time it takes Shemp hundreds of strokes and carriage returns before he is ready for more. Befuddled, Moe orders Shemp to read back the letter, and Shemp complies immediately, reciting his work thus far: "A gorg goggle yata benefucci timini garanga para dickman hee ha June 22nd."

Sweet and Hot (1958)

Third Stooge: Joe
Stooge Occupation(s): Psychiatrist (Moe); talent agent (Larry); brother (Joe)
Nemesis: Stage fright

Synopsis: Tiny Landers sings like an angel . . . but only for brother Joe. In front of a crowd she clams up, the victim of a terrible case of stage fright. Recognizing her immense potential for stardom—as well as her immense figure—savvy talent agent Larry offers Tiny all the food she can eat if she agrees to visit eccentric psychiatrist Hugo Gansamacher (Moe). After regressing the patient to childhood, Moe uncovers the source of Tiny's fears, and provides her with a powerful posthypnotic suggestion designed to generate confidence on the nightclub stage. Later, at a swank cabaret, Tiny unleashes a sizzling performance of "The Heat Is On," bringing down the house and causing Larry to fall head-over-heels in love after the fat lady sings.

Key Gag: Brilliant psychiatrist Hugo Gansamacher (Moe) is able to cure pudgy nightclub singer Tiny Landers's stage fright, largely by serving as a stellar example of bravery himself. But when a mouse appears after Tiny's triumphant nightclub debut, Gansamacher leaps onto a table, pulls up his pant cuffs, and cries, "A mice! Achtulieber, a mice!"

Tassels in the Air (1938)

Third Stooge: Curly

Stooge Occupation(s): Janitors; interior decorators

Nemesis: The great fashion designer Omay

Synopsis: Janitors Moe, Larry, and Curly take a well-deserved lunch break in the office of Omay, the great and trendy interior decorator. While Moe gives Curly expert instruction in how to speak pig Latin, a vogueish socialite bursts breathlessly into the office and declares that she simply must hire Omay to decorate her home. Moe, naturally, declares that he is Omay, and would be delighted to undertake the work. The transaction is marred only by Curly's violent reaction to the tassels that the lady wears, but Moe and Larry are able to restore order by tickling him under the chin. Later, at the woman's home, the Stooges become overconfident in their abilities, and priceless antiques suffer irreparably from their enthusiasm.

Key Gag: Moe and Larry have determined that Curly is ready to learn pig

Latin, and generously use their own names as teaching tools. Moe explains that in pig Latin, Moe is "O-may" and that Larry is "Arry-lay." Excited by the simplicity of the system, quick-study Curly retorts that his pig Latin name must therefore be "Curlycue."

Termites of 1938 (1938)

Third Stooge: Curly

Stooge Occupation(s): Exterminators; gentlemen escorts

Nemesis: Mice; high society

Synopsis: Socialite Muriel van Twitchett is at wit's end. Her husband's fishing trip will leave her without a date for a high-society party, and she simply cannot attend alone. A friend suggests that she call the Acme Escort Bureau, which is manned by a team of Ivy League gentlemen. But Muriel's maid mistakenly phones the Stooge-owned Acme Exterminating Company, and Moe, Larry, and Curly set out for the mansion believing that they have been hired to do battle with pests. While their table manners suggest that the Ivy League had little to do with their breeding, the Stooges nonetheless track down an infestation of mice that would have ruined the party even without the Stooges' pesty contribution.

Key Gag: Exterminator Moe has invented what appears to be a breathtakingly better mousetrap. His Simplex Rodent Exterminator works on the principle that a mouse will trip various wires laid outside its hole, causing a loaded cannon to discharge a deadly cannonball directly between the unfortunate rodent's eyes. (Moe has installed a hangman's noose over the mouse hole as a backup, but it appears that the cannon simply cannot miss.) When a mouse emerges from its hole and dances on the wires with impunity, Moe bends over to inspect the system, only to suffer the unfortunate cannonball experience he had so painstakingly reserved for the mouse.

They Stooge to Conga (1943)

Third Stooge: Curly
Stooge Occupation(s): Handymen
Nemesis: Power-hungry Axis spies

Synopsis: An enemy spy commits a major tactical error by hiring the Stooges to repair the doorbell at her hideout. At first, Curly appears to have found the faulty wire, but tugs on it so violently that he pulls Moe through a wall from the other end. Tracing the problem, Curly makes his way up the telephone pole outside, exercising insufficient caution as he digs his climbing spikes into Moe's eyeball and eardrum. Moe, in a forgivable moment of anger, lashes back by directing a flamethrower onto Curly's behind. None of this helps the doorbell problem. Back inside, the Stooges discover the Axis war room, where they use their curious approach to technology to

conquer the enemy. (Note: the scene in which Curly's climbing spikes dig deep into Moe's ear and eye are considered to be the most violent moments ever filmed by the Three Stooges, and still cause many television stations to refrain from showing *They Stooge to Conga*.)

Key Gag: The course of a strategically important German submarine is altered irreversibly when Curly takes over the boat via sophisticated remote controls. With Curly at the helm, the sub bobs and weaves like a punch-drunk boxer until Allied planes lock in on the enemy vessel and blow it to smithereens.

Three Arabian Nuts (1951)

Third Stooge: Shemp
Stooge Occupation(s): Warehouse men; genie masters
Nemesis: Cutthroat Arabian thieves

Synopsis: It took six months for John Bradley to accumulate his priceless collection of antiques and china, so naturally he is concerned about the crashing and smashing sounds emanating from the Stooge-owned Superior Warehouse and Storage Co. One item that doesn't break, however, is a copper lamp, which Shemp delightedly rubs free of dust. This is no ordinary lamp, and the magnificent genie that bursts forth in a puff of smoke is pleased to grant Shemp whatever wishes his heart desires. But Shemp is not the only one with an affection for genies. Arabian thieves have tracked the lamp to the Stooges' warehouse, and are more than willing to use four-foot sabres and razor-sharp daggers to express their displeasure with the genie's new masters.

Key Gag: Shemp has stumbled upon a treasure most men only dream about: a

As the crew can attest, Curly will endure any discomfort in the name of making great comedy (*They Stooge to Conga,* 1943).

magic lamp. When a genie bursts forth from a magnificent puff of smoke, Shemp cannot restrain his joy, and naturally asks for a new suit of clothes. The "genius," as Shemp calls him, delivers in style, fitting Shemp with a humdinger of an outfit that makes Larry green with envy. When Larry later finds the lamp and rubs it, he seizes upon the opportunity and makes his wish really count. The genie faithfully obeys . . . and returns Shemp to his old and dreary clothes.

Three Dark Horses (1952)

Third Stooge: Shemp
Stooge Occupation(s): Janitors; presidential convention delegates
Nemesis: Crooked presidential candidate Hammond Egger and his shady campaign manager, Bill Wick

Synopsis: Only one task remains for the crooks who run the shady presidential campaign of Hammond Egger: to recruit three delegates who are "too dumb to think and who will do what we tell them." Campaign manager Bill Wick sees potential in the Stooges, who are doing janitorial work inside Egger headquarters. At the presidential convention, however, the Stooges have a change of heart, deciding instead to vote for Egger's rival, Able Lamb Stewer, thereby disrupting the balance of world power—and Wick's sanity—forever.

Key Gag: Larry likes his coffee sweet, and is not bashful about adding nearly a pound of sugar to his modest mug of java. This time, however, it tastes a bit too sweet, so he passes the cup to pal Shemp, who tastes it himself and promptly adds many more spoonfuls of sugar. Larry stares at his sweet-toothed friend in disbelief, but Shemp is still not satisfied with the taste, and reaches into the sugar bowl,

removes a single additional grain of sugar, and drops it gingerly into the overdosed coffee cup. Now perfect, Shemp downs the drink happily, the perfect start to a wonderful day.

3 Dumb Clucks (1937)

Third Stooge: Curly
Stooge Occupation(s): Jailbirds; loyal sons
Nemesis: Their own father; their father's fiancée, Daisy; her band of thugs

Synopsis: While behind bars, the Stooges are informed that their pa intends to marry a blond hussy. Calling on an arsenal of jailbreak tools they had forgotten were under Moe's mattress, the Stooges bust out, travel to Popsie's home, and plead their case. Popsie, however, isn't keen on losing his "Daisy-Waisy," and goes for a wedding day haircut that transforms him into the spitting image of Curly . . . a dangerous turn of events given the fact that Daisy and her crew of thugs intend to kill Popsie the moment the pair gets married.

Key Gag: On the run from murderous crooks, the Stooges climb a skyscraper's flagpole, but fall several stories when the thugs release the latch. Miraculously, a store awning breaks their fall, and dumps them unceremoniously onto their father, whose woman-crazy antics started the chase in the first place.

Three Hams on Rye (1950)

Third Stooge: Shemp
Stooge Occupation(s): Stagehands; aspiring thespians
Nemesis: Impatient producer B. K. Doaks; notoriously harsh Broadway critic Nick Barker

Synopsis: Broadway producer B. K. Doaks has staged ten straight flops; if the critics pan his latest, "The Bride Wore Spurs," he'll be history. Doaks implores bit actors Moe, Larry, and Shemp to be on the lookout for top critic Nick Barker, who continually pans Doaks's shows and is known to show up to the theater in a disguise. After giving the works to nearly everyone in the theater except Barker (who has positioned himself conspicuously in the first row), the Stooges make a disaster of their Southern routine onstage, coughing up feathers from a Moe-baked cake. Barker's assessment: "Terrific! A sensation! The greatest satire I've ever seen!"

Key Gag: Broadway actors Moe, Larry, and Shemp cannot do their Southern routine without a cake, but Moe has forgotten to buy one. Acting quickly backstage, Moe decides to bake the cake himself. Shemp, however, carelessly tosses a potholder into the pan without considering the culinary consequences of his act. When the cake is later served by a lovely Southern belle, the Stooges haven't the heart to tell her about the dessert's unusual texture. Gentleman Moe does manage to remark that "this cake is as light as a feather!" But before long the Stooges succumb to coughing fits that produce a shower of feathers unlike any seen before on the Broadway stage.

Three Little Beers (1935)

Third Stooge: Curly
Stooge Occupation(s): Beer delivery men; golfers
Nemesis: The exclusionary policies of the Panther Brewing Company; fellow golfers

Synopsis: The Panther Brewing Company is throwing its annual golf tournament, but has neglected to invite its three new delivery men. The Stooges stumble across an invitation, however, and are thrilled to learn of the $100 first prize they are certain to win. Denied admission to the fancy golf course, the Stooges fashion media credentials from a nearby men's room. "Press!" declares Moe as the guard honors his button. "Press!" declares Larry as he flashes his badge. "Pull!" declares Curly, who flashes what must have been the only button left in the men's room. The Stooges prove to be as inept at golf as at beer delivery, however, and are chased into the street and out of the world of country clubs—forever, it seems.

Key Gag: As newcomers to golf, the Stooges prove that the game cannot be learned overnight. Moe causes hundreds of divots ("but they're getting smaller" he reassures an infuriated groundskeeper); Larry pulls up a weed that turns out to uproot the entire hole; and Curly takes time to do his laundry in a ball wash. Only after two furious groundskeepers contact the authorities and give spirited chase do the Stooges realize that they still haven't mastered the game.

Three Little Pigskins (1934)

Third Stooge: Curly
Stooge Occupation(s): Beggars; football stars
Nemesis: Football team owner Joe Stack; the rules of football

Synopsis: Cigar-chomping Joe Stack is worried. The big football game is just around the corner and his three star players are injured. A sassy blonde (played by Lucille Ball) suggests that he recruit the Three Horsemen, a trio of running backs who have been tearing up the college circuit. The Stooges, in the meantime, are mistaken by another of Stack's dames for the Three Horsemen, and are recruited to play in the big game. Wearing uniforms with numbers like "?" (Curly), "H_2O^2" (Moe), and "$^1/_2$" (Larry), the Stooges begin, curiously, by tackling the referee. Stack is understandably concerned, but goes overboard by shooting the Stooges in the hindquarters after Larry uses his head to block a kick.

Key Gag: Mistaken for three star football players, the Stooges are given royal treatment by three gorgeous girls whose mobster boyfriends stand to win a fortune on the upcoming game. With their boyfriends away, the girls dress the Stooges in women's lingerie and blindfolds, promising a big kiss if the Stooges can find them. Moe, Larry, and Curly grope desperately until they find the

three mobsters, who have just arrived and who the Stooges call "Sugarplum," "Baby," and "Cutie Pie." Unaccustomed to this type of affection from such fetchingly dressed men, the mobsters knock out Moe and Larry with a single punch; Curly, however, takes one look at his mobster's clenched fist and saves the man the trouble by fainting dead away.

Three Little Pirates (1946)

Third Stooge: Curly

Stooge Occupation(s): Shipwrecked stowaways; exotic wayfarers

Nemesis: The governor of Dead Man's Island; Black Louie, a knife-throwing pirate

Synopsis: The Stooges survive the shipwreck of Garbage Scow 188—NYC, but are captured and brought to the governor of Dead Man's Island, who sentences them to death after Curly flirts with his fiancée. The woman, however, is herself a captive and asks the Stooges to help her escape. Disguising themselves as

A rare glimpse of three athletes at the top of their games (*Three Little Pigskins*, 1934)

wayfarers bearing exotic gifts from strange lands, the Stooges mesmerize the greedy governor before escaping to Black Louie's Pirate Den, where the proprietor challenges the bifocaled Curly to a knife-throwing contest. Curly fares poorly, but the Stooges triumph in an action-packed swordfight in which Moe proclaims himself the new emperor of Dead Man's Island.

Key Gag: Sentenced to die for flirting with the fiancée of the governor of Dead Man's Island, the Stooges disguise themselves as wayfarers bearing fantastical gifts from mystical lands. They enchant the governor with their "Maha" routine, a dazzling exchange that goes like this:

> Moe: Maha?
> Curly: A-ha?
> Moe: You like to speak that?
> Curly: I like to *talk* that!
> Moe: Ras Bañas ya-tee benafucci a timi nicaronja. That, how you say, that Pickle Puss, he askee taskee what dee chit vat syke you gottik?
> Curly: Naathing!
> Moe: Naathing?
> Curly: Yooks!

Moe's translation: The maharajah says he is the bearer of a rare jewel.

Three Little Sew and Sews (1939)

Third Stooge: Curly
Stooge Occupation(s): Tailors; submarine stowaways
Nemesis: The U.S. Navy; enemy spies

Synopsis: Admiral Taylor agrees to a dangerous meeting with a top enemy spy, but naturally wants his jacket pressed first. At the navy tailor shop, clothier Curly tries the admiral's jacket on for size, likes the look, and decides to travel to the party himself. A sexy woman spy attempts to seduce Curly, but is momentarily sidetracked when Curly accidentally sits on a burning cigar. (The woman wonders aloud whether the smell emanating from the couch is burning rubbish, but Curly reassures her that it smells more like somebody's frying onions.) Soon, the spy has enough information to kidnap the Stooges, hijack a navy submarine, and experience one of the most explosive conclusions in Stooges history.

Key Gag: Disguised in a stolen admiral's uniform, Curly uses his newfound authority to free pals Moe and Larry from a navy jail cell—for the fee of five dollars each. When Moe and Larry express outrage at this charge, Curly orders a guard to put them on strict rations of bread and water. When that fails to engender the proper respect, Curly orders rations of just water, and then just salt water.

Three Little Twirps (1943)

Third Stooge: Curly
Stooge Occupation(s): Circus poster hangers; ticket scalpers; high-wire performers
Nemesis: Undercover detectives; a circus promoter; an angry spear-thrower

Synopsis: The circus is in town and the Stooges know a good ticket-scalping opportunity when they see one. Undercover detectives, however, don't appreciate Moe, Larry, and Curly's public service and attempt to place them under arrest. The Stooges flee the scene and disappear into various circus tents, but it is Curly's bad luck to end up in the lap of the bearded lady, who takes an instant shine to her "little bald-headed eagle." Soon captured, it looks like jail for the Stooges until the circus promoter remembers that he needs three human targets for the Sultan of Abadaba, an insane spear-thrower who dislikes people. After several close calls, Curly fires a spear back at the sultan and the Stooges make a high-wired and wobbly circus getaway.

Key Gag: On the run from furious circus promoters, Larry and Curly duck into a tent and hide themselves inside a horse costume. A nearsighted circus hand, told to make lion meat from the horse, mournfully does his duty by cutting off the horse's head. Only by good fortune, however, does the old man live through the horror of seeing Curly's yelping face pop out of the horse's "neck."

Three Loan Wolves (1946)

Third Stooge: Curly

Stooge Occupation(s): Pawnbrokers; fathers

Nemesis: Shakedown man Butch McGee and his dazzling dame, Molly the Glamour Girl

Synopsis: Sassy young Egbert doesn't dilly-dally with the truth; when he demands to know which of the Stooges is his father, the three pawnshop owners have little choice but to come clean. Long ago, they tell Egbert, shakedown man Butch McGee sent curvaceous confidence dame Molly the Glamour Girl to hock a phony diamond ring at the Stooges' pawnshop. Carrying her sister's baby to throw off the cops, Molly arrives

at the shop but cannot convince Larry to take the ring, especially after it shatters upon inspection. Panicked, Molly bolts from the shop, leaving Larry holding the child and later explaining to his bewildered partners, "The bag left me holding the babe!" And that, they tell an unsatisfied Egbert, is how he earned the privilege of having three fathers.

Key Gag: As pawnbrokers learning to care for the first infant their pawnshop has ever accepted, the Stooges try a variety of child care approaches not found in Dr. Spock. Their hideous facial contortions only make the baby cry, while Curly's gift of a loaded gun is too dangerous for such a small baby. Only after Curly fashions a bottle from a jug and a rubber glove does baby Egbert seem to settle in with his three new daddies.

Three Missing Links (1938)

Third Stooge: Curly

Stooge Occupation(s): Janitors; actors

Nemesis: A gorilla who doesn't like movie stars

Synopsis: B. O. Botswaddle is leaving to shoot a film in Africa, but he hasn't found a suitable actor to play the pivotal role of the gorilla. He is so uptight, in fact, that he fires his three janitors—the Stooges—simply for destroying his office. The Stooges beg for mercy, but it is Curly's face that makes an impression on Botswaddle; in a moment of epiphany, he decides to cast Curly as his gorilla, with Moe and Larry playing the parts of Stone Age Neanderthal men. On location in Africa, Curly steps away to change into his gorilla costume while a real gorilla wanders onto the set, creating a danger Moe and Larry never fully comprehend.

Key Gag: An angry gorilla has Curly cornered and all looks lost for the unlucky Stooge. Curly suddenly remembers that he still has some love candy that was prepared by a local witch doctor, and he offers it to the gorilla. The ape isn't biting, so Curly eats some himself to prove that the candy is safe. The witch doctor's recipe is potent, however, and Curly is soon in love himself, declaring to the confounded gorilla, "Darling, I love you! Give me a little kiss!" The ape is suddenly less interested in Curly and beats a hasty retreat.

Three Pests in a Mess (1945)

Third Stooge: Curly
Stooge Occupation(s): Inventors
Nemesis: Swindler I. Cheatham; various intimidating ghouls and goblins

Synopsis: Dollar signs dance in the crooked eyes of swindler I. Cheatham after he gets word that three men matching the Stooges' description have won big money in a recent sweepstakes. Moments later, Cheatham's dazzling dame spots the Stooges in a nearby hallway, and quickly goes to work wooing the new millionaires. But when she discovers that Moe, Larry, and Curly are simply aspiring inventors peddling a newfangled fly-catching machine (the fly is supposed to crawl up a flight of stairs, see its reflection in a mirror, attack it, and fatally smash its head), she turns unromantic, yells for help, and beats the daylights out of Curly. Cheatham, who doesn't like to be cheated, chases Moe, Larry, and Curly into a pet cemetery, allowing no creature—pet or Stooge—to rest in peace.

Key Gag: Curly has carelessly discharged a rifle and shot a mannequin, but the Stooges believe it's murder. Now they must dispose of the body before the cops get wise, and the Ever Rest Pet Cemetery looks like just the place. The plan works like a charm until the cemetery's proprietors get wind of a disturbance on the grounds and hide in an open grave in an attempt to nab the Stooges in the act. Curly bravely tosses the "corpse" into the open grave, but the proprietors throw it back out, traumatizing Curly and frustrating the impatient Moe. Curly makes another effort and again the corpse flies out. Finally, the proprietors jump out of the grave themselves, causing the Stooges' pant legs to spring up to their knees and the Stooges themselves to spring forth from their shoes.

Three Sappy People (1939)

Third Stooge: Curly
Stooge Occupation(s): Phone repairmen; psychiatrists
Nemesis: A millionaire named Rumsford

Synopsis: Jet-setting socialite Sheri Rumsford hungers for fun and will do anything—including driving a car into her own living room—for a laugh. Her husband, gravely concerned about his wife's mental health, places a call to Drs. Ziller, Zeller, and Zoller, three psychiatrists whose unorthodox methods are rumored to produce astounding results. The call, however, is answered by phone repairmen the Stooges, who cannot resist taking the case. Posing as Ziller, Zeller, and Zoller, they arrive at Rumsford's home and manage almost immediately to violate every code of professional psychiatric conduct. Sheri, however, is captivated by her doctors' strange behavior and might have been cured completely had her husband not lost his patience in the commotion and crowned her with a delicious-looking birthday cake.

Key Gag: Like any good doctor, Curly tests the reflexes of his patients by striking their knees at a precise angle. Unable to find a reflex in any guest at a swank party (including himself), a frustrated Curly strikes the knee of a statue of a glorious Greek athlete. The statue, however, demonstrates its healthy reflexes by kicking Curly in the stomach.

Three Smart Saps (1942)

Third Stooge: Curly
Stooge Occupation(s): Fiancés; undercover photographers
Nemesis: A high-living convict named Walker

Synopsis: The Stooges' fiancées, Stella, Nella, and Bella, are heartbroken because their father, the warden, has been overthrown by a convict named Walker, who is running the jail like a nightclub. The Stooges, determined to undo Walker's devious coup, bust into the jail and insinuate themselves into the black-tie party that's sprawling behind prison walls. While Curly rumbas with a willowy brunette, Moe swoops in with a spy camera to snap candid photos of the swank lawlessness that has overtaken the grounds. The Stooges' derring-do makes the front pages and they are rewarded with something money cannot buy: the hands in marriage of the lovely Stella, Nella, and Bella.

Key Gag: Curly has gone undercover at a party thrown by crooks, so his identity must be concealed at all costs. When his suit begins to unravel while dancing, Curly rumbas over to a nearby curtain, behind which Larry stands poised to mend it with needle and thread. Larry's hand, however, is unsteady, getting too much Curly and not enough fabric and causing squeals that nearly unravel the Stooges' covert operation.

The Three Stooges Go Around the World in a Daze (1963— feature-length film)

Third Stooge: Curly Joe
Stooge Occupation(s): Noble servants; world travelers
Nemesis: Upper-crust con man Vickers Cavendish; various foreign dignitaries unaccustomed to the Stooges' customs

Synopsis: Few con men look to the classics for inspiration, but Vickers Cavendish is no ordinary swindler. Reading Jules Verne's *Around the World in 80 Days,* he is struck by this inspiration: he will wager the great-grandson of that book's hero—Phineas Fogg III—that Fogg cannot make the same trip without spending a farthing. And for good measure, he'll also rob the bank that serves as escrow for the loot each man posts. Naturally, Fogg's honor is on the line and he accepts the bet, even bringing along faithful servants Moe, Larry, and Curly Joe to assist in the seemingly hopeless wager. Fogg and the Stooges set out on the trip, but Scotland Yard, believing Fogg to have been the culprit at the bank, puts out a worldwide warrant for his arrest. This leads to a series of uncomfortable predicaments and narrow escapes for the nobleman and his servants, including a bout with a sumo wrestling champ and a confrontation with master Chinese brainwashers.

Somehow, the team makes it back to London on the eightieth day, but the clock is ticking and only Curly Joe's pedal-to-the-metal driving style can beat the deadline and restore honor to the lineage of the Foggs.

Key Gag: Captured by Chinese military intelligence, the Stooges are taken to the infamous "back room" for a session of psychological torture and brainwashing. Terrible sounds of suffering emanate from behind closed doors, and it looks like curtains for whatever semblance of sanity the Stooges had carried in. But moments later, Moe, Larry, and Curly Joe emerge happy and unscathed; the three torturers, however, have suffered serious emotional harm, poking, slapping, and acting in every manner like the prisoners they were supposed to brainwash.

The Three Stooges in Orbit (1962—feature-length film)

Third Stooge: Curly Joe
Stooge Occupation(s): Transients; television stars

The combination helicopter-tank-submarine, the most effective anti-Martian weapon known to man (*The Three Stooges in Orbit*, 1962)

Nemesis: Unreasonable Martians Ogg and Zogg

Synopsis: Professor Danforth would make the perfect landlord if only he didn't talk so much about Martians and their coming invasion. Still, the Stooges need a place to live, and humor the old coot . . . until they see the space aliens for themselves. Now Professor Danforth's secret invention makes sense: the Earth will need a combination helicopter-tank-submarine to fight off the Martians who cannot wait to invade Earth. The machine looks utterly impractical, but Air Force Captain Andrews is so smitten with Danforth's daughter Carol that he recommends a full tryout to his commanding general. The Stooges, however, pilot the craft and soon Danforth is the laughingstock of the military, not a good result considering the imminent invasion planned by unreasonable Martians Ogg and Zogg. But when the Martians steal Danforth's machine, the Stooges go along for the ride, preventing disaster (and the destruction of Disneyland) before saving humanity from turning green forever.

Key Gag: The Stooges know that their hotel does not allow cooking on the premises. But when you're able—like the Stooges—to whip up fabulous gourmet meals, rules are but mere distractions. The biddy of a hotel manager, however, takes an instant dislike to the aromas wafting from the Stooges' room, and knocks angrily on the door to put an end to the recipes. Acting without hesitation, the Stooges hide the grub, using an ingenious trapdoor behind the television screen to stash the hash. But the manager smells a rat and, after fiddling to turn down the volume on the set, uncovers a veritable smorgasbord of items representing every major food group known to man.

The Three Stooges Meet Hercules (1962—feature-length film)

Third Stooge: Curly Joe

Stooge Occupation(s): Pharmacists; time travelers; galley slaves; fight promoters

Nemesis: Short-fused pharmacy owner Ralph Dimsal; Odius, bossy king of ancient Ithaca

Synopsis: The Stooges have their hands full working as pharmacists in Ithaca, New York, inventing items such as Larry's Pep Pills and Curly Joe's Calm-Down Pills. But they still manage to nurture their timid pal Schuyler, who works in the basement trying to perfect his time machine and to keep beautiful pharmacist Diane interested in him. But Diane can't play second fiddle forever; she gives Schuyler just two days to finish his time machine or she'll be finished with him. Worse, grouchy pharmacy owner Dimsal declares his intention to fire everyone in sight. With pressure boiling from all sides, the Stooges decide to assist in building the time machine while Schuyler is out of his lab. But the Stooges are better pharmacists than inventors, and soon the machine is smoking, bucking, and shooting fireworks. Schuyler and Diana rush to the scene and manage to step aboard the contraption just as it lifts off and travels back in time to Ithaca in ancient Greece. There, the Stooges and Schuyler manage to infuriate brutish King Odius and his muscle-bound right-hand man, Hercules. Odius seizes Diana for his bride and banishes Moe, Larry, Curly Joe, and Schuyler to

the galleys of a slave ship. But months of rowing produce an unexpected benefit: Schuyler's muscles bulge and he becomes as strong as twenty men, ultimately using his powers—and a few of Curly Joe's Calm-Down Pills—to defeat monsters of mythic proportions and to win Diane back from the clutches of Odius.

Key Gag: Hercules might be mighty, but his manners are ninety-eight pounds and weak. While King Odius attempts to make a dramatic speech during a feast in the palace, Hercules continues to annoy the king by cracking walnuts in his bulging biceps. But Curly Joe might be even more annoyed than the king; after spilling a goblet of wine on the legendary muscleman, the impatient Hercules shoves Curly Joe's head between his biceps and continues the cracking.

The Three Troubledoers (1946)

Third Stooge: Curly

Stooge Occupation(s): Drifters; fearless lawmen

Nemesis: The ruthless bandit Badlands Blackie

Synopsis: Badlands Blackie has kidnapped the lovely Nell's pappy and won't release him until Nell consents to become Mrs. Blackie. As in all great Westerns, a mysterious hero moseys into town at the darkest hour. "Coney Island Curly," however, demonstrates the kind of six-shooter skills that look certain to earn him an early grave. When Nell is dragged to Blackie's hideout for a shotgun wedding, Curly masterfully disguises himself as a justice of the peace, but blows his cover by reciting the unfamiliar vow, "Do you take this horse collar for your lawfully wedded harness?" Things look bleak for Sheriff Curly, but Deputy Moe manages to direct a bundle of dynamite that blows Blackie and his posse to smithereens.

Key Gag: With a deadly showdown between Badlands Blackie and Sheriff Curly only hours away, Deputy Moe earns his dough by advising the sheriff to sharpen his shooting eye. Curly reaches for a pair of inch-thick bifocals, but Moe isn't convinced he'll need them, deciding to test Curly's vision before any target practice commences. When Curly can't identify how many letters appear on a card Moe shows him, he is allowed to put on his spectacles for a closer look. This time when Moe asks him how many letters he sees on the card, the answer—"What card?"—does not bode well for his chances against the ruthless Blackie.

The Tooth Will Out (1951)

Third Stooge: Shemp
Stooge Occupation(s): Dentists
Nemesis: An ornery outlaw with a toothache

Synopsis: One certain method for avoiding police is to duck into a dental school and take lessons. The Stooges seem to know this rule instinctively and in a week are ready to take their practice to the western frontier. The bifocaled Shemp makes an interesting diagnosis on his first patient, a cowboy he says is suffering from "pungfauthadrednock with the bicuspid canafran." But only Moe's sobering pointer—"The mouth is in the front!"—allows the patient to escape with his life. The real test of Shemp's education, however, comes when a cutthroat bandit storms in, suffering immensely,

and demands an extraction. When Shemp consults the book *The Amateur Carpenter* instead of *Practical Dentistry*, the odds are not with the bandit.

Key Gag: Shemp has barely graduated from dental school when a murderous bandit demands an extraction—or else. Attempting to cram information he should have learned long ago, Shemp mistakenly reads from the book *The Amateur Carpenter*, and determines that "the next step is to sandpaper the chest." Myopic Shemp obliges by furiously rubbing sandpaper on the bandit's chest until Larry warns him to watch out for the man's tattoo. Shemp's reply: "He had a tattoo?"

Tricky Dicks (1953)

Third Stooge: Shemp
Stooge Occupation(s): Detectives
Nemesis: The underhanded killer of Slug McGurk

Synopsis: The Stooges run Section 13 of the detective bureau like they run their lives: no-nonsense and gritty to the bone. But B. A. Copper, their boss, isn't satisfied with attitude; he wants the killer of Slug McGurk captured and he wants it done now. The Stooges cross-examine top suspect Antonio Zucchini Salami Gorgonzola de Pizza, a British-accented Italian organ-grinder, but still cannot find a break in the case. Even the confession of Gilbraith Q. Tiddledewadder, a.k.a. Chopper, doesn't seem legit to the savvy gumshoes. When the real killer walks into the precinct ready to kill, however, the Stooges are bailed out by de Pizza's partner, an eagle-eyed monkey that handles a revolver like a seasoned Wild West gunslinger.

Key Gag: In a truly heroic act, detective Shemp confronts a ruthless killer and is shot in the chest repeatedly at point-blank range. Shemp, however, does not expire easily and flails about in dramatic death throes almost too agonizing to watch. Moe faithfully nurses his dying pal, feeding him an entire bottle of Old Panther whiskey. When Shemp shows miraculous signs of life, Moe shouts for a doctor and an ambulance, but Shemp insists instead on a plumber, as the whiskey gushes forth from the several bullet holes in his chest.

Triple Crossed (1959)
Third Stooge: Joe
Stooge Occupation(s): Jealous lovers (Moe and Joe); underwear salesman (Joe)

Nemesis: Homewrecker and pet shop owner Larry

Synopsis: A remake of *He Cooked His Goose*, with Joe playing Shemp's dual role of protective husband and underwear salesman.

Key Gag: See *He Cooked His Goose.*

Uncivil War Birds (1946)
Third Stooge: Curly
Stooge Occupation(s): Southern gentlemen; soldiers
Nemesis: The Union army; the Confederate army

Synopsis: Life is divine for the Stooges, who as Southern gentlemen bask in the glory of their thick accents and the

The sad effect of pressure on three detectives given just twenty-four hours to nab the killer of Slug McGurk (*Tricky Dicks,* 1953)

affections of fiancées Lulu Belle, Mary Belle, and Ringa Belle. But when the Civil War breaks out, the Stooges are forced to enlist. In the confusion, Moe and Larry join the Union while Curly signs on with the Confederacy. Never forgetting their brotherhood, the Stooges protect each other from enemy troops and even manage to infiltrate a meeting of Union officers while dressed as minstrels. Their heroism, like that of so many of history's soldiers, goes unrewarded when they return home, as Lulu Belle, Mary Belle, and Ringa Belle seem to have lost much of the whimsy they showered upon their fiancés before the war.

Key Gag: With Union soldiers closing in, Moe and Larry hide Confederate soldier Curlylocks (Curly) beneath a pile of straw in an innocent-looking barn. The soldiers see no trace of fugitive Curlylocks, but demonstrate solid instincts by vigorously stabbing their bayonets into the pile of straw—and into Curlylocks's behind. Curlylocks heroically attempts to restrain his yelps, but ultimately bursts forth into the arms of his captors and their now crumpled bayonet blades.

Uncivil Warriors (1935)

Third Stooge: Curly
Stooge Occupation(s): Union spies
Nemesis: The Confederate army

Synopsis: The Union army's position is precarious; without deep undercover work by Lieutenant Duck (Larry), Captain Dodge (Moe), and Major Hyde (Curly), all will be lost for the North. Inside the stately home of a Southern colonel, the Stooges turn on the charm and extract a devastating amount of intelligence from

the unwitting officer, even swallowing and coughing up a cake baked full of feathers by the colonel's daughter in order to preserve their cover. But the arrival of spy-hunting Major Filbert truly challenges the Stooges' powers of disguise, ultimately placing the fate of the nation in Curly's ability to convince the major that he is Moe's wife.

Key Gag: In order to sneak past an eagle-eyed guard, the Stooges pretend to look for their friend "Good-Time Charlie, a guy who walks like this. . . ." The Stooges imitate Charlie's heavy limp and slip by the bewildered guard.

Up in Daisy's Penthouse (1953)

Third Stooge: Shemp
Stooge Occupation(s): Loyal sons
Nemesis: Their own father; his fiancée, Daisy; her gang of murderous thugs

Synopsis: After all those years of raising three strapping boys, has it come to this? The Stooges' filthy rich father plans to leave their loving and loyal mother to marry a curvy blond hussy. But the Stooges aren't about to let it happen. With teeth gritted and Ma in mind, they travel to Popsie's home to plead their case. Popsie, however, is dreaming of nothing but blondes and has no intention of giving up his "Daisy-Waisy." In fact, to celebrate, Popsie goes for a wedding day haircut that transforms him into the spitting image of Shemp; bad news for everyone, given Daisy's plan to kill Popsie—or whoever looks like him—the moment the pair gets hitched. (A reworking of *3 Dumb Clucks,* with Shemp playing the demanding role of Popsie Howard.)

Key Gag: See *3 Dumb Clucks.*

Vagabond Loafers (1949)

Third Stooge: Shemp
Stooge Occupation(s): Plumbers
Nemesis: Water; cunning art thieves

Synopsis: What a terrible day for the pipes to leak at the stately Norfleet Mansion! Mr. and Mrs. Norfleet are moments from debuting their priceless Van Brocklin painting when water trickles ominously from an indoor pipe. Luckily, the Day and Nite Plumbers—Moe, Larry, and Shemp—are on duty and arrive at the scene in a flash. Still inexperienced with water, the three plumbers turn drops into tidal waves, nearly drowning everyone in the house. But there is a more serious problem: two cunning art thieves have made off with the Van Brocklin. Proving that they are better crime fighters than they are plumbers, the Stooges take full advantage of the mansion's slippery conditions to apprehend the thieves and return the painting—dry!—to the grateful but drenched Norfleets.

Key Gag: The Stooges' unorthodox approach to plumbing backfires in a mansion's kitchen, where faucets spin, flooded clocks run backward, and telephone receivers deliver water instead of voices. When asked about dinner, the unnerved and raincoat-clad cook responds, "Sorry, folks. Dinner's postponed on account of rain!"

Violent is the Word for Curly (1938)

Third Stooge: Curly
Stooge Occupation(s): Gas station attendants; Mildew College professors
Nemesis: Three snooty European professors; higher education

Synopsis: Mrs. Catsby, a blue-blooded patroness of academia, has made a lofty endowment to Mildew College, but insists that the money be spent on three esteemed professors due to arrive soon from Europe. The professors, however, make the mistake of stopping at the Acme Service Station, where the Stooges dish out a bit too much of their patented "super service" and blow the professors to kingdom come. On the run, the Stooges slip into the professors' clothes and wind up in the classroom at Mildew. It turns out that the Stooges have no patience for physics, and instead teach their students a jazzy version of the A-B-C's called "Swinging the Alphabet" that makes them the most popular instructors on campus.

Key Gag: The Stooges make a breathtaking escape from a gas station they have ruined but later find Curly frozen solid in the back of their getaway ice cream truck. Moe builds a roaring fire alongside the road and ties Curly to a spit above, rotating him in a valiant effort at defrosting. Using a stick to test his frozen friend, Moe calculates the enormity of the project: "Twenty minutes to a pound; we'll be here a month!" he says.

We Want Our Mummy (1939)

Third Stooge: Curly
Stooge Occupation(s): Detectives
Nemesis: The curse of King Rutentuten; mummy thieves

Synopsis: The curators at the Museum of Ancient History know that messing with the curse of King Rutentuten means certain death. Therefore, they hire the Stooges to travel to Egypt to rescue a kidnapped colleague and return the king's priceless mummy. After a pricey taxi ride to Cairo, the Stooges stumble upon an underground lair where they do battle with three toughguy crooks. Tragically, Rutentuten's mummy is crushed before the Stooges send the thugs sprawling down a secret trapdoor. With the professor freed, the Stooges are thrilled to learn that the damaged mummy was that of Rutentuten's wife, Queen Hotsytotsy. The king, it turns out, was a midget, and is safe and sound in the professor's grateful arms.

Key Gag: With murderous mummy thieves closing in, Moe and Larry wrap Curly in miles of bandage to disguise him as the priceless mummy of King Rutentuten. The ruse works perfectly until the boss crook finds a newspaper packed inside Curly's wrappings. His suspicion is slightly aroused when he reads the headline, "Yanks Win World Series," but he's not truly convinced the mummy's a fake until Curly replies, "Yeah, and I won five bucks!"

Wee Wee Monsieur (1938)

Third Stooge: Curly
Stooge Occupation(s): Parisian artists; deadbeat tenants; Foreign Legioneers
Nemesis: The finicky Parisian art community; the French Foreign Legion

Synopsis: Perhaps Paris has unjustly earned its reputation for nurturing artists. Although the Stooges are struggling to sell even a single painting, Parisian landlords still demand rent, fruit vendors still expect to be paid, and the police are still delighted to chase deadbeat tenants who steal watermelons. Only the French Foreign Legion embraces the Stooges,

even assigning them the critical task of protecting key military leader Captain Gorgonzola. After Gorgonzola is kidnapped moments later, the Stooges don Santa Claus suits and travel deep undercover to effect an extraction of the captain even more daring than their extraction of fruit-stand watermelons.

Key Gag: Although they feel silly doing so, the Stooges must convince an ornery king that they are sultry and seductive harem girls. Dressed fetchingly in veils (and Curly in a bikini top), the Stooges dance, strut, kick (each other), flap their arms, and perform daintily. The king's tentative response: "We have some new arrivals, I see."

Wham-Bam-Slam! (1955)

Third Stooge: Shemp
Stooge Occupation(s): Caretakers to an ailing Shemp
Nemesis: A flimflam friend named Claude A. Quacker; Shemp's frazzled nerves

Synopsis: A remake of *Pardon My Clutch.* New footage includes Larry's recommendation to use friend Claude A. Quacker to cure Shemp's nerves, Shemp eating powder puffs for breakfast and coughing up powder from his mouth and ears, and Shemp's footbath in a bucket of water containing a biting lobster. The final scene from *Pardon My Clutch,* in which a loopy millionaire tries to buy the Stooges' car, is replaced by a scene showing Shemp being cured by the noise and commotion made by their huffing-and-puffing car.

Key Gag: Larry never has full control over a feisty lobster he is handling, and

No one likes being mistaken for a stack of hotcakes (*Wham-Bam-Slam!*, 1955).

drops it into a bucket being used to bathe Shemp's aching feet. The hungry lobster takes a bite out of Shemp's toe, causing Shemp to declare that he has been "swallowed by an octopus." Moe saves the day by walloping the lobster with a sledgehammer, a heroic act that does little to distract the ungrateful Shemp from lamenting the injury to his "poor, dear, sweet, lovable toe."

Curly proves that the secret to becoming a top bullfighter is to work with a cooperative bull (*What's the Matador?*, 1942).

What's the Matador? (1942)

Third Stooge: Curly
Stooge Occupation(s): Bullfighters
Nemesis: A jealous husband named José; a humorless bull

Synopsis: The Stooges arrive in Mexico to debut their thrilling and hilarious bullfighting act. But at the bus terminal, Curly infuriates a native by flirting outrageously with his beautiful wife, Dolores. In the commotion, the Stooges and Dolores switch suitcases, forcing Moe, Larry, and Curly to make a risky trip to her apartment to swap bags. Her husband, however, does not understand why the Stooges are stuffed in, under, and around his bed, and nearly kills himself trying to kill them. Later, while the Stooges perform at the bullfighting arena, the man pays two animal handlers to release a real, snorting bull to teach Curly and his hindquarters a lesson about messin' with Dolores.

Key Gag: When a real bull chases Moe and Larry from their bull costume and out of the bullfighting ring, it looks like curtains for matador Curly. But after an initial bout of fear, Curly decides that the snorting, angry bull is no match for him. The bull kicks some dirt and lowers its horns. Curly does the same. And the collision at the center of the ring is a violent one from which the bull does not recover.

Who Done It? (1949)

Third Stooge: Shemp
Stooge Occupation(s): Detectives
Nemesis: The Phantom Gang and Nikko, the hideous monster who does their dirty work

Synopsis: The Phantom Gang has kidnapped another prominent citizen, causing jittery millionaire Old Man Goodrich to quake with terror. He wisely places a call to the Stooges at the Alert Detective Agency, but after hanging up is accosted by Nikko, a monstrous goon who works for three scheming crooks. The Stooges arrive on the scene in a bluster, but are quickly seduced by a blonde, who administers a near-lethal dose of poison to the amorous Shemp's drink. Moe and Larry revive Shemp and a spectacular chase ensues, culminating in a lights-out fight in which only Shemp is left standing.

Key Gag: No one appreciates the charms of a beautiful woman more than Shemp, but like most ace detectives he always keeps an eye open. When a crooked dame slips knockout pills into his drink, Shemp is prepared, secretly switching his spiked drink for her harmless glass while he points to a painting to distract her. The woman is no dummy and points to a different painting, clinking the two

glasses together but not switching them. Shemp has the last word, however, as he again points to a painting and switches the glasses, only this time he's given himself a Mickey Finn that has him gasping, groping, and heep-heeping on the floor.

Whoops, I'm an Indian! (1936)

Third Stooge: Curly
Stooge Occupation(s): Con men; Indians
Nemesis: The sheriff of Lobo City; Pierre, a hulking trooper

Synopsis: The Stooges run a dirty dice game in the Old West, but are forced to flee into the woods when a savvy sheriff offers a reward of $333.33 for their capture, "dead or in bad shape." Utilizing a unique approach to outdoor survival, the Stooges manage to avoid detection, even disguising themselves as Indians to fool the local authorities. But Pierre, a hulking trooper, dislikes Indians, especially after discovering that his wife has just run off with a chap named Chief Leaping Lizard. Pierre is ready to scalp the Stooges, but falls for Curly, who is disguised as an adorable squaw. Pierre marries Curly, but is ultimately unhappy to discover what his bride looks like without her wig.

Key Gag: On the run from the sheriff, the Stooges fashion brilliant Indian disguises for their getaway. Murderous Pierre, however, happens to be on the hunt for Indians and corrals the three braves and orders them to dance by firing his pistol at their feet. Not the kind of men to argue with an angry gunslinger, Moe and Larry break into a graceful waltz worthy of Fred Astaire and Ginger Rogers.

Woman Haters (1934)

Third Stooge: Curly
Stooge Occupation(s): Woman haters
Nemesis: Women

Synopsis: The Stooges' first short, done entirely in rhyme and starring Larry as the featured Stooge. The Woman Haters Club is in session, and welcomes its three newest members, Jackie (Curly), Jim (Larry), and Tommy (Moe). The Stooges vow, over drinks, never again to mix with women, and Jim even promises to break off his engagement with his fiancée, Mary. Jim, however, caves in and weds, taking a honeymoon trip on a romantic train. But Jackie and Tommy are also on the train, and don't take kindly to their friend's traitorous act. Mary is even angrier, and makes all three woman haters pay for a membership each of them probably regrets.

Key Gag: As part of his induction into the Woman Haters Club, Larry has made a solemn oath to avoid the fair sex, even staking his bankroll on his promise. But his fiancée's father persuades him to see things differently, pointing to the last man who had tried to cancel a wedding with one of his daughters: a sad sack with a mournful look who is bandaged head-to-toe and supported only by crutches.

Yes, We Have No Bonanza (1939)

Third Stooge: Curly
Stooge Occupation(s): Singing waiters; gold prospectors
Nemesis: Their boss, a bank robber named Maxey

Synopsis: The Stooges and three gorgeous waitresses make Maxey's Place swing with jazzy song-and-dance routines. But their bile-filled boss is cruel to the girls and impatient with the Stooges. Determined to get themselves and the girls out of Maxey's, the Stooges set out to prospect for gold, and stumble upon the very place where Maxey has hidden the loot from a recent bank robbery. Ecstatic at their discovery, they return to town to stake their claim, but are confronted by Maxey, who grabs the dough and makes off in a car. The Stooges, who have jumped out a window and onto a wooden horse, lasso Maxey's car and are pulled at death-defying speeds until the crook crashes just where he belongs: into the local jail.

Key Gag: Moe is hit in the head by a rock thrown by Curly, an act of treason he is not inclined to forgive. Naturally he fires back, not realizing that the missile he has thrown is a stick of dynamite with its fuse already lit. The TNT misses Curly and lands near Yorrick, the Stooges' trusty mule. A pet dog senses trouble and moves the dynamite away from Yorrick and under some steaks Curly is preparing for lunch. Hearing the hiss of the lit fuse but no longer able to see the dynamite, the Stooges conclude that Yorrick has swallowed the dynamite, an opinion that is cemented by a blast that showers steaks upon them all. Moe sums up his sorrow eloquently, saying, "Alas, poor Yorrick; I knew him well."

The Yoke's on Me (1944)

Third Stooge: Curly
Stooge Occupation(s): Farmers; war heroes
Nemesis: Escaped Japanese soldiers

Synopsis: With dreams of bountiful harvests, the Stooges pay $1,000 and their car for a farm not even Old McDonald could salvage. Even Moe's innovative plow—pulled by Larry and Curly—breaks down before it yields usable crops. But there's an even greater problem brewing near the Stooges' barn: escaped Japanese soldiers have made the farm their hideout, even using Stooge-carved jack-o'-lanterns as disguises. Curly, however, uncovers their ruse, leading to a dynamic—and explosive—confrontation. (Note: television program directors often refuse to air *The Yoke's on Me* due to the film's exaggerated portrayal of Japanese soldiers.)

Key Gag: As new farmers unfamiliar with animal nutrition, the Stooges allow an ostrich to feed on open cans of gunpowder. The matter is soon forgotten until the Stooges are surrounded by Japanese soldiers, and it occurs to the military-minded Moe that the nearby ostrich eggs might pack a wallop. Moe heroically lobs one of the eggs and blows the soldiers to smithereens.

You Nazty Spy (1940)

Third Stooge: Curly
Stooge Occupation(s): Dictators of Moronica
Nemesis: The Free World

Synopsis: Realizing that "there's no money in peace," three greedy cabinet members plot to overthrow the Kingdom of Moronica. But first they need a dictator, someone "stupid enough to do what we tell him." They decide on a paperhanger named Moe Hailstone (Moe), who accepts the job and declares, "We must make our country safe for hypocrisy!" and "Our motto shall be, 'Moronica for Morons!'" With Larry as his minister of propaganda and Curly as his field marshal, Moe terrorizes Moronica with his fascistic and foolhardy rule. Only an angry mob can undo the reign of Moe Hailstone, chasing the Stooges into a cage where lions salivate over their new three-course meal. (Note: Moe was the first American actor to portray Hitler in film. *You Nazty Spy* is biting satire, bravely acted and designed unflinchingly to make Hitler and the Axis powers look bumbling and dangerous.)

Key Gag: The Stooges are pitched the idea of becoming ruthless dictators of the country of Moronica. Larry and Curly seem indifferent, but the deep-thinking Moe takes great dramatic pause to evaluate the proposition. When he lifts his hand to rub his face in contemplation, a thick black feather affixes like a mustache to his upper lip, making him look eerily like a certain ruthless dictator of the time.

For information on the Official Three Stooges Fan Club or the Soitenly Stooges merchandise catalog, please write Comedy III Productions, Inc., P.O. Box 10666, Glendale, CA 91209-3666.

About the Author

Robert Kurson is a 1990 graduate of Harvard Law School and a Phi Beta Kappa graduate of the University of Wisconsin. He is currently a features writer for the *Chicago Sun-Times.*

Since his fifth birthday, Kurson has nurtured a love for the antics and language of the Three Stooges. Grade school teachers were baffled by his rendition of "Niagara Falls," a turn-of-the-century vaudeville routine popularized by Moe, Larry, and Curly in the film *Gents Without Cents.*

Kurson was born and raised in Chicago, and currently resides there with his wife.